AMERICAN HISTORY SINCE 1865

Birdsall S. Viault, Ph.D.
Winthrop College

An American BookWorks Corporation Project

McGraw-Hill Book Company

New York St. Louis San Francisco Auckland Bogotá Hamburg
London Madrid Mexico Milan Montreal New Delhi Panama
Paris São Paulo Singapore Sydney Tokyo Toronto

Birdsall S. Viault is Professor of History and Chairman of the Department of History at Winthrop College, Rock Hill, South Carolina. He received his B.S. degree from Adelphi University and an M.A. degree in Secondary Education from the same institution. Further graduate work at Duke University led to the award of the M.A. and Ph.D. in history. Professor Viault also holds a diploma from the Leibniz-Kolleg of the University of Tübingen, Federal Republic of Germany.

Prior to joining the faculty at Winthrop College, Professor Viault taught at Adelphi University. He has written numerous articles and reviews which have appeared in journals in the United States and Europe, and for close to a decade he wrote on subjects related to history and current affairs in a weekly column, "Perspective," which appeared in over thirty South Carolina newspapers. In addition, for more than a decade he has conducted summer travel seminars to western Europe and the Soviet Union.

Editor, Gary Ostrower, Ph.D., Alfred University

American History Since 1865

1 2 3 4 5 6 7 8 9 10 11 12 13 14 15 16 17 18 19 20 FGR FGR 8 9 2 1 0 9 8

ISBN 0-07-067426-4

Library of Congress Cataloging-in-Publication Data
Viault, Birdsall S.
        American history since 1865
        "An American BookWorks Corporation project."
        1. United States—History—1865–   . I.Title.
E661.V5 1988   973   88-13443
ISBN 0-07-067426-4

Preface

This volume, like its companion, is intended to serve two purposes. First, it provides an overview of the history of the United States since 1865 and may, therefore, be used as a textbook in its own right. Second, it may also be used as a review book in conjunction with the standard college texts in American history.

Throughout the book, an emphasis has been placed on providing readily accessible information. The time lines at the beginning of each chapter provide an introduction to the material covered in that chapter, while the subheadings within the chapter call the reader's attention to the major subjects considered.

No attempt has been made to cover the major interpretive or historiological debates relating to American history since the Civil War. Rather the reader is encouraged to consult the "Recommended Reading" section which appears at the end of each chapter. Here the reader will find detailed studies of subjects considered in the chapter. In selecting books to be included, emphasis has been placed on recent scholarship and classic works.

Acknowledgments

It is a pleasure for me to acknowledge the assistance of those who have done so much to make this book possible. Thanks must go, first, to Lewis Auerhaan, a student in my early teaching career who recommended me for this project. Judy Lassiter, the secretary to the History Department at Winthrop College, found time in the midst of a busy workload to do much of the typing and retyping of the manuscript, and her expertise helped make possible its completion on schedule. The student assistants in the History Department, Michelle Blythe, Tammie Harrell, Carol Willke, and especially Denise Cody, operated the microcomputer and printer with great skill in producing attractive copy for the editors and assisted in other ways in the preparation of the manuscript. The content editor, Professor Gary Ostrower of Alfred University, reviewed the manuscript with a keen eye and brought his considerable knowledge to bear in making many recommendations which have improved the final product considerably. My colleague, Jason Silverman, has provided continuing encouragement as he was busily at work on the first volume of this review of American history. Other colleagues, particularly Tom Morgan, Louise Pettus, and Ed Haynes, and Ross Webb, were generous in lending me books and in answering numerous questions. The staff of the Dacus

Library of Winthrop College, especially Susan Silverman and Nancy Davidson, have provided me with considerable help. Ben Morrison and Pat FitzGerald offered some useful suggestions. Fred Grayson provided encouragement and support throughout the project. I must also express my appreciation to the hundreds of students I have taught in close to thirty years. From them I have learned much about how to make history understandable and meaningful.

I owe my greatest acknowledgment to my wife, Sally, who provided me with support, encouragement, and enthusiasm throughout. She proofread the manuscript at every stage with great skill and checked the lists of recommended reading. I dedicate this book to her and to the memory of my mother, Christabel Scrymser.

Birdsall S. Viault
Rock Hill, SC
August 1988

Contents

CHAPTER 1

The Reconstruction Era

Time Line

1863	Lincoln proposes his moderate Ten Percent Plan for Reconstruction
1864	Loyal state governments are established in Louisiana, Arkansas, and Tennessee
	Congress passes the Wade-Davis Bill
1865	Congress approves the Thirteenth Amendment
	Congress creates the Freedmen's Bureau
	John Wilkes Booth assassinates Lincoln

Vice President Andrew Johnson succeeds to the Presidency

Former Confederate states are readmitted to the Union under Johnson's plan for Reconstruction

Southern states adopt Black Codes

Congress refuses to seat newly elected southern representatives and senators

1866   Congress overrides Johnson's veto of the bill that provided for the continuation of the Freedmen's Bureau

Congress passes the Civil Rights Bill

Congress approves the Fourteenth Amendment

The Radical Republicans win control of both houses of Congress

French Emperor Napoleon III ends his intervention in Mexico; the Mexicans execute Maximilian

The United States purchases Alaska from Russia

1867   Congress passes the Tenure of Office Act and the Command of the Army Act, restricting presidential power

1867–1868   The Reconstruction Acts establish the congressional plan for reconstruction of the South

1868	The House of Representatives impeaches Johnson, but the Senate fails to convict him
	Seven former Confederate states win readmission to the Union
	Republican Ulysses S. Grant wins the Presidency
1869	Congress approves the Fifteenth Amendment
1870–1871	Congress passes the Enforcement Acts
1871	Boss Tweed is convicted in New York
1872	Congress passes the Amnesty Act
	Grant wins reelection to the Presidency
	The *Alabama* Claims arbitration panel awards $15.5 million to the United States
1872–1875	Revelation of scandals discredits the Grant administration
1873	The Panic of 1873 leads to a general depression
1877	Republican Rutherford B. Hayes becomes President after a disputed election
	The Compromise of 1877 ends Reconstruction

The Reconstruction era includes the period from the end of the Civil War in April 1865 to the withdrawal of the last Union occupation forces from the South in early 1877. During this period, the Republican-controlled government in Washington at-

tempted to reshape the South. The moderate proposals for Reconstruction advanced by President Lincoln and his successor, Andrew Johnson, evoked strong opposition from the Radical Republicans in Congress, who favored harsher policies for dealing with the South and succeeded in putting their program into effect. Radical Reconstruction ended, however, without achieving its goal of carrying out a far-reaching political, social, and economic transformation of the South. Instead, white conservative rule was reestablished throughout the region.

Devastation of the South

Before the Civil War, the southern states had exercised a powerful influence over national affairs, but at war's end, they were devastated. Much public and private property had been destroyed. Georgia, South Carolina, and Virginia had suffered the most. General William T. Sherman's *March to the Sea* had laid waste the countryside, and Atlanta, Georgia, and Columbia, South Carolina, had been burned. In Virginia's Shenandoah Valley, General Philip Sheridan had carried out a similar scorched-earth policy. In much of the South, farmhouses and barns had been burned and plantations wrecked. Railroads and bridges had been systematically destroyed.

There was also enormous financial devastation: Banks had collapsed, and Confederate money and bonds were worthless. The plantation owners had lost their slaves, that represented an investment of over $2 billion. The entire economy of the South was in chaos.

The human toll of the war was tremendous. The war had taken the lives of 258,000 Confederate soldiers and civilians, and countless others had been wounded and maimed.

The Freed Slaves

While conditions were bad for southern whites, they were

even worse for the recently freed slaves. President Abraham Lincoln's *Emancipation Proclamation* of 1863 had abolished slavery throughout most of the South. Then, in February 1865, Congress passed the Thirteenth Amendment to the Constitution, making slavery unconstitutional in all of the United States; this amendment went into effect in December 1865. Four million blacks now emerged from slavery into freedom, but they had no land, few possessions, and little chance of finding work. Also, serious tensions existed between blacks and their former masters.

The Freedmen's Bureau

In March 1865, Congress created the Freedmen's Bureau, a branch of the War Department. This agency provided the freed slaves with emergency food and housing. It also found work for thousands of blacks and settled thousands of others on confiscated and abandoned land. In addition, the Freedmen's Bureau built thousands of schools. More than forty hospitals were constructed to provide much-needed medical care. It also attempted to protect the blacks' civil rights. But even with the work of the Freedmen's Bureau, blacks continued to face serious problems.

Lincoln and Reconstruction

During the Civil War, President Lincoln had begun to develop a plan for the readmission of the Confederate states to the Union. He took a moderate approach, rejecting suggestions that the southern states should be treated as conquered provinces. In Lincoln's view, secession was unconstitutional. Therefore, in a legal sense, the Confederate states had never left the Union.

In December 1863, Lincoln announced his plan for Reconstruction. The plan offered amnesty to white southerners who pledged their loyalty to the United States government, with the temporary exception of high-ranking Confederate civilian and military officials. Under what has been called the Ten Percent Plan, any former Confederate state could form a new government whenever a number equal to 10 percent of those who had voted in 1860 took an oath of loyalty to the Union. In Louisiana, Arkansas, and Tennessee, which were occupied by Union troops, state governments loyal to the Union were set up during 1864.

Radical Republican Opposition

Radical Republicans, led by Senator Charles Sumner of Massachusetts and Representative Thaddeus Stevens of Pennsylvania, rejected Lincoln's moderation. Congress refused to seat the representatives elected from Louisiana, Arkansas, and Tennessee and would not count their electoral votes in the 1864 presidential election.

The Wade-Davis Bill

In July 1864, Congress passed the Wade-Davis Bill, which stated that the Confederacy be treated as conquered territory. The bill authorized the President to appoint a governor for each state. Whenever a majority of the adult white males in that state took an oath of loyalty to the Union, the governor would call for the election of a state constitutional convention. Delegates elected to the convention would be required to take an "ironclad oath" that they had never borne arms against the Union and had never held any Confederate office. The Wade-Davis Bill required the new state constitutions to recognize the abolition of slavery, to deny voting rights to Confederate military and civilian leaders, and to repudiate debts incurred by the state during the Civil War. When these conditions were met, Congress would readmit the state to the Union.

Lincoln responded to the Wade-Davis Bill with a pocket veto, which enraged the Radical Republicans.

President Andrew Johnson

On April 14, 1865, President Lincoln was assassinated by John Wilkes Booth. Vice President Andrew Johnson succeeded to the Presidency. A former senator from Tennessee, Johnson was a Jacksonian Democrat who blamed the southern aristocracy for the Civil War. He was the only southern senator to remain in the Senate when his state seceded, and he was chosen as Lincoln's running mate in 1864.

Johnson's Plan for Reconstruction

Like Lincoln, Johnson favored a moderate approach to Reconstruction. The new President granted pardons to all supporters of the Confederacy who took an oath to support the United States Constitution, with the exception of some high officeholders and large property owners. Johnson accepted Reconstruction as complete in Louisiana, Arkansas, Tennessee, and Virginia. In the seven other states of the former Confederacy, he set up provisional governments. Loyal white citizens of these states were authorized to write new constitutions. Each state was required to declare secession null and void, repudiate state debts incurred under the Confederacy, and ratify the Thirteenth Amendment. By the end of 1865, every former Confederate state except Texas had met these requirements.

Southern Intransigence

In many cases, Southerners elected prominent supporters of the Confederacy to their state constitutional conventions and newly elected legislatures. When restored to the Union, the southern states elected many ex-Confederates to the House of

Representatives and the Senate. Alexander Stephens of Georgia, the former Vice President of the Confederacy, even won election to the Senate.

To make matters worse, the southern states adopted a series of Black Codes which imposed strict regulations on the former slaves. While some of the blacks' rights of citizenship were recognized, the Black Codes helped maintain white supremacy by limiting the political, legal, economic, and social rights of the freedmen. The Black Codes varied from state to state, but typically blacks were denied the right to vote or hold public office, barred from serving on juries, and forbidden to bear arms. Unless they secured a special license, blacks could not work in any occupation except that of agricultural laborer. Restrictions were also placed on the right of blacks to own property.

These actions by the southern states aroused resentment and anger in the North. The Radical Republicans insisted that the South obviously was unwilling to accept the consequences of its defeat and that stronger action was needed.

The Beginning of Radical Reconstruction

In 1865, Congress refused to seat the representatives and senators elected by the southern states. The Radical Republicans then established a congressional Joint Committee on Reconstruction to press their own solutions to the problem of the South. Congressional support of Radical Reconstruction intensified conflict between Congress and the President.

In February 1866, Congress adopted a bill to continue the work of the Freedmen's Bureau indefinitely and to expand the scope of its authority. (The Freedmen's Bureau had been scheduled to cease operations in June 1868.) Johnson believed that the Freedmen's Bureau represented an unwarranted interference by the federal government with the rights of the states. He issued a strongly worded veto of the Freedmen's Bureau Bill, and followed with a vehement outburst of criticism of the leading Radical Republicans. The Radical Republicans were furious but failed to win enough support in Congress to override the President's veto. In July, however, Congress passed a slightly modified version of the Freedmen's Bureau Bill and then overrode a second presidential veto.

The Civil Rights Bill

In March 1866, Congress passed the Civil Rights Bill, which struck out at the Black Codes. The Civil Rights Bill recognized the full citizenship of blacks and their equal civil rights. The federal government was authorized to intervene in the affairs of a state when it was necessary to do so in order to protect the rights of citizens. Johnson, who believed strongly in states' rights, vetoed the Civil Rights Bill. The President's action angered even many moderates in Congress, who then joined with the Radicals to override the veto. Congress was clearly gaining the upper hand in its conflict with the President.

The Fourteenth Amendment

In April 1866, the Joint Committee on Reconstruction proposed the adoption of the Fourteenth Amendment to the Constitution. The Fourteenth Amendment contained three major provisions:

Section One provided that all persons born or naturalized in the United States were citizens of the United States and of the state in which they resided. No state could impose restrictions on the rights of any citizen. No state could deprive any person of life, liberty or property without due process of law. No state could deny to any person the equal protection of the law.

Section Two provided that if any state denied voting rights to any of its adult male citizens, its representation in the House of Representatives and the electoral college would be reduced proportionately. This section has never been enforced.

Section Three prohibited former southern members of Congress and other officials who had supported the Confederacy from holding any state or federal office until this disability was removed by a two-thirds vote of each house of Congress.

After winning the endorsement of Congress, the Fourteenth Amendment was submitted to the states for ratification. Johnson urged the defeat of the amendment. Of the former Confederate states, only Tennessee ratified the Fourteenth Amendment, thereby gaining readmission to the Union. The other ten former Confederate states were joined by Kentucky and Delaware in refusing to ratify.

The Fourteenth Amendment failed to win ratification by the required three-fourths of the states and was thus defeated, but only temporarily. It ultimately went into effect in July 1868.

The 1866 Election

The South's defeat of the Fourteenth Amendment gave the Radical Republicans a powerful issue in the congressional election of 1866. This election involved, above all, a struggle for supremacy between the Radical Republicans and Johnson. Denouncing the Fourteenth Amendment, the President's supporters advocated a conciliatory policy toward the South. The President himself campaigned against candidates who opposed his policies. This was a mistake on two counts. First of all, in the nineteenth century, a president—or even a presidential candidate—did not campaign. It was considered undignified to do so. Second, Johnson's speeches were intemperate; they offended many people and caused the President to lose public support.

The Radicals argued that Johnson's moderate policies had failed. They pointed to the Black Codes and to race riots in

Memphis, New Orleans, and other southern cities as proof that a more determined Reconstruction program was needed.

The Radical Republicans won an overwhelming majority in both houses of Congress. They were now in a position to press forward with their own plan for Reconstruction in the ten former Confederate states that had not yet been readmitted to the Union.

Congressional Reconstruction

When Congress reconvened in December 1866, the Radical Republicans moved to impose their harsh program on the South.

A series of Reconstruction Acts, passed during 1867 and 1868, divided the ten former Confederate states that had not yet rejoined the Union into five military districts. These ten states were Virginia, North Carolina, South Carolina, Georgia, Florida, Alabama, Mississippi, Arkansas, Louisiana, and Texas. Thus, almost two years after the end of the Civil War, Congress established military government over the South. In each district, a general had full governmental authority to prepare the states in his district for readmission to the Union. In each state, new lists of registered voters, including former slaves, would be compiled. Whites who had actively supported the Confederacy would not be eligible to vote. These provisions made certain that the new state governments would be under Radical Republican control.

The Reconstruction Acts also established the terms for restoring the ten states to the Union. In each state, the newly registered voters would elect a constitutional convention. The new constitutions were required to provide guarantees of universal manhood suffrage. Once a state had adopted a constitution acceptable to Congress and had ratified the Fourteenth Amendment, its senators and representatives could take their seats in Congress.

In order to bar Johnson from removing Radical office holders, Congress passed the Tenure of Office Act of 1867. This

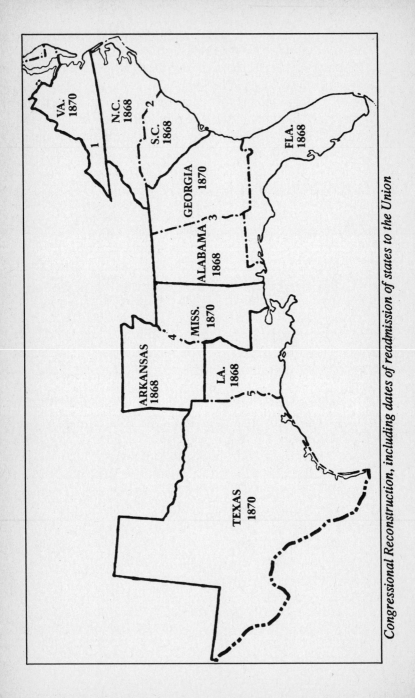

Congressional Reconstruction, including dates of readmission of states to the Union

law provided that the President could not remove any civil officials without the consent of the Senate. This law was intended,
in particular, to prevent the President from removing Edwin S.
Stanton, the Secretary of War, who was an ally of the Radicals.

The Command of the Army Act of 1867 required President
Johnson to issue orders to the military only through the General
of the Army, Ulysses S. Grant.

Congress passed these acts over the President's veto, as tension between Johnson and Congress mounted.

Impeachment of the President

In August 1867, Johnson removed Secretary of War Stanton,
because of Stanton's support of the Radicals and because the
President wanted to challenge the constitutionality of the Tenure
of Office Act.

The Radicals charged that the President's violation of the
Tenure of Office Act had provided grounds for impeachment.
Charges against the President were brought before the House of
Representatives, which voted in late February 1868 to impeach
Johnson because of his violation of the Tenure of Office Act and
because he had allegedly committed "high crimes and mis-
demeanors," the constitutional grounds for impeachment.

The impeachment of the President was followed by a trial in
the Senate, presided over by Chief Justice Salmon P. Chase.
During this trial, from March to May 1868, the President's
lawyers offered an able defense, arguing that the Tenure of Office Act was unconstitutional. Conviction of the President and
his removal from office required a two-thirds vote of the Senate.
Johnson was acquitted by a margin of only one vote.

Radical Reconstruction in the South

Under the terms of the Reconstruction Acts, new lists of
voters were prepared in the ten affected states. About 700,000

blacks were now voters, along with some 625,000 whites. About 150,000 whites lost their right to vote because of their support of the Confederacy.

Blacks won seats in most of the state constitutional conventions and also won election to the new state legislatures. It is an exaggeration, however, to speak of "Black Reconstruction," for the term suggests that blacks dominated the Reconstruction governments of the southern states. Only in South Carolina did blacks hold a majority of seats in the state legislature and then it was only for two years. When the southern states reentered the Union, several blacks won election to Congress. Mississippi elected two black senators, Hiram Revels and Blanche K. Bruce. But no state elected a black governor, and few blacks served as judges. Blacks thus played their major political role as voters rather than as officeholders. Throughout the South, the Union League, the Radicals' political organization, worked to recruit black voters as loyal supporters of the Republican party.

Among the whites in the new state governments were many "carpetbaggers" and "scalawags." A carpetbagger was a northern Republican. The name came from the fact that some of them had carried their possessions in cheap suitcases made of carpet material. The carpetbaggers had mixed motives. Many of them sincerely desired to help the South recover from the devastation of the war and to help blacks make the transition from slavery to a better life in freedom. In addition, many carpetbaggers brought valuable skills and much-needed capital to contribute to the South's economic recovery. Other carpetbaggers, however, had more selfish motives and came south primarily in hopes of gaining personal wealth and power.

The "scalawags" were native southern Republicans who supported Radical Reconstruction. Like the carpetbaggers, the scalawags acted from a mixture of motives. Many of them had opposed secession from the outset and now wanted to create a new South where blacks and poor whites would have a better life. Others were more interested in making personal gains.

Some of the new state governments acted irresponsibly, launching extravagant spending programs that resulted in enormous debts. There were also cases of fraud and corruption. But in this period of American history, the problem was hardly confined to Reconstruction governments in the South. Corruption afflicted many city administrations in the North—the Tweed Ring in New York is the most notorious example—as well as northern state governments and the administration of President Ulysses S. Grant.

Reconstruction governments in the South had a number of positive accomplishments to their credit. The new state constitutions provided for universal manhood suffrage, without property qualifications, and guaranteed civil liberties. The South acquired its first public school system, although the schools were racially segregated in fact if not by law. The practice of imprisonment for debt was ended. Public works projects resulted in the construction of much-needed roads, bridges, schools, and other public buildings. Taxes were reformed so that wealthier taxpayers would bear a larger part of the tax burden.

During 1868, seven states—North Carolina, South Carolina, Georgia, Florida, Alabama, Arkansas, and Louisiana—rejoined the Union. Georgia's readmission was rescinded, and the state did not gain reentry until 1870. Virginia, Mississippi, and Texas reentered the Union in 1870.

The Election of 1868

As their presidential candidate, the Republicans nominated the military hero, General Ulysses S. Grant. In 1868, the Republicans campaigned as supporters of a tough Reconstruction policy. In addition, the Republicans were identified with the interests of the northern industrialists, financiers, and railroad magnates in opposition to the agricultural interests of the South and West.

The Democrats nominated Horatio Seymour, the Civil War Governor of New York. The Democratic platform denounced Radical Reconstruction and endorsed the so-called Ohio Idea, a plan for the payment of the national debt in inflated greenbacks, rather than in gold. "Greenbacks" was the popular name given to the paper money issued during the Civil War. This proposal frightened many conservatives, even though Seymour repudiated this plank of his party's platform. The Republicans insisted that the national debt should be repaid in gold.

Even though the Republicans dominated the southern states readmitted to the Union in 1868, Grant won a relatively narrow victory, polling only 300,000 more votes than his opponent.

The Fifteenth Amendment

In February 1869, Congress approved the Fifteenth Amendment to the Constitution, which provided that no one could be denied the right to vote because of "race, color, or previous condition of servitude." Virginia, Mississippi, and Texas were required to ratify this amendment as a condition for their readmission to the Union in 1870. In the same year, the Fifteenth Amendment became a part of the Constitution.

The Southern Reaction to Radical Reconstruction

As the Civil War gradually receded in people's memories and as the North became increasingly concerned with its own political and economic problems, interest in Reconstruction began to decline. Gradually, conservative white southerners began to reassert their control.

This was a relatively easy task in those states where whites were a majority. All they had to do was to organize themselves politically and win elections. Presidential and congressional pardons restored voting rights to many individuals. Then, in 1872, Congress passed the Amnesty Act, which restored full political rights to about 150,000 whites.

In other states, where blacks held the majority or where the two races were about evenly balanced, whites frequently resorted to intimidation and violence to force blacks into submission. Secret white societies, such as the Ku Klux Klan and the Knights of the White Camellia, were established and carried out terroristic acts against blacks.

In an attempt to suppress these terrorist organizations, Congress passed a series of Enforcement Acts in 1870 and 1871, which were denounced by white southerners as the Force Acts. The first Enforcement Act imposed heavy penalties on persons convicted of interfering with any citizen's right to vote. The second of these laws placed congressional elections under the supervision of federal marshals and election supervisors. The third (popularly known as the Ku Klux Klan Act) outlawed such Klan activities as forming conspiracies, wearing disguises, and practicing intimidation. It also authorized the President to suspend habeas corpus (the Constitutional right of a citizen to have a court hearing before being imprisoned) when necessary to suppress what the act termed "armed combinations." President Grant invoked this act against members of the Ku Klux Klan in South Carolina in 1871. For the most part, however, these laws had no major impact.

Economic pressure was probably even more effective than terror in restoring white supremacy in the South. The former slaves had been freed, but they were still workers and remained dependent on whites. Blacks who would not readily submit to white domination lost their jobs, were unable to get credit, or were evicted from land on which they were tenants.

By 1871, Republican rule had ended in Virginia, North Carolina, and Georgia. White Democrats regained control of Texas in 1873, of Alabama and Arkansas in 1874, and of Mississippi in 1876. The rule of white Democrats was not restored in South Carolina, Louisiana, and Florida until the withdrawal of the last federal troops in early 1877.

The Grant Administration

The administration of Ulysses S. Grant has become virtually synonymous with graft and corruption, although the President himself was honest. After a career marked by forty years of failures, Grant had won both success and fame as commander of the Union armies during the Civil War. He came to the presidency without any political experience and made serious mistakes both in his appointments to office and in the choice of his personal associates. He regarded the presidency as an appropriate reward for the services he had rendered the nation and saw no reason why he should not share that reward with relatives and friends by giving them jobs, regardless of their qualifications. In its policies, the Grant administration strongly favored business, which was permitted to operate with little in the way of government interference and regulation. Businessmen regularly sought favors from the government and were often prepared to pay bribes to the officials capable of granting the favors. And many of Grant's appointees were more than willing to accept illegal payments in their efforts to use their offices to line their own pockets.

The Tweed Ring

One of the most notorious scandals of this scandal-ridden era did not, in fact, involve the Grant administration, but rather politicians in New York City, headed by "Boss" William M. Tweed, the leader of Tammany Hall, the Democratic party organization in the borough of Manhattan. The corrupt Tweed Ring bilked New Yorkers of $100 million—perhaps even as much as $200 million—before it was destroyed as a result of the investigative reporting of the *New York Times* and the biting cartoons drawn by Thomas Nast and published in *Harper's Weekly*. In 1871, Samuel J. Tilden won national notice by conducting the prosecution that resulted in Tweed's conviction.

Scandals of the Grant Administration

Having failed in business earlier in his career, President Grant greatly admired men who had built personal fortunes. Among his close associates were two notorious stock manipulators, Jim Fisk and Jay Gould, who quickly caused one of the first serious scandals of the Grant years.

In September 1869, Fisk and Gould attempted to make a quick fortune by cornering the nation's supply of gold. With the help of the President's brother-in-law, they spread a rumor that the government was ceasing the sale of gold from its reserves and bought as much gold as they could from private holders. The rapid increase in the price of gold forced many businessmen, who needed gold for their legitimate activities, into bankruptcy. Learning of the scheme, the President took belated action. On Black Friday, September 24, 1869, when the price of gold was at its height, the Treasury sold $4 million of its gold, forcing the price down.

The Crédit Mobilier scandal involved the Crédit Mobilier company, which had been formed in the 1860s to build the Union Pacific Railroad. The scandal broke during the years of 1872 and 1873, when it was revealed that members of Congress had been given stock in the Crédit Mobilier in an attempt to influence legislation affecting the railroads. Vice President Schuyler Colfax, who at the time had been Speaker of the House of Representatives, was implicated in the scandal.

In the Salary Grab scandal of 1873, Congress approved hefty salary increases for members of the three branches of the federal government, including 50-percent raises for representatives and senators which would be retroactive for the previous two years. A public outcry compelled Congress to revoke its own raise, although the others remained in effect.

In May 1874, a committee of the House of Representatives revealed the Sanborn contracts scandal. John D. Sanborn, a friend of Secretary of the Treasury William A. Richardson, had been paid a 50-percent commission for collecting unpaid taxes, with the commission money going to support Republican political activities. In order to avoid possible impeachment, Richardson resigned.

The Whiskey Ring scandal involved the disclosure that distillers had conspired with some treasury officials to avoid payment of excise taxes on whiskey. President Grant's private secretary was implicated in the scandal.

In March 1876, Secretary of War William W. Belknap resigned in order to avoid impeachment on charges that he had taken bribes in return for granting rights to establish trading posts in the Indian Territory.

The Election of 1872

As the presidential election of 1872 approached, the main opposition to Grant came from dissidents within his own Republican party, rather than from the Democrats. The anti-Grant rebels counted some prominent Republicans within their ranks. Among them was Senator Carl Schurz of Missouri, a German immigrant and a Civil War hero. The Liberal Republicans, as these dissidents called themselves, opposed high tariffs and believed that Radical Reconstruction should be ended and replaced by more conciliatory policies toward the South. They also favored civil service reform, which would put an end to favoritism and political patronage in appointments to public office.

The Liberal Republicans nominated Horace Greeley, the

respected but eccentric editor of the *New York Tribune*, for President. Instead of choosing a candidate of their own, the Democrats also nominated Greeley.

Although the Grant administration had showered favors on wealthy businessmen, the Republican campaign made a strong bid for the votes of working men. Grant won reelection by an overwhelming margin.

A few weeks after the election, Greeley died. His death symbolized the political demise of the Liberal Republicans.

The Panic of 1873

During Grant's second term, the scandals continued, and the President was also beset by an economic and financial collapse. The Panic of 1873 began with the failure in September of a major investment banking firm, Jay Cooke and Co., which had overextended itself by investing in railroad construction. As the panic spread, stock prices collapsed, and the New York Stock Exchange had to close for ten days. The panic soon became a general economic depression, which resulted primarily from an overexpansion of business and railroad building in the post-Civil War years. By 1874, 3 million workers were unemployed. A major political consequence of the depression came in the congressional elections of 1874, when the Democrats won control of the House of Representatives.

The Election of 1876

The year 1876 looked promising for the Democrats, for they could lay the blame for the depression at Grant's doorstep and condemn their Republican opponents for the scandals of the Grant administration. In addition, the nation was tiring of the harsh policies of Radical Reconstruction.

As their presidential candidate, the Democrats selected Samuel J. Tilden, the Governor of New York, who had gained fame for his successful prosecution of the Tweed Ring and was a strong advocate of reform.

The Republicans nominated Rutherford B. Hayes, the Governor of Ohio and a former Union general, who had a reputation for personal honesty.

The 1876 campaign was hard-fought and often bitter, although Tilden and Hayes agreed on the major issues. Both candidates favored the withdrawal of federal troops from the South. Both favored civil service reform. Both supported the gold standard and opposed government interference with private business. In addition, both had strong reputations for personal integrity.

The results of the election were indecisive. Tilden won a popular vote majority of about 250,000 and claimed 184 electoral votes, one short of the 185 needed for election. Hayes won 165 electoral votes. Twenty electoral votes were contested. Of these 20 contested electoral votes, 19 were in the three southern states—South Carolina, Florida, and Louisiana—which were still ruled by Republicans. Both parties claimed to have won these states, and two sets of rival electors appeared, one set pledged to Tilden, the other to Hayes. The remaining contested electoral vote was from Oregon. In order to win, Tilden needed only one of these contested votes, but Hayes needed all 20.

The Electoral Commission

Congress could not readily decide the disputed election since the Democrats controlled the House of Representatives and the Republicans dominated the Senate. In late January 1877, congressional moderates proposed that the dispute be submitted to an Electoral Commission of 15 members, five each from the House of Representatives, the Senate, and the Supreme Court. There would be seven Republicans, seven Democrats, and one nonpartisan Supreme Court justice. This plan was foiled when the Illinois legislature elected this justice to the Senate. His place on the Electoral Commission was taken by another justice, who was a partisan Republican.

Following party lines, the Electoral Commission voted by a margin of eight to seven to accept all the contested electoral votes as votes for Hayes, thus giving him the presidency. However, the decision of the Electoral Commission required the endorsement of the Democratic-controlled House of Representatives. The House Democrats balked until a compromise was worked out; the compromise ended Reconstruction in the South and gave Hayes the election.

The Compromise of 1877

White southern Democrats favored Tilden, the Democratic presidential candidate. However, when it seemed likely that Tilden would lose, the southerners decided to make the best deal possible. Under the terms of the Compromise of 1877, federal troops would be withdrawn from South Carolina and Louisiana, thus removing the main support of the Republican governments in those states. A southern Democrat would become Postmaster General in the Hayes cabinet, and southern Democrats would control appointments to federal offices in the South. In addition, the Republican administration in Washington would provide federal assistance to promote the South's economic development.

The Compromise of 1877 ended the dispute over the results of the 1876 election. Hayes was declared elected only two days before his inauguration on March 4, 1877.

In effect, the Compromise of 1877 involved the Republicans' acceptance of the white southerners' claims to home rule. The Republicans thus abandoned Reconstruction, ending their support of the former slaves, the carpetbaggers, and the scalawags, and agreed not to push for the enforcement of the

Civil Rights Act and the Fourteenth and Fifteenth Amendments. Few obstacles now remained in the path of the establishment of white conservative supremacy throughout the South. Nevertheless, the Fourteenth and Fifteenth Amendments, although forgotten for the moment, remained a part of the Constitution and were available to be invoked by a later generation of Americans.

Foreign Affairs Under Johnson and Grant

Presidents Johnson and Grant were ably served by their Secretaries of State, William H. Seward and Hamilton Fish, respectively. During Seward's tenure, the United States contended with French intervention in Mexico and purchased Alaska from the Russians. Among Fish's accomplishments was the resolution of several disputes with Great Britain.

French Intervention in Mexico

In 1862, the French Emperor, Napoleon III, collaborated with conservative Mexican landowners and churchmen in installing Archduke Maximilian of Austria as Emperor of Mexico. The United States regarded this as a violation of the Monroe Doctrine, and Secretary of State Seward demanded the withdrawal of the French troops, without which Maximilian could not stay in power. The Civil War prevented the American government from taking more vigorous action.

Following the end of the war, President Johnson and Secretary of State Seward sent troops commanded by General Philip Sheridan to the Rio Grande frontier, and the American government gave tacit support to Benito Juarez, the Mexican revolutionary leader.

Confronted by a stiffening American attitude, as well as by growing problems in Europe, Napoleon III withdrew the French troops in May 1866. With French support gone, Maximilian fell from power and was executed by a Mexican firing squad.

Territorial Expansion

In 1867, the United States purchased Alaska from the Russians for $7.2 million. Although opponents of the purchase denounced it as "Seward's Folly," reports of Alaska's vast riches in gold, fish, and furs convinced Congress to approve it. Also in 1867, the United States occupied the Midway Islands, located in the Pacific Ocean west of Hawaii.

The Treaty of Washington (1871)

Over the years, a number of disputes had developed between the United States and Great Britain. The most serious resulted from British sympathy for the Confederate cause during the Civil War. Lax enforcement of British neutrality made it possible for British shipyards to produce cruisers for the Confederacy. These ships, the most famous of which was the *Alabama,* preyed upon Union shipping. The American government demanded compensation from the British for the damage caused by the cruisers. For several years, the dispute over the so-called *Alabama* Claims remained unresolved.

The Treaty of Washington of 1871 settled this and several other Anglo-American disputes. The British acknowledged their partisan behavior during the Civil War and agreed that the *Alabama* Claims should be submitted to an international tribunal. Meeting in Geneva, Switzerland, in 1872, the arbitration panel awarded the United States $15.5 million.

Another provision of the Treaty of Washington led to an award of $2 million to Great Britain for property lost by British subjects during the Civil War. The treaty also provided for a new definition of the fishing rights of American fishermen in the North Atlantic off the shores of Newfoundland, while the arbitration panel awarded $5.5 million to Great Britain in settlement of claims against the United States resulting from previous American fishing in these waters. Yet another arbitration panel established the border between the United States and British Columbia in the area of Puget Sound.

The settlement of these disputes by peaceful means was important in establishing an improved relationship between the United States and Great Britain.

The end of Reconstruction in 1877 marked the failure of the Radical Republicans to reshape the South. In the states of the former Confederacy, the rule of conservative white Democrats was restored, and almost a century would pass before the Republican party became a significant factor in southern politics again. Despite the adoption of the Thirteenth, Fourteenth, and Fifteenth Amendments, Reconstruction also failed to establish the civil rights of black Americans. In national politics, the Republicans maintained their hold on the Presidency throughout the Reconstruction era, while the scandals of the Grant administration reflected the American people's growing obsession with wealth during what has come to be called the "Gilded Age."

In foreign affairs, the purchase of Alaska was the first acquisition of territory beyond the continental limits of the United States, while the resolution of differences with Great Britain helped lay the foundations of the Anglo-American "special relationship" which would play a central role in American foreign policy in the twentieth century.

Recommended Reading

Richard H. Abbott, *The Republican Party and the South, 1855–1877: The First Southern Strategy* (1986).

Herman Belz, *A New Birth of Freedom: The Republican Party and Freedmen's Rights, 1861 to 1866* (1976).

George R. Bentley, *A History of the Freedmen's Bureau* (1955).

William R. Brock, *An American Crisis: Congress and Reconstruction, 1865–1867* (1963).

Fawn Brodie, *Thaddeus Stevens: Scourge of the South* (1959).

LaWanda Cox and John H. Cox, *Politics, Principle, and Prejudice, 1865–1866: Dilemma of Reconstruction America* (1963).

Richard N. Current, *Those Terrible Carpetbaggers* (1988).

David H. Donald, *Charles Sumner and the Rights of Man* (1970).

David H. Donald, *The Politics of Reconstruction, 1863–1867* (1965).

W. E. B. DuBois, *Black Reconstruction* (1935).

Eric Foner, *Nothing But Freedom: Emancipation and Its Legacy* (1983).

John Hope Franklin, *Reconstruction After the Civil War* (1961).

William Gillette, *Retreat from Reconstruction, 1869–1879* (1979).

William B. Hesseltine, *Lincoln's Plan of Reconstruction* (1960).

Leon Litwack, *Been in the Storm So Long: The Aftermath of Slavery* (1979).

William S. McFeely, *Grant: A Biography* (1981).

Eric L. McKitrick, *Andrew Johnson and Reconstruction* (1960).

Rembert W. Patrick, *The Reconstruction of the Nation* (1967).

Michael Perman, *Reunion Without Compromise: The South and Reconstruction, 1865–1868* (1973).

Michael Perman, *The Road to Redemption: Southern Politics, 1869–1879* (1984).

Kenneth M. Stampp, *The Era of Reconstruction, 1865–1877* (1965).

Hans L. Trefousse, *Impeachment of a President: Andrew Johnson, the Blacks, and Reconstruction* (1975).

Hans L. Trefousse, *The Radical Republicans: Lincoln's Vanguard for Racial Justice* (1968).

Allen W. Trelease, *White Terror: The Ku Klux Klan Conspiracy and Southern Reconstruction* (1967).

Joel Williamson, *After Slavery: The Negro in South Carolina During Reconstruction, 1865–1877* (1965).

C. Vann Woodward, *Reunion and Reaction: The Compromise of 1877 and the End of Reconstruction* (1951).

CHAPTER 2

The New South and the New West

Time Line

1867	Nebraska acquires statehood
	Congress creates the Indian Peace Commission
1869	The first transcontinental railroad is completed
1873	Congress passes the Timber Culture Act
1874	Gold is discovered in the Black Hills of the Dakota Territory
1876	Colorado acquires statehood
	General George A. Custer's force is wiped out in the Battle of Little Big Horn
1877	The Nez Percé Indians resist relocation
	Congress passes the Desert Land Act
1878	Congress passes the Timber and Stone Act
1881	Booker T. Washington founds Tuskegee Institute in Alabama
1886	Henry W. Grady delivers his New South speech in New York
	Geronimo, the Apache leader, is captured
1887	Congress passes the Dawes Severalty Act
	A long-term drought begins in the Great Plains
1889	North Dakota, South Dakota, Montana, and Washington acquire statehood
1890s	Southern states restrict black voting rights and enact Jim Crow laws

1890	Wyoming and Idaho acquire statehood
	The Battle of Wounded Knee is fought in South Dakota
1893	Frederick Jackson Turner advances the Turner thesis
1895	Booker T. Washington proposes the Atlanta Compromise
1896	The *Plessy v. Ferguson* decision establishes the separate-but-equal doctrine
	Utah acquires statehood
1905	W. E. B. DuBois and his followers establish the Niagara Movement
1906	Congress passes the Burke Act
1907	Oklahoma acquires statehood
1910	The National Association for the Advancement of Colored People (NAACP) is established
1912	New Mexico and Arizona acquire statehood

The last years of the nineteenth century witnessed the emergence of the New South and the New West. Although still heavily agricultural, the New South strove to promote the development of industry and commerce. Dominated by conservative white Democrats, the New South was committed to the maintenance of white supremacy. Southerners restricted the political rights of blacks and their opportunities for economic, social, and educational advancement. At the end of the century, the South's development continued to lag behind that of the North. The

*region remained relatively poor and primarily agricultural, as
in the past.*

*The West, by contrast, experienced a remarkable growth and
development during the final years of the nineteenth century.
The story of the New West centers on railroad building and the
development of mining operations, cattle raising, and farming in
the lands beyond the Mississippi River which had been only sparsely settled by white Americans in the years before the Civil War.
It is the story of the triumph of white settlers in the face of great
natural obstacles. And it is also the tragic story of the often brutal suppression of the Indian tribes which once reigned supreme
in the Great Plains and the Desert Southwest.*

The New South

Politics in the New South

In the wake of the Compromise of 1877, conservative white
southern Democrats, the so-called Bourbons, moved to establish
their undisputed control of southern politics and government.
These Bourbons were also called Redeemers, because they had
"redeemed" their states from the rule of the Republican carpetbaggers and scalawags. By the end of 1877, white Democrats
had succeeded in reestablishing their control in every state which
had been subject to Reconstruction. Alongside the old planter
elite, bankers, merchants, industrialists, railroad men, and
lawyers came to exercise a powerful influence as members of
the southern ruling class.

While white southerners had condemned the state governments of the Reconstruction era for their fraud, corruption, and
extravagance, the new Bourbon-controlled governments were
also guilty of widespread graft and corruption. These new state
governments did practice financial retrenchment, however.
They reduced taxes, cutting back on support of public services.

While this policy benefited the industrialists and the owners of railroads and utilities, it did great harm to the public schools and also to the prisons. The state governments turned the prisons into an additional source of revenue by leasing prisoners out as cheap labor. This convict-lease system differed little from slavery and was often marked by extreme brutality in the treatment of the prisoners.

In the late nineteenth century, the South exerted considerably less influence on national politics than it had in the years prior to the Civil War, when southerners served as President for 50 of the 72 years—from the election of George Washington to the inauguration of Abraham Lincoln. In the half-century after 1865, Andrew Johnson was the only southerner to hold the office of President or Vice President. Few cabinet members, Supreme Court justices, and speakers of the House of Representatives were southerners. Throughout the post-Civil War era, few southerners supported the Republican party, which they regarded as the party of antislavery, the Union cause during the Civil War, and Radical Reconstruction. The one-party system thus remained entrenched in the South, which became known as the Solid South whose voters consistently supported Democratic candidates for both local and national office.

Industry in the New South

Henry W. Grady, the editor of the *Atlanta Constitution,* emerged as the most eloquent prophet of the New South. Grady believed that the South must develop an economy like that of the North, based on industry and commerce. In a famous speech in New York in 1886, Grady pictured a New South where there would be "a hundred farms for every plantation, fifty homes for every palace—and a diversified industry that meets the complex need of this complex age." Grady boasted, "We have fallen in love with work."

In the past, the South had shipped much of its cotton to textile mills in the North or to Europe. Now textile mills appeared in the South, especially in the Carolinas, Georgia, and Alabama.

The southern tobacco industry also flourished. The Duke family of North Carolina made a modest beginning at the end of the Civil War and, by the last years of the century, James B. Duke had built his American Tobacco Company, headquartered in Durham, North Carolina, into an industrial giant. By 1890, Duke had absorbed most of his competitors, and the American Tobacco Company held a near-monopoly of the processing of raw tobacco, producing close to 90 percent of the cigarettes sold in the United States.

In Alabama, where there were extensive deposits of iron ore and coal, an iron and steel industry developed, making Birmingham a major industrial center. Birmingham proudly called itself "the Pittsburgh of the South." By 1890, the capacity of southern iron and steel mills amounted to close to one-fifth of the nation's total.

Railroad building fostered the expansion of southern industry. In the decade from 1880 to 1890 alone, the South increased its railway mileage by 135 percent.

While the South expanded its industrial capacity, so, too, did the North. As a consequence, by 1900 the South's share of American industry amounted to only ten percent, the same as the share held by the South in 1860. Southern industrial wages remained low. In fact, low wages were an important element in attracting industry to the South. By 1900, the average income in the South was lower than it had been in 1860. Since much of the investment in the South's industrialization came from the North, with the profits returning northward, the South continued to have a largely colonial economy.

Agriculture in the New South

In the years after the Civil War, southern agriculture came to be characterized by tenancy. Most of the former slaves remained too poor to acquire land of their own and had to work land owned by large landowners. Some of these farmers were share tenants, who paid a specified share of the crop to the land-owners as rent. Others were sharecroppers, who were entitled only to whatever share of the crop remained after the landowners and merchants had sold the crop and taken their shares. In effect, sharecroppers and often tenants were left with little income. They depended on credit from local merchants, who charged an enormous rate of interest—often as high as 60 percent—on purchases of the necessities of life: clothing and food, as well as seed and tools. They had to pledge their share of the crop as security for this credit. This crop lien system trapped farmers in an unending cycle of debt and left them little better off than they had been under slavery. Meeting the debt to the merchants consumed most of the crop belonging to the sharecroppers and that of many tenants as well. Most of the tenants and sharecroppers were locked into debt peonage and had little chance of escaping.

In 1880, shortly after the end of Reconstruction, 36 percent of southern farmers were tenants or sharecroppers. By 1900, the figure had increased to 47 percent. By that point, 74 percent of all black farmers in the South and 35 percent of white farmers were tenants or sharecroppers.

Southern agriculture remained dependent on a few cash crops, like cotton and tobacco, and experienced little diversification. The crop lien system encouraged this dependence on cotton and tobacco, since these were commodities which could easily be stored and marketed by those to whom debts were owed. The South bought products it could have grown itself, from other areas of the country . To compound the problems of southern agriculture, much of the most productive farmland was in the hands of absentee owners. Southern farmers, like American farmers in general, suffered from the agricultural depression of the late nineteenth century, which reduced the income they received for their crops.

Southern society remained overwhelmingly rural and agricultural, as it had been before the Civil War. In 1890, more than 50 percent of the population of the North Atlantic states was classified as urban. Only 8.5 percent of the population of the South Atlantic states was so classified.

The Myth of the Old South

The emergence of the spirit of the New South was accompanied by a growth of nostalgia for a romanticized Old South. It is symbolic that Henry W. Grady, the prophet of the New South, and Joel Chandler Harris, the creator of "Uncle Remus," both worked for the *Atlanta Constitution*. According to the myth of the Old South, faithful slaves like Uncle Remus had lived happily alongside their noble white masters and the lovely southern belles and their handsome suitors in a world of plantation houses, magnolias, and mint juleps. As this myth of the Old South established itself in the minds of white southerners, the South moved into the future with one eye cast longingly on a past which had never truly existed.

Restriction of Black Voting Rights

The years following Reconstruction witnessed a gradual restriction of black voting rights. In some southern states, where blacks constituted close to half the population, white Democrats began early to restrict voting by blacks.

In other areas, voting by blacks continued for some years. Often, the conservative Bourbons would use a combination of bribery and intimidation to gain the votes of blacks in order to outweigh the votes of poor whites. Black voting also kept the

Republican party alive in some parts of the South. As long as blacks continued to vote, however, political control by the Bourbons was not secure.

By the 1890s, a full-scale assault on black voting rights got underway throughout the South. Because of the Fifteenth Amendment, which provided that the right to vote could not be denied because of race, white southerners had to find indirect ways to prevent blacks from voting. The poll tax offered one method. Few blacks had enough money to pay the tax, which was often cumulative. Another was the requirement of literacy and understanding tests. Voting registrars would administer difficult reading tests to prospective voters or else require them to explain a complex part of the Constitution.

These requirements affected both blacks and poor whites. In some cases, the Democratic elite was content to have poor whites barred from voting. In other cases, however, grandfather laws were adopted in order to permit more whites to vote. Under these grandfather laws, men who could not otherwise meet the requirements for voting could still be permitted to enter the voting booth if their ancestors had voted prior to Reconstruction or prior to the Civil War. Thus, poor whites were able to qualify as voters, while the former slaves and their descendants could not.

The United States Supreme Court did not interfere with the states' imposition of poll taxes or their adoption of literacy and understanding tests. In 1898, in the case of Williams v. Mississippi, the justices upheld the constitutionality of literacy tests.

The Supreme Court and Racial Segregation

During Reconstruction, the power of the federal government supported the cause of black rights. Subsequently, however, the Supreme Court came down on the side of white supremacy.

In the so-called Civil Rights Cases of 1883, the Supreme Court invalidated the Civil Rights Act of 1875, which had outlawed segregation in public facilities. While the Fourteenth Amendment prohibited states from discriminating on the basis of race, the justices held, this prohibition did not extend to individuals or private organizations. Racial segregation could therefore be legally enforced by railroads, hotels, theaters, and others serving the public.

The case of *Plessy v. Ferguson* in 1896 provided the most famous Supreme Court decision of the period on the question of segregation by race. The case involved a state law requiring the racial segregation of railroad passengers. The court ruled that this legally imposed segregation did not deprive blacks of equal rights so long as the separate accommodations were equal. The Supreme Court thus established the constitutional doctrine of separate-but-equal which provided a broad legal foundation for racial segregation generally and especially for the South's maintenance of racially segregated schools.

In 1899, the Supreme Court went beyond *Plessy v. Ferguson* in deciding the case of *Cummings v. County Board of Education*. The Court held that laws which established separate schools for whites were valid even if no comparable schools were provided for blacks.

With the backing of the Supreme Court, the southern states enacted laws, known as Jim Crow laws, enforcing racial segregation throughout the country. Schools, railroad trains, streetcars, waiting rooms, drinking fountains, public toilets, hospitals, prisons, and cemeteries were all segregated by race. Interracial marriage was prohibited.

Violence Against Blacks

By the 1890s, white violence against blacks showed a dramatic increase. Lynching was a national phenomenon, but it occurred more frequently in the South than elsewhere. During the 1890s, an average of 187 lynchings occurred each year in the

United States, 80 percent of them in the South. In the overwhelming majority of cases, the victims were black.

There were other instances of mob violence against blacks, as well. Race riots occurred in a number of cities, the most notorious of those of New Orleans in 1900 and Atlanta in 1906.

The Black Middle Class

Despite widespread discrimination and segregation, a black middle class emerged in the South, although it was proportionately smaller, poorer, and less influential than the white middle class. Middle-class blacks were able to acquire property, establish small businesses, and become professionals, such as teachers, lawyers, and physicians. A few blacks even became wealthy as founders of banks and insurance companies designed to serve a black clientele.

For the blacks who did succeed, the lesson was clear: Education provided the key to success. A number of black colleges were established, often with the assistance of northern churches and sometimes by southern state governments.

Booker T. Washington

In the late nineteenth century, Booker T. Washington emerged as the major black national leader, preaching a doctrine of hard work, thrift, sobriety, and self help. Born a slave in Virginia in 1856, Washington was educated at Virginia's Hampton Institute.

In 1881, with the help of northern philanthropists, Washington founded Tuskegee Institute in Alabama. Since Washington believed that most blacks would have to make their living by manual labor, Tuskegee specialized in vocational training in agriculture and the skilled trades.

In a famous 1895 speech, Washington set forth what came to be known as the "Atlanta Compromise." Blacks should not agitate for political or civil rights or social equality, Washington argued, and they should not challenge the system of racial segregation.   Instead, they should focus their attention on making economic gains.

White leaders accepted Washington as the leading spokesman for his race.   Presidents consulted him on issues dealing with blacks, and he maintained close relations with business leaders and philanthropists.

W. E. B. DuBois

W. E. B. DuBois became the most outspoken challenger of the moderation urged by Booker T. Washington and of the whole system of white supremacy.   Born in 1868 in western Massachusetts, DuBois was educated at the all-black Fisk University in Nashville, Tennessee, and then became the first American black to earn a Ph.D. at Harvard.   He became a professor at Atlanta University and then, in 1910, joined the faculty at the University of Pennsylvania.

At first, DuBois supported Washington's philosophy of black self help but later came to reject the Atlanta Compromise. Writing in The *Souls of Black Folk* in 1903, DuBois accused Washington of supporting white efforts to enforce racial segregation.   Blacks should not be content to be trained in agriculture and the skilled trades.   Instead, DuBois argued, blacks should seek a full university education and strive for careers in the professions.   Furthermore, blacks should reject segregation and agitate for a restoration of their civil rights.   In powerful words, DuBois proclaimed: "Separate schools for whites and blacks are not equal, can not be made equal, and . . . are not intended to be equal."

The Founding of the NAACP

In 1905, DuBois and a group of his followers met in Niagara

Falls, Canada, and founded the Niagara Movement. They called on black Americans to protest the denial of their civil rights and inequality in economic opportunity.

In 1910, the Niagara Movement joined with white supporters to establish the National Association for the Advancement of Colored People (NAACP), which pushed for a recognition of the civil rights of blacks.

The NAACP won one of its first victories in 1915, in the case of *Guinn v. United States,* with the Supreme Court ruling that Oklahoma's grandfather law was unconstitutional. Two years later, in 1917, the Supreme Court, in the case of *Buchanan v. Worley,* invalidated a Louisville, Kentucky, ordinance requiring residential segregation.

In the ensuing years, the NAACP continued its struggle on behalf of black Americans.

The New West

Settlement of the West

By the 1860s, a substantial number of white—and some black—settlers had crossed the Mississippi River into Arkansas, Missouri, Iowa, and Minnesota, and some had moved even further west into eastern Texas, Kansas, and Nebraska. In the Far West, along the Pacific coast, sizable white settlements had been established in California and Oregon.

The land in between remained the domain of the Indians. Then, in the years following the Civil War, Americans began to settle the New West. This area consisted of two regions. From a line drawn from the Dakotas southward through Texas, the Great Plains extended westward to the Rocky Mountains. Because of their semi-arid character, the Great Plains had become known as the Great American Desert and had attracted few settlers. West of the Rocky Mountains, a high arid Western Plateau reached westward to the Sierra Nevada and Cascade Mountains of California and the Pacific Northwest.

Extension of Statehood

During the Civil War and after, a host of new states gained admission to the Union. Kansas acquired statehood in 1861, with Nevada following in 1864 and Nebraska in 1867. During the 1860s, territorial governments were established in Dakota, Montana, Idaho, Wyoming, Colorado, and Arizona.

Of these territories, Colorado was the first to gain statehood, in 1876. By 1889, the Dakota Territory had been separated, and North and South Dakota entered the Union. Montana and Washington became states in the same year. In the following year, 1890, Wyoming and Idaho entered the Union. Utah gained statehood in 1896, after the state's Mormon religious leaders agreed to outlaw the practice of polygamy.

By the end of the century, only three territories had not acquired statehood: Oklahoma, New Mexico, and Arizona. Oklahoma, which had formerly been the Indian Territory, admitted white settlers and was granted territorial status in 1889–90. Oklahoma became a state in 1907, while New Mexico and Arizona entered the Union in 1912.

The Indians of the West

The western Indian tribes had different patterns of culture. In the southwest, the Pueblo Indians lived a settled life as farmers. They grew corn, developed methods of irrigation, and built adobe houses.

Other southwestern Indians, such as the Navaho and Apache tribes, lived a semi-nomadic life, moving their settlements from place to place and supporting themselves by farming, hunting, and raising sheep.

The Plains Indians were the most numerous of the western

tribes, numbering close to 250,000 at the end of the Civil War. The Plains Indians included the Comanche, Kiowa, Cheyenne, Arapaho, Crow, and Sioux tribes. The Plains Indians lived a nomadic life centered on the horse, the buffalo, and the open grasslands. Their horses were small, muscular animals descended from horses brought to America by the Spanish. As the Plains Indians roamed the open land in search of buffalo, they lived in tepees as their temporary dwellings.

The whole way of life of the Plains Indians focused on the American buffalo, or bison. In 1865, about 15 million of these huge grazing animals roamed the Great Plains. The Plains Indians ate buffalo meat, while the animal's skin provided the material for the Indians' clothing, shoes, blankets, and tepees. Dried buffalo manure ("buffalo chips") provided a ready source of fuel, while buffalo tendons were used for the strings of bows and buffalo bones were carved into tools.

The Indians of the Great Plains fought a prolonged and bitter struggle against the westward push of white civilization. They may have inflicted more casualties on their enemies than the whites inflicted on them. But in the end, the Indians were defeated. They were forced to accept whatever land was designated for them and to settle down as farmers.

Federal Relations with the Indians

The Indians' resistance to white encroachment on their land compelled the federal government to attempt to find a new approach to its dealings with the Indians.

In 1867, Congress established the Indian Peace Commission, consisting of both civilians and military men, with the task of developing a new and permanent Indian policy. The Indian Peace Commission proposed that the Plains Indians should be moved onto two large reservations. One would be in the Indian Territory, which later became Oklahoma. The other would be in

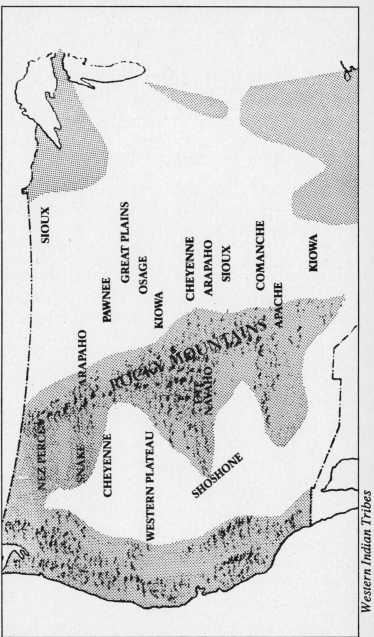

SIOUX

GREAT PLAINS

PAWNEE

OSAGE

KIOWA

CHEYENNE

ARAPAHO

SIOUX

COMANCHE

KIOWA

ARAPAHO

APACHE

NEZ PERCES

SNAKE

CHEYENNE

WESTERN PLATEAU

THE IDAHO

SHOSHONE

ROCKY MOUNTAINS

Western Indian Tribes

the Dakota Territory, comprising about two-thirds of what is today South Dakota. Reservations would also be established for the Navaho, Apache, and other Indians of the southwest and for the Indian tribes of the Rocky Mountain area.

Government agents cajoled, tricked, bribed, and otherwise compelled the leaders of the various tribes into accepting the treaties which created the new reservations. But this solution proved to be as unsatisfactory as the solutions which had preceded it.

Relations with the Indians, generally, and the administration of the reservations, specifically, were entrusted to the Bureau of Indian Affairs, an agency of the Interior Department. Even the bureau's best-intentioned officials had little understanding of the Indians and their culture. Other officials were guilty of corruption. Often the reservations were poorly administered. All of these things contributed to tension and conflicts between Indians and whites.

The Slaughter of the Buffalo

The problem was worsened by the whites' slaughtering of buffalo, which threatened the foundation of the whole way of life of the Plains Indians. A great demand for buffalo hides developed when buffalo robes and clothing made of buffalo skin became popular in the East. Other buffalo were hunted for sport. William F. "Buffalo Bill" Cody boasted that he had shot over 4,000 buffalo in the northern herd in less than two years.

By 1875, the northern herd had been virtually exterminated. A few years later, the smaller southern herd had also been almost totally eliminated. Fewer than 1,000 buffalo survived. Faced with the destruction of the buffalo and increasing white encroachment on their land, the Indians felt compelled to fight in an effort to preserve their way of life.

The Indian Wars

From the 1860s to the 1880s, Indian wars were being fought almost constantly.

During the Civil War, the eastern Sioux in Minnesota rose up in protest against the inadequacy of their reservation and the exploitation of corrupt whites. Led by Little Crow, the Sioux killed over 700 whites before their revolt was crushed and the tribe was forced to move to the Dakotas.

There was also trouble in Colorado during the Civil War, when the Indians became angry because white miners were moving onto their land. From 1861 to 1864, the Arapaho and Cheyenne Indians attacked stagecoaches and raided white settlements. This Indian war ended with the Chivington Massacre, when local militiamen killed over 450 Indian men, women, and children.

Following the Civil War, fighting broke out on several fronts. One of the most famous incidents in the Indian wars occurred when the Sioux rose up to oppose the encroachment of white miners in the Black Hills of the southwestern Dakota Territory. These lands had been reserved for the Indians by a treaty signed in 1868.

Under the leadership of Crazy Horse and Sitting Bull, the Sioux gathered in Montana, and army units were dispatched against the Sioux. General George A. Custer commanded one of these units. In 1876, at the Battle of Little Big Horn, the Indians surprised and wiped out Custer and his force of over 200 cavalrymen. In the wake of the battle, Sitting Bull escaped to Canada. Crazy Horse was taken prisoner in 1877.

In that same year, whites demanded that the Nez Percé Indians, who had a reputation for peacefulness, move to a smaller reservation. The Nez Percé refused. When troops began to move against them, Chief Joseph attempted to lead his followers to Canada. Moving against the Nez Percé, the troops caught them just before they reached the Canadian border. They were sent off to the Indian Territory, where most soon died of malnutrition and disease.

Further to the south, the Apaches resisted the white advance from the 1860s to the 1880s. The final resistance of the Apaches was led by Geronimo, who took refuge in the mountains of northern Mexico. For ten years, until he was captured in 1886, Geronimo led raids across the border.

The final great encounter between whites and Indians, the so-called Ghost Dance War, occurred in 1890. An emotional religious revival developed among the Indians, involving stories of the coming of a messiah and a ghost dance ritual. Agents on the Black Hills Sioux reservation feared a possible Indian uprising and called in troops. Some of the Sioux fled to the Badlands of South Dakota, where they joined others under the leadership of Chief Big Foot. The Indians fought the Seventh Cavalry at the Battle of Wounded Knee, South Dakota. Forty soldiers and 200 Indians, including women and children, died in the battle.

Federal Indian Land Policy

By 1885, about 170 Indian reservations had been established. In 1887, Congress passed the Dawes Severalty Act, which provided encouragement for Indians to settle down as individual farmers, emulating the lifestyle of the white settlers of the West. The Dawes Act proposed a gradual end of the ownership of land by Indian tribes and its replacement with individual ownership. It provided that tracts of land be allotted to individuals: A head of a family would receive 160 acres, while 80 acres would go to single adults, with 40 acres allotted to each dependent child. The Dawes Act also provided that adult landowners would receive citizenship and, after 25 years, would gain full title to their land.

Although well-intentioned, the Dawes Act failed to accomplish what it had set out to do. The Indians were not ready to give up their strong tribal bonds for the kind of individualism that was strange to them, however normal it was for white Americans.

In 1906, Congress passed the Burke Act in an attempt to provide greater incentives for the Indians to abandon their tribal membership in favor of individual citizenship. The Burke Act provided that the granting of citizenship should be deferred until the completion of the 25-year period provided for in the Dawes Act. However, Indians who proved they could adapt to the new lifestyle of individual farming could acquire both citizenship and title to their land in a shorter time. The Burke Act, like earlier legislation, did not provide the means for assimilating the Indians into the majority culture. A law adopted in 1924 granted citizenship to the Indians.

Government Encouragement of Western Settlement

Congress sought to encourage the settlement of the West and adopted legislation to further that end. Under the provisions of the Homestead Act of 1862, settlers could gain title to 160 acres of public land, paying only a small registration fee, if they promised to occupy and improve the land for at least five years.

In practice, the results of the Homestead Act were disappointing. One problem was that a farm of 160 acres was not large enough for the kind of agriculture—grain cultivation and cattle grazing—best suited to the semi-arid land of the Great Plains. Four hundred thousand homesteaders became owners of their land, but many more gave up and moved on.

In an effort to provide homesteaders with more land, Congress passed the Timber Culture Act of 1873. According to this law homesteaders could acquire an additional 160 acres if they promised to plant 40 acres of trees. About 10 million acres were allotted under this act.

The Desert Land Act of 1877 provided for the sale of 640 acre plots of federal land at $1.25 an acre to buyers who agreed to irrigate part of this land within three years.

The Timber and Stone Act of 1878 applied to land that was "unfit for cultivation." Buyers could purchase 160 acres of this land at $2.50 per acre.

Mining, lumber, and cattle companies often used fraud to acquire large tracts of land under these laws.

In addition to securing it from the federal government, there were other opportunities for acquiring land cheaply. Land could be bought from the great transcontinental railroads, which had received grants of millions of acres of federal land, and from state governments, which were also the beneficiaries of federal land grants. The Morrill Act of 1862 had granted land to the states for the endowment of agricultural and mechanical colleges.

By 1890, there had been such extensive settlement of the West that the Census Bureau announced the end of a frontier line.

The Turner Thesis

In 1893, historian Frederick Jackson Turner published an essay entitled "The Significance of the Frontier in American History." According to the Turner thesis, the isolation of the frontier and the qualities which people needed to push the frontier westward had promoted the development of American individualism and the nature of their democratic society and government. It was the existence of the frontier more than anything else, Turner claimed, that made America and Americans what they were.

Turner exaggerated. Frontier society was not as democratic as he claimed. And Turner attributed too much influence to the frontier in the shaping of American character and institutions.

At the same time, Turner had redirected attention to what he called the "really American part of our history."

The Building of the Transcontinental Railroads

The building of the transcontinental railroads did much to encourage the settlement of the West.

An 1862 act of Congress, amended in 1864, chartered two railroad companies, the Union Pacific and the Central Pacific. Two companies were then established to undertake the construction. The Crédit Mobilier built the Union Pacific westward from Omaha, Nebraska, while the Crocker Corporation built the Central Pacific eastward from Sacramento, California. The Crocker Corporation created four great California fortunes, those of Charles Crocker, Mark Hopkins, Collis P. Huntington, and Leland Stanford.

To assist the construction of the railroads, Congress provided land grants. The railroads would receive the right of way for their tracks, plus 20 square miles of land for each mile of track laid. These grants were given in alternate sections, laid out in checkerboard fashion along the right of way. The railroads sold much of this land to settlers at prices ranging from two to five dollars an acre.

Much of the construction was done by immigrant labor: Irish worked on the Union Pacific, while Chinese workers built the Central Pacific. The two lines met at Promontory Point, Utah, in 1869, with the driving in of a golden spike marking the occasion.

Other transcontinental railroad lines followed. The Southern Pacific Railroad, completed in 1883, joined San Francisco and New Orleans, by way of Yuma, Arizona, and El Paso, Texas. Further to the north, the Atchison, Topeka, and Santa Fe Railroad generally followed the course of the old Santa Fe Trail, joining Kansas City and Los Angeles by way of Santa Fe and Albuquerque, New Mexico. The railroad reached Santa Fe in 1882 and was joined with the Southern Pacific line to California the next year.

Two other transcontinental lines were built farther north. The Northern Pacific, from Duluth on Lake Superior and St. Paul, Minnesota, provided a link with Seattle, Washington, and Portland, Oregon; the route to Portland was completed in 1883. Construction of all of these railroads was undertaken with the assistance of federal land grants.

James J. Hill built the Great Northern Railroad without land grant assistance. Joining St. Paul, Minnesota, and Tacoma, Washington, the Great Northern was completed in 1893.

Branch lines of the great transcontinental railroads opened the West further to cattle ranching and farming.

Mining

The years from 1860 to 1890 witnessed a boom in mining in the West, especially in the mountain and plateau regions.

The great California gold rush had occurred back in 1849, and discovery in other areas followed. In 1858, gold was discovered in the Pike's Peak district near Denver in Colorado. By 1859, at least 100,000 prospectors arrived from all over the United States.

In 1859, both gold and silver were discovered at the Comstock Lode, beginning a great mining boom in the Washoe Mountains of western Nevada. As the "Fifty-Niners" rushed into the area, Virginia City became Nevada's major mining city. The flood of miners helped provide the basis for Nevada's gaining statehood in 1864.

During the 1860s, there were other strikes in Montana, Idaho, and Wyoming. In 1874, gold was found in the Black Hills of the southwestern Dakota Territory. Here Deadwood, the town of "Wild Bill" Hickock and Calamity Jane, won notoriety as one of the wildest of the mining towns. A decade later, rich deposits of silver were found in the Coeur d'Alene region of Idaho.

Almost everywhere, the fluctuating pattern of mining was similar. First, the prospectors rushed in, skimming the gold or silver from the surface of the earth and from streams. Then came the corporations, which had the necessary capital to dig mine shafts deep into the earth and to operate the crushing mills needed to extract the precious metals from the ore.

Gradually the ore deposits would dwindle. Mining would then come to a halt or else continue on a reduced scale. Once booming mining towns would begin to turn into ghost towns, cattle ranchers or farmers would begin to move into the area as permanent settlers.

Cattle Raising

The vast publicly owned grasslands of the Great Plains offered cattle raisers an opportunity to graze their herds free of charge, while the transcontinental railroads provided access to markets further east.

Western cattle raising had its beginnings in Texas. There, at the end of the Civil War, there were some five million head of cattle, largely unclaimed and running wild. These Texas longhorns were the descendants of cattle brought to America by the Spanish.

Texas also provided the small, rugged horses used by the cowboys who herded the cattle.

In 1866, a group of Texas cattlemen joined forces to drive their herds, totaling 260,000 head, northward to Sedalia, Missouri, on the Missouri Pacific Railroad. This was the first of the fabled long drives. Although there were heavy losses of cattle, the drive proved that herds of cattle could be moved great distances and allowed to graze along the way, with the cattle gaining weight during the drive.

There were several major trails leading to market facilities on the railroads. The Sedalia Trail went to Sedalia, Missouri, while a more western branch led to Kansas City, both on the Missouri Pacific Railroad. The famed Chisholm Trail led to Ellsworth, Abilene, and Wichita, all in Kansas, on the Kansas Pacific Railroad, a branch of the Union Pacific. The Western Trail ran to Dodge City, Kansas, on the Atchison, Topeka, and Santa Fe Railroad and further north to Ogallala, Nebraska, on the Union Pacific. The westernmost trail, the Goodnight-Loving Trail, reached Cheyenne and Laramie, Wyoming, also on the Union Pacific.

When railroads reached the Texas cattle country during the 1870s, the era of the long drives ended.

Gradually, the Texas longhorns were introduced in the upper Great Plains, where the hardy animals demonstrated their ability to survive the harsh winters. Crossbreeding with Angus and Hereford cattle brought in from the East produced improved beef cattle.

During the 1880s, the grazing of cattle on the open range came to an end. The overexpansion of cattle raising caused a severe drop in cattle prices beginning in 1882. Then vast herds of cattle died during the terrible winter of 1885–86, when snow and ice buried the grazing grass. Cattlemen began to gather hay to feed their cattle during the winter and to construct barbed wire fences around their land. No longer would cattle be left on the open range to fend for themselves. The age of the cattle ranch had begun.

Farming

Several years of higher than normal rainfall from 1878 to 1886 altered the reputation of the Great Plains as the Great American Desert, and an increasing number of farmers were encouraged to move into the area. While many of these settlers came from the older established areas of the Middle West, others were immigrants from Europe, especially Scandinavia and Germany. The opening of the Great Plains to farmers is one reason why more land was put into cultivation in the United States between 1870 and 1900 than in the previous 250 years.

From the late 1870s to the mid-1880s, the new western farmers experienced generally good times. With American farmers in the West and elsewhere producing more than ever before, however, there came to be an oversupply of agricultural produce and prices which began to decline. By the mid-1880s, an agricultural depression had begun.

The problems of the western farmers were intensified by a series of dry seasons which began in 1887. Large-scale irrigation, which was beyond the means of most farmers, was the only solution.

As the farmers' problems mounted, so, too, did their grievances. The railroads were a common object of the farmers' wrath. The farmers depended on the railroads to get their crops to market and complained about the high rates the railroads charged. To compound the problem, the railroads controlled the grain elevators and the warehouses where the farmers' produce was stored.

Farmers also had grievances against the banks and loan companies which charged them high rates of interest ranging from 10 to 25 percent. Farmers who borrowed money when conditions were good had problems repaying their loans in a time of agricultural depression.

The farmers complained, too, about prices: the low prices they received for their produce and the high prices they had to pay for manufactured goods.

As the farmers' grievances mounted, the foundations were being laid for a great national protest movement that would burst on the scene during the 1890s.

In the New South, political power remained solidly in the hands of conservative white Democrats, who gradually deprived blacks of their right to vote. The adoption of Jim Crow laws enforced racial segregation throughout southern society. While railroads and industry expanded, the South's industrial development continued to lag behind that of the North. Southern agriculture remained dependent on a few cash crops, such as cotton and tobacco, while most farmers—poor whites and blacks alike—were reduced to tenancy.

In the New West—the states and territories beyond the Mississippi River—white settlement increased dramatically during the final decades of the nineteenth century. As the West's population grew, a number of new states entered the Union. Throughout the West, the Indians were deprived of their land and confined to reservations. The federal government provided vast tracts of land to railroad builders and settlers, while mining, cattle raising, and farming came to form the backbone of the New West's economy.

Recommended Reading

The New South

W. J. Cash, *The Mind of the South* (1941).

Paul M. Gaston, *The New South Creed: A Study in Southern Myth Making* (1970).

Louis R. Harlan, *Booker T. Washington: The Making of a Black Leader, 1856–1901* (1972).

Louis R. Harlan, *Booker T. Washington: The Wizard of Tuskegee* (1983).

Stanley P. Hirshon, *Farewell to the Bloody Shirt: Northern Republicans and the Southern Negro, 1877–1893* (1962).

J. Morgan Kousser, *The Shaping of Southern Politics: Suffrage Restriction and the Establishment of the One-Party South, 1880–1910* (1974).

James M. McPherson, *The Abolitionist Legacy: From Reconstruction to the NAACP* (1976).

Raymond B. Nixon, *Henry W. Grady: Spokesman of the New South* (1943).

Howard N. Rabinowitz, *Race Relations in the Urban South, 1865–1890* (1980).

Roger L. Ransom and Richard Sutch, *One Kind of Freedom: The Economic Consequences of Emancipation* (1977).

Elliott M. Rudwick, *W. E. B. DuBois: Propagandist of the Negro Protest* (rev. ed., 1968).

Joel Williamson, *The Crucible of Race: Black-White Relations in the American South Since Emancipation* (1984).

C. Vann Woodward, *Origins of the New South, 1877–1913* (1951).

C. Vann Woodward, *The Strange Career of Jim Crow* (3rd rev. ed., 1974).

Gavin Wright, *Old South, New South: An Economic History Since the Civil War* (1986).

The New West

Ralph K. Andrist, *The Long Death: The Last Days of the Plains Indian* (1964).

Lewis Atherton, *The Cattle Kings* (1961).

Ray A. Billington, *Frederick Jackson Turner: Historian, Scholar, Teacher* (1973).

Ray A. Billington, *Westward Expansion: A History of the American Frontier* (2nd ed., 1960).

Dee Brown, *Bury My Heart at Wounded Knee: An Indian History of the American West* (1971).

Thomas D. Clark, *Frontier America: The Story of the Westward Movement* (2nd ed., 1969).

Robert R. Dykstra, *The Cattle Towns* (1968).

Gilbert C. Fite, *The Farmer's Frontier, 1865–1900* (1966).

Joe B. Frantz and Julian E. Choate, Jr., *The American Cowboy: The Myth and the Reality* (1955).

Frederick Merk, *History of the Westward Movement* (1978).

Rodman W. Paul, *Mining Frontiers of the Far West, 1848–1880* (1963).

Mari Sandoz, *The Buffalo Hunters: The Story of the Hide Men* (1954).

Fred A. Shannon, *The Farmer's Last Frontier* (1945).

Robert M. Utley, *Frontier Regulars: The United States Army and the Indian, 1866–1891* (1973).

Wilcomb E. Washburn, *The Indian in America* (1975).

CHAPTER 3

Industry and Labor
in the Late Nineteenth Century

Time Line

1859	America's first oil well is drilled in Pennsylvania
1866	William H. Sylvis establishes the National Labor Union
	Cyrus W. Field lays the first successful transatlantic cable
1869	The Knights of Labor is founded

1870	John D. Rockefeller establishes the Standard Oil Company
1873	The Panic of 1873 leads to a serious depression
1876	Alexander Graham Bell invents the telephone
1877	Railroad workers strike against the major eastern lines
	Swift and Co. ships the first refrigerator carload of beef from Chicago to Boston
1879	Thomas A. Edison develops the incandescent light bulb
	Terence V. Powderly becomes head of the Knights of Labor
1886	In the *Wabash Case*, the Supreme Court denies states the power to regulate the railroads
	The American Federation of Labor is established
	Labor protest results in violence in Haymarket Square, Chicago
1887	Congress passes the Interstate Commerce Act
1890	Congress enacts the Sherman Anti-Trust Act
1892	A strike at Pennsylvania's Homestead steel plant results in violence

1893	The Panic of 1893 leads to a serious depression
1894	Pullman Company workers go out on strike
1901	J. Pierpont Morgan organizes the United States Steel Corporation 1909
	Henry Ford begins to manufacture the Model T

During the years following the Civil War, the United States experienced tremendous economic growth. By 1890, industry had replaced agriculture as the most important sector of the economy. By 1900, the United States produced more than Great Britain and Germany—the world's top two economic powers—combined. The expansion of American industry was accompanied by major improvements in transportation and communication.

Economic expansion resulted in a growth of national wealth and an improvement in the standard of living. At the same time, industrial workers experienced hardships, including low wages, long hours, and unsafe and unhealthy working conditions. These hardships encouraged the development of unions which sought to organize workers for the promotion of their own interests.

The Civil War and Industrialization

Industrialization had begun in the United States well before the Civil War. Thus, the process of industrial expansion after 1865 was an intensification of trends which had been underway for several decades.

While the Civil War encouraged the expansion of industry

in the North, it disrupted the nation's important cotton textile industry and largely wrecked industry in the South. Whether the Civil War served to spur the nation's industrial development or, in fact, interrupted it is a matter of debate among economic historians.

Reasons for Industrial Growth

The availability of natural resources was an important factor contributing to the expansion of American industry. Minerals such as coal, iron, oil, lead, copper, zinc, and sulfur were present in abundance. Coal and, increasingly, oil were important sources of energy for industry and transportation. The country also had an abundant supply of labor, which was augmented by the flow of immigrants during the late nineteenth century. The growing population also provided a sizable market for the products of industry.

Large amounts of capital were available for investment in industry. Those who had acquired wealth in previous decades from their involvement in shipping and commerce were prepared to invest in new industrial enterprises. In addition, large amounts of capital were borrowed from European investors.

The post-Civil War political climate served to encourage industrialization. The defeat of the Confederacy removed for some years the political power of the heavily agricultural South. The Republican party, which dominated national politics for several decades, was strongly supportive of business interests, and the federal government provided business with both direct and indirect assistance.

The Morrill Tariff of 1861 imposed high tariffs which protected American industry against foreign competition. The National Banking Act of 1863 helped establish a stable banking system. The Bland-Allison Act of 1878 established a *de facto* gold standard, which served to maintain currency stability.

The federal government provided direct aid to the railroads in the form of generous land grants and also gave business interests effective control over much of the nation's mineral and timber resources. In addition, the federal government assisted business by refraining from efforts to regulate business activities and by opposing the activities of labor unions.

Technological Innovations and Inventions

New production techniques provided a stimulus for industrial growth. Although developed prior to the Civil War, standardized interchangeable parts began to be used extensively following the war. Shortly after the turn of the century, assembly line methods began to be applied to the production of agricultural machinery and automobiles.

While the telegraph had been invented by Samuel F. B. Morse prior to the Civil War, the first transcontinental telegraph service did not begin until 1861. Cyrus W. Field laid the first successful transatlantic cable in 1866. A decade later, in 1876, Alexander Graham Bell invented the telephone. In 1877, the American Bell Telephone Company was established. By 1880, more than 50,000 Bell telephones were in use. In 1885, the American Telephone and Telegraph Company (AT&T) was founded.

In 1879, Thomas A. Edison developed the incandescent light bulb, and in 1882, New York City introduced a system of electric power production.

The late nineteenth century witnessed a host of other important inventions, including the typewriter, the adding machine, the cash register, the carpet sweeper, the vacuum cleaner, and the phonograph.

The development of the internal combustion engine in the 1860s led to the production of the first successful automobiles in the 1890s. Henry Ford began the mass production of his famous Model T in 1909.

The Railroads

The late nineteenth century was a great era of railroad building, and by 1900, the United States had close to 200,000 miles of track—more than all of Europe.

In the thirty years from 1860 to 1890 alone, some 135,000 miles of track were laid. Railroad building was encouraged by the development of heavier steel rails and of larger and more powerful locomotives. Special livestock, tank, and refrigerator cars were introduced. In 1867, George M. Pullman established the Pullman Palace Car Company, which operated comfortable passenger coaches and sleepers, which were promoted as "gorgeous traveling hotels."

To facilitate scheduling, the railroads created four national time zones in 1883. This innovation eliminated the chaos created by the close to 70 local time zones that previously existed.

Railroad safety was promoted by the Westinghouse air brake, perfected in 1887, and by the development of automatic coupling devices to connect railroad cars.

Railroads did much to unify this country and to encourage the settlement of the West. Railroads also provided an economical means for the shipment of the products of industry and agriculture and, in addition, were large consumers of coal and steel, thereby promoting the growth of these key industries.

Railroad Regulation

As the railroads expanded, rates for carrying passengers and freight declined, especially in the East where competition was the greatest. In the West, however, farmers' complaints about high and discriminatory rates increased, and farm organizations, such as the Grange, began to press for state regulation of the railroads.

In 1869, Massachusetts established a commission to supervise the operation of railroads within its borders. Within a few years, a number of other states established similar commissions.

The movement to regulate the railroads was strongest in the Middle West, however. In 1871 and 1873, Illinois passed laws to control rates charged for passenger and freight service and to regulate the charges for the storage of grain in facilities owned by the railroads. Similar "Granger Laws" were adopted in several other states, including Iowa and Wisconsin. In the case of *Munn v. Illinois,* decided in 1877, the Supreme Court upheld the 1873 Illinois law which fixed rates for grain storage.

In 1886, however, state efforts to regulate railroads suffered a setback in the Supreme Court's decision in the so-called "Wabash Case." Declaring that the Constitution had granted Congress the exclusive right to control interstate commerce, the court denied to states the power to regulate railroads which were engaged in interstate commerce. In practice, this decision meant that states could not regulate railroads, since very few railroads operated within only one state.

For several years, Congress had been giving some attention to the question of regulating railroads. In 1874, for example, the House of Representatives passed the McCrary Bill, which provided for the establishment of a federal commission to regulate railroad rates. The bill failed to win Senate approval.

Following the Supreme Court's decision in the Wabash Case of 1886, the Senate established a committee headed by Republican Senator Shelby M. Cullom of Illinois to study the problem of railroad regulation and to make recommendations. The work of the Cullom committee led to the passage of the Interstate Commerce Act of 1887.

The Interstate Commerce Commission

In February 1887, President Grover Cleveland signed the Interstate Commerce Act. This law required railroads to publish their rate schedules and provided that rates be "reasonable and just." Railroads were banned from establishing rates which discriminated among localities and from charging more for short hauls than long hauls. Rebates and pooling were outlawed.

The Interstate Commerce Commission (ICC), composed of five members appointed by the President, had the responsibility for enforcing the Interstate Commerce Act. The law did not authorize the ICC to regulate rates. If the ICC questioned the reasonableness of a rate established by a railroad, the commission would have to prove its case in court. Often the courts proved to be unsympathetic to efforts to regulate the railroads. While the Interstate Commerce Act suffered from evident weaknesses, it did set an important precedent for regulation of economic activities by the federal government.

Problems of Railroad Overexpansion

Railroad overexpansion, combined with excessive speculation in railroad stock, had contributed to the financial Panics of 1857 and 1873. The bankruptcy of the Philadelphia and Reading Railroad in February 1893 helped produce the Panic of 1893. By the mid-1890s, many railroads were in serious financial trouble.

J. Pierpont Morgan, a powerful investment banker, played a central role in rescuing the railroads from their financial plight. During the period from 1894 to 1898, the Morgan firm reorganized many of the nation's leading railroads and helped restore order and efficiency to their operations.

The Textile Industry

The American textile industry had developed considerably

prior to the Civil War and remained important in the late nineteenth century. The textile industry was the largest employer of industrial labor and was second only to food and related products in the total value of its production. By 1900, almost 23,000 textile mills were operating in the United States, and the country had become a major exporter of cotton textiles.

The Food Industry

In the expansion of food processing, flour milling and meat packing were particularly important. Charles A. Pillsbury introduced new methods of milling the hard spring wheat produced in the northern Great Plains and developed a major milling industry centered in Minneapolis, Minnesota.

In Chicago in 1870, Philip G. Armour established Armour and Co., one of the nation's most important meat packing firms. Gustavus F. Swift perfected the refrigerator car, which made possible the shipment by rail of fresh meat to market. In 1877, Swift and Co. shipped the first carload of fresh beef from Chicago to Boston.

The Steel Industry

The Bessemer converter, invented in England, and a similar process developed by an American, William Kelly of Kentucky, made possible the mass production of steel and thus began one of the most important new industries. Rich deposits of iron ore in the Lake Superior region of northern Michigan and Minnesota were developed. Experiencing a tremendous growth, by 1900 the American steel industry produced as much steel as Great Britain and Germany combined.

Andrew Carnegie, an immigrant from Scotland, was the dominant figure in the American steel industry. During the 1870s and 1880s, he developed the steel industry in western Pennsylvania, and by 1900, Carnegie's mills were producing steel at an annual rate of three million tons.

J. Pierpont Morgan, the investment banker, began to expand his interests in steel during the 1890s and seemed to be on a competitive collision course with Carnegie. Then, in 1900, Carnegie sold his interests to Morgan for close to half a billion dollars. Morgan now brought the major American steel makers together and, in March 1901, created the United States Steel Corporation, which controlled 60 percent of the nation's steel production. Capitalized at $1.4 billion, United States Steel was the nation's first billion dollar corporation.

The Oil Industry

In 1859, Edwin L. Drake drilled the nation's first oil well near Titusville in western Pennsylvania. In 1870, John D. Rockefeller, who became the dominant figure in the oil industry in the late nineteenth century, established the Standard Oil Company. Often using ruthless methods against his competitors, Rockefeller was able to gain control of about 90 percent of the nation's oil refining business within a few years.

The story of Standard Oil provides a good example of the concentration of economic power and the development of monopoly in the late nineteenth century. At the beginning of the 1880s, Rockefeller created the Standard Oil Trust. Stockholders in some 40 corporations involved in the oil industry assigned voting rights in their stock to nine trustees, headed by Rockefeller. The stockholders received trust certificates which earned dividends but had no voting power. This left the trustees in complete control of the participating corporations. The Standard Oil Trust controlled most of the oil refineries in the United States along with much of the pipeline system and other activities related to the oil industry. The Standard Oil Trust provided a model for the establishment of similar trusts in other industries.

The development of trusts led to widespread public suspicion and hostility. By the late 1880s, law suits brought in state courts began to weaken the trusts. These law suits charged that trusts violated common law principles involving restraint of trade.

As the number of trusts declined, the holding company became a popular form of business consolidation in the 1890s. Holding companies often secured partial or full ownership of several firms which had previously competed with one another. Some of the nation's major industries were reorganized by holding companies. In 1899, Rockefeller established the Standard Oil Company as a holding company, chartered in New Jersey, which had very lenient laws regarding holding companies. Through this new holding company, Rockefeller was able to maintain his dominant position in the American oil industry.

The Sherman Anti-Trust Act

Opposition to the concentration of economic power gradually developed. In 1890, Congress passed the Sherman Anti-Trust Act. According to this law, "Every contract, combination in the form of trust or otherwise, or conspiracy, in restraint of trade or commerce among the several States or with foreign nations, is hereby declared illegal." In addition, the Sherman Anti-Trust Act provided that "every person who shall monopolize, or attempt to monopolize, or combine or conspire with any other person or persons, to monopolize any part of the trade or commerce among the several States, or with foreign nations, shall be deemed guilty of a misdemeanor."

This law empowered the government to bring civil or criminal suits against violators of the act. Only relatively weak penalties could be imposed on those convicted of a criminal violation: a maximum fine of $5,000 or a year's jail sentence or both.

The Sherman Anti-Trust Act was not an effective weapon in the struggle against monopolies. The specific definitions of "monopoly" and "restraint of trade" were left up to the courts, which continued to be generally sympathetic to business. In the 1895 case of *United States v. E. C. Knight Co.*, the Supreme Court held that the American Sugar Refining Company was not guilty of violating the Sherman Anti-Trust Act even though it controlled 99 percent of the nation's sugar refining business.

One unexpected use of the Sherman Anti-Trust Act came in its application against labor unions, which the courts held to be combinations in restraint of trade.

Social Darwinism

Successful businessmen had profited from laissez-faire economic policies and strongly opposed regulation. These businessmen were attracted by the arguments of those who contended that the principle of the survival of the fittest applied to human society just as it did to biology.

The idea that plants and animals had evolved through a process of natural selection, with the most fit surviving, had received its first expression in *The Origin of Species,* written by Charles Darwin and published in 1859.

The English philosopher Herbert Spencer drew a relationship between biology and society in a concept known as Social Darwinism. In his book *Social Statics,* Spencer argued that the process of evolution in society involved competition which produced winners and losers. Power and wealth resulted from ability and should not be denigrated as the product of undesirable business practices. Government intervention on behalf of the weak and disadvantaged would serve only to place obstacles in the path of a natural development. Spencer's ideas became very popular in America in the 1870s and the 1880s.

William Graham Sumner, a professor at Yale University,

was the major American exponent of Spencer's views, arguing that individuals should have complete freedom to compete and to pursue their self-interest. Sumner, adding religious overtones to Spencer's Social Darwinism, suggested that those who succeeded in acquiring power and wealth were virtuous and had succeeded because they practiced the virtues of piety, temperance, hard work, and frugality.

The Gospel of Wealth

Not all of those who gained great wealth were content to be cast in the role of "robber barons." Some believed that possession of wealth carried with it social responsibility.

The successful industrialist Andrew Carnegie wrote "The Gospel of Wealth," published in the *North American Review* in 1889. Carnegie endorsed the doctrine of laissez-faire, insisting that the only proper function of government is to protect private property. Those who profited and became wealthy, he believed, had earned their success. The wealthy did, however, have an obligation to be philanthropic. Carnegie took his own advice and gave away some $350 million to support philanthropic endeavors which included the establishment of libraries.

Opposition to Laissez-Faire

Although the principle that the government should not seek to regulate economic activity was widely accepted in late nineteenth century America, there were some dissenters. Henry George, a journalist and social reformer, published his book *Progress and Poverty* in 1879. Troubled by the unequal distribution of wealth, George was especially opposed to the holding of land in the hope that its value would increase as a result of social development rather than because of improvements made by the landowner. George proposed a "single tax" which would deprive landowners of any unearned increment in the value of their land. While the single tax idea did not win much support, *Progress and Poverty* represented an expression of the growing dissent from laissez-faire doctrine. Henry George ran for mayor of New York City in 1886 and was only narrowly defeated.

The sociologist Lester Frank Ward attacked the ideas of Herbert Spencer, repudiating the view that there was a relationship between the process of evolution in nature and human society. In *Dynamic Sociology,* published in 1884, Ward argued that human beings can make rational choices and thus are not limited by natural selection: human beings are not simply the victims of natural forces beyond their control. Ward believed that government intervention in economic and social issues was both necessary and desirable.

In his utopian novel *Looking Backward,* published in 1888, Edward Bellamy urged the elimination of competition and the creation of a socialist society based on cooperation. Bellamy devoted the final decade of his life to promoting his humanitarian, and non-Marxist brand of socialism.

Henry Demarest Lloyd, a journalist, wrote a bitter attack on John D. Rockefeller and Standard Oil in *Wealth Against Commonwealth,* published in 1894. Rejecting laissez-faire, Lloyd argued that Social Darwinism represented nothing more than an attempt to legitimize the greed of the industrialists.

Workers in the Late Nineteenth Century

In the early nineteenth century, most American workers had been employed in agriculture. Between 1860 and 1910, the percentage of workers engaged in agriculture declined from 60 to just over 30 percent. During the same period, the percentage of workers employed in industry grew from 18 to 28 percent.

In the late nineteenth century, there were few laws to protect the factory workers who were frequently exploited by large and impersonal corporations. In the 1890s, ordinary unskilled workers earned an average wage of $9 a week. Most industrial workers worked a ten-hour day and a six-day week. In steel and some other industries, workers worked six 12-hour days a week, for a total work week of 72 hours.

Many working men could not earn enough to support their families, and their wives and children also had to work in order for the family to survive. Instead of finding employment outside the home, many married women earned money by taking in sewing and laundry and by caring for boarders in their homes. In 1890, only slightly more than 3 percent of married women had jobs outside the home, but many unmarried women did. In 1870, 11 percent of all workers in manufacturing were women. By 1900, 20 percent were. In some industries, like textiles, women were an important part of the labor force. Women workers in industry earned considerably lower wages than men, sometimes as low as $5 or $6 a week.

Factory jobs paid women more than they could earn in many other jobs, such as domestic work. Women working as domestic servants received room and board and between $2 and $5 in wages a week. Domestic servants had little free time, generally one evening a week and part of Sunday off.

Women high school graduates, whose numbers were increasing in the late nineteenth century, often found jobs working as salespersons and cashiers in the new department stores and increasingly replaced men in many office jobs, operating the recently invented typewriter. Women who worked in stores and offices frequently earned more money than most women factory workers, and their working conditions were better. But women white collar workers had few opportunities for advancement, since managerial positions were generally reserved for men.

Many college-educated women entered the teaching profession, while some were able to enter other professions such as medicine and law. But medical and law schools accepted very

few women students. Most upper middle-class women continued to see their primary role in life as wives and mothers.

Black women customarily worked both before and after marriage. In southern cities in 1880, about three-quarters of single
black women and one-third of married black women worked outside the home, most of them as domestic servants or laundres-
ses.

Child labor was common. In 1880, 20 percent of the nation's
children between the ages of ten and 14 worked in factories and
on farms. As late as 1900, about 13 percent of America's textile
workers were under the age of 16. Some state legislatures sought
to restrict child labor, but the laws proved ineffective for the most
part.

For most American workers—men, women, and children—
wages were low, hours were long, and working conditions were
unsafe and unhealthy. While efforts were made to unionize
workers, labor unions remained weak. Fewer than 10 percent of
the country's industrial workers joined unions in the last years
of the nineteenth century.

The National Labor Union

In 1866, William H. Sylvis, a leader of the Iron Moulders
Union in Pennsylvania, launched the first attempt to organize a
truly national union. The National Labor Union (NLU) emphasized efforts to establish the eight-hour day for industrial
workers. In 1871, the National Labor Union founded the National Labor Reform Party. This party's poor showing in the 1872
election weakened the NLU, which then collapsed during the
depression following the Panic of 1873.

The Knights of Labor

In 1869, Uriah Stephens founded the Noble and Holy Order
of the Knights of Labor. A secret fraternal order with elaborate

rituals, the Knights of Labor sought to recruit both skilled and unskilled workers. It called for the eight-hour day, equal pay for men and women, an end to contract labor by prisoners, and the abolition of child labor. In addition, the Knights favored the passage of an income tax, the issuance of paper money, the abolition of the national banking system, and prohibition. In these demands, the Knights resembled the farmers' organizations of the late nineteenth century.

In 1879, Terence V. Powderly became the Knights' Grand Master Workman. At that time, the union claimed 9,000 members. By 1882, the membership had increased to more than 40,000.

Although the Knights of Labor discouraged the use of strikes as a weapon in their struggle, strikes in the mid-1880s helped the Knights make their greatest gains in membership. In 1884, unorganized shopworkers called a strike against the Union Pacific Railroad. The railroad recognized the shopworkers' new union, which then affiliated with the Knights of Labor. Other strikes contributed to the growth of the Knights, and the union's membership increased rapidly from about 100,000 to over 700,000 members. A decline soon set in, however, and by 1890 the Knights' membership had dropped to about 100,000. The Knights of Labor was near collapse when Powderly retired in 1892.

The American Federation of Labor

In the meantime, Samuel Gompers of the Cigarmakers' Union joined with other labor leaders in 1881 to form a new federation of unions. Reorganized in 1886, the federation became the American Federation of Labor (AFL). Samuel Gompers served as the AFL's president until his death in 1924.

Gompers and the AFL leaders were relatively conservative in their approach. They accepted the American system of private enterprise but wanted to get a larger share of the benefits for labor. The AFL emphasized "bread and butter" unionism, seeking higher wages, shorter hours, and better working conditions for its members, rather than promoting more far-reaching reforms of the basic economic and social structure.

The AFL focused its organizing efforts on skilled workers who possessed more bargaining power than unskilled laborers, who could easily be replaced. The labor federation did not attempt to organize workers in the developing mass-production industries such as coal, steel, and oil. The AFL remained a loose alliance of national craft unions in which each member union retained a considerable degree of autonomy in managing its own affairs and had the authority to call its own strikes. The AFL regarded strikes and boycotts as legitimate weapons.

During the 1890s, the AFL experienced slow growth. By 1902, it had over one million members, and by 1914 the membership exceeded two million.

The Railroad Strike of 1877

The development of labor unions in the late nineteenth century was accompanied by bitter and sometimes bloody labor-management conflict. In July 1877, a series of wage cuts led to strikes affecting four major railroads connecting the east coast and Chicago: the Baltimore and Ohio, the New York Central, the Pennsylvania, and the Erie. As tension mounted, acts of violence occurred in the Pittsburgh area. The governor of Pennsylvania sent the state militia to the area, and violence increased, resulting in several deaths. President Rutherford B. Hayes then sent army troops to Pittsburgh, and the strike collapsed.

The Haymarket Riot

The year 1886 was filled with considerable labor unrest, as workers pushed for the adoption of the eight-hour day. The situation became especially tense in Chicago, where a major strike was called against the McCormick Harvester Company. On May 4, 1886, a demonstration protesting police brutality took place in Chicago's Haymarket Square. A bomb, perhaps thrown by an anarchist, resulted in the death of seven policemen and the wounding of 67 other people. The police fired into the crowd, killing four.

The events in Chicago led to a wave of antilabor and antiradical hysteria. Although the identity of the bomb-thrower was never established, eight anarchists were charged with responsibility for the policemen's deaths, since they had been inciting hostility toward the police. A jury found all eight guilty, and four were hanged.

The Homestead Strike

In 1892, 3,800 members of the Amalgamated Association of Iron and Steel Workers went on strike at Andrew Carnegie's Homestead Plant in Pennsylvania, protesting against wage cuts and bad working conditions. In an effort to break the strike, Henry C. Frick, the plant manager, brought in 300 Pinkerton detectives. In the ensuing violence, seven detectives and nine workers were killed. While there was considerable sympathy for the strikers, the strike failed completely. Union activity in the steel industry did not resume for a number of years.

The Pullman Strike

The Panic of 1893 led to a new depression and a new wave of wage cuts and strikes. In 1894, more workers were unemployed as a result of strikes than in any previous year.

The most serious strike in 1894 occurred among railroad workers and was centered around Chicago. It began with the workers in George M. Pullman's company town south of Chicago. A series of wage cuts, combined with the Pullman

Company's unwillingness to reduce rents for company-owned houses, enraged the workers. The Pullman workers had recently joined the new American Railway Union, led by Eugene V. Debs. The union urged arbitration of the dispute. When the company rejected arbitration, the workers went on strike.

Railroad workers who were also members of the American Railway Union would not handle Pullman cars unless the company agreed to arbitration. The company continued to refuse. The Railroad Managers' Association supported the Pullman Company by firing switchmen who would not handle Pullman Cars. In response, the union called a strike against the railroads. By the end of June, nearly all the workers on the railroad lines running west from Chicago went on strike.

The Railroad Managers' Association appealed for intervention by the federal government. The Association convinced President Grover Cleveland and Attorney General Richard Olney that troops should be used against the striking workers since the strike interfered with the delivery of the mail. Olney went to court and secured an injunction under the Sherman Anti-Trust Act against the union. This was the first time an injunction was used in a labor dispute. In order to enforce the injunction against the defiant union, Cleveland sent 2,000 troops to Chicago. John L. Altgeld, the pro-labor Governor of Illinois, protested the use of troops.

The intervention of the troops, however, broke the strike. The failure of the strike greatly weakened the American labor movement. Debs and several other officials of the union were tried and sentenced to jail for defying the injunction. The Supreme Court upheld the convictions. As a result of the strike, Debs became a prominent national figure and soon became the leader of the American socialist movement, running for President as the Socialist party's candidate on five occasions.

During the final decades of the nineteenth century, the United States developed from a predominantly agricultural country to the world's leading industrial power. New inventions and the construction of railroads encouraged industrial development. Industries such as textiles, food processing, steel, and oil employed a growing number of workers. With the adoption of the Interstate Commerce Act (1887) and the Sherman Anti-Trust Act (1890), the federal government began efforts to regulate the railroads and restrict the development of monopolies. Also during these years, workers began to organize labor unions to promote their interests in negotiations with the owners and managers of industry. The efforts of organized labor and the growing maturity of American industry joined to improve health and safety conditions in the workplace and the standard of living of workers and their families.

Recommended Reading

Paul Avrich, *The Haymarket Tragedy* (1984).

Robert V. Bruce, *Bell: Alexander Graham Bell and the Conquest of Solitude* (1973).

Carl N. Degler, *The Age of the Economic Revolution, 1876–1900* (1967).

William M. Dick, *Labor and Socialism in America: The Gompers Era* (1972).

Melvyn Dubofsky, *Industrialism and the American Worker, 1865–1920* (1975).

John A. Garraty, *The New Commonwealth, 1877–1890* (1968).

Ray Ginger, *Age of Excess: The United States from 1877 to 1914* (1965).

William H. Harris, *The Harder We Run: Black Workers Since the Civil War* (1982).

David F. Hawkes, *John D.: The Founding Father of the Rockefellers* (1980).

Richard Hofstadter, *Social Darwinism in American Thought* (rev. ed., 1955).

David M. Katzman, *Seven Days a Week: Women and Domestic Service in Industrializing America* (1978).

Stuart Kaufman, *Samuel Gompers and the Origins of the American Federation of Labor, 1848–1896* (1973).

Alice Kessler-Harris, *Out to Work: A History of Wage-Earning Women in the United States* (1982).

Edward C. Kirkland, *Industry Comes of Age: Business, Labor, and Public Policy 1860–1897* (1961).

Gabriel Kolko, *Railroads and Regulation, 1877–1916* (1965).

Harold C. Livesay, *Andrew Carnegie and the Rise of Big Business* (1975).

Harold C. Livesay, *Samuel Gompers and Organized Labor in America* (1978).

David Montgomery, *Workers' Control in America: Studies in the History of Work, Technology, and Labor Struggles* (1979).

Daniel Nelson, *Managers and Workers: Origins of the New Factory System in the United States, 1880–1920* (1975).

Glenn Porter, *The Rise of Big Business, 1860–1910* (1973).

Nick Salvatore, *Eugene V. Debs: Citizen and Socialist* (1982).

Robert Smith, *Women and Work in America* (1959).

Philip Taft, *The A.F. of L. in the Time of Gompers* (1957).

Peter Temin, *Iron and Steel in Nineteenth Century America* (1964).

John L. Thomas, *Alternative America: Henry George, Edward Bellamy, Henry Demarest Lloyd and the Adversary Tradition* (1983).

Norman J. Ware, *The Labor Movement in the United States, 1860–1895* (1929).

Barbara M. Wertheimer, *We Were There: The Story of Working Women in America* (1976).

Robert Wiebe, *The Search for Order, 1877–1920* (1967).

Harold F. Williamson and A.R. Daum, *The American Petroleum Industry: The Age of Illumination, 1859–1899* (1959).

CHAPTER 4

Immigration and Urbanization in the Late Nineteenth Century

Time Line

1860–1890	Ten million immigrants arrive in the United States; most are northern and western Europeans
1868	The Burlingame Treaty permits unrestricted immigration of Chinese
1871	Andrew S. Hallidie invents the cable car
1882	The Chinese Exclusion Act is adopted

1883	The Brooklyn Bridge, the world's longest suspension bridge, opens
1886	Montgomery, Alabama, opens the nation's first streetcar line
	The first settlement house is established in New York City
1887	The anti-Catholic American Protective Association is founded in Iowa
1889	Jane Addams establishes Hull House in Chicago
1890–1920	Fifteen million immigrants arrive in the United States; most are southern and eastern Europeans
1894	Membership in the American Protective Association reaches 500,000
	Congress passes a bill requiring a literacy test for immigrants; it is vetoed by President Cleveland
	The National Municipal League is formed to promote reforms in city government
1898	New York City is enlarged by adding Brooklyn, Queens, the Bronx, and Staten Island to Manhattan
1901	Boston opens the nation's first subway system

During the late nineteenth century, millions of immigrants came to the United States seeking, above all, greater economic oppor-

tunities. *While most were Europeans, many others were from Latin America and Asia. These immigrants provided an important source of labor for America's industries, mines, and farms. Gradually, however, opposition to immigration developed among native-born white Americans and by the final years of the nineteenth century an active movement for immigration restriction had developed.*

The years after the Civil War were also a time when the United States experienced a period of rapid urbanization, although it was not until 1920 that a majority of the American population was classified as urban. As cities grew in size, problems of city life intensified. The rapidly growing cities gave rise to political bosses as well as to movements promoting both political and social reform.

Immigration

During the nineteenth century, immigrants to the United States numbered in the millions. Between 1860 and 1920, the number of immigrants totaled 25 million, with most coming from Europe. These immigrants had different motives for leaving the lands of their birth. Some wanted to escape political or religious persecution. Others sought to avoid compulsory military service. Most hoped to find better opportunities for economic advancement. Many immigrants originally planned to spend a few years in America, to make some money, and then return home. Most remained, however, although close to a third of all immigrants ultimately did return to their homelands or move on to some other country.

There were three great waves of immigration during the nineteenth century. The first was prior to the Civil War, when about five million immigrants arrived between 1820 and 1860.

From 1860 to 1890, the second wave of immigration brought ten million people to the United States. More than two-thirds of these immigrants were from western and northern Europe. They included both Protestants and Catholics from Great Britain, Ireland, Germany, and Scandinavia. Most of the immigrants from Great Britain and Ireland remained in the cities along the Atlantic seaboard. Many Scandinavians and Germans settled on farms in the Middle West or in cities like Chicago, Cincinnati, Milwaukee, and Minneapolis. Both in this period and later, relatively few immigrants found new homes in the South.

Between 1890 and 1920, another 15 million immigrants came to the United States. The great majority were of southern and eastern European origin—from Italy, Greece, Hungary, Poland, Russia, and other countries—and were largely of the Catholic, Jewish, and Eastern Orthodox faiths. Prior to 1880, only about 200,000 people of southern and eastern European origin lived in the United States. While most of these immigrants from southern and eastern Europe were originally rural, peasant people, in America the majority settled in the cities of the Northeast and Middle West, finding work in factories, mills, and mines.

Catholic Immigration

In 1850, Catholics in the United States numbered only 1.6 million. As a result of immigration, the number of Catholics grew to over 12 million by 1900. In mid-century, most American Catholics were of Irish and German origin. After 1880, however, the number of Catholics from Italy, Hungary, Poland, and Lithuania grew substantially. As Catholic immigration increased, so, too, did the anti-Catholic attitudes of many native-born American Protestants.

Jewish Immigration

As late as 1870, there were only about 250,000 Jews in the United States. By 1920, the number had increased to 3.5 million. Early Jewish settlers in America were mainly Sephardic (of Spanish and Portugese origin) or German. Most were relatively well-educated and well-assimilated. In the late nineteenth century, there was a great influx of Orthodox Jews from eastern Europe—Rumania, Hungary, Poland, Lithuania, and Russia. For many native-born Americans, the customs of these eastern European Jews seemed strange, and anti-Semitism increased.

Opposition to Immigration

At the beginning of the nineteenth century, most white Americans were Protestants of English, Scotch-Irish, and German ancestry. A large proportion of immigrants in the years before the Civil War were of similar background and were assimilated with few problems, although Irish Catholic immigrants encountered considerable prejudice and discrimination.

During the late nineteenth century, antagonism mounted toward the growing number of Catholic and Jewish immigrants from southern and eastern Europe. American nativism became more openly racist, and there were warnings that the racial purity of white Anglo-Saxon America was endangered by the influx of the supposedly racially inferior southern and eastern Europeans.

Josiah Strong, a Congregational minister, believed that these immigrants, especially the Catholics, posed a threat to the American way of life. In *Our Country: Its Future and Possible Crisis* (1885), Strong warned his fellow Protestants about the "perils which threaten our Christian and American civilization."

In 1887, Henry F. Bowers of Iowa organized the American Protective Association (APA) which opposed Catholic immigration in particular. Operating mainly in the upper Middle West, the APA promoted fantastic rumors about Catholic conspiracies and recruited half a million members by 1894.

American Protestants often were inclined to regard the United States as a Protestant country, whatever the Constitution said about the separation of church and state. American Catholics wanted their own schools because they believed—often with good reason—that the public schools operated, in effect, as Protestant schools. Many Protestants reacted with hostility in the face of Catholic efforts to create a system of Catholic parochial and private schools. Ohio, for example, passed a law requiring all students to attend public schools, and several other states attempted to place restrictions on Catholic schools.

In addition to religious prejudice, other factors encouraged efforts to restrict immigration. Labor leaders often supported immigration restriction because they feared competition for jobs by immigrants willing to work for low wages. Advocates of temperance were offended by patterns of heavy alcohol use by members of some immigrant groups. Feminists were antagonized by the fact that many European women were willing to accept traditional patterns of male domination.

As early as the 1870s, laws were passed to bar the immigration of those persons regarded as undesirable. An 1875 law denied entry to prostitutes and those convicted of crimes, while a law of 1882 barred immigrants who were insane or mentally retarded or who were likely to become public charges.

By the 1890s, opponents of immigration wanted to impose broader restrictions which would limit the number of immigrants from southern and eastern Europe. In 1894, the New England-based Immigration Restriction League found a spokesman in the recently elected Republican senator from Massachusetts, Henry Cabot Lodge. Lodge won congressional passage of a bill providing for a literacy test for immigrants, which would have severely restricted immigration by southern and eastern Europeans, who had had few educational opportunities. President Grover Cleveland vetoed this bill, and congressional foes of immigration could not muster enough votes to override the veto.

Chinese Exclusion

By the 1850s, between four and five thousand Chinese came to the western United States each year. Many of these immigrants found work as miners. The Burlingame Treaty of 1868 permitted unrestricted Chinese immigration; this was designed to provide a work force for the building of the Central Pacific Railroad. By 1880, Chinese comprised about 17 percent of California's population. White Americans feared Chinese competition for jobs and were hostile to what they regarded as the strange ways of the Chinese. Anti-Chinese agitation led to a new treaty in 1880 which permitted the United States to "regulate, limit, and suspend" Chinese immigration. In 1882, President Chester A. Arthur signed the Chinese Exclusion Act, which banned Chinese immigration for ten years. This ban was extended periodically and then became permanent in 1904.

The Growth of the Cities

In the late 1860s, less than a quarter of the American population lived in cities. By 1890, the proportion had risen to about one-third and by 1910, to nearly a half.

In 1860, only New York City had a population in excess of one million, and only seven other cities had more than 100,000 inhabitants. By 1870, 15 cities had a population of over 100,000. By 1920, the number had grown to 68.

New England and the Middle Atlantic states were the most heavily urbanized. Among the major cities in this area were Boston, New York, Brooklyn (a separate city until 1898), Philadelphia, and Baltimore. All of these cities had a population of 100,000 or more by 1860, and all were seaports. In the Middle West, several major cities developed, including Chicago, Cleveland, Cincinnati, St. Louis, Milwaukee, and Minneapolis. Farther west, Denver, San Francisco, Los Angeles, and Seattle became major cities during the late nineteenth century. There was less urbanization in the South, although old cities like New Orleans and Memphis grew in size, and industrial expansion promoted the growth of newer cities like Birmingham and Houston. The South remained predominantly rural, however. As late as 1910, only slightly more than 20 percent of the South's population was classified as urban.

Reasons for the Growth of the Cities

Annexations, migration, and immigration all contributed to the process of urbanization. Annexing adjacent areas served to increase a city's size. The most dramatic example of annexation occurred in 1898, when New York City, previously limited to Manhattan, annexed Brooklyn, Queens, the Bronx, and Staten Island. This annexation doubled New York's population from 1.5 million to three million. In most cases, however, while the annexation of outlying areas increased a city's territorial extent, it did not substantially increase the population.

The migration to the West during the late nineteenth century was accompanied by a migration to the cities. Many farmers and their families abandoned their failing farms in times of agricultural depression and moved to cities in the hope of finding greater economic opportunities.

Black migration contributed significantly to the growth of cities, especially as blacks in search of economic opportunity and greater personal freedom began to move in growing numbers from the rural South to the North and West. By 1900, almost 80 percent of American blacks outside the South lived in cities, and 32 cities had a black population in excess of 10,000. While industries hired many immigrants, discrimination in employment gpersisted against blacks, the majority of whom found themselves restricted to service occupations.

Some of the millions of immigrants to the United States settled in rural areas, but most became urban dwellers. By 1890, four out of five New Yorkers were foreign born. In the cities, immigrants tended to settle in segregated ethnic neighborhoods where they could more easily maintain their traditional culture and way of life. Some ethnic neighborhoods were inhabited primarily by people from a particular province or even a specific town. Gradually the immigrants and their children learned English, and American lifestyles began to merge with European traditions.

Cities and Industry

In the late nineteenth century, American industry was concentrated in the larger cities. The growing urban population provided both labor for factories and a market for the products of these factories. In turn, the possibility of securing employment in industry drew increasing numbers of people to the nation's cities. By 1900, urban factories produced about 90 percent of the country's total industrial output.

Some specialization developed in urban industry. Several New England cities became centers for the production of textiles and shoes. In New York City, tens of thousands of immigrants found work in factories producing men's, women's, and children's ready-to-wear clothing. Pittsburgh and Birmingham became centers of the steel industry. Milwaukee became famous for its beer, while Minneapolis became a center for flour milling.

Cities and Opportunity

In the late nineteenth century, America was, for many, a land of opportunity. People leaving failing farms, blacks moving from the South, immigrants coming from overseas—all headed to American cities in search of opportunity. While wages for factory workers were low, manual workers were often able to rise to white collar jobs. Others took pride in their manual ability and achieved success as skilled craftsmen. Still others succeeded in saving a few hundred dollars, enough to establish themselves in business as owners of small shops or taverns.

A Baptist minister from Philadelphia, the Reverend Russell Conwell, summed up the opportunities presented by America in his famous sermon "Acres of Diamonds," which he preached to some 6,000 audiences. Opportunity, Conwell declared, was available for everyone to grasp. "I say you ought to get rich, and it is your duty to get rich."

Urban Mass Transit

The development of mass transit systems did much to make the growth of cities possible. Prior to the Civil War, horse and mule-drawn streetcars provided much of the public transportation in the nation's cities. Not only were these streetcars slow, but cleaning up after the animals was a problem.

During the 1870s, mechanization of urban transit systems had begun. In 1871, Andrew S. Hallidie, a Scottish immigrant, invented the cable car. Cable cars operating on rails were pulled through the streets by an underground cable. San Francisco, whose cable cars are still in use, introduced the country's first cable car system in 1873. Soon thereafter, a number of other American cities, including New York, Philadelphia, and Chicago, developed cable car systems.

The development of electric-powered streetcars, invented by Stephen Dudley Field, made it possible for the middle class to move to the outer limits of cities and to the emerging suburbs and to commute to work in the downtown areas. Streetcars, also called trolley cars, were powered by electricity transmitted through overhead power lines. In 1886, streetcar service began in Montgomery, Alabama, and Richmond, Virginia, inaugurated its streetcar system in 1888. By 1890, streetcar lines were operating in more than fifty cities. Between 1890 and 1902, the mileage of electrified streetcar track increased from 1,300 to 22,000.

Some cities also constructed elevated railways for urban rapid transit. New York City's "El," originally operated with steam engines, began service during the 1870s, and elevated railways were also built in Boston, Philadelphia, Chicago, and Kansas City. Boston began operation of its subway system in 1901, and New York and Philadelphia also built subway systems around the turn of the century.

Cities also benefitted from bridge construction, with the new bridges replacing ferry lines. The Brooklyn Bridge, the engineering masterpiece of John Roebling, opened in 1883. The world's longest suspension bridge at the time, the Brooklyn Bridge, joining Brooklyn with Manhattan, began a boom in residential development in Brooklyn. Another important bridge was James B. Eal's cantilevered steel bridge built across the Mississippi River at St. Louis and opened in 1874.

Other Technological Advances in Urban Life

Urban living was improved by advances in street paving, which included the use of cobblestones, brick, and asphalt. By the late 1880s, electric streetlights began to replace gas lamps, and during the same period, the construction of central electric power stations made possible the gradual introduction of electric lighting into homes. Cities also began to develop central water supply systems, as well as sewage disposal systems. These water and sewage disposal systems helped promote an improvement in public health and reduced the incidence of diseases such as typhoid fever, diphtheria, scarlet fever, and cholera. Cities also improved their systems for fighting fires, and by the end of the nineteenth century, most cities had professional fire departments.

The introduction of steel-frame construction made it possible to construct taller buildings, which made for more efficient use of the expensive land in downtown areas. The development of skyscrapers first occurred in Chicago, which had to rebuild after the great fire of 1871. Elevators provided ready access to the new skyscrapers. The Otis Elevator Company installed the first electric elevator in 1889.

Urban Housing

Since most urban workers earned relatively low wages, their choice of housing was limited. Most urban dwellers rented apartments in crowded tenement buildings, which were usually four to six stories high. Each floor was divided into several poorly lit and poorly ventilated apartments. In many instances, two or three—or even more—families lived in an apartment that was designed for a single family. These conditions resulted in the creation of dirty and dangerous slums. In the mid-1890s, New York City's Lower East Side, crowded with immigrants, had a population of 702 people per acre, one of the highest population densities in the world.

Jacob Riis, a Danish-born social reformer, made the public aware of just how terrible living conditions in the slums were in his book *How the Other Half Lives*, published in 1900. In an attempt to improve the housing of the poor, New York City enacted building codes dealing with light, ventilation, and safety standards in new tenement buildings.

Urban Poverty

The low wages paid to most workers meant that many city dwellers lived at a bare subsistence level. A widespread attitude in American society at this time was that people who were willing to work hard could raise themselves out of poverty. Therefore, those who were poor had only themselves to blame.

This attitude encouraged a reluctance to provide public assistance to the poor. If such assistance were made available, it was feared, the poor would become dependent on it and would have less incentive to improve their lot by working hard. Some cities did provide limited assistance for the poor, often requiring work on public projects in exchange for help. Private agencies also provided some assistance to the poor.

The City Bosses

Urban political leaders also helped provide aid to the poor. The so-called "bosses" who headed the political machines in many cities provided jobs, fuel, food, and legal aid for those in need. The bosses also held picnics and provided other entertainment for their supporters and advocated public improvements, such as parks and streetcars. City dwellers who benefited from the bosses' help expressed their appreciation with their votes. In particular, those who held city jobs were expected to get the voters out to the polls on election day.

The urban bosses were also in a position to hand out favors in return for money. Bribery was commonly practiced by those who sought city contracts for construction and other projects and by those who sought franchises for providing gas, electricity, and water and for operating streetcar lines and other transportation services. The bosses, and often the police, collected bribes from those who could benefit from lax enforcement of laws that related to gambling and prostitution.

The most famous American political machine was New York City's Democratic political organization, Tammany Hall. While the most infamous of the Tammany Hall bosses, William M. Tweed, fell from power in the early 1870s, there were others to succeed him, including "Honest John" Kelly and Richard Croker.

Other cities also produced political machines and bosses. Some were Democrats, while others were Republicans. Jim

Pendergast became the political boss in Kansas City. (His successor in later years, Tom Pendergast, was President Harry Truman's mentor during his early political career.) In Cincinnati, there was George Cox, while Omaha produced Tom Denison. Martin Behrman was the political boss in New Orleans, while Edward H. Crump dominated Memphis politics for many years.

While the urban political machines participated in widespread graft and corruption, they also served to involve city government more directly in people's welfare than ever before. The bosses were able to build their political machines, above all, because they knew their people and their needs and tried to serve them. The record of the city bosses is thus mixed. On the one hand, the bosses lined their own pockets by bribery and often outright theft. On the other hand, they helped make the cities work by meeting the needs of the immigrants and other urban poor.

Urban Reform

Middle- and upper-class city dwellers reacted against the political bosses and their machines and launched reform campaigns in an effort to root out corruption and to establish city government on the basis of sound business principles. To eliminate political favoritism, the reformers believed that city jobs should be given out on the basis of competitive civil service examinations. Many reformers favored putting the day-to-day operation of city government into the hands of a professional city manager who would operate under the general supervision of the elected city council and mayor. In January 1894, reformers from several cities met in Philadelphia and established the National Municipal League with the purpose of fighting the bosses and promoting reform policies. The efforts of the National Municipal League achieved only a limited success.

Urban Social Reformers

Some reformers realized that efforts to reform urban politics could not succeed unless more was done to deal with the social problems of the cities.

Educational reformers worked to promote public education. As a result of their efforts, the United States came close to establishing a system of universal public elementary education. By 1900, 31 states and territories had enacted compulsory school attendance laws. In 1870, the United States had only 160 public high schools. By 1900, the number had risen to 6,000. Illiteracy in the United States declined considerably, but as late as 1900, the average American adult had attended school for only five years.

McGuffey's Readers played an important part in the education of America's children. Prepared by William Holmes McGuffey, a professor at Miami University in Ohio, and introduced in 1836, some 100 million copies were sold in the second half of the nineteenth century. *McGuffey's Readers* taught religion and ethical values along with reading.

The kindergarten movement began to develop in the United States during the 1870s, with the first kindergarten opening in St. Louis in 1873. Fundamental to the kindergartens was the idea that four- and five-year-old children could learn by playing.

During the late nineteenth century, teacher training became more professional. On the eve of the Civil War, the country had only ten normal schools (specialized colleges for teacher training). In 1900, there were close to 350 of these schools.

The Social Gospel movement expressed the growing social consciousness of middle-class Protestants. Washington Gladden, one of the first proponents of the Social Gospel, insisted that the problems created by modern industrial capitalism could be solved only by applying the teachings of Jesus. Gladden supported labor's right to organize and suggested that labor-management conflict could be eliminated by creating an industrial partnership which would provide the workers with a share of the profits of industry.

Walter Rauschenbusch, a Baptist and professor at the Colgate-Rochester Theological Seminary in upstate New York, was the most prominent advocate of the Social Gospel. In *Christianity and Social Crisis* (1907) and other books, Rauschenbusch urged the Protestant churches to carry Christian principles into action by supporting the cause of social reform. In particular, he believed, the churches should be more responsive to the needs of the workers. The principles of the Social Gospel movement represented a repudiation of the doctrines of Social Darwinism and had a significant impact on the major Protestant denominations.

A number of middle-class Americans found an outlet for their social concerns in the settlement house movement. Settlement houses were community centers intended to help urban workers improve their education and vocational skills and to assist them in getting better jobs. Settlement houses frequently offered child care services and health care clinics. They also provided opportunities for studying art and music and sponsored other recreational activities.

Stanton Coit and Charles B. Stover opened the first settlement house in New York City in 1886. Originally called the Neighborhood Guild, it later became known as the University Settlement. Another well-known settlement house in New York was the Henry Street Settlement, founded by Lillian Wald. Wald later played an active role in the campaign that led to the creation of the federal Children's Bureau in 1912.

The most famous settlement house was Hull House in Chicago, founded by Jane Addams and Ellen Gates Starr in 1889. In addition to her settlement house work, Addams was active in the efforts which led to the enactment of the Illinois Factory Act of 1893. This law prohibited the employment of children under the age of 14 for more than eight hours a day.

During the late nineteenth century, the promise of a better life in America attracted increasing numbers of immigrants from Europe and elsewhere. While immigration from northern Europe continued, additional millions of immigrants arrived from southern and eastern Europe, as well as from Latin America and Asia. Some Americans began to fear that immigration presented a threat to their traditional way of life, and demands for immigration restriction mounted.

Immigrants provided a ready source of labor for the nation's expanding industry, which also drew the workers it needed from rural areas of the United States. Industrialization stimulated the process of urbanization, and the nation's cities grew in number and size. Widespread urban poverty resulted in efforts to improve economic and social conditions in the cities. Urban bosses gained greater power in state and national politics, while demands for reform of city government increased.

Recommended Reading

Jane Addams, *Twenty Years at Hull House* (1910).

Josef J. Barton, *Peasants and Strangers: Italians, Rumanians, and Slovaks in an American City, 1890–1950* (1975).

John W. Briggs, *An Italian Passage: Immigrants to Three American Cities, 1890–1930* (1978).

Alexander B. Callow, Jr., ed., *The City Boss in America* (1976).

Alexander Chudacoff, *The Evolution of American Urban Urban Society* (2nd ed., 1981).

Robert D. Cross, *The Church and the City, 1865–1910* (1967).

Allen F. Davis, *American Heroine: The Life and Legend of Jane Addams* (1973).

Allen F. Davis, *Spearheads for Reform: The Social Settlements and the Progressive Movement, 1890–1914* (1967).

Leonard Dinnerstein and David M. Reimers, *Ethnic Americans: A History of Immigration and Assimilation* (1975).

John B. Duff, *The Irish in the United States* (1971).

Elizabeth Ewen, *Immigrant Women in the Land of Dollars: Life and Culture on the Lower East Side, 1890–1925* (1985).

Nathan Glazer and Daniel P. Moynihan, *Beyond the Melting Pot: The Negroes, Puerto Ricans, Jews, Italians, and Irish of New York City* (2nd ed., 1970).

Oscar Handlin, *The Uprooted* (2nd ed., 1973).

John Higham, *Send These to Me: Jews and Other Immigrants in Urban America* (1975).

John Higham, *Strangers in the Land: Patterns of American Nativism, 1860–1925* (1955).

Charles H. Hopkins, *The Rise of the Social Gospel in American Protestantism, 1865–1915* (1940).

Irving Howe, *World of Our Fathers* (1976).

Francis L. K. Hsu, *The Challenge of the American Dream: The Chinese in the United States* (1971).

Maldwyn A. Jone, *American Immigration* (1960).

Alan M. Kraut, *The Huddled Masses: The Immigrant in American Society, 1880–1921* (1982).

Seymour J. Mandelbaum, *Boss Tweed's New York* (1965).

Gwendolyn Mink, *Old Labor and New Immigrants in American Political Development: Union, Party, and State, 1875–1920* (1986).

Gary R. Mormino, *Immigrants on the Hill: Italian-Americans in St. Louis, 1882–1982* (1986).

James S. Olson, *Catholic Immigrants in America* (1987).

Gilbert Osofsky, *Harlem: The Making of a Ghetto, Negro New York, 1890–1930* (1966).

Kathy Lee Peiss, *Cheap Amusements: Working Women and Leisure in Turn-of-the-Century New York* (1986).

Jacob A. Riis, *How the Other Half Lives: Studies Among the Tenements of New York* (1890).

Moses Rischin, *The Promised City: New York's Jews, 1870–1914* (1962).

Arthur M. Schlesinger, *The Rise of the City, 1878–1898* (1933).

Allan H. Spear, *Black Chicago: The Making of a Negro Ghetto, 1890–1920* (1967).

John G. Sproat, *The Best Men: Liberal Reformers in the Gilded Age* (1968).

David B. Tyack, *The One Best System: A History of American Urban Education* (1974).

Sam Bass Warner, Jr., *Streetcar Suburbs: The Process of Growth in Boston, 1870–1900* (1962).

CHAPTER 5

Conservative Government and Agrarian Revolt

Time Line

1867	The Grange is established
1873	Congress discontinues the coinage of silver
1877	Republican Rutherford B. Hayes is declared the winner of the disputed 1876 presidential election
1878	The Bland-Allison Act authorizes limiting the coinage of silver

1880	Republican James A. Garfield wins the presidential election
1881	Garfield's assassination; Vice President Chester A. Arthur becomes President
1883	Congress passes the Pendleton Act, reforming the civil service
1884	Democrat Grover Cleveland wins the Presidential election
Late 1880s	Depression hits American agriculture
1888	Republican Benjamin Harrison wins the presidential election
1890	Congress passes the Sherman Silver Purchase Act, increasing the Treasury's purchase of silver
	Congress passes the McKinley Tariff
1892	The Populist party is established
	Cleveland wins his second presidential term
1893	The Panic of 1893 leads to a serious depression
	Congress repeals the Sherman Silver Purchase Act
1894	Congress passes the Wilson-Gorman Tariff
	Coxey's Army demands government assistance for the unemployed
1896	Republican William McKinley defeats his Democratic opponent, William Jennings Bryan, for the Presidency

1897	Congress passes the Dingley Tariff
Late 1890s	The American economy begins to revive
1900	Congress passes the Gold Standard Act

During the two decades following the disputed presidential election of 1876, Republican and Democratic administrations alike pursued conservative, pro-business policies. The two major parties put more emphasis on winning elections and dispensing patronage than on the promotion of particular policies, although questions of civil service reform, the regulation of the railroads and monopolistic business, and tariff policy produced some controversy.

The most controversial issue during these years involved monetary policy, first the greenback question and then the conflict between supporters of the gold standard and those who advocated unlimited coinage of silver ("free silver"). Until the mid-1890s, controversy over monetary policy was not a partisan issue, but rather one that cut across party lines.

America's discontented farmers, who created the Populist movement, came to identify their cause with free silver. In 1896, the Democrats endorsed free silver and nominated William Jennings Bryan for the Presidency. William McKinley, the conservative Republican candidate, inflicted a crushing defeat on Bryan and the Democrats. McKinley's victory marked the beginning of over thirty years of Republican domination of national politics.

An Era of Small Government

In the late nineteenth century, the federal government operated on a small scale, and the citizens expected it to do so.

Its activities were so limited, in fact, that the federal treasury posted a surplus for a number of years. The major financial problem facing the government seemed to be how to reduce revenues rather than increase them.

Federal agencies performed mainly routine administrative tasks, and the government was not extensively involved in social welfare, education or the regulation of the economy. The diplomatic service was small. The army performed service on the frontier, fighting occasional small-scale Indian wars. The navy functioned mainly as a coastal patrol force, although an expansion of the navy did begin in the 1890s.

The nation's presidents, the Republicans and Grover Cleveland, the only Democrat elected to the Presidency during these years, regarded their work as primarily executive— supervising the federal government's operations—and had only small White House staffs at their disposal. They did not play an active role in originating legislative proposals, and, generally, they did not attempt to lead Congress in the development of policy.

Party Politics

From the mid-1870s to the mid-1890s, the Republican and Democratic parties were about equal in strength, even though the Republicans held the Presidency for most of the period. People identified themselves strongly with one of the two major parties, and voter turn-out was high. Close to 80 percent of the eligible voters cast their ballots in presidential elections, while congressional elections brought a 60 to 80 percent participation.

Although elections were hard-fought, neither party was inclined to identify itself strongly with divisive issues. Historically, the Democrats tended to favor states' rights and limited activity on the part of the federal government, as well as tariffs for revenue only. The Republicans were more active in encouraging the development of business and industry and favored protective tariffs. In practice, both parties were pro-business and opposed anything which bore any resemblance to economic radicalism or socialism. At the same time, leaders of business and industry supported the Republicans more than they did the Democrats.

The Republicans maintained their identification with the Union cause during the Civil War. Republican campaigners continued to "wave the bloody shirt," reminding northern voters that the Democrats had been the party of rebellion. Five Republican presidents—Grant, Hayes, Garfield, Harrison, and McKinley—were Union veterans of the Civil War, and during the 1880s, a third of the Republicans in Congress were veterans of the Union army.

Following the Compromise of 1877, which gave Rutherford B. Hayes the Presidency, the Republicans agreed to abandon Reconstruction and, with it, their support of southern blacks.

On the major issues of the two decades after 1876—civil service reform, the regulation of railroads and monopolies, and monetary policies—the major differences were within the parties, rather than between them, until the Democrats adopted a strong free silver position in 1896.

The five presidential elections from 1876 to 1892 were all decided by narrow margins, and neither party succeeded in establishing decisive control over Congress.

The Congress

While the Presidents of the late nineteenth century did not play an active role in the development of policy, Congress was also content to remain relatively passive. In both the House of Representatives and the Senate, the party leaders had trouble trying to control the membership, while the rules of the House were so complex that business often ground to a halt. The situation improved after "Czar" Thomas B. Reed became Speaker in 1889 and established his firm control over the House of Representatives. Reed served as Speaker from 1889 to 1891 and again from 1895 to 1899. The failure of either party to establish decisive control over Congress also served to prevent vigorous congressional action. From the mid-1870s to the mid-1890s, the Republicans generally dominated the Senate, while the Democrats usually controlled the House of Representatives. During this period, neither party succeeded in winning control of both houses of Congress for more than a single two-year congressional term.

The Hayes Administration

A Republican, Rutherford B. Hayes served as President from 1877 to 1881. An officer in the Union army during the Civil War, Hayes had served one term in the House of Representatives before winning the governorship of Ohio in three consecutive elections. As President, Hayes opposed the spoils system and endorsed civil service reform, which led to a feud with some of the leaders of his own Republican party.

The Stalwarts and the Half-Breeds

During the late 1870s and early 1880s, a bitter factional conflict raged within the Republican party. The conflict did not involve differences over issues, but rather revolved around a personal feud and disputes over the distribution of patronage. Senator Roscoe Conkling, the Republican boss of New York state, led one faction, the Stalwarts. Representative James G. Blaine of Maine headed the other faction, the Half-Breeds.

Eventually the differences were resolved, and the party was unified.

The Garfield Administration

In 1880, Hayes decided not to seek the Republican nomination for a second term. If he had, his effort to win renomination might have been blocked by Conkling and the Stalwarts.

Hayes' withdrawal opened a hotly contested battle for the Republican nomination. After 36 indecisive ballots, the Republican national convention chose James A. Garfield as the party's standard-bearer. Another Ohioan, Garfield, had served in the Union army prior to becoming a member of the House of Representatives in 1863. In 1880, shortly before his nomination for the Presidency, he won election to the Senate.

Although Garfield won by a narrow plurality of only 10,000 votes over his Democratic opponent, a relatively obscure Civil War general named Winfield Scott Hancock, his margin in the electoral college was substantial: 214 electoral votes for Garfield to Hancock's 155.

In July 1881, only four months after taking office, Garfield was assassinated by Charles Guiteau, a seemingly deranged man who had been denied a patronage appointment.

The Arthur Administration

Garfield was succeeded by his vice president, Chester A. Arthur, who held the Presidency from 1881 to 1885. A product of Roscoe Conkling's New York political machine, Arthur came to the office of the President with an uncertain reputation, although he performed responsibly in office.

Like other Republican presidents of this era, Arthur supported increased pensions for veterans of the Union army. From $27 million in 1878, the federal government's expenditures on pensions increased to $66 million in 1883. The Grand Army of the Republic (GAR), the major organization of Union veterans, had good reason for its consistent support of the Republican party. While the GAR initially pushed for pensions for Union veterans with service-connected disabilities, it came to favor pensions for veterans with any disability and ultimately called for pensions for all Union veterans. Spending money on pensions proved to be a convenient and politically rewarding way to dispose of the embarrassing surplus in the federal budget.

Civil Service Reform

One of the major functions of American presidents was to dispense political patronage, handing out government jobs to the party faithful. There were about 100,000 jobs to be distributed, most of them in the post office, which was the only large federal agency in the nineteenth century. Garfield's assassination in 1881 by a disappointed office seeker increased support for civil service reform, and Arthur urged passage of the Pendleton Act of 1883.

The Pendleton Act created the Civil Service Commission, composed of three members appointed by the President. The Civil Service Commission was charged with filling certain government jobs on the basis of competitive examinations. At first, only about 10 percent of the jobs were covered, but the Pendleton Act empowered the President to extend the merit system to other positions. A president frequently did this toward the end of his term in order to protect his appointees from being replaced by his successor. During his second term, President Grover Cleveland doubled the number of federal employees covered by the merit system from about 40,000 when he took office in 1893 to about 80,000 in 1897. An increasing number of jobs thus came to be covered by the merit system, but dispensing patronage remained an important—and often annoying—presidential task.

The Pendleton Act also prohibited the solicitation of campaign contributions from federal employees.

The 1884 Election

In 1884, the Republicans refused to renominate Arthur and instead gave their presidential nomination to James G. Blaine of Maine. A longtime congressman, Blaine had served as Speaker of the House from 1869 to 1875 and had then won election to the Senate. While Blaine's supporters hailed him as the "plumed knight," he was still under a cloud of suspicion resulting from charges of corruption leveled against him in the mid-1870s. His opponents were not convinced that Blaine had told the truth when he denied the charges and denounced him as "the Continental Liar from the State of Maine."

Anti-Blaine Republicans, known as the Mugwumps, supported the Democratic nominee, Grover Cleveland, who had served as the reform mayor of Buffalo before winning election as Governor of New York.

The campaign was hard-fought, although Blaine and Cleveland did not disagree significantly on issues. While Cleveland's supporters questioned Blaine's honesty, the Republicans accused Cleveland, a man of great public honor, of having fathered an illegitimate child. A Republican campaign verse ran: "Ma, Ma, where's my Pa? Goin' to the White House, ha, ha, ha!"

During the campaign, Blaine was hurt by a statement made by one of his supporters, Samuel D. Burchard, a Protestant minister from New York. Burchard denounced the Democrats as the party of "Rum, Romanism, and Rebellion." Blaine failed to disassociate himself strongly enough from this remark, and the failure hurt him at the polls. While winning a popular vote plurality of only 23,000, Cleveland polled 219 votes in the Electoral College to Blaine's 182 votes.

Grover Cleveland's First Term

Grover Cleveland was the only person in American history to serve two nonconsecutive presidential terms, from 1885 to 1889 and from 1893 to 1897. He was also the first President, since Grant, to win a second term in the White House.

As the first Democrat to win the Presidency since 1856, Cleveland performed his duty to his party by replacing Republican office holders with faithful Democrats. In an effort to heal some of the wounds of the Civil War, he named two former Confederates to his cabinet and appointed southerners to a number of positions. His effort to return captured Confederate battle flags encountered heavy public opposition, however, and had to be abandoned.

Cleveland was probably the most active of the late nineteenth century presidents, although his was a largely negative activism. Cleveland vetoed a record number of bills, especially private bills sponsored by representatives and senators to provide pensions to Union army veterans whose applications for pensions had been rejected by the Bureau of Pensions.

Although Cleveland was basically conservative and sympathetic to business, he did sign the Interstate Commerce Act of 1887, which established the basis for government regulation of the railroads.

The Democratic party traditionally supported tariffs for revenue purposes only and criticized the Republicans for their endorsement of protective tariffs, which were intended to protect American industry from the competition of cheaper imports. In 1887, Cleveland called for a reduction of the high tariffs enacted during earlier Republican administrations. When Congress did not respond to his appeal, Cleveland made the tariff question a major issue in the 1888 election.

The Election of 1888

In 1888, Cleveland faced Benjamin Harrison, the Republican nominee. A grandson of President William Henry Harrison, he had served as a colonel in the Union army and had represented Indiana in the U. S. Senate since 1881.

Cleveland's advocacy of tariff reform served to push the leaders of business and industry, who benefitted from high protective tariffs, even more solidly into the Republican camp, and they contributed heavily to Harrison's campaign.

While Cleveland won a popular vote plurality of over 100,000, he polled only 168 electoral votes to Harrison's 233. For the first time since 1874, the Republicans won control of both houses of Congress.

The Harrison Administration

Benjamin Harrison served as President from 1889 to 1893. He approved the passage of the Dependent Pension Act of 1890, which provided pensions to all Union veterans who were unable to support themselves, as well as pensions for the dependents of veterans. Expenditures for pensions nearly doubled during Harrison's term of office from $81 million to $157 million. The total cost of pensions paid to Union veterans by the federal government ultimately exceeded the cost of fighting the Civil War.

The Republicans continued their support of protective tariffs, and the McKinley Tariff of 1890 raised rates to an average of nearly 50 percent. Also in 1890, the Sherman Anti-Trust Act was passed, although it proved to be ineffective in controlling monopolistic business practices.

The Elections of 1890 and 1892

During the early 1890s, the political pendulum showed signs

of swinging in favor of the Democrats, although that trend proved to be brief.

The strength of the Democrats had gradually been increasing, especially in the cities of the Northeast and Middle West. In these cities, with their large immigrant populations, ethnic and cultural issues, especially those of liquor and immigration restriction, benefitted the Democrats. The growing movement for prohibition had been pulling many Republicans, especially in rural areas, to the new Prohibition party. In order to hold on to its rural supporters, the Republican party began to move in favor of prohibition and to show some concern for immigration reform.

In the congressional elections of 1890, the Republicans' once substantial majority in the Senate was reduced to only eight seats. In the House of Representatives, the Democrats increased their seats from 159 to 235, leaving only 88 seats to the Republicans.

Two years later, in the presidential election of 1892, Grover Cleveland defeated Harrison's bid for reelection. Winning a popular vote plurality of almost 400,000, Cleveland polled 277 electoral votes to Harrison's 155. The Populist candidate, James B. Weaver, won about one million votes. For the first time since 1878, the Democrats won control of both houses of Congress.

Grover Cleveland's Second Term

During his second term from 1893 to 1897, Cleveland failed in his efforts to obtain a significant reduction of the tariff. The Wilson-Gorman Tariff of 1894 reduced rates only slightly. Even though the Democrats, who favored tariff reduction in principle, controlled both houses of Congress, representatives and senators were concerned above all about protecting the economic interests of their constituents. Although opposed to the new tariff, Cleveland allowed it to become law without his signature.

In order to make up for the revenue which would be lost as a result of tariff reduction, the Wilson-Gorman Act provided for a modest income tax of 2 percent on all income in excess of $4000 a year. In the 1895 case of *Pollock v. Farmers' Loan and Trust Co.*, the Supreme Court ruled that the income tax provision was unconstitutional.

The Panic of 1893

Cleveland's return to the office virtually coincided with the Panic of 1893, which plunged the nation into a severe depression. In March, the month of Cleveland's inauguration, the Philadelphia and Reading Railroad went bankrupt. Then in May, the National Cordage Company collapsed. A number of banks failed, and the resulting shortage of credit led to the failure of many businesses which were dependent on loans.

About 20 percent of the labor force became unemployed. The depression also affected the farmers of the South and the Great Plains. Prices for agricultural products that had been declining for several years now dropped further, hitting new lows.

Coxey's Army

In the spring of 1894, Jacob S. Coxey of Masillon, Ohio, led a group of unemployed workers to Washington to call for the enactment of a national public works program to provide jobs. "Coxey's Army" totaled only about 500 men, and the march collapsed after Coxey and two of his associates were arrested for trespassing on the grounds of the Capitol.

The Election of 1894

As the party in power, the Democrats had to take the blame for the depression, and suffered a major setback in the 1894 congressional election. The Democrats lost a third of their seats in Congress.

A major political realignment was getting underway. At the center of this realignment was growing agricultural discontent which increasingly came to be linked with economic problems, such as declining income and increasing debt.

American Agriculture in the Late Nineteenth Century

The years following the Civil War witnessed a great expansion of American agriculture. From 1860 to 1890, the number of farms increased from two million to 4.5 million, while the rural population grew from 25 million to almost 41 million. In the South, most farmers were tenants or sharecroppers, but elsewhere farmers were usually independent farm owners. Rural America, therefore, consisted mostly of family farms, with the average farm comprising somewhat less than 150 acres.

America's farmers had begun to concentrate on the production of a cash crop. The production of wheat was centered in the Great Plains, while the corn belt ran slightly to the east through most of the Middle West. Dairy products were produced especially in the area extending eastward from Minnesota and Wisconsin to upstate New York, while cotton production was centered in the area running from the Carolinas westward to Texas.

Problems of Agriculture

America's farmers faced many problems. While most farmers were independent, they were not selfsufficient. They depended on the railroads for storage of their crops and for shipment to market. They depended on the commodity exchanges that established the prices for agricultural produce. And they depended on the processors—the flour millers, the meat packers, and the canners. They also depended heavily on banks and mortgage companies for credit.

Farmers lived a difficult life. They had to work hard, with the average farmer's work week totaling 68 hours, as compared to the average industrial worker's week of 56 hours. As late as 1900, farm children spent only two-thirds as many days a year in school as city children, and farm children left school at an earlier age.

Farmers often felt a powerful sense of isolation. This was particularly pronounced in the Great Plains where the winters were long, distances were great, and communication was difficult. Farmers did not benefit from the technology—paved roads, indoor plumbing, electricity—which improved life in the city.

Above all, the farmers confronted immense economic uncertainty, since the prices of agricultural products were subject to wide fluctuations.

The Grange

In order to promote the farmers' interests, Oliver H. Kelley, a former official of the Agriculture Department, established the National Grange of the Patrons of Husbandry in 1867. Open to both men and women, the Grange became an important social center in farm communities and also helped increase the farmers' knowledge of scientific agriculture. By 1874, the Grange had recruited some 1.5 million members.

During the 1870s, the Grange worked to promote the development of cooperatives among farmers, and all sorts of cooperatives were established: stores, creameries, warehouses, grain elevators, and insurance companies. Most of these cooperatives were not successful, however. Private business opposed them, and the cooperative managers often were inexperienced. Also contributing to the cooperatives' failure was the farmers' strong tradition of individualism.

The nation's first mail-order house, Montgomery Ward and Co., was founded in 1872 to meet the needs of the Grangers.

The Grange also had political impact, working in the 1870s to secure the adoption by state legislatures of the so-called Granger Laws to regulate the railroads. In the late 1870s, the Grange grew weaker, and its membership gradually declined to 100,000.

The Farmers' Alliances

Producers of grain in the Middle West and Great Plains suffered particularly from the uncertainties which beset agriculture. Grain prices fluctuated considerably. After dropping in the late 1870s, grain prices increased substantially in the early 1880s. As grain prices rose and fell, so, too, did the price of land. When grain prices declined in 1883–84, farmers who had bought land earlier at high prices could not earn enough to meet their mortgage payments and were threatened with foreclosure.

Angry and frustrated farmers established the National Farmers' Alliance of the North West. In the South, similar organizations emerged among the tenants and sharecroppers, including the Southern Farmers' Alliance and the Colored Farmers' Alliance. The latter organization had only a limited impact, since most blacks were barred from voting in the South. In addition, white racist attitudes made any effective cooperation impossible between the two southern alliances.

The alliances were originally designed to operate as social and mutual aid organizations and, like the Grange before them, established farmers' cooperatives. When these cooperatives failed, the alliances began to turn toward political action. In the late 1880s, the western and southern alliances began to cooperate. In 1890, the farmers' alliance gained control of several state legislatures in the West. In the South, the farmers' alliance found vigorous leaders, including Benjamin F. "Pitchfork Ben" Tillman of South Carolina and Thomas Watson of Georgia. In 1890, the Southern Farmers' Alliance captured four governorships, won control of seven state legislatures, and elected 44 pro-Alliance congressmen and several senators. The protest of the farmers was clearly having a significant political impact.

The Populists

In 1892 representatives of the western and southern alliances met in St. Louis and established the People's Party, known as the Populists. The Populist platform called for a graduated income tax, the nationalization of the railroads, the secret ballot, veterans' pensions, the direct election of senators, and restrictions on immigration. The Populists endorsed the sub-treasury plan, originally proposed by the Souther Farmers' Alliance. This plan, if enacted, would enable farmers to borrow money at 2 percent interest, with crops serving as collateral. The Populists proposed the abolition of the national banks, which they believed were an instrument used by eastern bankers to exploit the farmers. Finally, the Populists called for the unlimited coinage of silver at the ratio of 16 ounces of silver to one ounce of gold.

In 1892 the Populists nominated James B. Weaver, and Iowa congressman, as their presidential candidate. Weaver polled 1 million votes and carried four states—Kansas, Colorado, Idaho, and Nevada—winning 22 electoral votes.

The Silver Issue

After 1892 the Populists increasingly focused their attention on the issue of the unlimited coinage of silver—free silver. Western and southern Populists believed strongly that most of the eastern bankers, and the Populists became obsessed with the evil influence of what one of their manifestoes described as "the money power."

In their decision to emphasize free silver, the Populists were influenced by William H. Harvey's pamphlet, *Coin's Financial School*, published in 1894. Harvey insisted that all of the nation's problems resulted from an inadequate supply of money. The solution was simple: unlimited coinage of silver at a ratio of 16 to 1.

Background of the Money Question

The money question proved to be the most explosive political issue in the United States in the post-Civil War years.

Ever since the end of the Civil War, deflationary pressures had been operating. By 1880, the wholesale price index was 30 percent lower than it had been in 1870. By 1890, it was 20 percent lower than in 1880. This decline worked to the disadvantage of debtors, who wanted an increase in the money supply. They faced the opposition of those who defended the cause of sound money, believing that tampering with the currency would endanger the nation's economic stability.

The Greenback Issue

The battle over money following the Civil War was fought first over the greenback issue. In order to help finance the war, the Lincoln administration had issued paper money, which came to be called greenbacks. After the war, the advocates of sound money wanted to remove some of the greenbacks from circulation and to back those that remained with gold. In other words, the Treasury would exchange gold for greenbacks. This proposal was designed to end the inflationary threat posed by the greenbacks. With the support of President Rutherford B. Hayes, this proposal was put into effect in 1879.

In the meantime, those who supported keeping all of the

greenbacks in circulation had turned to political action. In 1875, the National Greenback Party, later renamed the Greenback Labor Party, was formed. This party won its major support from discontented farmers in the Middle West and Great Plains, but also found some backing from labor. Greenback congressional candidates won a total of over one million votes in the 1878 election, but as economic conditions improved, the party lost strength. In 1880, James B. Weaver, the Greenbacks' presidential candidate, won slightly over 300,000 votes. (Weaver was the Populists' presidential candidate in 1892.) In 1884, the Greenback candidate, Benjamin F. Butler, a former Union general, polled only 175,000 votes in the Presidencial race.

Free Silver

As the greenback issue began to subside, the issue of free silver moved to the forefront of the money question.

Until 1873, the United States had operated on a bimetallic standard; that is, both silver and gold had been recognized as the basis for the dollar. The official value of silver and gold had been established at the ratio of 16 ounces of silver to one ounce of gold. Silver came to be in short supply, however, and the actual market value of silver exceeded the value established by the government. The United States Mint stopped coining silver, and silver coins disappeared from circulation. In 1873, Congress officially recognized this situation by adopting a law ending the coinage of silver which, in fact, had already occurred. This law, in effect, put the United States on the gold standard.

At the time, the issue was not particularly controversial. Within a few years, however, large deposits of silver were discovered in Colorado, Nevada, and other western states. The increase in the supply of silver led to a decline in the price of silver in relation to gold.

If the government returned to the bimetallic standard and

coined silver once again at the old ratio of 16 to 1, the amount of money in circulation would be greatly expanded. The expansion of the nation's money supply would halt the deflationary trend and lead to inflation. This inflation would, in turn, benefit the nation's debtors, especially the farmers, who would have more "cheaper money" to pay off their debts. The discontented farmers and other debtors now began to protest against what they called the "Crime of '73" and to demand free silver. Producers of silver also supported bimetallism since the ratio of 16 to 1 would cause the Treasury to pay considerably above the market price for the silver it bought. By 1893, in fact, the market value of silver stood at a ratio of 26 to 1 and by 1894, it was 32 to 1.

In 1878 a coalition of pro-silver Democrats and Republicans pushed through the Bland-Allison Act. Under its terms, the Treasury would purchase a limited amount of silver each month (from $2 to $4 million) and coin silver dollars.

This act did not satisfy the advocates of silver who succeeded in securing the passage of the Sherman Silver Purchase Act of 1890. The act authorized the Treasury to purchase and coin 4.5 million ounces of silver each month. The Treasury would pay for this silver with treasury notes, which were redeemable in either gold or silver. While the Sherman Silver Purchase Act led to an expanded money supply, it also opened the way to an assault on the nation's gold reserve.

President Cleveland and the Money Question

The money question continued to cut across party lines, with both Democrats and Republicans joining the cause of free silver, while other Democrats and Republicans remained committed to sound money and the gold standard. By the 1890s, however, the Republicans were becoming more determined in their support of the gold standard, while the advocates of free silver increased their hold on the Democratic party.

President Grover Cleveland, a Democrat, was fundamentally conservative and remained an advocate of the gold standard. Nevertheless, he found it difficult to maintain the gold standard in the face of increasing pressures on the nation's gold reserve. In 1893, Cleveland convinced Congress to repeal the Sherman Silver Purchase Act. He believed that the act's provision permitting the redemption of treasury notes in gold or silver presented the major threat to the nation's gold supply. The advocates of free silver were furious.

The pressure on the gold reserve continued as holders of greenbacks redeemed them for gold and as foreign investors cashed in American securities. In early 1895, the Treasury's gold reserve reached a new low of $41 million.

Cleveland now turned to a syndicate of private bankers, including J. Pierpont Morgan and August Belmont, who represented the Rothschild banking interests. The bankers helped finance purchases of gold to replenish the Treasury's reserve. Cleveland's action angered many, including Democrats who had come to share the Populists' mythology about the evil eastern bankers, "the money power."

The 1896 Election

The issue of free silver dominated the 1896 election. The Democrats rejected Cleveland and the gold standard and embraced the cause of free silver. When the Democratic national convention met in Chicago, it chose William Jennings Bryan, a 36-year-old Nebraska congressman, as its presidential candidate. Bryan electrified the convention with his "Cross of Gold speech," proclaiming, "You shall not press down upon the brow of labor this crown of thorns: you shall not crucify mankind upon a cross of gold."

The Democratic convention produced a remarkably progressive platform. In addition to calling for the unlimited coinage of

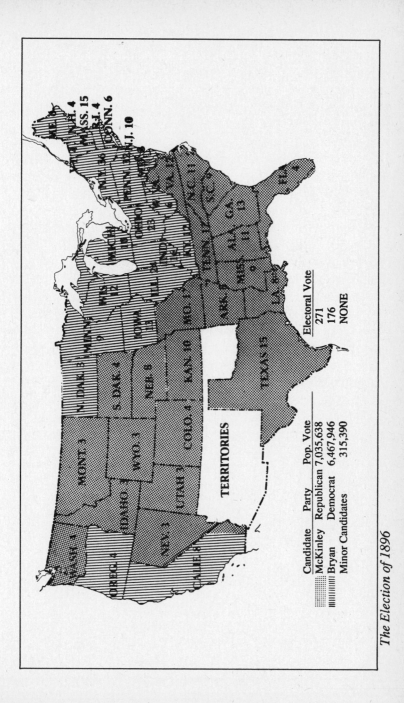

Candidate	Party	Pop. Vote
McKinley	Republican	7,035,638
Bryan	Democrat	6,467,946
Minor Candidates		315,390

Electoral Vote	
	271
	176
	NONE

The Election of 1896

silver, the Democrats endorsed a tariff for revenue only (rather than a protective tariff designed to protect American industry from foreign competition), the adoption of a graduated income tax, and tougher enforcement of the Interstate Commerce Act. The platform denounced Cleveland's use of the army to break the Pullman strike and the use of the injunction against labor unions.

With the Democrats endorsing free silver, the Populists decided to back Bryan for the Presidency.

Meeting in St. Louis, the Republican national convention nominated William McKinley, a long time congressman who had been elected Ohio's governor in 1890. McKinley was as ardent an advocate of sound money as Bryan was of free silver.

Probably the most important figure in the 1896 campaign was Marcus A. Hanna, the Republican boss of Ohio. Hanna had engineered McKinley's nomination and then proceeded to manage the candidate's campaign, which McKinley conducted from his front porch in Canton, Ohio. Bryan, on the other hand, campaigned actively all over the country. McKinley appeared as a safe and responsible individual and also benefited from huge contributions from bankers and industrialists who were terrified by the Democrats' advocacy of free silver and their progressive platform.

McKinley polled just over seven million votes and won 271 electoral votes to Bryan's almost 6.5 million popular votes and 176 electoral votes. Bryan did well in the South, the Populist West, and the silver-mining states. McKinley swept the Northeast and Middle West, as well as California and Oregon. He made inroads into Democratic strongholds, capturing such cities as Boston, New York, Chicago, and Minneapolis. Following Bryan's defeat in 1896, the Populist party disintegrated.

The 1896 election ended the virtual equality of the two parties which had prevailed for two decades. The Republicans clearly emerged as the majority party, a position they would hold until Franklin D. Roosevelt's victory in 1932.

The Recovery of the Farmers

In the late 1890s, the situation of the nation's farmers improved, despite the defeat of free silver. In the 1890s, major discoveries of gold occurred in Alaska, South Africa, and Australia. In addition, the development of the cyanide process made it possible to extract gold from low-grade ore. In 1898, more than twice as much gold was produced than in 1890. The increased supply of gold resulted in inflation. From 1897 to 1914, prices increased by almost 50 percent, and the farmers' debt burden began to ease. The prosperity of American farmers lasted for more than two decades, until the 1920s.

The McKinley Administration

William McKinley was the last of the Union army veterans to serve in the Presidency. As President, he presided over a conservative and generally inactive administration. The Republicans remained faithful to their commitments to high protective tariffs and sound money. The Dingley Tariff of 1897 raised tariffs to a very high average of 57 percent, and the Gold Standard Act of 1900 reaffirmed the nation's adherence to the gold standard.

Between the end of the Civil War in 1865 and the mid-1890s, the Republican and Democratic parties were relatively equal in strength. Nevertheless, the Republicans held the Presidency for all but eight years. The Democrats dominated the Solid South, while the Republicans built a solid power base in much of the Northeast, the Middle West, and the West.

While the politicians debated civil service reform, the tariff, and pensions for Civil War veterans, discontent mounted among the nation's farmers. The Populist movement won increasing support in rural areas, especially in the West, and stepped up its demands for the unlimited coinage of silver. The farmers believed that the resulting inflation would ease their financial plight. In 1896, the Democratic party embraced the cause of free silver. The victory of Republican William McKinley over William Jennings Bryan, his Democratic opponent for the Presidency, not only defeated the campaign for free silver but also solidified the Republicans' dominant position in national politics.

Recommended Reading

Harry Barnard, *Rutherford B. Hayes and His America* (1954).

Sean D. Cashman, *America in the Gilded Age: From the Death of Lincoln to the Rise of Theodore Roosevelt* (1984).

Pãolo E. Coletta, *William Jennings Bryan: Political Evangelist, 1860–1908* (1964).

Kenneth Davison, *The Presidency of Rutherford B. Hayes* (1972).

Vincent P. DeSantis, *Republicans Face the Southern Question: The New Departure Years, 1877–1897* (1959).

Robert F. Durden, *The Climax of Populism: The Election of 1896* (1965).

Harold U. Faulkner, *Politics, Reform, and Expansion, 1890–1900* (1959).

Gilbert C. Fite, *The Farmer's Frontier, 1965–1900* (1966).

John A. Garraty, *The New Commonwealth, 1877–1890* (1968).

Ray Ginger, *Age of Excess: The United States from 1877 to 1914* (1965).

Paul W. Glad, *McKinley, Bryan and the People (1964)*.

Lawrence Goodwyn, *Democratic Promise: The Populist Movement in America* (1976).

Lewis L. Gould, *The Presidency of William McKinley* (1980).

John D. Hicks, *The Populist Revolt: A History of the Farmers' Alliance and the People's Party* (1931).

Richard Hofstadter, *The Age of Reform: From Bryan to F.D.R.* (1955).

J. Rogers Hollingsworth, *The Whirligig of Politics: The Democracy of Cleveland and Bryan* (1963).

Ari Hoogenboom, *Outlawing the Spoils: A History of the Civil Service Reform Movement, 1865–1883* (1961).

Paul Kleppner, *The Cross of Culture: A Social Analysis of Midwestern Politics, 1850–1900* (2nd ed., 1970).

Margaret Leech and Harry J. Brown, *The Garfield Orbit* (1978).

Robert D. Marcus, *Grand Old Party: Political Structure in the Gilded Age* (1971).

Robert McMath, *Populist Vanguard: A History of the Southern Farmers' Alliance* (1975).

H. Wayne Morgan, *From Hayes to McKinley: National Party Politics, 1877–1896* (1969).

Allan Peskin, *Garfield: A Biography* (1978).

Thomas C. Reeves, *Gentleman Boss: The Life of Chester Alan Arthur* (1975).

David J. Rothman, *Politics and Power: The United States Senate, 1869–1901* (1966).

David Rubinstein, *Before the Suffragettes: Women's Emancipation in the 1890s* (1986).

Theodore Saloutos, *Farmer Movements in the South, 1865–1933* (1960).

Barton C. Shaw, *The Wool-Hat Boys: Georgia's Populist Party* (1984).

Harry J. Sievers, *Benjamin Harrison, (3 vols.)* (1952–1968).

Francis B. Simkins, *Pitchfork Ben Tillman, South Carolinian* (1944).

Allen Weinstein, *Prelude to Populism: Origins of the Silver Issue 1867–1878* (1970).

R. Hal Williams, *Years of Decision: American Politics in the 1890s* (1978).

C. Vann Woodward, *Tom Watson: Agrarian Rebel* (1938).

CHAPTER 6

The New American Empire

Time Line

1889	The first Pan-American Congress meets
1890	Captain Alfred Mahan publishes *The Influence of Sea Power Upon History*
1895	American pressure leads to arbitration of the British boundary dispute with Venezuela
	A revolt against Spanish rule breaks out in Cuba
1898	The United States annexes Hawaii
	The New York Journal publishes the de Lôme letter

The battleship *Maine* explodes in Havana harbor

The United States declares war on Spain

Commodore George Dewey takes the Philippines

American forces take Cuba and Puerto Rico

The Treaty of Paris ends the Spanish-American War; Cuba becomes independent; the United States annexes Puerto Rico, the Philippines, and Guam

Opponents of American expansionism form the Anti-Imperialist League

1899   The Senate ratifies the Treaty of Paris

Germany and the United States divide the Samoan Islands

Secretary of State Hay issues his first Open Door note

1900   The Foraker Act establishes a government for Puerto Rico

The citizens of Hawaii receive American citizenship

The Boxer Rebellion breaks out in China

Secretary of State Hay issues his second Open Door note

1901   The Platt Amendment is approved by Congress

William Howard Taft becomes the first civilian Governor of the Philippines

1912   Alaska receives territorial status

The history of the United States during the nineteenth century is, in large part, the history of expansion. The acquisition of Louisiana, Florida, Texas, New Mexico, California, Oregon, the Gadsden Purchase, and Alaska expressed the expansionist spirit of Americans and extended the United States from the original thirteen colonies along the Atlantic seaboard westward to the Pacific Ocean.

From early in its history, the United States demonstrated a concern about the affairs of the western hemisphere, a concern expressed by the issuance of the Monroe Doctrine in 1823. This concern with hemispheric affairs increased in the years following the Civil War. American involvement in the Caribbean, in particular, caused the United States to go to war with Spain in 1898.

That war, in turn, led to the American acquisition of the Philippines. This, combined with the annexation of Hawaii and other island possessions in the Pacific, established an American presence in East Asia and a growing involvement in the affairs of China. By the early years of the Twentieth century, the United States had become a major power, playing an active role in world affairs.

Motives for Overseas Expansion

By the 1890s, the United States had completed its transcontinental expansion, and there was now a growing quest for a new frontier and the opportunities it could provide. The country's expanding industries needed new markets and additional sources of raw materials. Many Americans wanted to find new arenas for missionary activity of both the political and religious variety, while others glorified expansion for its own sake, regarding it as a symbol of the nation's strength and vitality.

The Economic Motive

The late nineteenth century witnessed a great expansion of the American economy. By 1900, the United States gained first place in manufacturing among the nations of the world, whereas in 1870, it had ranked fourth. With more land coming under cultivation, there was a tremendous increase in agricultural production, especially of cotton, wheat, and corn.

As America's industrial and agricultural output increased, there was a movement to create a commercial empire for the United States in the Caribbean, in Central and South America, and farther to the west in Asia. Acquiring new markets for American products would increase the profits of the nation's industrialists, farmers, and merchants. In addition, these overseas areas were the source of commodities desired by Americans: coffee, sugar, fruits, oil, rubber, and minerals.

In the period from 1865 to 1900, American exports more than tripled, and direct investments abroad also increased dramatically. The United States was clearly becoming a major factor in the world economy.

The Missionary Motive

Faith in America and its values and faith in God combined to create a spirit among Americans which gave further support to the cause of expansionism. Josiah Strong, a Congregational minister, emerged as an eloquent spokesman for this missionary spirit. In his *Our Country*, published in 1885, Strong asserted that the Anglo-Saxons (the British and Americans) represented two great ideas: political liberty and "a pure spiritual Christianity." He argued that the Anglo-Saxons had been "divinely commissioned" to spread the blessings of freedom and Protestant Christianity throughout the world. Strong boldly predicted, "This powerful race will move down upon Mexico, down upon Central and South America, out into the islands of the sea, over upon Africa and beyond."

Overseas missionary activity grew markedly in the post-Civil War years. In China, which became the favorite object of America's missionary fervor, the number of missionaries increased by over 1,000 percent between the mid-1870s and 1914; from fewer than 500 to more than 5,000. Although these missionaries won relatively few Chinese converts, the missions produced a group of young, western-educated, and reform-minded individuals, many of whom played leading roles in the Chinese Revolution of 1911, which overthrew the Manchu dynasty.

The Quest for National Glory

In the late nineteenth century, people in many countries believed that overseas expansion was the most natural way to demonstrate a nation's vitality and greatness. These people also believed that failure to expand was a sign of weakness and decadence.

In America in the late 1890s, this spirit of expansionism was expressed by nationalistic young political leaders like Assistant Secretary of the Navy Theodore Roosevelt and Senator Henry Cabot Lodge of Massachusetts. A truly great America, they believed, must assert itself in world affairs.

These expansionists were aware of the empire building of the European powers, who were carving out imperial domains for themselves in Africa and Asia. For people like Roosevelt and Lodge, the pursuit of "national honor," to use Roosevelt's term, was far more important than achieving any economic gains.

Captain Mahan and the Role of Sea Power

Captain Alfred Thayer Mahan had a powerful impact on the thinking of American expansionists. In his book *The Influence of Sea Power Upon History* (1890), Mahan argued that the development of sea power was the key to promoting a nation's greatness and prosperity. The United States, he urged, should "look outward." The nation should develop a great navy and a substantial merchant fleet, and it should promote its foreign trade. The United States should acquire naval bases and colonies both in the Caribbean and the Pacific. And, Mahan asserted, the new American empire should be united by an American-built and operated canal joining the Caribbean and the Pacific.

Naval Expansion

The American navy grew during these years. In 1883, Congress approved the construction of three cruisers. Three years later, in 1886, Congress appropriated the funds for 20 more ships, including two battleships, the *Maine* and the *Texas*.

While this expansion occurred, the navy remained primarily a force to defend the American coasts. The passage of the Naval Act of 1890 marked the beginning of the development of an American high-seas fleet. This act authorized the construction of a number of new ships, including three additional battleships, the *Indiana*, the *Oregon*, and the *Massachusetts*.

Latin America

In the early 1880s, Secretary of State James G. Blaine emerged as an advocate of increased trade with Latin America and closer cooperation between the countries of the western hemisphere. Blaine also hoped to acquire naval bases in the Caribbean and favored the construction of a Central American canal.

In 1881, Blaine invited the countries of the western hemisphere to attend a conference designed to promote peace and commerce. Following President James A. Garfield's assassination and the succession of President Chester A. Arthur, however, Blaine resigned and the conference was never held.

Blaine became Secretary of State once again in the cabinet of Benjamin Harrison. An inter-American conference, held in 1889, did not reach any agreement on Blaine's proposals concerning trade and arbitration treaties, although it did agree to establish an information bureau which subsequently became the Pan-American Union.

An incident in 1891 led to strained relations between the United States and Chile. In October 1891, a group of American sailors on shore leave in Valparaiso, Chile, became involved in a barroom brawl. Two Americans were killed and several others injured. President Harrison issued an ultimatum, demanding "prompt and full reparation" from Chile. Faced with the threat of American force, Chile had to comply. The incident left resentment in its wake.

The Venezuelan Boundary Dispute

For some years, a boundary dispute had simmered between Venezuela and Great Britain, which ruled the colony of British Guiana. By 1895, the discovery of gold in the disputed territory raised the prospect of British action against Venezuela.

The United States was generally anxious in these years to assert its influence and power in inter-American affairs. In addition, President Grover Cleveland, who was experiencing domestic political difficulties because of the depression, welcomed an opportunity for vigorous international action to curry favor with public opinion.

Cleveland instructed Secretary of State Richard Olney to send a note to London. The strong message he sent had the tone of an ultimatum. Invoking and expanding the Monroe Doctrine, Olney asserted that the United States was "practically sovereign on this continent" and demanded that the British agree to submit the dispute with Venezuela to arbitration.

Lord Salisbury, the British Foreign Secretary, flatly rejected Olney's broad interpretation of the Monroe Doctrine, as well as the demand for arbitration. The British response angered American opinion, and some Americans went so far as to advocate war against Great Britain.

The British did not want a conflict with the United States and bowed to American demands for arbitration of the boundary dispute with Venezuela. The arbitration tribunal awarded most of the territory in question to British Guiana.

Although tension between Washington and London had run high, the peaceful resolution of the conflict contributed to an improvement in Anglo-American relations.

The Pacific

In 1878, the United States acquired rights to a naval base at Pago Pago in the Samoan Islands in the South Pacific. The United States had to share the base with Great Britain and Germany.

In the late 1880s, a German attempt to take over Samoa nearly resulted in an conflict between German and American ships. A typhoon wrecked both fleets, and the crisis passed. A conference held in Berlin in 1889 saw the establishment of a tripartite American, German, and British protectorate over the Samoan Islands. A decade later, in 1899, the British pulled out in exchange for concessions elsewhere. The Americans and Germans then divided the islands, with the United States acquiring exclusive rights to Pago Pago.

In the late 1880s, a dispute broke out in the Bering Straits, located between Alaska and Siberia, where the United States claimed exclusive rights over the fur seals. When the United States seized several Canadian ships, the British threatened naval action. An arbitration tribunal resolved the conflict, rejecting the American claims and requiring the United States to pay damages.

Hawaii

Hawaii ultimately proved more important to the United States than either Samoa or the Bering Straits. American commercial interests in Hawaii dated back to the late Eighteenth century, and American missionaries had followed the traders into the islands. During the nineteenth century, Americans acquired a substantial degree of control over sugar growing in Hawaii.

A reciprocity treaty, concluded in 1875, admitted Hawaiian sugar to the United States without the payment of tariffs. In 1887, the United States Senate ratified the renewal of this treaty, and the United States acquired the rights to a naval base at Pearl Harbor on the island of Oahu.

The growing American influence caused resentment among the Hawaiians, who also objected to the bringing in of a large number of Japanese and Chinese immigrants to work in the sugar fields.

In 1891, the nationalistic Queen Liliuokalani became Hawaii's ruler and began to promote a campaign of "Hawaii for the Hawaiians." The Queen was determined to assert her authority and to reduce American influence.

In 1893, with the aid of the U.S. Navy and Marines, American sugar growers staged a revolt, overthrew the Queen, proclaimed the establishment of a republic, and called for the annexation of Hawaii by the United States. President Harrison submitted the annexation treaty to the Senate. Before the treaty could be ratified, however, Grover Cleveland became President for the second time.

Cleveland halted the ratification process and sent a special commissioner to investigate the situation in Hawaii. The commissioner reported that an overwhelming majority of Hawaiians supported their Queen.

Despite this report, the Queen was not restored to her throne and the revolutionary government remained in power, awaiting a more opportune moment to press for annexation. That moment came in July 1898, during the Spanish-American War, when American expansionist fever was at its peak. Hawaii now became an American possession.

Cuba

Cuba, lying some 90 miles off the coast of southern Florida, almost inevitably attracted the interest of Americans, especially when Spanish misrule provoked Cuban revolts.

When a new Cuban revolt broke out in 1895, the Spanish government refused to grant concessions to the Cubans. Instead, Madrid sent General Valeriano "Butcher" Weyler to Cuba with 50,000 troops and orders to crush the revolt.

In Cuba, Weyler followed a policy of reconcentration. The Spanish army rounded up thousands of Cubans and imprisoned them in towns surrounded by barbed wire and armed guards. Many Cubans died of famine and disease.

News from Cuba enraged Americans, many of whom felt an almost religious obligation to help the oppressed. Rallies were organized to raise money for Cuban relief. Some Americans wanted military intervention for the humanitarian purpose of helping the Cubans, while others—like Captain Mahan, Theodore Roosevelt, and Senator Lodge—favored war for the glory and territorial gains it would bring. American economic interests were also at stake, since there was heavy American investment in Cuban sugar plantations and the United States conducted a substantial trade with Cuba.

President Cleveland and his successor, William McKinley, who took office in 1897, hoped to avoid a war over Cuba.

In mid-1897, there were signs that a full-scale conflict with Spain might be averted. A new government in Madrid recalled Weyler and appeared ready to carry out reforms. The Spanish even offered the prospect of granting some degree of self-government to the Cubans. Few reforms were accomplished, however, and hopes for a peaceful resolution of the conflict faded.

Early in 1898, the Spanish responded to renewed rioting in Havana with repressive measures. Spanish repression, in turn, served to intensify American anger.

The Yellow Press

American popular newspapers, the so-called yellow press, did much to inflame American opinion. In New York, William Randolph Hearst's *Journal* and Joseph Pulitzer's *World* were locked in a circulation war and vied with each other in search of sensational stories to win readers. Hearst and Pulitzer filled their papers with stories of Spanish atrocities in Cuba.

The yellow press and the sense of outrage it helped stimulate among Americans had some influence on McKinley as he contemplated the course of action he should follow. Even McKinley's major political opponent, Democrat William Jennings Bryan, who was in principle a pacifist, favored intervention in Cuba as a moral obligation.

The de Lôme Letter

In a letter, stolen by Cuban rebels and written by the Spanish minister to the United States, Enrique Depuy de Lôme, to a friend in Cuba, de Lôme described McKinley as "weak" and "a bidder for the admiration of the crowd." The letter was published in Hearst's *New York Journal* on February 9, 1898. Publication of the de Lôme letter further intensified American anger.

The Sinking of the *Maine*

The United States government sent the battleship *Maine* to Havana harbor to protect American life and property. On February 15, 1898, the *Maine* blew up, killing 260 officers and sailors. The cause of the explosion has never been determined. An official board of inquiry concluded that the explosion resulted from an underwater mine. In fact, however, the explosion may have been caused by a defective boiler or by a coal fire that spread to the magazine.

It is unlikely that the Spanish were responsible, since Spain wanted to avoid war with the United States. The Spanish government denied any part in the destruction of the *Maine*, offered condolences, and proposed a joint Spanish-American investigation.

Americans who favored war blamed the Spanish, and the yellow press promoted the slogan "Remember the *Maine*."

The Coming of War

Continuing public fury at the sinking of the *Maine* compelled McKinley to act. On April 11, 1898, the President sent a warlike message to Congress. On April 19, Congress adopted a resolution recognizing Cuba's independence and approving the use of troops against Spain. These actions by Congress were tantamount to a declaration of war. Congress also approved the Teller Amendment, which declared that the United States did not intend to annex Cuba and that the Cubans should have the right to determine their own form of government.

Spain responded to these American actions a few days later with a formal declaration of war on the United States.

The Spanish-American War

Hailed as "a splendid little war" by Secretary of State John Hay, the Spanish-American War was short and popular. Some 385 Americans lost their lives in combat, and more than 5,000 others died as a result of disease and tainted food.

Shortly before the outbreak of hostilities, Theodore Roosevelt, the Assistant Secretary of the Navy, took advantage of the absence of Secretary of the Navy John D. Long and sent a message to Commodore George Dewey, the commander of the Pacific fleet, then at Hong Kong. Roosevelt ordered Dewey to sail to the Philippines in the event of war with Spain. The Philippines were a Spanish colony.

On May 1, 1898, Dewey won a tremendous victory in Manila Bay, destroying a weaker Spanish squadron without losing any of his own men in the battle. Dewey then established a blockade in Manila, awaiting the arrival of army troops, which took the Philippine capital on August 14, the day after the signing of the armistice which officially ended the fighting.

The United States Army proved to be less prepared for war than the Navy. Chaos reigned in Tampa, Florida, as the troops prepared to sail for Cuba. Fortunately for the Americans, the Spanish were even less prepared.

Anxious to participate directly in combat, Theodore Roosevelt resigned his post in the Navy department and took a commission as a lieutenant colonel in the Army. As second in command to Colonel Leonard Wood of the Rough Riders, Roosevelt led the famous charge up Cuba's San Juan Hill. The unit's horses had not arrived in Cuba, so the Rough Riders had to fight as infantrymen.

Victories in the battles of San Juan Hill and El Caney, both fought on July 1, 1898, placed the American forces in position to take Santiago, the Spanish stronghold in Cuba.

Faced with American troops advancing on Santiago and an American naval blockade of the city's harbor, Admiral Pascual Cervera, the commander of Spain's Caribbean fleet, decided to go down fighting. On July 3, he sailed his fleet out of Santiago harbor and engaged a superior American force. The battle ended a few hours later, with 400 Spanish dead and one American killed. On July 17, Santiago surrendered.

The Americans quickly seized the Spanish island colony of Puerto Rico in the Caribbean in the face of little resistance. In the Pacific, Guam was also easily taken.

The Treaty of Paris

The Treaty of Paris, signed on December 10, 1898, ended the Spanish-American War. Spain recognized the independence of Cuba. And Spain ceded Puerto Rico, Guam, and the Philippine Islands to the United States, which agreed to pay the Spanish $20 million for the Philippines.

Whether or not the United States would demand the cession of the Philippines had been questionable. And when the Senate debated the ratification of the Treaty of Paris, controversy centered on the issue of the Philippines.

The Annexation of the Philippines

The debate over the annexation of the Philippines extended beyond the Senate to become a major national issue in late 1898 and early 1899.

President McKinley had been uncertain about whether the United States should demand the Philippines. He finally decided to include the annexation in the Treaty of Paris, he explained, because of his belief that the United States had an obligation to uplift and civilize the Filipinos. This attitude, shared by many Americans, reflected their sense of superiority and pride.

Furthermore, McKinley reasoned, the United States could not simply return the Philippines to Spain. Nor could the United States leave them to be taken over by France, Germany, or another European power. Nor could the Filipinos be left to govern themselves, since they were believed to be incapable of doing so.

Supporters of annexation echoed the President's arguments and pointed to the strategic and economic advantages to be gained by American possession of the Philippines. They also stressed the importance of the United States playing an active role in world affairs.

Opponents of annexation organized the Anti-Imperialist League, which counted a number of prominent Americans among its leaders. These opponents argued that occupying and ruling a foreign people without their consent represented an action contrary to the spirit of the Declaration of Independence. The antiannexationists also contended that taking a territory without any intention of eventually granting it statehood was both unprecedented and unconstitutional. Furthermore, they argued that governing and defending the Philippines would be costly. Just as racism was a factor for those favoring annexation, so, too, did those opposed offer a racist argument: the United States could not easily assimilate the nonwhite and inferior Filipinos.

After a long and often acrimonious debate, the Senate ratified the Treaty of Paris on February 6, 1899, with only two votes more than the required two-thirds majority.

The Election of 1900

The presidential election campaign of 1900 revealed the strongly nationalistic mood of the American electorate. A rematch of 1896, President William McKinley, a Republican, was pitted against the Democratic nominee William Jennings Bryan.

Bryan began his campaign by attempting to make his opposition to American imperialism the central issue. This quickly proved to be a mistake. The Spanish-American War had been very popular, and a substantial majority of Americans supported the acquisition of overseas possessions.

The Democrats then tried to focus on economic issues, condemning monopolies and advocating free silver. But prosperity had returned to the country, and the voters were not greatly interested in economic issues.

The Republicans could claim credit for the revival of the economy and for the growth of American prestige and power in the world. McKinley defeated Bryan even more decisively than he had four years earlier, polling 52 percent of the popular vote and 292 electoral votes. While losing even his home state of Nebraska, Bryan took 46 percent of the popular vote and 155 electoral votes.

The Status of America's Overseas Possessions

By the beginning of the new century, the United States had acquired an empire, including Alaska, Hawaii, part of Samoa, Puerto Rico, the Philippines, Guam, and some smaller Pacific islands.

An almost immediate question involved the issue of whether the people of these territories had the same rights as Americans. At the time, the question was phrased: "Does the constitution follow the flag?"

In the so-called "Insular Cases" of 1901–03, the Supreme Court answered this question in the negative. The justices decided that the inhabitants of these territories would acquire

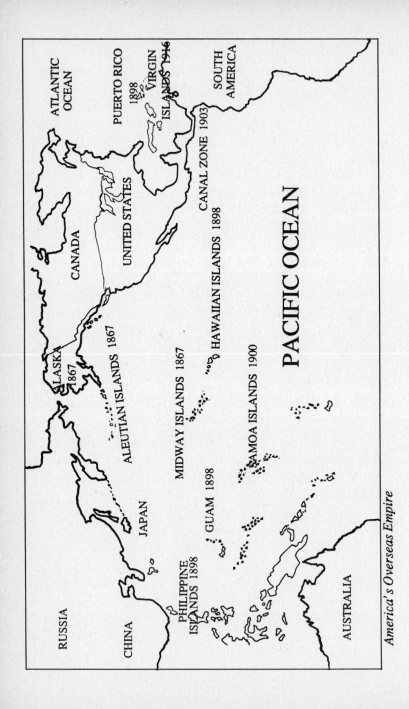

America's Overseas Empire

citizenship and constitutional rights only when Congress decided they should.

Congress soon granted territorial status to Hawaii, Alaska, and Puerto Rico. Under a 1900 law, all citizens of Hawaii received American citizenship. The Hawaiians were authorized to elect a two-house legislature, while executive authority was vested in a governor appointed by the President.

Since its 1867 purchase from Russia, Alaska had been administered by appointed officials. In 1912, Alaska received territorial status. Citizenship was extended to the inhabitants of Alaska, who would elect the territory's legislature, while the governor would be a presidential appointee.

Following a brief military occupation, Puerto Rico attained a civilian government. Under the Foraker Act of 1900, Puerto Rico became an unincorporated territory. The President would appoint Puerto Rico's governor and the upper house of the legislature. Puerto Rico's voters would elect the lower house. The Jones Act of 1917 granted citizenship to the Puerto Ricans and made the upper house elective.

Smaller possessions, like Guam, were administered by naval officials.

Cuba After Independence

American forces, commanded by Major General Leonard Wood, remained in Cuba until 1902, left with the task of preparing Cuba for independence. The Cubans drafted their new constitution under American guidance.

In 1901, Congress approved the Platt Amendment and required the Cubans to include it in their constitution. The Platt Amendment restricted Cuba's ability to make treaties and borrow money. It also granted the United States the right to intervene in Cuba to preserve the country's independence and the security of life and property. In addition, the Platt Amendment

obliged Cuba to sell or lease to the United States the land for a
naval base. This provision resulted in the establishment of an
American naval base at Guantanamo Bay, which the United
States continues to operate. While independent in principle,
Cuba was, in fact, under a substantial degree of American con-
trol.

War in the Philippines

The Filipinos did not universally accept annexation by the
United States. From 1898 to 1902, Filipino insurgents fought
the Americans in a costly struggle that resulted in the death of
some 5,000 Americans and perhaps at least 50,000 Filipinos.
Both sides were guilty of committing atrocities.

Emilio Aguinaldo, the leader of the insurgency who had earlier led a Filipino revolt against the Spanish, was captured by the
Americans in March 1901. Aguinaldo called on his followers to
stop fighting, although the conflict continued in some parts of
the Philippines until 1902.

In 1900, while the war in the Philippines was in progress,
McKinley sent a special commission to the islands. Headed by
William Howard Taft, the commission had the task of establishing a civilian government in the Philippines. In 1901, Taft
became the Philippines' first civilian governor.

The intention of the United States was to prepare the Philippines for independence, and the new civilian government gave
the Filipinos considerable local autonomy. The Philippines acquired full independence on July 4, 1946, following World War
II.

American Policy in China

The acquisition of the Philippines increased the interest and
role of the United States in East Asia. Concerned about the possibility that the imperialist powers might partition China into ex-

clusive spheres of influence, Secretary of State John Hay issued his first Open Door note in September 1899. He addressed it to Great Britain, Germany, and Russia and later sent it to France, Italy, and Japan. In this note, Hay called on these various powers to accept the principle of equal access by all nations to trade in China.

The British gave conditional acceptance to Hay's proposal, while the Russian response was vague. The German, French, Italian, and Japanese acceptances were all conditional on the full agreement of all the other powers. Hay's proposal of the Open Door policy thus gained a less positive response than he had hoped for, but the Secretary of State nevertheless announced that all the powers had accepted the American proposal.

In May 1900, the Boxer Rebellion broke out in China. The Boxers were young Chinese who opposed both the Manchu dynasty and the growing foreign influence in their country. During the summer of 1900, the Boxers killed over 200 missionaries and other foreigners and laid siege to the western legations in Peking, China's capital. The western powers joined with Japan to send a military force to China. Of the 19,000 troops, some 5,000 were Americans, dispatched from the Philippines. In August, the international force ended the siege in Peking.

Foreign military intervention in China caused Hay to fear that the imperialist powers might be tempted to carve out domains for themselves. In July, 1900, Hay issued his second Open Door note, calling on other countries to join the United States in promising to respect the "territorial and administrative" integrity of China. Only Great Britain, France, and Germany responded positively, but Hay's initiative did help prevent more strongly punitive action against China in the aftermath of the Boxer Rebellion. The countries that intervened in China agreed to accept financial reparations, rather than demand Chinese territory.

By 1900, the United States had become a major world power, with substantial interests in Latin America, the Pacific, and East Asia. The United States constructed a powerful high seas fleet and took the lead in creating the Pan-American Union. In the Pacific, the United States acquired part of the Samoan Islands and annexed Hawaii. Victory in the Spanish-American War in 1898 resulted in the addition of the Philippine Islands and Puerto Rico to the growing American empire, as well as the establishment of an American protectorate over Cuba. The United States now had special interests in the Caribbean region, which it would soon expand with the construction of the Panama Canal and a policy of intervention in the affairs of Caribbean and Central American states. In East Asia, Secretary of State John Hay's promotion of the Open Door policy reflected the growth of American commercial interests in China. The acquisition of empire and increased influence in the world filled Americans with pride and reaffirmed their traditional belief in the nation's mission.

Recommended Reading

Robert L. Beisner, *From the Old Diplomacy to the New, 1865–1900* (1975).

Robert L. Beisner, *Twelve Against Empire: The Anti-Imperialists, 1898–1900* (1968).

Charles S. Campbell, *The Transformation of American Foreign Relations, 1865–1900* (1976).

Kenton J. Clymer, *Protestant Missionaries in the Philippines, 1898–1916: An Inquiry into the American Colonial Mentality* (1986).

Frank Freidel, *The Splendid Little War* (1958).

Willard B. Gatewood, Jr., *Black Americans and the White Man's Burden, 1898–1903* (1975).

David F. Healy, *U. S. Expansionism: The Imperialist Urge in the 1890s* (1970).

David F. Healy, *The United States in Cuba, 1898–1902: Generals, Politicians, and the Search for Policy* (1963).

Walter R. LaFeber, *The New Empire: An Interpretation of American Expansion, 1860–1898* (1963).

Gerald F. Linderman, *The Mirror of War: American Society and the Spanish-American War* (1974).

Ernest R. May, *Imperial Democracy: The Emergence of America as a Great Power* (1961).

Thomas J. McCormick, *China Market: America's Quest for Informal Empire, 1893–1901* (1967).

Stuart Creighton Miller, *"Benevolent Assimilation": The American Conquest of the Philippines, 1899–1903* (1982).

H. Wayne Morgan, *America's Road to Empire: The War with Spain and Overseas Expansion* (1965).

Thomas J. Osborne, *"Empire Can Wait": American Opposition to Hawaiian Annexation, 1893–1898* (1981).

Daniel B. Schirmer, *Republic or Empire: American Resistance to the Philippine War* (1972).

David F. Trask, *The War with Spain in 1898* (1981).

Paul A. Varg, *The Making of a Myth: The United States and China, 1879–1912* (1968).

Paul A. Varg, *Missionaries, Chinese, and Diplomats: The American Protestant Missionary Movement in China, 1890–1952* (1958).

Richard E. Welch, Jr., *Response to Imperialism: The United States and the Philippine-American War, 1899–1902* (1979).

Joseph E. Wisan, *The Cuban Crisis as Reflected in the New York Press, 1895–1898* (1934).

CHAPTER 7

The Progressive Era

Time Line

1873	The Women's Christian Temperance Union (WCTU) is established
1900	Robert LaFollette wins the first of three terms as Governor of Wisconsin
	Republican William McKinley wins his second presidential term
1901	Theodore Roosevelt becomes President following the assassination of McKinley
1902	*McClure's Magazine* begins publication of

muckraking articles by Lincoln Steffens, Ida Tarbell, and others

Roosevelt appoints Oliver Wendell Holmes to the Supreme Court

Roosevelt initiates antitrust action against the National Securities Company

Roosevelt promotes mediation to settle the anthracite coal strike

Congress passes the Newlands Act

1903   The Department of Commerce and Labor is established

The Hay-Buneau-Varilla Treaty authorizes the United States to construct the Panama Canal

1904   Roosevelt wins the presidential election

1905   Roosevelt mediates the settlement of the Russo-Japanese War

The United States intervenes in the Dominican Republic

The Industrial Workers of the World (IWW) is founded

1906   Upton Sinclair's novel *The Jungle* is published

Congress passes the Hepburn Act, strengthening the Interstate Commerce Commission

	Congress passes the Pure Food and Drug Act
	Congress passes the Meat Inspection Act
1908	Republican William Howard Taft wins the presidential election
1909	Congress passes the Payne-Aldrich Tariff
	Herbert Croly publishes *The Promise of American Life*
	The United States intervenes in Nicaragua
1910	Roosevelt delivers his "New Nationalism" speech in Osawatomie, Kansas
1912	Roosevelt launches his Bull Moose campaign for the Presidency, dividing the Republican party
	Democrat Woodrow Wilson wins the presidential elction
1913	Congress creates the Federal Reserve System
	Congress passes the Underwood Tariff
	The Department of Commerce and Labor is divided into two separate departments
	The Sixteenth Amendment is ratified
	The Seventeenth Amendment is ratified
1914	Congress establishes the Federal Trade Commission
	Congress passes the Clayton Antitrust Act
	The United States intervenes in Haiti

A United States naval force intervenes in Vera Cruz, Mexico

1916   Wilson appoints Louis D. Brandeis to the Supreme Court

The United States intervenes in the Dominican Republic

1919   The Eighteenth Amendment is ratified

1920   The Nineteenth Amendment is ratified

The 1900 presidential election resulted in an overwhelming re-election victory for the Republican candidate, William McKinley. McKinley's triumph apparently represented the nation's strong support of the President and his conservative policies.

In reality, however, Americans were not as satisfied as the election returns suggested. Beneath the apparently tranquil surface of American politics, there was a growing desire for political, economic, and social change. This pressure for reform gradually intensified, resulting in the Progressive Movement.

In the political realm, progressives wanted to make government, at local, state, and national levels, more responsive to the will of the people, and there were growing demands for extending the right to vote to women. In economic affairs, the progressives wanted to reduce the power of monopolistic enterprise by extending the scope of governmental regulation of business. In the social sphere, the progressives sought to improve the lot of the poor and underprivileged. Many reformers also sought to promote prohibition as a remedy for the social and economic problems that resulted from the consumption of alcohol.

In foreign policy, the progressive era witnessed a continuation of the more active involvement of the United States in world affairs that had begun in the final years of the nineteenth century. The United States intervened in the affairs of several countries in Latin America and also constructed the Panama Canal, linking the Caribbean Sea with the Pacific Ocean. In Asia, the United States continued its support of the Open Door policy and sought, in particular, to place obstacles in the path of Russian and Japanese expansion in China. While focusing much of its attention on Latin America and Asia, the American government tended to overlook the significance of developments in Europe, developments which led to the outbreak of a major war in the summer of 1914.

The Muckrakers

A group of crusading journalists, known as muckrakers, gave impetus to the movement for reform by investigating political, economic, and social abuses. One of the most important muckraking publications was *McClure's Magazine*, published by S. S. McClure. In late 1902, *McClure's* published the first of a series of articles by Lincoln Steffens, who had studied political corruption in a number of American cities. In 1904, Steffens published his book *The Shame of the Cities*. Also, in late 1902, *McClure's* carried Ida Tarbell's first article on the Standard Oil Company. These articles were followed by Tarbell's publication of the two-volume *History of the Standard Oil Company* in 1904.

Other important muckrakers included Ray Stannard Baker and David Graham Phillips. Baker wrote about conditions among workers and blacks, while Phillips tackled corruption on the national level in *The Treason of the Senate*, published in 1906.

Writers of fiction also joined the ranks of the muckrakers.

Upton Sinclair revealed the shocking conditions in the meat-packing industry in *The Jungle* (1906). In *The Octopus* (1901), Frank Norris criticized the power of the railroads, and he exposed the greed of grain speculators in another novel, The Pit (1903). In novels like *The Financier* and *The Titan*, Theodore Dreiser assaulted the wealthy for their greed and lack of social responsibility. Jack London proved to be even more radical, describing class warfare between the exploiting capitalists and exploited workers in his novel *The Iron Heel* (1907).

Progressives and City Government

A number of progressives focused their zeal for reform on city government, striving in particular to destroy the political bosses and their machines. Political bosses generally profited from their connections with business, large and small, legal and illegal. Railroads, public utilities, banks, insurance companies, and other private corporation frequently paid bribes to get franchises, lax enforcement of the laws, and other preferential treatment. So, too, did saloon owners and operators of houses of prostitution.

In their effort to destroy the relationship between bosses and special interest groups, the progressives favored giving the voters more effective control over city government and giving the cities more power to control special interests. A movement in favor of home rule developed, designed to encourage state legislatures to allow cities greater freedom in determining the nature of their governments. By 1912, some form of home rule for cities had been approved in twelve states.

Progressive reformers promoted two forms of city government: the commission form and the city manager form. In the commission form, city government was run by a group of qualified officials who headed the major departments, police, fire, water, sanitation, etc. Generally one of the commissioners acted as mayor. In the city manager form, a professional administrator ran the operations of a city's government under the general supervision of an elected council and mayor. This was a part of a general progressive faith in specialization and expertise.

Progressives and State Government

In addition to combatting the urban bosses, progressives also turned their attention to the reform of state government, seeking to reduce the power of the party organizations and state legislatures and to increase the power of the voters. In particular, progressives pushed for the adoption of the initiative, the referendum, and the recall. The initiative made it possible to bypass legislatures entirely by providing that legislation could be initiated by petition and then submitted directly to the voters for their approval. The referendum provided that certain actions taken by state legislatures would be brought to the voters for their approval or disapproval. The recall gave voters the power to remove officials and judges before their terms of office had expired. Progressives also encouraged the introduction of the direct primary, which gave voters the power to select candidates for office, thereby reducing the influence of political bosses and machines.

Other progressive reforms at the state level included placing restrictions on the activities of lobbyists, prohibiting political contributions by corporations, and forbidding railroads to give free passes to legislators and other public officials.

As the progressive movement gained momentum, state legislatures enacted a wide range of social legislation. There were laws to prohibit child labor and to regulate work by women. Other laws established minimum wages and maximum hours, as well as health and safety standards in factories. Several states enacted workmen's compensation laws, providing insurance benefits to workers injured on the job. Other goals of the progressives at the state level included the direct election of senators, prohibition, and women's suffrage.

Several progressive governors became major national figures. Among them were Hiram Johnson of California, Charles Evans Hughes of New York, and Woodrow Wilson of New Jersey.

Robert M. LaFollette of Wisconsin

Probably the most famous of all the progressive governors was Robert M. LaFollette of Wisconsin. Elected governor in 1900, LaFollette promoted a broad program of progressive reform. In developing his program, LaFollette secured the advice of professors at the University of Wisconsin, establishing a practice which would later be followed by state and national leaders, including President Franklin D. Roosevelt who often turned to his so-called Brain Trust for guidance in tackling complex problems.

Prior to LaFollette's election to the Senate in 1906, Wisconsin had adopted the initiative and referendum, as well as the direct primary. Wisconsin established stricter controls over railroads and public utilities and imposed higher taxes on railroads and other corporations. Restrictions were placed on the activities of lobbyists, and a merit system was established in state employment. A workmen's compensation law was enacted, as well as legislation regulating standards of health and safety in factories. LaFollette also pushed for the enactment of a state income tax, which was approved after he left the governorship. This extensive program of reform caused progressives to look to Wisconsin as a laboratory of reform.

Prohibition

Many reformers regarded the excessive use of alcohol as a

major social problem, destroying family life, and promoting disease, unemployment, and poverty. Led mainly by women, the temperance movement began to gain momentum in the 1870s. In 1873, the Women's Christian Temperance Union (WCTU) was established, finding its major leader at the end of the decade in Frances Willard. By 1911, the WCTU had recruited close to a quarter of a million members. During the 1890s, the Anti-Saloon League emerged to give further impetus to the temperance movement.

Advocates of temperance began to promote the cause of prohibition, urging a complete ban on the production and sale of alcoholic beverages. By 1916, prohibition laws had been adopted in 19 states. In 1917, Congress approved the Eighteenth Amendment to the Constitution, establishing prohibition throughout the United States. The ratification process was completed in 1919. Congress then passed the Volstead Act, providing for the enforcement of prohibition.

Women's Suffrage

During the progressive era, the movement for women's suffrage gained momentum. In the mid-nineteenth century, Elizabeth Cady Stanton and Susan B. Anthony had pioneered demands for granting women the right to vote. Later in the century, Carrie Chapman Catt and Anna Howard Shaw developed the National American Woman Suffrage Movement into a major force, increasing its membership from about 13,000 in 1893 to more than two million in 1917.

Four sparsely populated western states—Wyoming, Utah, Colorado, and Idaho—granted women voting rights between 1869 and 1896. Washington passed a women's suffrage law in 1910, the first state to do so in fourteen years. California followed suit in 1911, while Arizona, Kansas, and Oregon extended the right to vote to women in 1912. In 1913, Illinois became the first state east of the Mississippi to allow women to vote. By 1919, women possessed at least some voting rights in 39 states, while 15 states had granted full suffrage to women. The Nineteenth Amendment to the Constitution, extending full voting rights to women, was ratified in 1920.

Some activist women were not content merely with securing the right to vote. Alice Paul, a Quaker and ardent advocate of women's suffrage, organized the National Women's Party during World War I. In 1923, Paul and her followers began a campaign to promote the adoption of an equal rights amendment. Some leaders of the women's movement opposed this, fearing that it would deprive working women of the benefits of protective legislation which had been enacted only after a long struggle. Such protective legislation included laws limiting the number of hours women could work. In the case of *Muller v. Oregon*, decided in 1906, the Supreme Court upheld a law establishing a ten-hour work day for women.

Socialism

While most progressives advocated reform of the existing economic system, radicals insisted that reform would not be sufficient. In their view, capitalism would have to be eliminated and replaced with socialism.

During the first years of the twentieth century, the socialist movement in America won considerable support. In 1900, Eugene V. Debs, the presidential candidate of the Socialist party, polled less than 95,000 votes. In 1912, Debs' vote increased to almost 900,000. Other leading Socialists of this era included Victor Berger of Milwaukee and Morris Hilquit of New York. During these years, several hundred Socialists won election to state and local offices.

Some socialists were relatively moderate, advocating the nationalization of large enterprises, while smaller businesses would remain in the hands of private owners. Others favored a more radical transformation of the economy and society. One of the most radical socialist organizations was the Industrial Workers of the World (IWW), led by William "Big Bill" Haywood, the elderly radical Mother Jones, and Elizabeth Gurley Flynn, who later became a prominent figure in the American Communist party. Known as the Wobblies, the IWW advocated uniting all workers in a single union. Militant in its policies, the IWW favored using strikes and industrial sabotage as weapons in the struggle to destroy the "wage slave system." The IWW remained relatively small, with its membership probably never exceeding 150,000.

The Assassination of President McKinley

On September 6, 1901, while attending an exposition in Buffalo, New York, President William McKinley was shot by anarchist Leon Czolgosz. McKinley died eight days later. Vice President Theodore Roosevelt succeeded to the Presidency. At the age of 42, he was the youngest man ever to become President.

Theodore Roosevelt's Background

In McKinley's first administration, Roosevelt had served as Assistant Secretary of the Navy. He resigned that office to serve with the Rough Riders during the Spanish-American War. In 1898, he won election as Governor of New York and, two years later, was picked to be McKinley's vice-presidential running mate. Some Republican leaders had opposed the choice of Roosevelt, believing him to be too independent and unorthodox. As President, Roosevelt quickly proved his unorthodoxy by appointing Oliver Wendell Holmes to the Supreme Court. Holmes became one of the most outstanding liberal justices in the Supreme Court's history.

Roosevelt and the Regulation of Business

Unlike his predecessors during the late nineteenth century, Theodore Roosevelt believed that the President and the federal government should play an active role working in behalf of the public interest. In particular, Roosevelt favored government regulation of big business, and his policy toward business won him the title of trustbuster.

Roosevelt did not oppose business consolidation as such, but he did want to regulate it in order to prevent abuses of corporate power. In other words, the President made a distinction between "good trusts" and "bad trusts." Large scale business enterprises, he believed, promoted efficiency and brought other benefits. Through regulation, government could protect the interests of the public.

In particular, Roosevelt favored the establishment of a federal agency that would have the power to investigate the activities of corporations and to inform the public about those corporations acting against the public interest. The pressure of an informed public opinion, Roosevelt believed, would force corporations to curtail their undesirable practices.

The Department of Commerce and Labor

In 1903, Congress created a new cabinet-level department, the Department of Commerce and Labor. The Bureau of Corporations, part of the new department, had the authority to investigate the activities of corporations engaged in interstate commerce and to report its findings to the President. The President would then determine what action, if any, the federal government should initiate.

The Northern Securities Company Case

In 1902, Roosevelt instructed the Justice Department to invoke the Sherman Antitrust Act in an antitrust suit against the Northern Securities Company. A gigantic railroad holding company, created by J. Pierpont Morgan, Edward H. Harriman, and James J. Hill, the Northern Securities Company controlled most railroads west of the Mississippi.

In a 5-4 decision, issued in 1904, the Supreme Court held that the Northern Securities Company was an unlawful combination in restraint of trade and ordered it dissolved.

During his Presidency, Roosevelt initiated 44 antitrust suits. Nevertheless, he did not make a major effort to reverse the trend toward business consolidation but rather continued to stress the importance of regulation.

The Elkins Act

Passed in 1903, the Elkins Act tightened government regulation of the railroads by requiring railroads to adhere to their published rates. This act served, in particular, to eliminate the practice of railroads giving rebates to favored customers.

The Anthracite Coal Strike

In May 1902, the United Mine Workers, led by John Mitchell, went on strike in the anthracite coal fields of northeastern Pennsylvania. The miners demanded a 20 percent wage increase, an eight-hour day, and recognition of their union by the mine operators. The mine operators, led by George F. Baer, refused to have any dealings with the union.

As the strike continued, the threat of coal shortages in the coming winter mounted. In fact, shortages of coal created problems for some communities by September. Roosevelt threatened to send federal troops to seize the mines and produce coal. The President's threat forced the coal operators to agree to mediation, and the workers returned to the mines in late October.

Roosevelt appointed the Anthracite Strike Commission,

which awarded workers a 10 percent raise and established the nine-hour day. But the United Mine Workers did not win recognition from the operators.

The 1904 Election

While the Republicans unanimously nominated Theodore Roosevelt for reelection, the Democrats chose as their presidential nominee the conservative Judge Alton B. Parker of New York. During the campaign, Roosevelt proclaimed that, as President, he had acted to provide all of the people with a Square Deal.

Roosevelt polled over 7.6 million votes, winning 336 electoral votes, while Parker won slightly over five million votes and 140 electoral votes. The Republicans maintained their solid control of both houses of Congress.

The Hepburn Act

Following his reelection victory, Roosevelt resumed his efforts to promote more extensive regulation of business by the federal government. In June, 1906, Congress passed the Hepburn Act, which gave the Interstate Commerce Commission (ICC) the power to establish reasonable and just railroad rates. The act also restricted the right of railroads to grant free passes. The ICC was expanded from five to seven members, and its jurisdiction was extended to express and sleeping-car companies, oil pipeline companies, ferries, terminal facilities, and bridges.

The Pure Food and Drug Act

In June, 1906, Congress passed the Pure Food and Drug Act, which banned the interstate sale of adulterated or fraudulently labelled food and drugs.

The Meat Inspection Act

The revelation of unhealthy conditions in meat-packing plants led to the adoption, in June, 1906, of the Meat Inspection Act, which provided for the enforcement of sanitary conditions in meat-packing establishments and for federal inspection of meat sold in interstate commerce. The act passed with the support of the large meat packers, whose products had been excluded from foreign markets because of the poor quality of American beef and pork.

Conservation

As President, Theodore Roosevelt gave strong support to the conservation movement, which developed as a result of growing concern about the threat of unregulated exploitation of the nation's wilderness and natural resources. In his efforts on behalf of conservation, Roosevelt had the able support of Gifford Pinchot, who since 1898 had headed the Forest Service in the Department of Agriculture. Pinchot believed that development should be carefully controlled by experts in forestry and resource management.

Under the terms of the Forest Reserve Act of 1891, Roosevelt's predecessors had banned settlers from about 46 million acres of land owned by the federal government. Roosevelt increased this to about 150 million acres. Roosevelt also withdrew coal, oil, and phosphate lands from public sale and established five new national parks.

In 1902, Congress passed the Newlands Act (also known as the National Reclamation Act) which provided that the income received from the sale of public land in the West would be used to finance irrigation projects.

The Panic of 1907

At the beginning of 1907, the nation appeared to be prosperous. But industry was producing more than domestic and foreign markets could absorb. As inventories mounted, stock and commodity prices began to decline. By early autumn, credit was scarce. On October 22, the Knickerbocker Trust Company of New York collapsed, promoting panic selling the following day on the New York Stock Exchange. Banks and businesses failed. Industries which continued to operate cut production, reduced wages, and laid off workers.

One consequence of the Panic of 1907 was the passage of the Aldrich-Vreeland Act of 1908. This act established the National Monetary Commission to study the nation's banking and currency systems. Headed by Senator Nelson W. Aldrich, the commission produced a report urging major improvements in the nation's financial structure. This report led to the adoption of the Federal Reserve Act of 1913.

The Foreign Policy of the Roosevelt Administration

Theodore Roosevelt believed in activism in foreign affairs just as in domestic policy: the United States should "walk softly and carry a big stick." He supported Secretary of War Elihu Root in his efforts to modernize the army. In 1901, Root established the Army War College to provide special training for officers. An advocate of a strong navy, Roosevelt demonstrated the United States' growing importance as a naval power by sending a flotilla of 16 warships—the great white fleet—on a voyage around the world.

The President promoted a policy of intervention in the affairs of Caribbean and Central American countries when it appeared desirable to do so in order to protect and promote the interests of the United States.

The Venezuelan Debt Crisis

Early in his Presidency, Roosevelt's attention was drawn to Venezuela, which owed sizable debts to European and American creditors. In December 1902, Germany and Great Britain attempted to collect their debts by force and blockaded several Venezuelan ports. Roosevelt was alarmed, in particular, by the prospect of Germany acquiring a foothold in Latin America.

Roosevelt joined Venezuela's President Cipriano Castro in urging arbitration to settle the dispute. The British and Germans agreed, and the Hague Tribunal produced a settlement in 1904. In the Venezuelan Debt Crisis, Roosevelt had made it clear that he would not permit European powers to intervene in western hemisphere affairs in any way that might endanger American interests.

The Roosevelt Corollary

Roosevelt continued to be concerned about the possibility of future intervention by European powers in the western hemisphere, especially in the Caribbean and Central America. Such intervention, he believed, could be prevented only if the United States assumed the responsibility for maintaining political and economic stability throughout the region.

In his annual message to Congress in May, 1904, Roosevelt set forth what became known as the Roosevelt Corollary to the Monroe Doctrine. Not only did the United States have the right to oppose European intervention in the western hemisphere, as President James Monroe had declared in 1823, but the United States also had the right to intervene in the domestic affairs of the western hemisphere states to maintain order and to prevent intervention by others. Roosevelt declared, "Chronic wrongdoing, or an impotence which results in a general loosening of the ties of civilized society, may in America, as elsewhere, ultimately require intervention by some civilized nation, and in the

Western Hemisphere the adherence of the United States to the Monroe Doctrine may force the United States, however reluctantly, in flagrant cases of such wrongdoing or impotence, to the exercise of an international police power."

Intervention in the Dominican Republic

The President found his first opportunity to invoke the Roosevelt Corollary in dealing with the problem of the Dominican Republic (also known as Santo Domingo). By 1903, the Dominican Republic was virtually bankrupt and owed debts to several European countries. France and Italy threatened to intervene. Under American pressure, the Dominican Republic agreed, in 1905, that the United States would take control of the country's customs houses and use 55 percent of the customs receipts for the repayment of the foreign debt.

The Panama Canal

Roosevelt strongly supported efforts to build a United States-controlled canal across Central America, providing a direct water route between the Atlantic and Pacific Oceans.

Before the United States could undertake such a project, it was necessary to cancel the Clayton-Bulwer Treaty of 1850. In this treaty, the United States and Great Britain agreed on joint Anglo-American construction and operation of a Central American canal. The Hay-Pauncefote Treaty of 1901 ended this agreement, enabling the United States to proceed on its own. The United States promised to maintain the neutrality of the canal and agreed that it would be open to ships of all nations on equal terms.

There were two possible routes for a Central American canal, one through Nicaragua, the other across Panama. The rights to construct a canal in Panama were owned by a French company, the New Panama Canal Company, headed by Philippe Buneau-

Varilla. This company had attempted to construct a canal in the 1880s. Buneau-Varilla demanded over $100 million for his company's rights. This exhorbitant price caused Roosevelt to favor the route through Nicaragua.

When Buneau-Varilla realized that a canal in Nicaragua would make his rights in Panama worthless, he reduced his price to a more reasonable $40 million. In June, 1902, Congress approved the Spooner Amendment, endorsing the Panama route if the French would sell their rights for $40 million and if Colombia would agree. (At this time, Panama was a part of Colombia.)

Under the terms of the Hay-Herran Treaty of 1903, Colombia authorized the United States to construct a canal in Panama. The United States agreed to pay Colombia $10 million, plus an annual rental of $250,000 for a nine-mile-wide canal zone. The lease had a term of 99 years, with an option for renewal. The Colombian Senate wanted at least $25 million and refused to ratify the treaty.

Colombia's action infuriated Roosevelt, who considered a forcible American seizure of Panama. This proved unnecessary, however, since Buneau-Varilla organized a revolt in Panama in November, 1903. Aware of the plot, Roosevelt ordered American warships into the area to keep Colombia from dispatching troops to Panama in an effort to suppress the revolt.

When Panama declared its independence from Colombia, the United States promptly recognized the new government. Buneau-Varilla represented Panama in negotiating a new treaty with the United States, the Hay-Buneau-Varilla Treaty of 1903. Under the terms of this treaty, Panama granted the United States a perpetual lease to a ten-mile-wide canal zone. The United States agreed to pay Panama $10 million, plus an annual rental of $250,000 beginning nine years following the ratification of the treaty. The United States also pledged to maintain Panama's independence.

The United States began construction of the Panama Canal in 1904. The project was completed a decade later.

The Russo-Japanese War

Theodore Roosevelt supported the maintenance of the Open Door policy in China and, in particular, sought to promote a balance of power in East Asia between China, Japan, and Russia.

Russia's advance into Manchuria presented a threat both to the territorial integrity of China and to Japan's interests in the area. In 1904, Japan went to war against Russia.

Roosevelt believed that the complete defeat of either power would endanger the balance of power in the region, and he offered his services as a mediator. In August, 1905, Japanese and Russian representatives met with Roosevelt at the navy yard in Portsmouth, New Hampshire. Having defeated the Russian navy in the Battle of Tsushima Strait in late May, Japan was in a strong position.

Shortly before the meeting convened in Portsmouth, Secretary of War William Howard Taft, on a mission to the Philippines, met with the Japanese Foreign Minister, Count Katsura. In the Taft- Katsura Memorandum, the United States agreed to the establishment of Japanese control over Korea in exchange for a Japanese declaration that they had no aggressive designs on the Philippines.

In the Treaty of Portsmouth, signed in August, 1905, Russia recognized Japan's predominant position in Korea and southern Manchuria, including the Liaotung Peninsula. In addition, Russia ceded to Japan the southern half of Sakhalin Island. Roosevelt received the Nobel Peace Prize in 1906 in recognition of his work as mediator.

In 1908, in the Root-Takahira Agreement, the United States and Japan promised to preserve the *status quo* in the Pacific region. In fact, however, Japan's power in East Asia would continue to grow.

The 1908 Election

In 1908, William Howard Taft won the Republican presidential nomination. For the third time, the Democrats chose William Jennings Bryan as their candidate for the Presidency.

Taft won easily, polling almost 7.7 million popular votes and 321 electoral votes. Bryan's popular vote totalled 6.4 million, and he won 162 electoral votes. The Republicans retained control of both houses of Congress.

Taft as President

Taft was basically conservative, although he sounded a moderately progressive note in his inaugural address, calling for the regulation of big business and the conservation of the nation's resources. Taft proved to be a less active President than Roosevelt had been, and he quickly became unpopular with progressive Republicans.

The Payne-Aldrich Tariff

Although the House of Representatives passed a bill, introduced by Henry C. Payne, providing for substantial tariff reductions, protectionist senators, led by Senator Nelson W. Aldrich, pushed for higher rates. The resulting compromise, the Payne-Aldrich Tariff of 1909, established average rates of about 40 percent. The tariff angered advocates of lower tariffs and split the Republican party. Taft supported the Payne-Aldrich Tariff, and progressives charged him with abandoning Roosevelt's policies and supporting reactionaries.

The Revolt against Speaker Cannon

Relations between Taft and the progressives worsened when the President refused to support efforts to reduce the power of the dictatorial Speaker of the House of Representatives, Joseph "Uncle Joe" Cannon of Illinois. Led by George W. Norris, a progressive Republican from Nebraska, Cannon's foes wanted to revise the rules of the House of Representatives and remove the Speaker from the powerful Rules Committee, which controlled the flow of legislation in the House. In addition, the reformers proposed an enlargement of the Rules Committee and called for the election of its members, instead of their appointment by the Speaker. A coalition of insurgent Republicans and Democrats approved the reforms. The bitter dispute further damaged Republican unity.

The Ballinger-Pinchot Affair

The Ballinger-Pinchot Affair of 1910 did further harm to the relationship between Taft and the progressives. As his Secretary of the Interior, Taft appointed Richard A. Ballinger, a conservative corporation lawyer. Ballinger reopened to public entry several waterpower sites in Montana and Wyoming which had been withdrawn from sale by the Roosevelt administration.

This action angered conservationists. Gifford Pinchot, the chief of the Forest Service, accused Ballinger of damaging the conservation movement and supported charges of corruption which had been leveled at Ballinger. Taft defended his Secretary of the Interior and fired Pinchot. Progressive Republicans began to consider supporting Roosevelt for the Presidency in 1912.

Despite the Ballinger-Pinchot Affair, Taft generally supported conservation. In 1909, the President withdrew over three million acres of oil lands in California and Wyoming from public entry.

The 1910 Congressional Elections

The congressional elections of 1910 went badly for the Republicans. For the first time in 16 years, Democrats won control of the House of Representatives by a margin of 226 seats to 161. While the Republicans kept their majority in the Senate, the upper house was actually dominated by a coalition of Democrats and progressive Republicans.

Taft and the Regulation of Business

The Roosevelt administration had initiated 44 suits under the Sherman Antitrust Act. The Taft administration started 90. Major suits were launched against the Standard Oil Company and the American Tobacco Company. In the case of *Standard Oil Co. et al. v. U.S.*, decided in 1911, the Supreme Court upheld the dissolution of the company which had been ordered by a lower court. In the case of *U.S. v. American Tobacco Co.*, also decided in 1911, the Supreme Court ordered the company's reorganization rather than its dissolution.

The Mann-Elkins Act of 1910, which Taft supported, strengthened the Interstate Commerce Commission (ICC) by giving it jurisdiction over telephone, telegraph, cable, and wireless companies. The act also established a special Commerce Court to hear cases involving rate disputes.

Other Reforms of the Taft Administration

In 1910, Congress passed legislation establishing a Postal Savings System. Under this law, certain post offices were authorized to receive deposits and to pay 2 percent interest on these accounts.

The Mann Act of 1910 (also known as the White Slave Traffic Act) prohibited the transportation of women across state lines for immoral purposes.

The Publicity Act of 1910 required members of the House of Representatives to make their list of campaign contributions public. Senators were required to do so in 1911.

In 1912, the Children's Bureau was established within the Department of Commerce and Labor.

In 1913, the Department of Commerce and Labor was divided into two separate departments. Taft signed this bill just a few hours before leaving office.

The Sixteenth Amendment

In 1909, Congress proposed the Sixteenth Amendment to the Constitution, authorizing an income tax. The ratification process was completed in early 1913. The introduction of a federal income tax provided the government with the means to raise the revenue it needed to support its expanding activities.

The Seventeenth Amendment

After several years of debate, Congress approved the Seventeenth Amendment to the Constitution in 1912. This amendment provided that U.S. senators be elected by direct popular vote, rather than by state legislatures. The amendment was ratified in 1913.

The Foreign Policy of the Taft Administration

While Taft and his Secretary of State, Philander C. Knox, did not believe that the United States should be involved in European political affairs, they promoted American political and economic interests in both Latin America and Asia. This policy became known as "Dollar Diplomacy."

In neglecting Europe, the United States was attempting to ignore the fact that the European balance of power had contributed to the maintenance of American security for many years. If that balance of power were upset—particularly, if Germany should defeat Great Britain in what some believed was an approaching European war—the security of the United States would be endangered.

Dollar Diplomacy in Latin America

Like Roosevelt, Taft believed that political and economic stability in the Caribbean and Central America was essential for the security of the United States. In order to promote stability in this area, the Taft administration encouraged greater private American investment. The investors expected, in return, that the American government would act diplomatically and militarily to safeguard their investments.

When a revolution occurred in Nicaragua in 1909, American marines intervened to support the rebels, and the administration urged bankers to extend loans to the new government. Mounting turmoil in 1912 caused the marines to return to Nicaragua. The marines were withdrawn in 1925 but returned the following year. They remained in Nicaragua until 1933.

Dollar Diplomacy in Asia

In 1909, the administration encouraged American bankers to join in a consortium with British, French, and German financiers to construct a railroad in China. While the administration wanted to maintain the Open Door policy in China, this proved difficult to do in the face of the greater power and interests of Japan and others in the area. At the same time, the effort of the United States to assert influence in China served to promote a further deterioration of American-Japanese relations.

The Progressive Revolt Against Taft

After leaving the Presidency in early 1909, Theodore

Roosevelt went on a hunting safari in Africa and then toured Europe. When he returned to New York in June, 1910, he avoided making a public statement on the growing rift between Taft and the progressives. Roosevelt did meet with Gifford Pinchot, however, while declining an invitation to visit Taft at the White House. Few could doubt where Roosevelt stood.

During the summer of 1910, Roosevelt set out on a national speaking tour, identifying himself strongly with the progressive cause. In a speech on "The New Nationalism," delivered in Osawatomie, Kansas, on August 31, 1910, Roosevelt reaffirmed his support of the Square Deal. Declaring that "property shall be the servant and not the master of the commonwealth," he stated that the New Nationalism "maintains that every man holds his property subject to the general right of the community to regulate its use to whatever degree the public welfare may require it." Roosevelt's views revealed the influence of Herbert Croly's book *The Promise of American Life*, which had been published in 1909.

Many progressive Republicans were convinced of the need for a progressive candidate to oppose Taft in 1912. While some favored Senator Robert M. LaFollette of Wisconsin, most supported Roosevelt, who declared his candidacy in February, 1912. Roosevelt won all of the thirteen Republican presidential preference primaries. But Taft held on to the support of most of the party's leaders.

On the eve of the Republican national convention, which met in Chicago in June, 1912, Roosevelt declared, "I'm feeling fit as a bull moose." The bull moose now became Roosevelt's political symbol. When Taft won the Republican nomination, Roosevelt made clear his willingness to accept the presidential nomination of a new Progressive party.

Roosevelt and the Progressive Party

In August, 1912, the Progressive party held its convention in Chicago and nominated Roosevelt for President. The Progressives denounced both the Republican and Democratic parties as "tools of corrupt interests." The Progressive platform called for stronger regulation of big business, legislation to protect workers, banning the use of the injunction in labor disputes, and conservation.

The Democrats Nominate Woodrow Wilson

The Republican split gave the Democrats the best chance they had had in years to win the Presidency. When the Democratic national convention met in Baltimore in June, Champ Clark, the Speaker of the House of Representatives, was the front-runner, but he failed to win the required two-thirds vote of the delegates. On the 46th ballot, the Democrats nominated Woodrow Wilson, the former president of Princeton University and the Progressive Governor of New Jersey. Wilson advocated what he called the New Freedom.

The Democratic platform expressed the party's traditional support of a tariff for revenue only. The platform also called for more regulation of business, new banking legislation and increased control over the "money trust," legislation to benefit workers and farmers, and conservation.

The 1912 Election

With Taft conducting no real campaign, the main contest in 1912 was between Roosevelt and Wilson. The primary difference between Roosevelt's New Nationalism and Wilson's New Freedom involved their views on the regulation of business. As he had earlier, Roosevelt distinguished between "good trusts" and "bad trusts," believing that business consolidation was not necessarily undesirable. In contrast, Wilson believed that the concentration of economic power was an inherent evil and wanted the government to act to restore free competition.

Wilson polled 6.3 million votes, 42 percent of the total. With 435 electoral votes, however, his electoral college majority was greater than that achieved by any President up to that time in American history. Roosevelt won 4.1 million popular votes and 88 electoral votes. Taft won 3.5 million popular votes and carried only two states, Vermont and Utah, with eight electoral votes. The Democrats won control of both houses of Congress.

The Underwood-Simmons Tariff

As President, Wilson pushed for a reduction of the tariff and sought to combat the special interests which attempted to maintain protection of particular industries. In support of his position, Wilson addressed a joint session of Congress. This was the first time a President personally appeared before Congress since John Adams had done so in 1800.

The Underwood Tariff (also known as the Underwood-Simmons Tariff) of 1913 brought the first substantial reductions in the tariff since the Civil War. The legislation also enacted a graduated income tax at modest rates to compensate for the loss of revenue resulting from the tariff reductions. The income tax had been authorized by the recently ratified Sixteenth Amendment.

Banking and Currency Reform

During the progressive era, there was a growing movement for reform of the banking system and for the establishment of controls over what was called the "money trust." Two major problems had been identified: the inelasticity of the currency and the concentration of credit facilities. The National Banking Act, adopted in 1863 during the Civil War, had made no provision for the expansion and contraction of credit to meet the needs of agriculture and business. In addition, most of the credit facilities were concentrated in banks located in Chicago and the East.

In the aftermath of the Panic of 1907, Congress had established the National Monetary Commission (also known as the Aldrich Commission), headed by Senator Nelson W. Aldrich. In its report, issued in 1912, the Aldrich Commission called for the creation of a National Reserve Association.

In late 1913, Congress passed the Federal Reserve Act (also known as the Glass-Owen Act), creating the Federal Reserve System. The nation was divided into twelve districts with a Federal Reserve Bank in each district. All national banks were obliged to participate in the system; state-chartered banks had the option of joining. The Federal Reserve Board, consisting of seven members appointed by the President, supervised the system.

The Federal Reserve System provided a means for the expansion of the money supply and of credit when business activity increased or when demands for credit grew. In addition, the federal government would now play a more active role in the country's economic and financial affairs. This was a significant development.

Wilson and the Regulation of Business

Unlike Theodore Roosevelt, who accepted business consolidation as long as it did not threaten the public interest, Wilson believed in the importance of free competition. Toward that end, the President urged a revision of the Sherman Antitrust Act which would specify the business practices that were illegal.

In September, 1914, Congress passed the Federal Trade Commission Act, which established a commission of five members appointed by the President with the power to take action against unfair trade practices. The Federal Trade Commission

(FTC) replaced the Bureau of Corporations, which had been created during the Roosevelt administration as a division of the Department of Commerce. Wilson's support of this act reflected his increasing acceptance of the idea of controlled competition in place of his earlier advocacy of free competition.

Having changed his position, Wilson was not an enthusiastic supporter of the Clayton Antitrust Act, which Congress adopted in October, 1914. The Clayton Antitrust Act strengthened the Sherman Antitrust Act by making certain business practices illegal, including price discrimination, interlocking directorates, and corporations acquiring stock in competing corporations. Farm and labor organizations were declared exempt from prosecution under the antitrust laws insofar as they could not be regarded as unlawful combinations in restraint of trade. Furthermore, injunctions could not be invoked in labor disputes unless they were "necessary to prevent irreparable injury to property."

Other Progressive Actions of the Wilson Administration

In January, 1916, Wilson appointed Louis D. Brandeis, a progressive, to the Supreme Court. Brandeis was the first Jew ever to serve on the nation's highest court. The Brandeis appointment symbolized Wilson's continuing commitment to the cause of progressivism.

The Federal Farm Loan Act of 1916 established a system of twelve Federal Land Banks, paralleling the Federal Reserve System, which offered farmers long-term loans—from five to forty years—at low interest rates. This made cheap credit, which the Populists long advocated, available to farmers.

The Warehouse Act of 1916 also eased credit for the nation's farmers by making it possible for them to use warehouse receipts for stored agricultural produce as collateral for bank loans.

Farmers also benefitted from the Smith-Lever Act of 1914

and the Smith-Hughes Act of 1917. The first provided federal matching funds for states for the support of agricultural extension education carried out by farm demonstration agents (county agents). The second provided federal matching funds for the teaching of home economics and agriculture in the nation's high schools.

The Federal Highway Act of 1916 provided federal matching funds to states for the construction of rural post roads.

The Kern-McGillicuddy Act of 1916 established a program of workmen's compensation for federal employees, while the Keating-Owen Child Labor Act of 1916 prohibited the interstate shipment of goods produced by children under the age of 14. The Supreme Court declared the Keating-Owen Act unconstitutional in the 1918 decision in the case of *Hammer v. Dagenhart*.

The Adamson Act of 1916 established the eight-hour day for railroad workers.

The Foreign Policy of the Wilson Administration

Neither President Wilson nor his first Secretary of State, William Jennings Bryan, had any direct experience with foreign affairs. They set out on an effort to promote a higher standard of morality in international relations. Toward this end, during 1913 and 1914, Bryan negotiated a series of 30 bilateral treaties which committed the signatories to refrain from going to war over any dispute until the end of a twelve-month cooling-off period. The hope was that the period of one year would provide time for tempers to subside and for the diplomats to find a satisfactory compromise solution. These treaties were quickly forgotten as international relations deteriorated in the period immediately preceding the outbreak of the First World War in the summer of 1914.

Wilson's Policy in Latin America

Although Wilson had opposed Taft's Dollar Diplomacy, the United States continued its interventionist policy in the Caribbean. In 1915, American marines intervened in Haiti to restore order; they remained until 1934. The marines intervened in the Dominican Republic in 1916, remaining until 1924.

Wilson's Intervention in Mexico

For a number of years, Mexico had been ruled by Porfirio Diaz, a dictator with close ties to American business interests. In 1911, Francisco Madero overthrew Diaz. Madero promised reforms, but his policies frightened American businessmen who feared their interests were threatened.

In early 1913, General Victoriano Huerta seized power and executed Madero. The killing of Madero angered Wilson, who refused to recognize the Huerta government. Instead, the United States provided arms to Venustiano Carranza, who opposed Huerta.

In April, 1914, an incident occurred at Tampico, Mexico, where several American sailors were arrested. Mexican authorities quickly released them and offered apologies. Nevertheless, Wilson ordered a naval force to the Mexican port of Vera Cruz to stop the landing of arms destined for Huerta's forces.

In August, 1914, Carranza took power in Mexico and Huerta fled. The Americans ended their occupation of Vera Cruz in November, although tension continued. Finally, the United States and several Latin American countries recognized the Carranza government in October, 1915.

Trouble in Mexico continued, however. In particular, Pancho Villa emerged as the leader of an anti-Carranza movement. In January, 1916, Villa's forces killed 18 Americans in northern Mexico. In March, Villa conducted a raid across the border into New Mexico, killing 17 more Americans. Wilson now secured Carranza's permission to send an American force, commanded by General John J. Pershing, into northern Mexico in an unsuccessful pursuit of Villa. Pershing's forces were withdrawn in January, 1917, and Carranza gradually restored order in Mexico.

During the Progressive era, the spirit of reform extended into many areas of American life. Progressives promoted political reform in the hope that government on all levels would become more responsive to the needs of the people. These reforms included the initiative, the referendum, the recall, direct election of United States senators, and women's suffrage. Progressive reformers failed, however, to devote much attention to the issue of discrimination against black Americans.

Above all, progressivism involved a substantial expansion of the activities of the federal government. Controls were placed on money and banking, the regulation of the railroads was expanded, and restrictions on business consolidation were strengthened. Progressive legislation provided increased protection for labor, extended assistance to farmers, and established guarantees of the purity of food and drugs. The enactment of an income tax helped provide the federal government with the financial resources it needed to support its growing activities.

In foreign affairs, the United States played an increasingly active role. The Panama Canal was constructed, and the United States pursued an interventionist policy in the Caribbean region and Mexico. While the United States acted as a mediator in the war between Russia and Japan, it sought to avoid involvement in European affairs.

Recommended Reading

John M. Blum, *The Republican Roosevelt* (1954).

John M. Blum, *Woodrow Wilson and the Politics of Morality* (1956).

Frederick S. Calhoun, *Power and Principle: Armed Intervention in Wilsonian Foreign Policy* (1986).

G. Wallace Chessman, *Theodore Roosevelt and the Politics of Power* (1969).

Paolo E. Coletta, *The Presidency of William Howard Taft* (1973).

John Milton Cooper, Jr., *The Warrior and the Priest: Woodrow Wilson and Theodore Roosevelt* (1983).

Robert Crunden, *Ministers of Reform: The Progressives' Achievement in American Civilization, 1889–1920* (1982).

Melvyn Dubofsky, *We Shall Be All: A History of the Industrial Workers of the World* (1969).

Raymond A. Esthus, *Theodore Roosevelt and the International Rivalries* (1970).

Louis Filler, *The Muckrakers: Crusaders for American Liberalism* (1968).

Eleanor Flexner, *Century of Struggle: The Woman's Rights Movement in the United States* (1959).

Robert B. Fowler, *Carrie Catt: Feminist Politician* (1986).

Dewey W. Grantham, *Southern Progressivism: The Reconciliation of Progress and Tradition* (1983).

William H. Harbaugh, *Power and Responsibility: The Life and Times of Theodore Roosevelt* (1961).

Samuel P. Hays, *Conservation and the Gospel of Efficiency: The Progressive Conservation Movement, 1890–1920* (1959).

Akira Iriye, *Pacific Estrangement: Japanese and American Expansion, 1897–1911* (1972).

Jack Temple Kirby, *Darkness at the Dawning: Race and Reform in the Progressive South* (1972).

Gabriel Kolko, *The Triumph of Conservatism: A Reinterpretation of American History, 1900–1916* (1963).

Aileen S. Kraditor, *The Ideas of the Woman Suffrage Movement, 1890–1920* (1965).

Walter LaFeber, *The Panama Canal: The Crisis in Historical Perspective* (1978).

David W. Levy, *Herbert Croly of the New Republic: The Life and Thought of an American Progressive* (1985).

Arthur S. Link, *Woodrow Wilson and the Progressive Era, 1910–1917* (1954).

Christine A. Lunardini, *From Equal Suffrage to Equal Rights: Alice Paul and the National Woman's Party, 1910–1928* (1986).

George E. Mowry, *The Era of Theodore Roosevelt, 1900–1912* (1958).

Nell I. Painter, *Standing at Armageddon: The United States, 1877–1919* (1987).

David P. Thelen, *Robert M. LaFollette and the Insurgent Spirit* (1976).

Harold S. Wilson, *McClure's Magazine and the Muckrakers* (1970).

CHAPTER 8

The Era of the First World War

Time Line

1914	Archduke Francis Ferdinand is assassinated; World War I begins in Europe
	The United States declares its neutrality
1915	German submarines sink the *Lusitania*
	Secretary of State Bryan resigns; he is succeeded by Robert Lansing
	Germany issues the *Arabic* Pledge
1916	Congress passes the National Defense Act
	Colonel Edward M. House's peace mission

to Europe results in the House-Grey Memorandum

Germany issues the *Sussex* Pledge

Woodrow Wilson wins reelection to the Presidency

1917   Germany resumes unrestricted submarine warfare

The Zimmermann Telegram is intercepted

The March Revolution results in the fall of Tsar Nicholas II of Russia

The United States declares war on Germany

Congress passes the Selective Service Act

The War Industries Board is established

Congress passes the Lever Food and Fuel Control Act

Congress passes the Revenue Act

The Committee on Public Information is established

Congress passes the Espionage Act

Congress passes the Trading with the Enemy Act

Japan presents China with the Twenty-One Demands

The United States and Japan conclude the Lansing-Ishii Agreement

	The November Revolution in Russia brings V. I. Lenin and the Bolsheviks to power
1918	Wilson presents the Fourteen Points to Congress
	Congress passes the Sedition Act
	Soviet Russia makes a separate peace with Germany
	The Republicans win control of Congress
	Emperor William II of Germany abdicates
	The armistice ends World War I
1919	The peace conference opens in Paris
	Wilson suffers a stroke
	The Senate rejects the Treaty of Versailles
	The United States experiences a wave of strikes and racial violence
1919–1920	The Red Scare sweeps the United States

When war broke out in Europe in the summer of 1914, most Americans believed the war did not concern them. Gradually, however, the United States was drawn into the conflict because of the possible threat a German victory would present to the balance of power and, more specifically, because of Germany's campaign of unrestricted submarine warfare.

For the United States, the war proved to be brief and victorious. The United States raised and equipped a large army and carried out an unprecedented mobilization of industry, agriculture, and labor which involved the federal government more extensively in the lives of the American people than ever before in the nation's history.

The war also proved to be disappointing and frustrating for Americans. What President Woodrow Wilson had hailed as "a war to end all wars" and as the prelude to a new age of international peace and justice resulted, instead, in two decades of uncertainty which ended in a second world war—more world encompassing and more destructive than the first.

The Outbreak of War in Europe

On June 28, 1914, a South Slav nationalist assassinated the Archduke Francis Ferdinand, the heir to the throne of Austria-Hungary, and his wife in Sarajevo, the capital of the Austrian province of Bosnia. The assassination set in motion a chain of events which, within a few weeks, led to the outbreak of a general European war.

For the Austrians, the assassination of Francis Ferdinand proved to be the last straw. They were now determined to crush South Slav nationalist agitation backed by Serbia. The Russians, for their part, were equally determined to support Serbia. If they did not, the consequence might be the end of Russian influence in the Balkans.

Germany was resolved to support Austria-Hungary, its only reliable ally. When France, Russia's ally, refused to provide the Germans with assurances of neutrality, Germany attacked France through Belgium. The German war plan, known as the Schlieffen Plan, called for a quick defeat of France, whereupon the German war machine would turn its full force against Russia. The German violation of Belgian neutrality brought an immediate British declaration of war.

By September 1914, the war on the western front began to turn into a stalemate. The Germans failed to achieve a quick defeat of France, but the Allies were not able to turn the tide against Germany.

The Allies and the Central Powers

The Allies of World War I included, first of all, the nations of the Triple Entente: France, Russia, and Great Britain. Serbia was numbered among the Allies, as well, and Italy, Rumania, and Greece ultimately supported the Allied cause. So, too, did Japan. Although the Japanese had no interests at stake in Europe, they hoped to acquire Germany's concessions in China, as well as the German-held islands in the North Pacific.

The Central Powers, Germany and Austria-Hungary, won the support of Bulgaria and the Ottoman Empire (Turkey).

American Neutrality

When the European war began, President Woodrow Wilson issued a proclamation of American neutrality on August 4, 1914. Wilson also appealed to the American people to be "impartial in thought as well as in action."

While most Americans shared Wilson's view that the war did not directly affect the interests of the United States, few were completely impartial. Many immigrants and first-generation Americans supported the cause of the countries of their origin. Many German-Americans sympathized with Germany, as did many Irish-Americans, who were hostile to Great Britain.

Americans of British ancestry and other old-line Americans tended to support the Allies. They were influenced by powerful ties of tradition and culture. The Allies benefited in particular from the fact that the American power structure still consisted almost exclusively of Protestants of Anglo-Saxon origin. These Americans generally regarded Germany as autocratic, militaristic, and aggressive and believed that a German victory would present a fundamental threat to European civilization and its values.

Hundreds of young Americans volunteered in support of the Allied cause. Some served in ambulance units on the front in France, while others joined Allied military services such as the French Foreign Legion or the Lafayette Escadrille, a group of American pilots who volunteered to help France fight the German invaders.

The Impact of Allied Propaganda

When the war began, the British cut the transatlantic cable to Germany. The British and French were thus able to promote their view of the war in the United States with little competition. Allied propaganda, with its tales of German atrocities—some genuine, some fabricated—had a powerful impact on American public opinion which was already favorable to the Allies. Many German actions served to reinforce Allied propaganda: the invasion of neutral Belgium, the destruction of the historic Belgian university city of Louvain, the execution of the British nurse Edith Cavell, the shelling of Paris, and submarine assaults on unarmed merchant and passenger ships.

The British Challenge to Freedom of the Seas

American relations with Great Britain were not completely harmonious, however. Soon after the war began, British actions presented a challenge to American support of the doctrine of freedom of the seas. Taking advantage of their naval power, the British began a blockade of the sea routes to limit the shipment of goods to Germany. British warships halted American merchant vessels bound for German and neutral ports and searched them for contraband. The term "contraband" refers to goods which may be seized by a belligerent if they are being shipped to another belligerent by a neutral. Wilson protested strongly against these British violations of neutral rights, but he eventually acquiesced in the restrictions imposed by the British. The Germans regarded this American acquiescence as a distinctly unneutral attitude.

American Economic and Financial Relations with the Allies

At an early point in the war, British and French orders for supplies from the United States began to fuel the prosperity of American industry and agriculture. American trade with the Allies grew from about $800 million in 1914 to about $3 billion in 1916.

The matter of American loans to the Allies proved to be more complicated. When the war began, Wilson responded to the urging of Secretary of State William Jennings Bryan and prohibited private American loans to countries at war, although the State Department did permit short-term credits to the Allies. By 1915, however, it became evident that the Allies would no longer be able to make substantial purchases in the United States without access to American loans. New York bankers had been urging the government to remove the restrictions on loans to belligerents, and Wilson did so in the autumn of 1915. By the time the United States entered the war in April, 1917, American banks had bought over $2 billion in Allied bonds (and only about $20 million in German bonds). American bankers thus had a heavy stake in an Allied victory.

German Submarine Warfare

Unable to win a decisive victory over the British and French at the front, the Germans decided to use their submarine fleet to establish a blockade of Great Britain. On February 4, 1915, the German government announced the establishment of a war zone around the British Isles. Within this war zone, submarines would attack every ship on sight. The Germans added that they could not guarantee the safety of neutral ships.

Since submarines were basically defenseless when on the surface, they could not observe the traditional rules of maritime warfare. In particular, a submarine could not give a warning of an impending attack so that passengers and crew could safely abandon ship. A submarine also could not rescue survivors.

In response to the German announcement, Wilson warned the Germans that the United States would regard any attack on American ships or any loss of American lives as "an indefensible violation of neutral rights" and would "hold the Imperial German Government to strict accountability."

On March 28, 1915, a German submarine sank the British ship *Falaba* in the Irish Sea and one American was killed. On May 1, the American tanker *Gulflight* was hit by a German torpedo near the Scilly Isles off the southwestern coast of England; two Americans died.

The Sinking of the *Lusitania*

In April 1915, the German embassy in Washington placed a warning notice in New York newspapers advising Americans not to sail on British ships. On May 7, a German submarine sank the British luxury liner *Lusitania* off the coast of Ireland. Twelve hundred people lost their lives, including 128 Americans.

In the first *Lusitania* note, sent to the Germans on May 13, 1915, the United States demanded that Germany end its unrestricted submarine warfare and pay damages for the loss of American lives. The note repeated the American intention to hold Germany to "strict accountability." In their reply at the end of May, the Germans contended that the *Lusitania* was not an ordinary passenger ship since it had been carrying guns and munitions.

The Resignation of William Jennings Bryan

The issue of the American response to Germany's unrestricted submarine warfare caused a split in the Wilson administration. While some advocated taking a strong stand against Germany, others, including Secretary of State Bryan, urged moderation. Bryan believed that Americans should be prohibited from traveling on belligerent ships.

Rejecting Bryan's view, the President drafted a second, more strongly worded note of protest rejecting the German claim that special circumstances made unrestricted submarine warfare necessary. Bryan resigned on June 7 and Wilson named Robert Lansing, a New York lawyer with strong pro-Allied sympathies, to succeed him. On June 9, the second *Lusitania* note was sent to Berlin. In the third *Lusitania* note, dispatched on July 21, the United States warned that it would regard any further sinkings as "deliberately unfriendly."

The Arabic Pledge

Hoping to avoid a break with the United States, the German government instructed its submarine commanders on June 6, 1915, not to sink any passenger liners without warning. Nevertheless, on August 19, a German submarine sank the British liner *Arabic* with the loss of two American lives. On September 1, the German ambassador to Washington, Count Bernstorff, offered the so-called *Arabic* Pledge, promising that passenger ships would not be sunk without warning and without providing for the safety of noncombatants. On October 5, the German government apologized for the loss of American lives in the sinking of the *Arabic* and offered to pay damages. During the final weeks of 1915, German submarines restricted their attacks to merchant ships.

The Preparedness Movement

During 1915, there was an increase in American opinion favoring a preparedness program, and Wilson endorsed proposals calling for a substantial expansion of the armed forces. While the National Security League sought to promote greater public support of preparedness, opponents of the program established the American Union Against Militarism.

In January, 1916, Wilson embarked on a national speaking tour to promote preparedness. In June, Congress passed the National Defense Act, providing for the expansion of the army to 175,000 men and for an army of 223,000 after five years. The National Guard would be expanded to 450,000 men, and the Reserve Officer Training Corps (ROTC) was established in colleges and universities. Other legislation started a major naval construction program.

The House Mission

While Wilson endorsed preparedness, he also initiated an effort to secure a negotiated end to the war. Colonel Edward M. House, Wilson's closest adviser, had held inconclusive talks in London, Paris, and Berlin in early 1915. In early 1916, House returned to Europe for a new round of talks with British, French, and German statesmen. At the end of February, House and the British Foreign Secretary, Sir Edward Grey, agreed on the text of the House-Grey Memorandum. The memorandum provided that, at some moment which the British and French found opportune, Wilson would propose a conference to end the war. If the Allies agreed and Germany refused, the United States "would probably enter the war against Germany."

Both the Allies and the Central Powers continued to believe in the possibility of winning a decisive military victory, and hopes for a negotiated settlement faded.

The Gore-McLemore Resolutions

In February, 1916, the Germans announced their intention to sink armed enemy merchant ships without warning. This intensified fears that more American lives would be lost and that the United States would be drawn into the war.

Representative Jeff McLemore, a Texas Democrat, and Senator Thomas P. Gore, a Democrat from Oklahoma, introduced resolutions designed to keep Americans from traveling on armed belligerent ships. Wilson strongly opposed the McLemore-Gore resolutions, citing the doctrine of freedom of the seas, and in early March, Congress rejected both resolutions.

The *Sussex* Pledge

A secret order, issued in November, 1915, authorized German submarine commanders to regard all ships sailing in the English Channel as troop transports subject to being sunk without warning. On March 24, 1916, a German submarine torpedoed a French passenger ferry, the *Sussex*, injuring several Americans. The United States regarded the attack as a violation of the *Arabic* Pledge, and Secretary of State Lansing urged that diplomatic relations with Germany be broken.

Resisting this advice, Wilson sent a strongly worded ultimatum to the Germans, warning that if they did not cease their attacks on passenger ships, the United States would break relations.

At this point, the Germans did not have sufficient submarines available to force Britain out of the war. They decided to make concessions to the United States in order to avoid an open break. In the so-called *Sussex* Pledge, the Germans promised that their submarines would not attack unresisting passenger ships without warning and without providing for the safety of survivors.

The Election of 1916

In 1916, the Democrats nominated Wilson for reelection to the Presidency and, despite the President's hesitation, centered their campaign around the slogan "He kept us out of war." To oppose Wilson, the Republicans chose Charles Evans Hughes, the progressive former Governor of New York who was now an associate justice of the Supreme Court. In their platform, the Republicans called for neutrality and preparedness.

The election was very close. Wilson was reelected, carrying the South and several key states in the West, including California, with a plurality of only 4,000 votes. Polling 9.1 million popular votes, Wilson won 277 votes in the electoral college to Hughes' 8.5 million popular votes and 254 electoral votes. The Democrats maintained their control of both houses of Congress by a narrow margin.

Attempted Mediation of the War

Following his reelection victory, Wilson made another attempt to secure a negotiated peace. On December 18, 1916, Wilson called on both sides to state their war aims, with the hope that some common ground might be found. Distrusting Wilson, the Germans failed to respond, while the Allies made demands that would clearly be unacceptable to the Central Powers. There was no hope of a compromise settlement. On both sides, the human and material losses had been so great that neither side could settle for anything less than total victory.

Addressing the Senate in January 1917, Wilson expressed his own views on peace, calling for "peace without victory" and the creation of a world organization to maintain peace.

Unrestricted Submarine Warfare

By early 1917, the Germans were coming to the conclusion

that victory depended on their ability to starve the British into surrender. The German government thus decided to renew its campaign of unrestricted submarine warfare on February 1. Two days later, Wilson broke diplomatic relations with Germany. The Germans realized that war with the United States was inevitable. They hoped that Great Britain could be forced out of the war before the United States could place an army in France.

On February 25, a German submarine sank the British passenger liner *Laconia* with the loss of two American lives. The following day Wilson requested the Congress to authorize the arming of American merchant ships. While the House of Representatives passed the Armed Ship Bill on March 11, a filibuster led by Robert M. LaFollette prevented Senate action on the bill. Wilson used his executive authority to order the arming of merchant ships.

The Zimmermann Telegram

British intelligence intercepted a message sent by Arthur Zimmermann, the German Foreign Minister, to the German ambassador to Mexico. In this telegram, Zimmermann proposed an alliance between Germany and Mexico in the event of a German-American war. Under its terms, Mexico would regain the territory in the American Southwest which it had lost to the United States as a consequence of the Mexican War. The British provided a copy of the Zimmermann telegram to the Americans. Its publication on March the 1st outraged American opinion.

The American Declaration of War

As the German campaign of unrestricted submarine warfare continued, a growing number of ships were sunk. On March 16 alone, the sinking of three American ships was reported. Demands for war were increasing, both among the American public and within the Wilson administration.

On April 2, 1917, Wilson presented his war message to Congress, condemning Germany's submarine warfare as "warfare against mankind." The President declared: "The world must be made safe for democracy." On April 4, the Senate adopted the war resolution by a vote of 82 to 6. The House of Representatives followed suit on April 6, approving the resolution by a vote of 373 to 50.

Revolution in Russia

While the United States was moving toward intervention in the war, revolution began to engulf Russia. The strain imposed by total war had produced an almost complete political, economic, and social breakdown of underdeveloped Russia. A spontaneous uprising against the tsarist government resulted in the abdication of Nicholas II in March 1917. A provisional government was established, headed first by Prince George Lvov and then, as of the summer of 1917, by Alexander Kerensky.

At first, Wilson was enthusiastic about the developments in Russia. Russia had overthrown its autocracy and was in the process of creating a democratic republic. Wilson hoped that Russia's new government would intensify the war effort against Germany. But the provisional government failed to establish its effective control over Russia. In November, V. I. Lenin and the Bolsheviks seized power and set out to establish the world's first communist society.

Intervention in Russia

In an effort to keep stores of arms from falling into German hands should the Bolsheviks withdraw from the war, Wilson sent 5,000 American troops to participate in an Allied intervention at Archangel in northern Russia. Some 10,000 American troops also participated in an Allied intervention in Siberia in order to prevent a Japanese takeover of eastern Siberia. In addition, the

Allies hoped to rescue the marooned Czechoslovak Legion, composed of war prisoners captured earlier by the Russians, and to keep military supplies from falling into the hands of the Bolsheviks. Fighting in both Archangel and Siberia resulted in several hundred American casualties. The Soviets have never forgotten these western invasions of their country in 1918.

American Mobilization

When the United States entered the war in April, 1917, there was little that the Americans could do to provide immediate aid to the Allies. The United States Navy did put destroyers on antisubmarine duty in the North Atlantic, and American warships began to escort merchant ships. The effectiveness of Germany's submarine warfare was reduced dramatically.

What the European Allies needed most in 1917, however, was manpower. The United States Army numbered only about 200,000 men in the summer of 1917. It would take some time before a sizable number of American troops could be recruited, trained, and transported to Europe.

The War Department, headed by Secretary of War Newton D. Baker, planned to organize an army of four million men. The Selective Service Act, passed in May 1917, required all men between the ages of 21 and 30 to register for the draft. In August, 1918, the age range was changed to include men between the ages of 18 and 45. During the war, 24 million men registered for the draft, and about 2.8 million were actually drafted into the army. In addition, about 2 million men enlisted in the armed forces. Ultimately just over 2 million American soldiers served in France, with close to 1.7 million serving in combat.

In addition to mobilizing manpower, the United States also mobilized its economy. The Army Appropriation Act of 1916 had created the Council of National Defense, consisting of six cabinet members under the chairmanship of Secretary of War

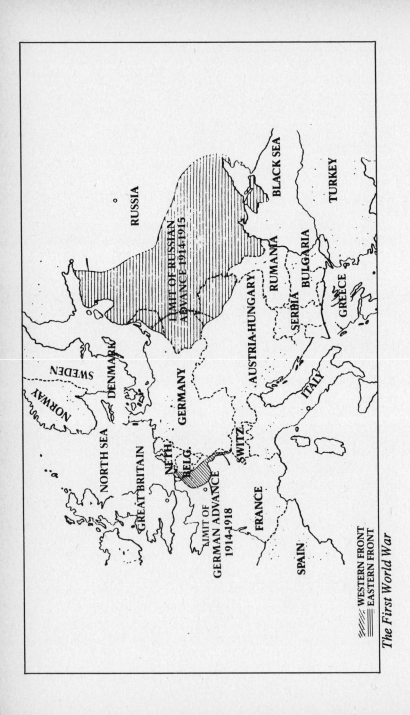

The First World War

Baker. The Council of National Defense was authorized to prepare for the mobilization of American industry in the event of war. To assist it in this task, the Council of National Defense had an advisory commission of seven experts drawn from among the nation's industrial and labor leaders.

In July, 1917, the Council of National Defense established the War Industries Board, which proved relatively ineffective in winning the full cooperation of industry and the armed forces. In March 1918, Wilson reorganized the War Industries Board, placing the financier Bernard M. Baruch at its head and giving the board more extensive authority to allocate resources and to organize industry for the war effort.

The Shipping Act, adopted in September, 1916, had created the United States Shipping Board to build, purchase, and lease ships through the Emergency Fleet Corporation. Even though this program was established several months prior to the American entry into the war, ships could not be constructed quickly enough to have any real impact on the course of the war.

The Lever Food and Fuel Control Act, passed in August, 1917, gave the President extensive authority in the areas of food and fuel production and conservation. Herbert Hoover, who had earlier directed the Belgian Relief Commission, became head of the Food Administration with the task of mobilizing agriculture to provide enough food for the American people, the U.S. armed forces, and the Allies, especially the French. Hoover placed his main emphasis on achieving these goals by promoting patriotism among American farmers and consumers rather than by regulation. American farmers prospered during the war, as farm income increased from $4 billion in 1914 to $10 billion in 1918. The Fuel Commission, headed by Harry A. Garfield, sought to control the price of coal and to allocate scarce coal supplies.

The United States Railroad Administration, created in December, 1917 and directed by Secretary of the Treasury William G. McAdoo, placed the nation's railroads under govern-

ment control in order to handle the increased volume of freight.
The Cost of the War

World War I cost the United States about $33 billion. Of
this total, about $10 billion was raised by taxes, and $23 billion
was borrowed. The Revenue Act of 1917 made the personal income tax the major source of revenue. In addition, the Revenue
Act imposed an excess profits tax, increased postal rates, and
provided for increases in excise taxes on alcohol, tobacco,
amusements, and luxury goods. In addition to borrowing from
banks, the federal government also sold Liberty Bonds to the
American public.

Labor and the War

In April, 1918, Wilson established the National War Labor
Board (NWLB) to help resolve labor-management disputes.
Under the joint chairmanship of former President William
Howard Taft and Frank P. Walsh, a labor lawyer, the NWLB
banned strikes and lockouts but recognized the workers' rights
to collective bargaining. In addition, efforts were made to
promote the eight-hour day and decent wages and working conditions, and to prevent the exploitation of women and children.

An increasing number of American workers became
unionized during the war. Unions affiliated with the American
Federation of Labor (AFL) increased their membership from 2.7
million in 1914 to over 4 million by the end of the war.

American workers benefited more from full employment
than they did from wage increases. As a result of wartime inflation, the cost of living in 1919 was 77 percent above prewar
levels. Wages did not keep pace with the rapidly rising prices.

Blacks and the War

The war improved employment opportunities for American
blacks. Faced with a shortage of labor, industry began to employ

large numbers of blacks for the first time. In the hope of finding work in northern factories, close to 500,000 blacks left the South in what has been called the Great Migration. Black migration to the North continued in the postwar decades.

Some 400,000 blacks served in the armed forces during the war, and over 40,000 saw combat. Black soldiers did not receive equal treatment, however. They served in segregated units and often were restricted to performing menial tasks, although a few blacks were commissioned as junior officers.

Emmett J. Scott, the Secretary of Tuskegee Institute in Alabama, became a special assistant to Secretary of War Baker to help the War Department deal with racial problems.

Racial tensions mounted during the war. In 1917, race riots broke out in Houston, East St. Louis, and Philadelphia. In 1919, racial antagonism intensified. In the South, lynchings increased, and more than 70 blacks were lynched during the year. A serious race riot in Chicago led to the deaths of 15 whites and 23 blacks.

Women and the War

Women found more opportunities for employment during the war and worked both for patriotic reasons and out of economic necessity. At the same time, only about 5 percent of the women who were employed during the war years were newcomers to the work force. Many of these women left their jobs following the war. In 1910, 8 million women were in the labor force. By 1920 the figure had increased to only 8.5 million.

Propaganda for the War Effort

To mobilize public opinion in support of the war effort and to promote the official point of view, the Committee on Public Information was established in April, 1917. Headed by George Creel, a progressive journalist, the Creel Committee produced a flood of propaganda emphasizing that the United States was fighting for the cause of democracy and that the Germans were barbarians. In addition to releasing 75 million pieces of printed material, the Committee on Public Information produced short propaganda movies and organized a corps of volunteer speakers, the Four-Minute Men, to promote the war effort.

Suppression of Dissent

In addition to drumming up support for the war effort, steps were taken to suppress opposition to the war. The Espionage Act of 1917 provided for fines of up to $10,000 and prison terms up to 20 years for those found guilty of aiding the enemy or spreading "false reports or false statements" which might impede the conduct of the war.

The Trading with the Enemy Act of 1917 not only prohibited trade with enemy countries but also gave the government sweeping powers to restrict the foreign language press in the United States.

The Sedition Act of 1918 extended the penalties of the Espionage Act of 1917 to those who obstructed the sale of Liberty Bonds or who might use "any disloyal, profane, scurrilous or abusive language" against the American government, the Constitution, the flag or the uniform of the armed services.

Attorney General Thomas W. Gregory vigorously enforced these laws, launching prosecutions against almost 2,000 individuals. In the case of *Schenk v. United States* decided in 1919, the Supreme Court upheld the conviction of Charles T. Schenk, the General Secretary of the Socialist party, who had advocated resistance to the draft. The Schenk case produced Associate Justice Oliver Wendell Holmes' famous judgment that Schenk was not entitled to the protection of the constitutional guarantees of freedom of speech since his words had presented "a clear and present danger" to national security.

Two prominent Socialists, Eugene V. Debs and Victor L.

Berger, were the best known individuals convicted under the espionage and sedition laws. In a speech delivered in Canton, Ohio, in June, 1918, Debs defended the principle of freedom of speech, attacked capitalism, and predicted the ultimate triumph of socialism. Charged with inciting resistance to the government, Debs was sentenced to ten years' imprisonment.

Berger, the editor of the *Milwaukee Leader*, had published editorials opposing the war. In February, 1919, Berger received a prison sentence of 20 years. While Berger's sentence was reversed on appeal to the Supreme Court, Debs remained in prison until December, 1921, when President Warren G. Harding granted pardons to him and close to two dozen other political prisoners.

Anti-German Hysteria

During the war, anti-German hysteria often went to ridiculous extremes. Not only did German-Americans suffer from discrimination, but superpatriots sought to ban everything German. In some areas, the teaching of the German language and the performance of German music were prohibited. German books were burned. German china was smashed. Sauerkraut was renamed "liberty cabbage." And some even called German measles "liberty measles."

Vigilante groups were formed to ferret out suspected disloyalty. The largest of these organizations, the American Protective Association, recruited some 250,000 members to work in its campaign to enforce conformity in support of the war effort.

Relations with Japan

In August, 1917, Japan declared war on Germany, and Japanese forces occupied the German-held Shantung Peninsula in northern China and the German islands in the North Pacific, the Carolines, Marianas, and Marshalls. The Japanese also presented China with the Twenty-One Demands, which would give the Japanese substantial political and economic control over China. Facing Japanese pressure, China accepted some of these demands, including the recognition of Japanese control over the Shantung Peninsula.

The United States wanted to uphold the Open Door policy in China (the principle that all nations should have equal opportunity to develop trade and industry in China) and, at the same time, avoid a confrontation with Japan. In May, 1915, Secretary of State Bryan warned the Japanese that the United States would refuse to recognize any treaty imposed on China which infringed upon Chinese territorial integrity, American treaty rights or the Open Door.

To counter the United States, Japan induced its European allies in October 1915 to recognize Japan's claims to the Shantung Peninsula and the German islands in the North Pacific.

In September, 1917, Japan sent a special mission to the United States headed by Viscount Kikujiro Ishii. Ishii and Secretary of State Lansing reached an ambiguous accord. The Lansing-Ishii Agreement of November 1917 provided American recognition of the fact that "Japan has special interests in China, particularly in that part to which her possessions are contiguous." At the same time, Japan pledged to respect the Open Door policy and China's independence and territorial integrity. Putting these conflicting statements in the same agreement stripped the agreement of any real meaning.

The Fourteen Points

In 1915, a group of Americans had created the League to Enforce Peace to promote the idea of establishing an international organization designed to prevent future aggression. In an address to a meeting of the League to Enforce Peace in May, 1916, Wilson endorsed American participation in a postwar world or-

ganization.   The President reaffirmed this commitment in a
speech to the Senate on January 22, 1917.

In September, 1917, following America's entry into the war,
Wilson established The Inquiry, a group of experts to advise him
on the development of a statement of American war aims.

Wilson presented his program of the Fourteen Points to a
joint session of Congress on January 8, 1918. He called for open
diplomacy, freedom of the seas, free trade, a reduction of arma-
ments, and urged self-determination for the subject peoples of
the German, Austro-Hungarian, and Ottoman empires. In the
14th point, Wilson endorsed the creation of "a general association of nations affording mutual guarantees of political independence and territorial integrity to great and small states alike."
The League of Nations would become the central part of
Wilson's vision of the postwar world, and the Fourteen Points as
a whole put the United States on a collision course with the
European Allies who had already made commitments to one
another in a series of secret treaties.

Wilson and the Secret Treaties

Wilson refused to be bound by the secret treaties concluded
by the Allies. In order to maintain his freedom of action, the
President refused to make a formal alliance with Great Britain
and France and insisted on regarding the United States officially as an Associated Power, rather than as an ally. Wilson expected that the Allies would come to be so dependent on
American military and economic aid that he could compel them
to accept his views on the peace settlement.

The American Expeditionary Force

To contribute to victory over Germany, the United States organized the American Expeditionary Force (AEF) under the
command of General John J. "Black Jack" Pershing. The first

American troops arrived in France in June, 1917, and the first American units went to the front in October. Large numbers of American troops did not reach France, however, until early 1918.

While the British and French wanted the AEF to be integrated with their forces, the Americans insisted that the AEF be left intact and be given its own sector on the French front.

Victory in Europe

In March, 1918, Soviet Russia dropped out of the war, signing the Treaty of Brest-Litovsk with Germany. No longer having to fight on the eastern front, the Germans prepared to launch an offensive in the West. The German assault, which began on March 21, represented their final desperate effort to achieve victory. By the end of May, the Germans had pushed across the Marne River, reaching a point about 50 miles from Paris. In the face of the German advance, the British, Americans, and French agreed to name French General Ferdinand Foch as the supreme commander on the western front.

In early June, the German advance was slowed. At Chateau-Thierry, the AEF helped the French halt the German drive. In their first substantial action, the Americans drove the Germans from Belleau Wood later in June. During the summer and fall of 1918, the AEF played a major role in the Aisne-Marne, Oise-Aisne, St. Mihiel, and Meuse-Argonne offensives which, together with French and British offensives on other sectors of the front, broke the back of the German resistance.

The Armistice

At the end of September, Germany's military leaders called on their government to seek an armistice. On October 6, a new German government headed by Prince Max of Baden asked for an armistice based on Wilson's Fourteen Points. Two factors delayed agreement on the armistice. First of all, the British and

French were reluctant to agree to the Fourteen Points until the Americans threatened to negotiate separately with the Germans. Second, Wilson was not prepared to deal with a German government that did not clearly represent the German people. On November 9, German Emperor William II abdicated and went into exile in Holland, and a German republic was proclaimed.

On November 11, 1918, the armistice was signed at Compiègne, France.

American Losses in the War

Some 49,000 Americans died as a result of combat, while another 63,000 service personnel succumbed to disease, primarily influenza and pneumonia. In 1918, a terrible influenza epidemic engulfed the world, killing a total of 21 million people, including about 500,000 Americans.

British war dead totaled 900,000, while the French lost 1.7 million.

Wilson and the Peace Conference

Wilson and a large American delegation sailed for France aboard the *George Washington* on December 4, 1918. Wilson thus became the first President ever to go overseas on a diplomatic mission. In Europe, Wilson received a tumultuous reception, and he mistakenly concluded that the people of Europe shared his view of what the postwar world should be like.

The Paris Peace Conference began its deliberations on January 12, 1919. Delegations from 32 countries were in attendance, but neither Germany nor Soviet Russia was represented. The main work of the peace conference was accomplished by the Council of Four: President Woodrow Wilson of the United States, Premier Georges Clemenceau of France, Prime Minister David Lloyd George of Great Britain, and Premier Vittorio

Orlando of Italy. Despite Wilson's earlier advocacy of open diplomacy, the four leaders negotiated in secret.

The Treaty of Versailles

The Paris Peace Conference produced five treaties for Germany, Austria, Hungary, Bulgaria, and Turkey. The most important was the Treaty of Versailles, the peace settlement with Germany.

In drafting this treaty, a major controversy developed over French demands regarding the German Rhineland. Clemenceau wanted to separate the Rhineland from Germany in order to create a buffer state along the Franco-German border. Wilson objected, citing the principle of national self-determination. A compromise was reached, providing that the Allies would occupy the Rhineland for a period of fifteen years and that the Rhineland would be permanently demilitarized. In addition, in the Pact of Guarantees, the United States and Great Britain promised to come to the defense of France in the event of a future German attack. However, neither Great Britain nor the United States ever ratified this pact.

The Treaty of Versailles restored the provinces of Alsace and Lorraine to France. The treaty provided further that the coal-rich area of the Saar in western Germany would be placed under the control of the League of Nations for fifteen years. During this period, the coal of the Saar would be the absolute property of the French state. This was done to compensate France for the damage done during the war to the coal mines in northern France. At the end of the fifteen-year period, a plebiscite (vote) would be held to determine the Saar's future. When the plebiscite was held, the people of the Saar voted to return to German control.

Germany also suffered small territorial losses to Belgium and Denmark, but the most extensive territorial losses occurred in the East. The newly recreated Poland received a large piece

TERRITORY LOST BY:

GERMANY

BULGARIA

AUSTRIA–HUNGARY

RUSSIA

Peace Settlements in Europe, 1919

of eastern Germany. In particular, the Polish Corridor was created to give Poland access to the Baltic Sea. The Polish Corridor separated East Prussia from the rest of Germany. The Germans greatly resented this, as they resented the Allies' decision to make the port city of Danzig, at the head of the Polish Corridor, into a free city. Although Danzig was largely German in population, it was separated from Germany in order to provide Poland with access to a seaport which was not under German control.

The disarmament clauses of the Treaty of Versailles also caused resentment among the Germans. The German army was restricted to 100,000 men, to be raised by long-term enlistments, while the navy was reduced to the status of a coastal defense force. Germany was to be allowed no air force, no tanks, and no submarines.

Article 231 of the Versailles Treaty became known as the war-guilt clause. Under its terms, Germany and its allies accepted the responsibility for causing the war. This provided the justification for requiring Germany to pay reparations to the Allies. Germany's reparations obligation was eventually set at $33 billion.

The Mandate System

The Treaty of Versailles also deprived Germany of its colonies in Africa and the Pacific. The German colonies in Africa were assigned to Great Britain, the Union of South Africa, and France as mandates under the nominal supervision of the League of Nations. The mandate system was designed to protect the indigenous populations, but in practice the system proved to be little more than disguised annexation.

In the Middle East, the Arab lands which had previously belonged to Germany's ally, Turkey, were assigned as mandates to France and Great Britain. France acquired Syria and Lebanon, while the British received Palestine, Transjordan, and Iraq. Germany's islands in the North Pacific went to Japan as mandates. The Japanese also claimed the Shantung Peninsula in China, but Wilson insisted that, with Germany's defeat, China should regain control of the area. The British and French supported the Japanese claim, and Wilson had to give in.

Self-Determination in Eastern Europe

The collapse of the Central Powers made it possible for the subject nationalities of Germany and Austria-Hungary to achieve their independence. Wilson strongly supported the principle of national self-determination; however, it proved difficult to draw boundaries in areas where national groups were intermingled with one another, which was generally the case throughout east Central Europe. Czechoslovakia acquired the province of the Sudetenland, which had previously been a part of Austria, even though the area was inhabited mainly by German-speaking people. Rumania gained Transylvania which had a large Hungarian minority. Elsewhere, it was difficult to draw lines clearly separating Germans from Poles, Poles from Czechoslovaks, etc.

Conflict Over Italy's Claims

Italy's claims for territory at the expense of the former Austro- Hungarian Empire caused a major conflict at the Paris Peace Conference. Italy demanded and received the Trentino, a former Austrian possession with a large German minority, and Istria, with its seaport of Trieste. This area had also belonged to Austria. Although the population of Trieste was predominantly Italian, Istria itself was overwhelmingly Slovene and, on the basis of national self-determination, should have been assigned to the new country of Yugoslavia.

Wilson resisted the Italian demand for Fiume, which was to

be Yugoslavia's major seaport. In April, 1919, Wilson appealed to the Italian people on the question of Fiume, and the Italian delegation walked out of the peace conference in protest. Two weeks later, the Italians returned, but the statesmen in Paris never resolved the Fiume question. Instead it was left to be settled by direct negotiations between Italy and Yugoslavia.

The League of Nations

For Wilson, the most important issue at the Paris Peace Conference was the creation of the League of Nations. According to a plan proposed by the French, the League was intended, above all, to preserve the European balance of power and insure French security. Wilson conceived of the League differently. In his view, it was to be an association of nations which would replace traditional power politics with a commitment to use peaceful means in the resolution of international disputes. The Covenant of the League of Nations produced by the peace conference embodied Wilson's conception.

The Covenant provided for the creation of an Assembly, representing all the members of the League of Nations, a Council, a smaller body with the major powers as permanent members along with several other members elected by the Assembly, and a Secretariat, which would be the League's administrative body. The Assembly, Council, and Secretariat would all be headquartered in Geneva, Switzerland. The Permanent Court of International Justice (PCIJ) operated under a protocol separate from the Convenant of the League. Popularly known as the World Court, the PCIJ had its headquarters in the Dutch capital of The Hague.

For Wilson the heart of the Covenant was Article X, which obligated all members of the League of Nations "to respect and preserve against external aggression the territorial integrity and existing political independence of all Members of the League."

In effect, Article X made the League of Nations into a mutual security alliance. At Wilson's insistence, the Covenant of the League was included as a part of the Treaty of Versailles and the other four peace treaties drafted at Paris.

The Signing of the Treaty of Versailles

When the drafting of the Treaty of Versailles was completed, a German delegation was summoned to Paris, where the treaty was signed in the Hall of Mirrors of the Palace of Versailles on June 28, 1919.

The Debate on the Ratification of the Treaty of Versailles

In July, 1919, Wilson began his campaign to win Senate ratification of the Treaty of Versailles. The debate over ratification centered on the Covenant of the League of Nations rather than on the terms of the peace settlement with Germany.

Wilson had already made some major political miscalculations. During the 1918 congressional election campaign, the President had asserted that the election of a Republican-controlled Congress would represent a repudiation of his leadership. The Republicans won control of both houses of Congress. The President made a further error when he failed to include any senators or any prominent Republicans among his major advisers at the Paris Peace Conference.

Senator Henry Cabot Lodge of Massachusetts, the chairman of the Foreign Relations Committee, was the key figure among Senate Republicans. Lodge was not an isolationist and did not oppose a world organization in principle. But he disliked Wilson personally and believed that the League of Nations proposed by Wilson presented a threat to American sovereignty. In March, 1919, Lodge drafted his so-called Round Robin Resolution, declaring that the Treaty of Versailles was not acceptable to the Senate. Thirty-seven Republicans signed the resolution. This was more than enough to block ratification by the necessary two-thirds of the 96 senators.

Under Lodge's guidance, the Republicans drafted a series of reservations (proposed amendments) to the League Covenant. These reservations provided that the United States would not accept any mandate and would not use its armed forces in support of League actions without the consent of Congress. In addition, the reservations provided that the Monroe Doctrine would remain outside the League of Nation's jurisdiction. If these reservations were accepted, Lodge and most of the other Republican senators were prepared to support the Treaty of Versailles.

Fourteen other Republican senators, known as the irreconcilables, opposed the League of Nations in any form. The irreconcilables were mainly western progressives, including Hiram Johnson of California, William C. Borah of Idaho, and Robert LaFollette of Wisconsin. For the time being, at least, the irreconcilables agreed to support the Lodge reservations rather than conduct a direct attack on the League.

As the debate progressed in the summer of 1919, the majority of the American people appeared to support the moderate Republican position which favored American membership in the League of Nations if the Lodge reservations were accepted.

Wilson refused, however, to entertain any notion of a compromise, even though several of his advisers urged him to do so. In an attempt to win the support of public opinion, Wilson embarked on a national speaking tour in September, 1919, delivering 37 speeches in 29 cities. He collapsed at Pueblo, Colorado on September 25. Canceling the rest of his tour, the exhausted President returned to Washington, where he suffered a major stroke on October 2. Wilson remained largely incapacitated during his final 17 months in office.

The Defeat of the Treaty of Versailles

Wilson's illness intensified his unwillingness to compromise on the League of Nations. In November, 1919, he called on the Democratic senators to oppose all reservations. The Republican majority proceeded to approve the Lodge reservations. The increasingly intransigent Wilson responded by urging the Democrats to vote against the treaty containing the Lodge reservations. On November 19, the Senate defeated the treaty by a vote of 35 in favor of to 55 against, with the irreconcilables joining the Wilson Democrats in opposition. The Democrats then proposed the ratification of the Treaty of Versailles without the Lodge reservations. The treaty was again defeated, by a vote of 38 in favor of to 53 against.

In March, 1920, the Senate voted on the Treaty of Versailles for the last time. Many Democrats now broke ranks with the President and voted for the treaty with the Lodge reservations. With 49 votes for the treaty and 35 against, the treaty fell 7 votes short of the required two-thirds majority. The United States thus decided not to join the League of Nations.

Labor-Management Conflict

During 1919, more than 3,000 strikes took place in the U.S., involving over 4 million workers. While the striking workers demanded wage increases in the face of rapidly rising prices, management asserted that the labor leaders were promoting subversion. In early 1919, labor unions in Seattle, Washington, called a general strike in support of striking shipyard workers. Endorsing management's position, Mayor Ole Hanson charged that the general strike represented a Communist-inspired attack on the American system rather than a normal labor-management dispute.

In September, 1919, a police strike in Boston alarmed the public. Massachusetts Governor Calvin Coolidge ordered the national guard to Boston in an attempt to break the strike. Coolidge became a national hero when he declared: "There is no right to strike against the public safety by anybody, anywhere, any time."

Also in September, close to 350,000 steelworkers went on strike in several midwestern cities protesting low wages and the 12-hour day. Judge Elbert H. Gary, the chairman of the United States Steel Corporation, charged that Communists were behind the strike. When the steel company sought to employ strikebreakers in the steel mills in Gary, Indiana, a riot occurred. Fighting between strikers and the national guard, which had been called in to protect the strikebreakers, resulted in the deaths of 18 strikers. In January, 1920, the steelworkers' union admitted defeat. Unionization of the steel industry did not take place until 1937.

In another strike in late 1919, the United Mine Workers, led by John L. Lewis, demanded raises and shorter hours for miners in the bituminous coal fields. When Attorney General A. Mitchell Palmer secured a court injunction, Lewis called off the strike. The general failure of the unions in 1919 resulted in a considerable weakening of the influence of organized labor in American industry.

The Red Scare

During 1919 and 1920, a fear of radicalism and subversion swept the United States. Now that victory over Germany had been achieved, the Communists in Russia, who were promoting world revolution, seemed to pose a new threat.

In the spring of 1919, rumors spread that radicals were planning to assassinate public officials and other prominent Americans. In April, a bomb damaged the home of Senator

Thomas W. Hardwick of Georgia. Explosions occurred in several cities in early June, and a bomb damaged the Washington home of Attorney General A. Mitchell Palmer. These bombings were seen as part of a vast revolutionary conspiracy, rather than as sporadic acts of violence by a small group of anarchist extremists.

Beginning in the autumn of 1919, agents of the Justice Department, acting on orders from Attorney General Palmer, arrested hundreds of radicals, including the remnants of the leadership of the Industrial Workers of the World (IWW). In December, over 200 alien radicals, including the anarchist Emma Goldman, were deported to Soviet Russia. On January 2, 1920, one of the largest of the Palmer Raids occurred when federal agents arrested 2,700 individuals. When the Red Scare was at its height, the New York state legislature expelled five Socialist members. Assistant Secretary of Labor Louis F. Post voided several hundred deportation orders issued by Mitchell's Justice Department when it became evident that membership in a radical organization alone, rather than some specific alleged activity, was the only basis for deportation. During the spring of 1920, the Red Scare began to subside.

While the United States sought to avoid involvement in the First World War and attempted to mediate the conflict, Germany's unrestricted submarine warfare provoked the American declaration of war in April, 1917. The war resulted in a massive mobilization of both American manpower and economic resources and served to increase the influence of the federal government over the lives of the American people. Participation in the war served to stimulate both the patriotism of the American people and an effort to restrict the expression of dissent.

In the Fourteen Points, President Woodrow Wilson set forth his program for a peace based on principles of justice. Above all, Wilson urged the creation of a League of Nations, which he hoped would provide a means for the peaceful resolution of future international disputes. The Paris Peace Conference of 1919 drafted the Treaty of Versailles, which provided for the establishment of the League. But isolationist opposition to American participation in the League and Wilson's refusal to agree to any compromise resulted in the Senate's failure to ratify the treaty.

Recommended Reading

Arthur E. Barbeau and Florette Henri, *The Unknown Soldiers: Black American Troops in World War I* (1974).

Edward M. Coffman, *The War to End All Wars: The American Military Experience in World War I* (1968).

John Milton Cooper, Jr., *The Vanity of Power: American Isolation and the First World War, 1914–1917* (1969).

Robert H. Ferrell, *Woodrow Wilson and World War I, 1917–1921* (1985).

Frank Freidel, *Over There: The Story of America's First Great Overseas Crusade* (1964).

Robert L. Friedheim, *The Seattle General Strike* (1964).

Lloyd C. Gardner, *Safe for Democracy: The Anglo-American Response to Revolution, 1913–1923* (1984).

Lawrence E. Gelfand, *The Inquiry: American Preparations for Peace, 1917–1919* (1963).

Otis L. Graham, Jr., *The Great Campaigns: Reform and War in America, 1900–1928* (1971).

Maureen Weiner Greenwald, *Women, War, and Work: The Impact of World War I on Women Workers in the United States* (1980).

Ellis W. Hawley, *The Great War and the Search for a Modern Order: A History of the American People and Their Institutions, 1917–1933* (1979).

David M. Kennedy, *Over Here: The First World War and American Society* (1980).

N. Gordon Levin, Jr., *Woodrow Wilson and the Paris Peace Conference* (1972).

N. Gordon Levin, Jr., *Woodrow Wilson and World Politics: America's Response to War and Revolution* (1968).

Arthur S. Link, *Wilson the Diplomatist* (1957).

Seymour W. Livermore, *Politics Is Adjourned: Woodrow Wilson and the War Congress, 1916–1919* (1966).

Ernest R. May, *The World War and American Isolation, 1914–1917* (1959).

Robert K. Murray, *The Red Scare: A Study in National Hysteria, 1919–1920* (1955).

William Preston, *Aliens and Dissenters: Federal Suppression of Radicals, 1903–1933* (1963).

Elliott Rudwick, *Race Riot at East St. Louis, July 2, 1917* (1964).

Francis Russell, *A City in Terror, 1919: The Boston Police Strike* (1975).

Daniel M. Smith, *The Great Departure: The United States and World War I, 1914–1920* (1965).

Daniel M. Smith, *Robert Lansing and American Neutrality, 1914–1917* (1956).

Gene Smith, *When the Cheering Stopped: The Last Years of Woodrow Wilson* (1964).

Barbara J. Steinson, *American Woman's Activism in World War I* (1982).

Ralph A. Stone, *The Irreconcilables: The Fight Against the League of Nations* (1970).

Arthur Walworth, *Wilson and His Peacemakers: American Diplomacy at the Paris Peace Conference, 1919* (1986).

Edwin A. Weinstein, *Woodrow Wilson: A Medical and Psychological Biography* (1981).

James Weinstein, *The Decline of Socialism in America, 1912–1923* (1967).

CHAPTER 9

The Twenties:
The Era of "Normalcy"

Time Line

1915	The Ku Klux Klan is reestablished
1920	Prohibition begins
	Republican Warren G. Harding wins the Presidency
	KDKA, the nation's first commercial radio station, begins broadcasting
1921	The Emergency Immigration Act imposes restrictions on immigration

	Sacco and Vanzetti are convicted of murder and robbery
1922	Congress adopts the Fordney-McCumber Tariff
1923	President Harding dies; Vice President Coolidge succeeds to the Presidency
1924	The Teapot Dome scandal and other scandals of the Harding administration are revealed
	The National Origins Act places further limits on immigration
1925	A Tennessee law forbidding the teaching of evolution leads to the Scopes trial
1927	Charles A. Lindbergh makes his transatlantic solo flight
	The Jazz Singer, the first feature-length talking picture, is released
1928	Coolidge issues his second veto of the McNary-Haugen Bill
	Republican Herbert Hoover wins the Presidency
1929	Congress establishes the Federal Farm Board
	The stock market crash marks the beginning of the Great Depression
1930	Congress passes the Hawley-Smoot Tariff

The Republican party dominated the politics of the "New Era" of the 1920s. The Republican Presidents—Warren G. Harding, Calvin Coolidge, and Herbert Hoover—won election with over-whelming majorities, and the Republicans held solid control of both houses of Congress.

The nation experienced substantial prosperity, although it was uneven. Much of American agriculture remained in a depressed state, and many poorly paid workers did not share in the nation's growing wealth. The partnership of government and business, which had begun during World War I, continued and expanded, as did the process of business consolidation.

The 1920s were also a time of growing conflict between the traditional values of rural America and the country's increas-ingly more urban way of life. This conflict was expressed in the movement for immigration restriction, the revival of the Ku Klux Klan, prohibition, and the tension between fundamentalism and modernism in religion.

The 1920 Election

Woodrow Wilson considered seeking a third presidential term in 1920, hoping to make the election a great national referendum on the League of Nations. But Wilson's failing health made a campaign impossible.

James M. Cox, the Governor of Ohio, won the Democratic presidential nomination. Cox supported the League and opposed prohibition. As Cox's running mate, the Democrats selected Franklin D. Roosevelt, the Assistant Secretary of the Navy in the Wilson administration.

The Republican national convention was divided between supporters of General Leonard Wood and Governor Frank Low-den of Illinois. Breaking the deadlock, the Republicans turned to a dark horse, Senator Warren G. Harding of Ohio. The

Republicans nominated Massachusetts Governor Calvin Coolidge for the Vice Presidency. Coolidge had won national attention during the Boston police strike of 1919.

Harding's call for a return to "normalcy" struck a responsive chord among the American electorate. The Republican won an overwhelming victory, capturing over 60 percent of the popular vote. Harding polled 16 million votes to Cox's 9 million. In the electoral college, the count was 404 for Harding to 127 for Cox. The Republicans won sizable majorities in both houses of Congress, gaining a majority of 22 seats in the Senate and 167 seats in the House of Representatives.

The Harding Administration

While Harding was personable and attractive, he proved to be a weak and ineffective leader. He appointed several outstanding individuals to his cabinet, but other appointees lacked both ability and character.

Former Supreme Court Justice and Republican presidential nominee Charles Evans Hughes became Secretary of State, while Andrew W. Mellon, a Pittsburgh banker, served as Secretary of the Treasury. As Secretary of Commerce, Herbert Hoover became one of the most important figures in the federal government during the Harding and Coolidge administrations.

Under Mellon's guidance, the Harding administration pushed for less government regulation of business, a high protective tariff, and tax reductions, primarily to benefit business and the wealthy. In addition, Mellon sought to reduce the federal budget and the national debt by cutting expenditures and promoting more efficient administration. In practice, however, while the budget was balanced and national debt was reduced, federal spending increased considerably and the federal bureaucracy grew in size. By 1925, the federal budget was 250 percent more than it had been in 1915.

The Fordney-McCumber Tariff

The Fordney-McCumber Tariff of 1922 increased tariffs substantially, especially on chemical and metal products to protect American industry against a feared revival of German industries which had previously dominated these fields. In addition, high tariffs were imposed on agricultural products in an effort to assist the nation's farmers.

The Harding Scandals

The nation was shocked by revelations of misconduct by several major figures in the Harding administration.

Charles R. Forbes, the head of the Veterans Bureau, stole millions of dollars from his agency before he resigned under fire in 1923. Indicted for fraud, conspiracy, and bribery, Forbes was sentenced in 1925 to a two-year prison term and a $10,000 fine.

Convicted of conspiracy to defraud the government, Colonel Thomas W. Miller, the Alien Property Custodian, was also sent to prison.

Attorney General Harry M. Daugherty, the leader of the Ohio Gang, was forced to resign in 1924 in the face of charges that he had taken bribes from violators of the prohibition laws and had failed to prosecute corruption in the Veterans Bureau. In order to avoid self-incrimination, Daugherty did not testify at his own trial, which ended in a hung jury.

Jesse Smith, an influence peddler and close friend of Attorney General Daugherty, was charged with bribery and committed suicide.

The Teapot Dome scandal was the most notorious scandal of the Harding administration. Secretary of the Interior Albert B. Fall controlled the oil reserves at Teapot Dome, Wyoming, and Elk Hills, California, which Presidents Taft and Wilson had set aside for the Navy. Fall illegally leased these lands in 1922 to two private oil operators, Harry F. Sinclair and Edward L. Doheny.

When these leases became public knowledge in 1923, a Senate investigation revealed that the oilmen had given Fall close to $500,000 in cash, bonds, and prize cattle. The government sued to cancel the leases in 1927. While Fall and the oilmen were acquitted of charges of conspiracy to defraud the government, Fall was convicted of bribery in 1929. Sentenced to a one-year jail term, Fall became the first cabinet member ever to be imprisoned.

Harding's Death

The nation was still largely unaware of the scandals when Harding embarked on a tour of the West and Alaska in June 1923. On August 2, Harding suffered a heart attack and died in San Francisco. Vice President Calvin Coolidge succeeded to the Presidency.

A man of few words who believed in minimal activity by the federal government, Coolidge pushed for a full investigation of the Harding scandals. To replace disgraced Attorney General Daugherty, Coolidge appointed Harlan Fiske Stone, the dean of the law school of Columbia University. Stone later became a Supreme Court justice.

The 1924 Election

Economic prosperity benefitted Calvin Coolidge and the Republicans in the 1924 presidential election.

The Democrats were deeply divided. The party's eastern urban wing backed Governor Alfred E. Smith of New York for the party's presidential nomination, while the southern and western rural wing supported William G. McAdoo, who had served as Secretary of the Treasury in the Wilson administration. The Democratic national convention lasted for 17 days and went through 103 ballots before finally nominating John W. Davis, a Wall Street lawyer who had served as a congressman from West Virginia and ambassador to Great Britain.

A third party emerged in 1924 as a group of dissidents, including elements of the farm bloc, Socialists, and the American Federation of Labor, revived the Progressive party and nominated Senator Robert LaFollette of Wisconsin for the Presidency.

With 15.7 million popular votes and 382 electoral votes, Coolidge won reelection. Davis polled 8.4 million popular votes and won 136 votes in the electoral college. LaFollette won 5 million popular votes but carried only his home state of Wisconsin with its 13 electoral votes.

The Prosperity of the 1920s

Following a recession in 1921–1922, the nation achieved considerable economic prosperity for the balance of the decade. During the 1920s, the nation's industrial production grew by 64 percent, promoted by a great increase in labor productivity. From 1922 to 1929, the gross national product (GNP) increased some 40 percent, from $74.1 billion to $103.1 billion. Per capita income, which stood at $641 in 1921, rose to $847 in 1929. Unemployment remained low, in the range of 3 to 4 percent. While prices had tripled in the period from 1914 to 1920, there was little inflation in the 1920s.

The benefits of prosperity were unevenly divided, however. The wages of most workers remained relatively low. Close to two-thirds of the nation's families had annual incomes of less than $2,000, while the average family income for the lowest 40 percent of the population was only $725 per year. Low wages restricted the workers' share in the nation's prosperity, since the workers were limited in their ability to consume the products of American industry and agriculture.

There were, in addition, some weaknesses in the economy, despite the general prosperity. Agricultural overproduction caused economic hardship for the nation's farmers, and the coal and textile industries also experienced problems. The coal industry was declining because of increasing competition from foreign coal producers, while the emergence of synthetics, especially rayon, created difficulties for the cotton and wool textile industries. In both coal and textiles, unemployment ran well above the national average.

Government and Business

The Republican administrations of the 1920s were strongly probusiness, and these policies won widespread support among the people.

Secretary of Commerce Herbert Hoover actively supported a partnership between government and business, a policy he believed would promote the expansion and continued prosperity of the nation's private enterprise economy. In particular, Hoover encouraged a policy known as associationalism, which involved the establishment of trade associations. In 1919, about 700 such associations existed. By 1929, there were more than 2,000, representing virtually every significant industry and commodity. By sharing information and promoting trade practice controls, the trade associations hoped to encourage stability in the economy and increase profits. While some of the practices of the trade associations could have been challenged under the antitrust laws, the Republican administrations followed a policy of lax enforcement of those laws. In fact, the Antitrust Division of the Justice Department encouraged the activities of the trade associations. Government policy on taxation also benefitted business and the wealthy. In 1926, Secretary of the Treasury Mellon won congressional approval of his proposal to cut income tax rates for wealthy taxpayers from 46 percent to 26 percent and to reduce inheritance taxes by 50 percent.

The Supreme Court and Business

The Supreme Court was also strongly probusiness during the 1920s. In the 1920 case of *United States v. United States Steel Co.*, the Supreme Court decided that it was not improper for the giant United States Steel Co. to dominate the steel industry as long as some competitors continued to operate.

In the case of *United States v. Maple Flooring Association*, decided in 1925, the Supreme Court held that trade associations were legal if they did not act to eliminate competition.

Led by its new Chief Justice William Howard Taft, appointed by Harding in 1921, the Supreme Court upheld the use of injunctions against labor unions. In the case of *Duplex Printing Press Co. v. Deering*, decided in 1921, the Supreme Court ruled that injunctions could be invoked against boycotts imposed by organized labor. In the case of *Truax v. Corrigan*, also decided in 1921, the court invalidated a state law which prohibited the use of injunctions against picketing.

In two other cases, the Supreme Court voided laws designed to benefit workers. In its 1922 decision in the case of *Bailey v. Drexel Furniture Co.*, the Supreme Court invalidated a national law regulating child labor. Then, in the case of *Adkins v. Children's Hospital*, decided in 1923, the court voided a District of Columbia law establishing a minimum wage for women workers.

Business Consolidation

During the 1920s, earlier trends in the direction of business consolidation continued. By 1929, 200 corporations controlled about half of the nation's corporate assets. The Big Three automakers—Ford, General Motors, and Chrysler—produced about 90 percent of the cars and trucks manufactured in the United States. Four tobacco companies produced over 90 percent of the country's cigarettes. A revolution was underway in retailing, as chain stores expanded at the expense of small, family-owned and operated stores. Supermarket chains, including A & P, Piggly Wiggly, and Safeway, grew, as did other chains, such as Woolworth, Kresge, J.C. Penney, and Western Auto. By the end of the 1920s, chain stores accounted for about 20 percent of the nation's retail sales.

The New Look of Business

American business during the 1920s began to take on a "new look." Businessmen emphasized the idea of self-regulation. While self-regulation sometimes meant no regulation at all, some businessmen recognized economic and social responsibilities which the robber barons of an earlier generation had not. These concerned businessmen stressed the importance of business ethics, philanthropic activity to benefit the community, and the welfare of their workers. A number of corporations began to employ professional personnel managers and labor relations specialists. Insurance and pension plans for workers were inaugurated, as were plans to promote employee stock ownership. Wages paid to workers increased, although generally not as much as profits, and the work week became shorter.

The businessmen's motives were by no means entirely altruistic, since improved working conditions and fringe benefits would make workers less inclined to join unions. The unsuccessful strikes following World War I had weakened unions. In 1920, slightly more than 5 million workers belonged to unions. By 1926, union membership had declined to 3.6 million. Corporations which established procedures for consultation between management and elected representatives of the workers hailed this system as the American Plan. The clear implication was that labor unions which represented workers through collective bargaining were somehow un-American.

Bruce Barton

Advertising executive Bruce Barton emerged during the 1920s as a major spokesman for business. A pioneer in the modern advertising industry, Barton founded in 1920 the advertising agency which ultimately became Batten, Barton, Durstine & Osborne (BBD&O). In 1925, Martin published the best seller *The Man Nobody Knows*, which portrayed Jesus as a businessman. He wrote that Jesus "picked up twelve men from the bottom ranks . . . and forged them into an organization that conquered the world." For Barton, businessmen who built a successful business were fulfilling a Christian obligation.

Problems in Agriculture

In 1929, net farm income in the United States was $3 billion less than in 1919. As the depression in agriculture persisted, a number of attempted remedies produced little in the way of substantial results.

George Peek, a plow manufacturer from Moline, Illinois, advanced a dramatic proposal which began to win support. First of all, Peek proposed that high tariffs be established on imported agricultural goods in order to preserve the domestic market for the nation's farmers. The farmers would then sell all they could in this protected market. The federal government would buy the remaining surplus and sell it abroad for whatever price it would bring. The farmers would pay a small tax—an equalization fee— to reimburse the government for any losses it incurred.

Peek's plan was embodied in the McNary-Haugen Bill, which Congress passed twice, in 1927 and again in 1928. On both occasions, Coolidge vetoed the bill. Among his reasons for vetoing the bill Coolidge cited his fear that it would lead to overproduction and profiteering and would antagonize foreign producers of agricultural products and lead to retaliation against the United States.

The Automobile Industry

During the 1920s, the United States entered the automobile age in a big way. In 1921, 1.5 million cars were sold. By 1929, car sales increased to 9 million. In 1920, 8 million cars were registered in the United States. By 1929, the figure had risen to 23 million, with an average of one car for every five people.

By 1929, 3.7 million workers were employed in jobs directly or indirectly related to the automobile. The expansion of the automobile industry promoted the expansion of related industries, including steel, rubber, gears, tools, and gasoline, while road construction became a major industry in its own right.

The country's most famous auto maker, Henry Ford, was producing 9,000 of his famous Model T's every day and had cut the car's price to below $300. In the late 1920s, Ford introduced his new Model A. By 1930, Ford had manufactured more than 20 million cars. Ford and other leaders of American business became cultural heroes with a popularity rivaling that of prominent sports figures.

The Airplane

The first flight by a heavier-than-air craft took place on December 17, 1903, at Kitty Hawk on the Outer Banks of North Carolina. An airplane designed by Orville and Wilbur Wright, with Orville at the controls, remained airborne for 12 seconds and flew 120 feet.

Although the airplane was of little economic importance to the United States in the 1920s, the air age had clearly begun. In 1920, the first transcontinental airmail route, from New York to San Francisco, was established.

The greatest event in aviation of the decade came in May, 1927, when Charles A. Lindbergh succeeded in making the first solo flight across the Atlantic. The "Lone Eagle" flew his *Spirit of St. Louis* from New York's Long Island to Paris in 33 hours and 39 minutes. Lindbergh became the greatest American hero of the decade.

Radio

In the 1890s, Guglielmo Marconi, an Italian, invented wireless telegraphy. The next step was to develop a means for the wireless transmission of the human voice. In the years prior to World War I, Lee DeForest, an American, played a major role in this development.

The age of radio began in the United States on November 2, 1920, when KDKA in Pittsburgh, Pennsylvania went on the air, broadcasting the presidential election returns. By 1923, over 500 radio stations were operating, and by 1929, the number had grown to over 800. Some 40 percent of the nation's homes had a radio by 1929, and two major national networks, the Columbia Broadcasting System (CBS) and the National Broadcasting Company (NBC) had been formed.

In keeping with the American tradition of private enterprise, radio broadcasting remained in the hands of private companies and was supported by advertising, rather than being government-owned-and-operated.

The Movies

The 1920s also witnessed the emergence of the movies as a central feature of American life. Thomas A. Edison and other inventive geniuses developed motion pictures in the late nineteenth century, and a few movies were produced in the 1890s. In 1902, the first story sequence was produced: the eight-minute-long *The Great Train Robbery*. By 1912, the country had close to 13,000 movie theaters, most of them nickelodeons, charging five cents for admission and operating in converted storefronts.

One of the most famous early full-length feature films was D. W. Griffith's *The Birth of a Nation*. Produced in 1915, the movie presented a glorified view of the Ku Klux Klan during Reconstruction and helped promote a revival of the Klan.

The movie industry had originally been centered in the New York area. By the 1920s, however, the industry had moved to southern California, which offered moviemakers the advantages of its warm and sunny climate and its scenic diversity.

In 1927, the first feature-length talking picture was released. *The Jazz Singer* starred Al Jolson, one of the country's most popular vaudeville stars. Talkies quickly made silent movies obsolete.

By the end of the 1920s, the United States had 23,000 movie theaters selling an average of 100 million tickets a week.

Mass Circulation Magazines

Radio and the movies helped bring the American people together more closely by creating a truly national culture. So, too, did mass circulation magazines. By 1922, ten magazines claimed a circulation of a least 2.5 million. Among the most popular magazines of the 1920s were the *Saturday Evening Post*, *Collier's Weekly*, *Good Housekeeping*, the *Ladies Home Journal*, and the *American Mercury*. The latter's acid-penned editor H. L. Mencken became noted for his caustic comments on the contemporary American scene. Three other widely-read magazines—the *Reader's Digest*, *Time*, and the *New Yorker*—began publication during the decade. The Book of the Month Club, founded in 1926, also helped in the creation of a national culture.

Sports

During the "Roaring Twenties", the American people became more ardent sports fans than ever. Professional boxing produced heavyweights Jack Dempsey and Gene Tunney, while Bobby Jones and Bill Tilden won popularity in professional golf and tennis, respectively.

College football became truly popular for the first time, and the professional National Football League was established in 1922. Among the nation's football heroes was Red Grange who played for the University of Illinois before signing a contract with George Halas' Chicago Bears.

Baseball, the national sport, entered the 1920s under a cloud. In 1919, the Chicago White Sox won the American League pennant and were expected to win an easy World Series victory over the Cincinnati Red Stockings, the National League pennant winner. But the White Sox lost. A subsequent investigation revealed that several White Sox players had conspired with gamblers to throw the series.

The Black Sox scandal was forgotten, however, as baseball entered its golden age. Babe Ruth, the greatest baseball hero of all, hit 60 home runs for the New York Yankees in 1927, and the new Yankee Stadium in the Bronx became known as "the house that Ruth built."

Urbanization

The 1920 census revealed that, for the first time in the nation's history, a majority of the American people lived in urban areas. In 1870, fifty years earlier, only 28 percent of the population was classified as urban. An intensifying conflict between rural and urban America accompanied the process of urbanization. Rural America both feared and resented the cities with their material advantages, large immigrant populations, political bosses, and ways of life that seemed to challenge traditional American values.

Immigration Restriction

Rural, white, Protestant America expressed fear of the threat to the "American way of life" presented by immigrants, especially the more recent Catholic and Jewish immigrants from southern and eastern Europe. Many Americans also feared the immigrants' competition for jobs.

The emergence and popularization of pseudoscientific ideas about supposedly superior and inferior races gave added impetus to the movement to restrict immigration. In *The Passing of the Great Race* (1916), for example, Madison Grant warned of the threat posed by the Latins and Slavs of southern and eastern Europe to the racial purity of the Nordic peoples of northern European origin.

In the years preceding World War I, an average of about 1 million immigrants a year entered the United States. In 1919, only 110,000 immigrants arrived, but in 1920, the figure rose to 430,000. In 1921, the figure nearly doubled, to 805,000. Fearing a flood of immigrants, Congress passed the Emergency Immigration Act of 1921. This law established quotas for immigrants, restricting new immigrants each year to 3 percent of the foreign-born residents of any nationality as shown in the 1910 census.

In 1924, Congress passed the National Origins Act which reduced the figure to 2 percent based on the 1890 census. This law assigned higher quotas to Great Britain, Ireland, Germany, and the Scandinavian countries than they were able to fill, and, at the same time, greatly restricted immigration from southern and eastern Europe. The 1924 law also placed a complete ban on immigration from East Asia. At the same time, no restrictions were placed on immigration from the Western Hemisphere, which had the ironic effect of substantially increasing the nation's population of Hispanic Catholics.

The Sacco and Vanzetti Case

American antiforeignism (nativism) also expressed itself in the Sacco and Vanzetti case, which remained a major public issue for several years.

Two Italian immigrants, Nicola Sacco and Bartolomeo Vanzetti, were charged with the 1920 murder of a paymaster in South Braintree, Massachusetts. While both men were admitted anarchists, the evidence against them was less than conclusive and their 1921 trial was conducted in an atmosphere of antiradical hysteria. Both men were convicted and sentenced to death. (Modern ballistic studies of Sacco's gun suggest that he may indeed have been guilty.)

Supporters of Sacco and Vanzetti charged that they had been convicted for their political beliefs. Demands for a new trial and for pardons were rejected, and despite international protests Sacco and Vanzetti died in the electric chair in August, 1927.

The Ku Klux Klan

In 1915, William J. Simmons of Georgia revived the Ku Klux Klan as an organization of "native born, white, gentile Americans." The new Klan was antiblack, antiforeign, anti-Catholic, and anti-Semitic.

The Klan spread from the South to the Middle West, Southwest, and Far West and by 1924 claimed well over 4 million members.

In many states, the Klan gained a powerful influence on politics. In 1924, the Democratic national convention was deeply divided over a resolution condemning the Klan, which was defeated in a close vote.

In 1922, the Klan endorsed an initiative proposal in Oregon

to require all children between the ages of 8 and 16 to attend public schools. The effect would be to compel the closing of Catholic and other private schools. The initiative was adopted, and Walter Pierce, the Klan-endorsed Democratic candidate, won the governorship. The Supreme Court overturned the Oregon School Law in the 1925 case of *Pierce v. Society of Sisters*

The Klan became particularly powerful in Indiana, although events in that state also hastened the Klan's decline. David Stephenson, the Grand Dragon of the Indiana Klan, gained considerable influence in the state's Republican party. Stephenson became the central figure in a scandal when he kidnapped and raped his secretary and then prevented her from getting medical assistance when she attempted suicide; this resulted in her death. In 1925, Stephenson was convicted of manslaughter and sentenced to life imprisonment. Stephenson demanded that Governor Ed Jackson, who had been elected with Klan support, grant him a pardon. When Jackson refused to do so, Stephenson retaliated by making revelations that led to the conviction of a congressman and several other public officials.

This and other Klan-related scandals helped hasten the organization's decline. By 1928, Klan membership had fallen to 200,000.

Prohibition

Nationwide prohibition became effective on January 16, 1920, under the terms of the Eighteenth Amendment to the Constitution. The manufacture, sale, and transportation—but not the possession or consumption—of "intoxicating liquors" in the United States was now illegal. The Volstead Act of 1919 provided for the enforcement of prohibition, defining as "intoxicating" any beverage containing more than 0.5 percent alcohol. Prohibition had broad popular support in the South and

Middle West but was strongly opposed in the eastern cities. But most Americans expected that prohibition would remain a permanent feature of national life. Enforcement of prohibition proved difficult, however. How could the authorities enforce a law which made a crime out of something which millions of people had never regarded as a crime? The agents charged with enforcement were relatively few in number, and many of them could be readily bribed.

With the onset of prohibition, the old saloons disappeared and were replaced by speakeasies (illegal bars). Rumrunners smuggled liquor into the country from Canada, Mexico, and the West Indies, and bootleggers distributed it to their customers. Some Americans produced their own alcoholic beverages (bathtub gin) at home.

In some states, little effort was made to enforce prohibition. In 1923, in fact, New York repealed the state law which provided for the enforcement of prohibition, and by 1930 six other states had followed New York's example. Other states, however, attempted to promote strict enforcement. Michigan, for example, mandated life imprisonment for anyone convicted for the fourth time of violating prohibition.

By the late 1920s, national sentiment in favor of repealing prohibition was clearly growing.

Organized Crime

Prohibition did not create organized crime, but it did provide organized crime with a new impetus. Illegal alcohol offered the prospect of huge profits, and rival criminals engaged in gang wars to insure their control of the business. In Chicago alone during the 1920s, gang wars resulted in the deaths of over 500 individuals. In 1925, "Scarface" Al Capone began his effort to win control of the crime syndicate in the Windy City. The authorities suspected Capone of being responsible for the notorious St. Valentine's Day Massacre of 1929, when seven members of a rival gang were gunned down, but there was insufficient evidence to charge Capone with this or other crimes. Capone was finally convicted of income tax evasion and sentenced to 11 years in a federal penitentiary.

In addition to profiting from the sale of alcohol, organized crime engaged in gambling, prostitution, and narcotics, as well as protection rackets and labor racketeering. Organized crime became big business. By 1930, its annual income was estimated at $12 to $15 billion, more than the income of the federal government.

The Scopes Trial

During the 1920s, there was a resurgence of religious fundamentalism, particularly among rural Protestant Americans. Fundamentalists believed in the literal truth of the Bible, including the story of Creation as set forth in the Book of Genesis, and therefore opposed the theory of evolution advanced by Charles Darwin in *The Origin of Species* (1859) and advocated by his followers. In Tennessee, fundamentalists won the adoption of a law prohibiting the teaching of evolution in the state's public schools and colleges. In 1925, John T. Scopes, a biology teacher in Dayton, Tennessee, deliberately violated this law.

The American Civil Liberties Union (ACLU) recruited the noted criminal lawyer and professed agnostic Clarence Darrow to defend Scopes, while William Jennings Bryan, the three-time Democratic presidential candidate and an ardent fundamentalist, went to Dayton to lead the prosecution. During the trial, Scopes sank into the background as the debate raged between Darrow and Bryan.

Scopes was found guilty, although the trial discredited both Bryan and the antievolutionists in the public mind. The Tennessee Supreme Court upheld the antievolution law on appeal, but overturned Scopes' sentence (a $100 fine) on a technicality.

Blacks in the 1920s

The black migration from the rural South to the cities of the North had become substantial during World War I, and this Great Migration continued through the 1920s. During the decade, 1.5 million blacks moved northward, and the black populations of New York, Philadelphia, Cleveland, Detroit, and Chicago more than doubled. In the northern cities, the black population tended to be concentrated in areas that came to be called ghettos. The most famous ghetto was New York's Harlem.

The urban ghettos provided many supporters for the black nationalist movement led by Marcus Garvey, an immigrant from Jamaica in the West Indies who had established the Universal Negro Improvement Association in 1914. Garvey believed that God and Jesus Christ were blacks, held whites in contempt, and opposed integration, which was favored by the National Association for the Advancement of Colored People (NAACP). In Garvey's view, integration was a white plot to assure a supply of cheap labor. He insisted that blacks should return to Africa and establish a black empire. Garvey won millions of black followers, and encouraged them to invest in his ventures, including the Black Star Steamship Company which he created to transport blacks to Africa. Garvey proved, however, to be a poor businessman. In 1923, the steamship company collapsed, and Garvey was convicted of defrauding his supporters. He served two years in prison and was then deported to Jamaica.

During the 1920s, New York's Harlem became a major cultural center as the Harlem Renaissance developed among black writers, artists, actors, and musicians. The major figures of the Harlem Renaissance included the poets Langston Hughes, Countee Cullen, and Claude McKay. James Weldon Johnson portrayed the black Mecca in *Black Manhattan*, while Jean Toomer's powerful novel *Cane* dealt with black life in Georgia and Washington.

In the political realm, blacks scored two victories. In 1928, Oscar DePriest won election to Congress from a district in Chicago. He was the first black congressman since 1901. In 1930, blacks campaigned against Hoover's nomination of John J. Parker for a seat on the Supreme Court. As the Republican candidate for the governorship of North Carolina in 1928, Parker had declared that black voting was "a source of evil and danger." Parker was denied Senate confirmation by a vote of 39 to 41. These successes, however, had little impact on the lives of most American blacks, who continued to suffer from political, legal, economic, and social discrimination.

Women in the 1920s

Although the Nineteenth Amendment to the Constitution extended the right to vote to women, women came only gradually to take an active part in the political life of the nation. In the presidential election of 1920, only about one-third of the eligible women voted. The major political parties moved to grant at least token positions to women. In 1920, Harriet Taylor Upton, who had been an officer of the National American Woman Suffrage Association, was named vice chairman of the Republican National Committee. In 1924, Emily Newell Blair became vice chairman of the Democratic National Committee.

In 1924, two women won election as state governors. Miriam "Ma" Ferguson became Governor of Texas. Her husband had previously held that office but had been impeached in 1917. Nellie Taylor Ross replaced her late husband as Wyoming's Governor. About two-thirds of the women in Congress were filling their late husbands' unexpired terms.

During the 1920s, women gradually increased their presence

in the nation's labor force. In 1920, some 8.4 million women were employed. That number grew to 10.8 million by 1930.

The 1928 Election

In 1928, the Democrats nominated Governor Alfred E. Smith of New York as their presidential candidate. Smith was a grandson of Irish immigrants, a Catholic, a wet (an opponent of prohibition, as opposed to a dry), and a product of Tammany Hall (the Democratic organization of New York's Manhattan borough). He also spoke with a gruff New York accent. In other words, Al Smith was a red flag waved in the face of the rural, Protestant, dry bull.

The Republican national convention nominated Secretary of Commerce Herbert Hoover, the intellectual leader of the Republican New Era of the 1920s.

Winning strong support among rural, Protestant, dry voters, Hoover carried such traditionally Democratic states as Virginia, North Carolina, Florida, Oklahoma, and Texas. With 21.4 million popular votes and 444 votes in the electoral college, Hoover overwhelmed Smith, who polled 14 million popular votes and 87 electoral votes.

Although he lost the election, Smith ran well in the nation's cities. In 1924, the Republicans had carried the country's 12 largest cities. Smith won them all in 1928. The Democrats' gains in the cities proved to be more enduring than Hoover's victories in the Democratic South. In 1932, Franklin D. Roosevelt recaptured the South and, building on Smith's gains in 1928, began to construct a new Democratic majority that dominated the nation's politics for the next 20 years.

The Hoover Administration

When Hoover took office on March 4, 1929, the nation was

at the height of its prosperity. But two groups were not getting their share: unorganized workers and the farmers.

To benefit the farmers, Congress passed the Agricultural Marketing Act of 1929, which was designed to help farmers establish producers' cooperatives. A Federal Farm Loan Board was created with a revolving fund of $500 million. The Board would lend money to commodity cooperatives which bought, stored and sold surplus agricultural products. When prices rose, the cooperatives would sell the surplus and repay the government. In 1930, the Federal Farm Board established the Grain Stabilization Corporation and the Cotton Stabilization Corporation, which were intended to prop up declining prices by buying up surpluses. But the two corporations were not able to cope effectively with the huge surpluses being produced by the country's farmers. The depression in agriculture continued and would soon merge with the Great Depression of the 1930s.

Hoover also sought to protect American farmers from foreign competition by raising tariffs on the products of agriculture. The Hawley-Smoot Tariff of 1930 provided for increasing protective tariffs on 75 farm products and 925 industrial products. The act raised tariff rates from the 26 percent average of the Fordney-McCumber Tariff of 1922 to 50 percent, a new high. Rather than helping the American farmer, or the nation's economy in general, the Hawley-Smoot Tariff led to reprisals by foreign governments, which reduced the market for the products of both American agriculture and industry.

For the Republican Presidents of the 1920s, "normalcy" meant, above all, reducing the scope of the federal government's activities. President Coolidge's remark, "The business of America is business," became a motto of the decade, and the federal government promoted the interests of private enterprise. The economic prosperity of the 1920s proved to be both considerable and uneven. Workers' wages remained relatively low, the nation's farmers experienced hardships, and some industries, especially coal and textiles, declined.

The 1920s witnessed major changes in American life. For the first time in the nation's history, a majority of the American people lived in urban areas. The automobile, radio, the movies, and sports became national passions. The challenges presented to the traditional way of life of a predominantly rural America led to antiforeignism and efforts to restrict immigration, as well as to a resurgence of the Ku Klux Klan. The controversy over prohibition, the Scopes trial, and the presidential election of 1928 all served as symbols of the conflict between the old America and the new.

Recommended Reading

Frederick Lewis Allen, *Only Yesterday: An Informal History of the 1920s* (1931).

Jervis Anderson, *This Was Harlem: A Cultural Portrait, 1900–1950* (1982).

Irving Bernstein, *The Lean Years: A History of the American Worker, 1920–1933* (1960).

David Burner, *Herbert Hoover: A Public Life* (1979).

David Burner, *The Politics of Provincialism: The Democratic Party in Transition, 1918–1932* (1968).

Paul A. Carter, *The Twenties in America* (1968).

David M. Chalmers, *Hooded Americanism: The History of the Ku Klux Klan* (1981).

Norman H. Clark, *Deliver Us from Evil: An Interpretation of American Prohibition* (1976).

E. David Cronon, *Black Moses: The Story of Marcus Garvey and the Universal Negro Improvement Association* (1955).

Jonathan Daniels, *The Time Between the Wars: Armistice to Pearl Harbor* (1966).

Robert A. Divine, *American Immigration Policy, 1924–1952* (1957).

Martin L. Fausold, *The Presidency of Herbert C. Hoover* (1985).

Roberta Strauss Feuerlicht, *Justice Crucified: The Story of Sacco and Vanzetti* (1977).

Ray Ginger, *Six Days or Forever? Tennessee v. John Thomas Scopes* (1958).

Oscar Handlin, *Al Smith and His America* (1958).

John D. Hicks, *Republican Ascendency, 1921–1933* (1960).

Kenneth T. Jackson, *The Ku Klux Klan in the City, 1915–1930* (1965).

Isabel Leighton, ed. *The Aspirin Age, 1919–1941* (1949).

J. Stanley Lemons, *The Woman Citizen: Social Feminism in the 1920s* (1973).

William E. Leuchtenberg, *The Perils of Prosperity, 1914–1932* (1958)

Lawrence Levine, *Defender of the Faith, William Jennings Bryan: The Last Decade, 1915–1925* (1965).

David L. Lewis, *When Harlem Was in Vogue* (1981).

Allan J. Lichtman, *Prejudice and the Old Politics: The Presidential Election of 1928* (1979).

Donald J. Lisio, *Hoover, Blacks, and Lily-Whites: A Study of Southern Strategies* (1985).

Donald R. McCoy, *Calvin Coolidge: The Quiet President* (1967).

Robert K. Murray, *The Politics of Normalcy: Governmental Theory and Practice in the Harding-Coolidge Era* (1973).

Francis Russell, *The Shadow of Blooming Grove: Warren G. Harding in His Times* (1968).

Arthur M. Schlesinger, Jr., *The Crisis of the Old Order, 1919–1933* (1957).

Judith Stein, *The World of Marcus Garvey: Race and Class in Modern Society* (1986).

Joan Hoff Wilson, *Herbert Hoover: Forgotten Progressive* (1975).

CHAPTER 10

The Great Depression and the New Deal

Time Line

1929	The stock market crash signals the beginning of the Great Depression
1930	The depression deepens; by year's end, unemployment reaches 4 million
	The Democrats win a majority in the House of Representatives; the Republicans hold a slim majority in the Senate
1932	Congress establishes the Reconstruction Finance Corporation

Federal troops disperse the Bonus Army in Washington, D.C.

Democrat Franklin D. Roosevelt wins the Presidency; the Democrats take control of both houses of Congress

1933   The Hundred Days produces a flood of New Deal legislation

The Twentieth Amendment is ratified

The Twenty-First Amendment is ratified

1934   The Democrats win increased majorities in both houses of Congress

The Wheeler-Howard Act revises federal policy toward the American Indians

1935   The Second New Deal results in a series of new relief, recovery, and reform programs

Proponents of industrial unionism establish the Committee for Industrial Organization (CIO)

1936   Roosevelt wins reelection to the Presidency

1937   Roosevelt fails in his effort to pack the Supreme Court

1938   Congress passes the Second Agricultural Adjustment Act and the Fair Labor Standards Act

The Republicans make gains in the congressional elections, although the Democrats retain control of both houses

The Great Depression plunged the nation from the height of apparent prosperity and optimism about the future into the depths of despair. The most serious economic crisis in American history, the Great Depression began in the wake of the stock market crash of October, 1929 and lasted until 1940, when the outbreak of war in Europe provided a stimulus for increased economic activity in the United States.

In November, 1932, when the depression had thrown more than 10 million workers into the ranks of the unemployed, the American people elected Franklin D. Roosevelt to the Presidency. Roosevelt insisted that the crisis called for action on a broad front and promised the American people a "New Deal," with a three-pronged emphasis on relief, recovery, and reform.

The Stock Market Crash

The stock market crash of October, 1929 opened the floodgates to a series of economic disasters. Stock prices had begun to increase significantly in 1924, as was to be expected in a time of general prosperity. In late 1927, stock prices began to rise rapidly. As the indexes of stock performance shot upward, so, too, did the speculative fever of American investors.

Speculative buying of stock was encouraged by the margin rules in force at the time, when stock buyers had to make a down payment of as little as 10 percent of the cost of the stock, with brokers borrowing the balance. Expecting the bull market to continue, speculators pushed stock prices to unprecedented levels.

Soon after President Herbert Hoover's inauguration in March, 1929, Secretary of the Treasury Andrew Mellon sought to cool down the speculative fever, urging investors to buy more bonds and fewer stocks. But Mellon's advice fell largely on deaf ears. Banks continued to lend money to speculators buying on margin and stock prices continued to climb. By the autumn of 1929, stock prices were about twice what they had been two years earlier.

In September, 1929, prices on the New York Stock Exchange began to ease. On Wednesday, October 23 and Thursday, October 24, the declines in stock prices were considerable, and the New York exchange was thrown into near panic for several hours as speculators tried to unload stock. Major financiers, including Thomas Lamont of the Morgan banking firm, John D. Rockefeller, Jr., and John J. Raskob, made reassuring statements and the panic abated, but only briefly.

On Black Tuesday, October 29, 1929, investors traded 16 million shares of stock and the bottom fell out of the bull market. (During this period, a day when three million shares were traded was considered busy.) The slide in stock prices continued and, by mid-November, stocks had dropped to about 50 percent of their September value.

The Impact of the Stock Market Crash

The fall in stock prices ruined many investors. But only about one million Americans were active stock traders in 1929. Hopes were widespread that the stock market crash would not have a destructive impact on the American economy as a whole. Before long, however, industrial production began to decline, construction ground to a halt, banks and businesses failed, already low farm income declined further, and unemployment grew steadily. The Great Depression had begun.

Why the Depression Happened

This is still not an easy question to answer. There were some basic weaknesses in the American economy, which were intensified by the stock market crash. If these weaknesses had not been present, the economy might have been able to ride out the stock market crash without suffering great damage. Instead, the collapse of the stock market put pressure on the weak spots in the economy, and a general loss of confidence spread rapidly among the American people.

To a substantial degree, the prosperity of the 1920s was more apparent than widespread. Wealth continued to be concentrated in the hands of relatively few people. Business kept its profits high and the wages of workers and the cost of raw materials low. This served to reduce the purchasing power of the workers and farmers.

American agriculture, which had expanded greatly before and during World War I, suffered the consequences of overexpansion in the 1920s. The decline of farm income thrust American agriculture into a depression which persisted through most of the decade. Some industries, such as coal mining and textiles, also did not share in the prosperity of the 1920s.

The expansion of the productivity of American agriculture and industry depended upon mass consumption. The inequality in the distribution of wealth and depressed conditions in agriculture and some areas of industry, however, served to limit consumption, particularly consumption of the increasingly more available durable consumer goods such as automobiles, radios, and refrigerators. Workers who earned low wages could not afford to buy what they produced. This ultimately had a negative impact on American industry.

Loose, ill-coordinated, and often reckless banking practices also hurt the American economy and diminished people's confidence. Even in a time of supposed prosperity, from 1927 to 1929, some 1,600 banks failed. With the onset of the depression, over 4,000 banks collapsed from 1930 through 1932. The Great Depression resulted from a combination of these elements.

Hoover's Response to the Depression

In his speech accepting the Republican presidential nomination in 1928, Herbert Hoover had looked forward to the day "when poverty shall be abolished from this nation." When the depression began, Hoover blamed the economic downturn on a failure of business confidence. In an effort to restore confidence, the President made a series of encouraging statements. In November, 1929, he met with leaders of business and industry and urged them not to reduce employment, wages, and building programs.

As the economic crisis intensified, Hoover began to push for a more active role on the part of the federal government in combating the depression. This represented a change from the practice of the government in the past. At the same time, however, the actions of the Hoover administration remained relatively small-scale and tentative when compared to the extent of the economic downturn.

At the President's urging, Congress moved to reduce income taxes, in order to put more private money into the economy, and to enact expanded public works programs, including the construction of Boulder Dam on the Colorado River. Hoover also encouraged state and city governments to increase their spending on public works. The President knew that unemployment would increase, but he wanted to keep it at a minimum and to use public expenditures to create new jobs.

At the same time, Hoover refused to consider certain measures. He maintained a firm faith in the gold standard and would not permit any inflation of the currency in an effort to prime the economic pump. In addition, the President rejected the idea that the federal government should take any direct action to provide relief to the needy; that should remain the responsibility of private charities and of state and city governments. Hoover felt that instead of providing direct relief, the federal government should aid the recovery efforts of industry and banks.

The Depression During 1930

At the end of 1929, there were about 3 million unemployed. In early 1930, the employment picture brightened somewhat and, by spring, the stock market had recovered about half its losses.

Hoover's program did not, however, stimulate the recovery he had expected. Public works projects created relatively few jobs, and income tax cuts resulted in only a small increase in purchasing power. As the economy contracted, industry laid off more workers in order to avoid increases in inventories of unsold goods. Banks and brokerage houses continued to fail. By late spring, stock prices began to slip again, and the unemployment figures moved upwards. By the end of 1930, unemployed numbered 4 million.

The Election of 1930

During the congressional election campaign of 1930, the Democrats blamed Hoover and the Republicans for the depression and demanded direct federal assistance to the unemployed, a measure which the President continued to oppose. Hoover sought to reassure the voters that the economic downturn was only a temporary phenomenon and that prosperity would soon return.

Although the voters were obviously unhappy, there was no mass revolt against the Republicans. The Democrats did win a narrow majority in the House of Representatives, and John Nance Garner, a Texas Democrat, became Speaker. The Republicans maintained technical control of the Senate, with 48 Republicans, 47 Democrats, and one Farmer-Laborite from Minnesota holding seats in the upper house. In fact, however, a coalition of Democrats and progressive Republicans dominated the Senate. For the next two years, Hoover had to deal with a hostile Congress that called for stronger measures against the depression than the President was prepared to take.

The Deepening Depression

The year 1931 began with an intensifying banking crisis on both sides of the Atlantic. In an attempt to restore order to international finance, Hoover proposed a one-year moratorium on all intergovernmental debts, which primarily involved German reparations and Allied war debts owed to the United States.

The financial and economic crisis in Europe in 1931 had an impact on the United States, helping to push stock prices down well below the levels reached in the 1929 crash.

During 1931, unemployment continued to mount, reaching 7 million by October. Those who still had jobs had to accept wage cuts. From 1929 to 1932, the average wage of factory workers dropped by 60 percent.

The national debt increased from $16.2 billion in 1930 to $22.5 billion in 1932, while national income dropped from $81 billion in 1929, to $53 billion in 1931, to $41 billion in 1932.

Bank and business failures increased. From 1929 to 1932, 5,000 banks failed, while 85,000 businesses went under. During the same period, net investment slumped from $10 billion to $1 billion, and industrial production dropped by 50 percent. For millions of Americans, life became increasingly more desperate.

The Reconstruction Finance Corporation

Although Hoover continued to oppose direct federal assistance to the needy, the President sought to do more to promote the recovery of private business.

In January, 1932, Congress passed legislation establishing a new federal lending agency, the Reconstruction Finance Corporation (RFC), which was authorized to make loans to banks, insurance companies, other financial institutions, and also to railroads. The President hoped that these loans would combat deflation in industry and agriculture and contribute to an increase in employment and an expansion of purchasing power.

The Relief and Construction Act of July, 1932 expanded the scope of the RFC's activity by authorizing the agency to make loans to state and city governments for public works projects. In addition, the RFC could also lend money to states and cities whose relief funds had run out.

The Farm Holiday

As people became more desperate, they were willing to take more direct action. In Iowa, farmers led by Milo Reno began a farm holiday. In what amounted to a farmers' strike, they tried to keep produce off the market in an attempt to force an increase in prices. They slaughtered hogs and dumped milk and used force in efforts to prevent the sale of farms whose mortgages had been foreclosed. The farm holiday failed, and farm prices continued to slump. By 1933, the purchasing power of farmers was 40 percent below the level of 1929—and that was already a time of depression for American agriculture.

The Bonus March

For some time, the American Legion and other veterans' groups had been calling for more help for the veterans of the First World War. In 1931, overriding a presidential veto, Congress enacted a law which allowed veterans to borrow as much as 50 percent of the value of endowment policies they had received in 1924. As the depression deepened, the veterans began to demand full payment in cash.

In the late spring of 1932, a Bonus Army of some 12 to 15 thousand veterans descended on Washington and camped in vacant government buildings and in shacks on Anacostia Flats along the Potomac River.

The House of Representatives approved legislation to make full payment to the veterans, but the bill died in the Senate. The government then provided assistance to help the bonus marchers return home. Most accepted the aid, but about 2,000 refused to leave the city. Fearing a flare-up of revolutionary violence, Hoover ordered the army to drive them from Washington. General Douglas MacArthur, the army's Chief of Staff, used tanks, cavalry, and tear gas in carrying out his mission. The forced dispersal of the bonus marchers damaged Hoover's popularity still further.

The Election of 1932

By late 1932, the number of unemployed reached 10 or 11 million and may have been even higher. Given the extent of the depression, it was almost certain that the Democrats would win the Presidency.

Renominating Hoover, the Republicans called for cuts in government expenditures, a balanced budget, and maintenance of the gold standard. They also proposed a public referendum on the controversial issue of prohibition.

The Democrats selected Governor Franklin D. Roosevelt of New York as their presidential nominee. After serving as Assistant Secretary of the Navy in the Wilson administration, Roosevelt was the Democrats' unsuccessful vice presidential candidate in 1920. In 1921, Roosevelt suffered an attack of poliomyelitis, which paralyzed him from the waist down. Refusing to retire to the life of a country gentleman, Roosevelt returned to politics, winning election as New York's Governor in 1928 and reelection in 1930. Roosevelt selected John Nance Garner, the Speaker of the House of Representatives, as his vice presidential running mate.

Declaring that the federal government had a "continuous responsibility . . . for human welfare," the Democratic platform proposed aid to the farmers, a system of unemployment compensation and old age pensions, reform of banking, and regulation of the stock exchanges. Calling, somewhat inconsistently, for reduced government spending, the Democrats promised to balance the budget. In addition, they called for the outright repeal of the Eighteenth Amendment, which had established prohibition.

During the campaign, Hoover tried to defend his record and that of his administration, while accusing the Democrats of being irresponsible. Roosevelt appeared energetic and confident in the face of the national climate of uncertainty, but he avoided making specific promises beyond pledging help to the farmers and endorsing cuts in government expenditures and a balanced budget.

Roosevelt won close to 28 million popular votes, some 12 million more than Hoover's. Roosevelt captured 42 states with 472 electoral votes, while Hoover's electoral votes totaled 59. The Democrats also won comfortable majorities in both houses of Congress.

Hoover's Last Months in Office

Congress had approved the Twentieth Amendment and had sent it to the states for ratification. The amendment provided that Congress would convene each year on January 3 and that the President would be inaugurated every four years on January 20.

However, the ratification process was not completed until February, 1933. Therefore, the nation would be "on hold" for four months, from the election in early November, 1932 until Roosevelt's inauguration on March 4, 1933.

While the nation marked time, Hoover tried to get Roosevelt

to commit himself to the maintenance of the gold standard and a balanced budget. The new President wanted to keep his options open, however, and refused to make commitments.

The Repeal of Prohibition

During this period, Congress approved the Twenty-First Amendment, repealing prohibition. The ratification process was completed in December, 1933.

The Banking Crisis

The nation's banks sank deeper into crisis. In February, 1933, Michigan proclaimed an eight-day bank holiday, ordering the state's banks to close in order to forestall a financial collapse. As inauguration day approached, banks in 22 states were closed.

Roosevelt's Inauguration and the National Bank Holiday

Taking the oath of office on March 4, 1933, Roosevelt pledged "direct, vigorous action" to combat the Great Depression. He assured Americans that "the only thing we have to fear is fear itself."

To forestall a collapse of the nation's banking system, the new President proclaimed, on March 5, a national bank holiday and called the Congress into special session.

During the following days, the Reconstruction Finance Corporation put $1 billion into the banking system. When Congress met on March 9, it promptly approved the Emergency Banking Act, which provided for an examination of the banks and authorized the reopening of those that were sound.

On March 12, in the first of his many fireside chats (informal radio reports to the American people), Roosevelt assured the nation that most of the country's banks would reopen the following week. About 10 percent of the banks remained closed for at least a while longer, but many of these subsequently reopened.

The Hundred Days

The special session of Congress lasted from March 9 to June 16, 1933. During these Hundred Days, Congress approved a flood of major legislation, action virtually without precedent in American history.

This activity was directed by the President, his cabinet, and the Brain Trust, a group of Roosevelt's close advisers. The Brain Trust included three Columbia University professors, Adolf A. Berle, Jr., Raymond Moley, and Rexford G. Tugwell.

The main emphasis of the Hundred Days was on relief and recovery. The new legislation established a series of alphabet agencies, so-called because they were customarily referred to by their initials.

A sincere believer in government economy, Roosevelt convinced Congress to reduce federal government salaries and military pensions. He also secured congressional approval for taking the country off the gold standard, a move which would counter the deflationary trend.

During the Hundred Days, Congress also amended the Volstead Act, legalizing the production and sale of light wine and beer.

Major Legislation of the Hundred Days:

March	Establishment of the Civilian Conservation Corps
May	The Federal Emergency Relief Act
May	The Agricultural Adjustment Act
May	The Tennessee Valley Act

June   The Home Owners' Loan Act

June   The Farm Credit Act

June   The Glass-Steagall Banking Act

June   The National Industrial Recovery Act

The Civilian Conservation Corps

Established in March, 1933, the Civilian Conservation Corps (CCC) was designed to provide work for unemployed young men, aged 18 to 25. Ultimately some 3 million people were put to work on reforestation, flood control, erosion control, and road construction projects.

The Federal Emergency Relief Act

Passed in May, 1933, this act created the Federal Emergency Relief Administration (FERA) to provide matching funds for states and cities to distribute as direct relief to those in need. Harry Hopkins, a former social worker and friend of the President, headed the FERA.

The Agricultural Adjustment Act

The Agricultural Adjustment Act, passed by Congress in May, 1933, established the Agricultural Adjustment Administration (AAA). In an attempt to increase severely depressed farm prices, the AAA paid subsidies to farmers who agreed to decrease their production of basic agricultural commodities, including wheat, corn, cotton, rice, hogs, and dairy products. These subsidies were financed by a tax levied on the industries which processed agricultural products, the so called processing tax.

The efforts of the AAA served to reduce the production of agricultural products. As a consequence, farm prices and farmers' incomes increased. Nevertheless, agricultural production continued to be higher than the forecasts called for, and the increases in prices and incomes were less than anticipated.

Following the harvest in the autumn of 1933, the AAA established the Commodity Credit Corporation. This agency accepted crops as security for loans. In order to qualify for these loans, farmers had to agree to reduce their production the following year. The creation of the Commodity Credit Corporation represented a further effort to reduce production in order to increase prices and farm incomes.

In January, 1936, in the case of *United States v. Butler*, the Supreme Court, by a vote of 6 to 3, declared the processing tax unconstitutional, thus making it impossible for the AAA to continue to function. In an attempt to fill the gap, Congress passed, in February, the Soil Conservation and Domestic Allotment Act. This act used soil conservation measures as a means to reduce the production of crops which were in chronic surplus. Payments would be made to farmers who practiced soil conservation by withdrawing land from the cultivation of soil-depleting crops, such as wheat, corn, and cotton.

The Tennessee Valley Authority

The creation of the Tennessee Valley Authority (TVA) in May, 1933 brought to fruition the long-standing dream of Senator George W. Norris, a progressive Republican from Nebraska. Encompassing parts of seven states—Tennessee, Kentucky, Virginia, North Carolina, Georgia, Alabama, and Mississippi—the TVA was designed to promote the development of the valley of the Tennessee River. The TVA built a total of 20 dams for flood control and for the production of cheap electric power. Rates for TVA-produced and sold electricity served as a yard stick to measure the rates charged by private utilities. The TVA also promoted soil and forest conservation and developed new recreation areas. The activities of the TVA raised the standard of living of the three million people who lived in the Tennessee valley.

The Home Owners' Loan Act

Passed by Congress in June, 1933, this act created the Home Owners' Loan Corporation (HOLC), which helped homeowners refinance their mortgages at lower rates. This program served not only to prevent the foreclosure of home mortgages, it also provided banks with the liquid assets they needed.

The Farm Credit Act

Also adopted in June, 1933, this act established the Farm Credit Administration (FCA), which reorganized the agricultural credit system and helped farmers refinance their mortgages at lower rates.

The Glass-Steagall Banking Act

This law, also passed in June, 1933, separated investment and commercial banking in an effort to prevent speculative abuses which had been a common occurrence before the onset of the banking crisis. In addition, this act also created the Federal Deposit Insurance Corporation (FDIC), which insured bank deposits up to a maximum of $5,000 for each account.

The National Industrial Recovery Act

June, 1933, when the Hundred Days drew to a close, also produced the National Industrial Recovery Act (NIRA), designed to promote the recovery of industry and trade and a reduction of unemployment.

The NIRA established the National Recovery Administration (NRA), headed by Hugh Johnson, a former general. The NRA assisted industry and business in developing codes of fair competition. These codes regulated production, competitive practices, and wages and hours in the major areas of industry and business and involved a suspension of the antitrust laws.

Participating businesses displayed the symbol of the NRA, the blue eagle, and used the NRA's motto "We Do Our Part" in their advertising.

Section 7a of the NIRA recognized the right of workers "to organize and bargain collectively through representatives of their own choosing . . . free from interference, restraint, or coercion of employers." This gave considerable encouragement to the efforts of labor unions to organize American workers.

In practice, the NRA had some early successes. Drafting codes proved to be difficult, however, and before long complaints of code violations, unfair competition, and illegitimate price-fixing became common.

In the 1935 case of *Schechter Packing Corp. v. United States*, often called the Sick Chicken Case, the Supreme Court unanimously ruled the NRA unconstitutional.

The Public Works Administration

The NIRA also established the Public Works Administration (PWA), directed by Harold Ickes, the Secretary of the Interior. The PWA was designed to create jobs by building roads, dams, post offices, hospitals, schools, and other public buildings. From 1933 to 1939, the PWA spent $5 billion on some 35,000 projects which provided jobs for more than 500,000 people.

Other Early New Deal Legislation

1933	The Civil Works Administration
1934	The Security Exchange Act
1934	The National Housing Act
1934	The Frazier-Lemke Farm Bankruptcy Act
1934	The Communications Act

The Civil Works Administration

The persistence of unemployment required the establishment of a new agency to carry on what had been intended to be the temporary work of the Federal Emergency Relief Administration (FERA). Created in November, 1933, the Civil Works Administration (CWA) developed make-work programs like street sweeping, leaf raking, and ditch digging. Directed by Harry Hopkins, who had headed the FERA, the CWA put several million people to work during the winter of 1933–34.

The Security Exchange Act

This 1934 act established the Securities and Exchange Commission, which had the responsibility of regulating stock exchanges and trading in most securities to prevent manipulation of prices and other abuses. The act also empowered the Federal Reserve Board to impose restrictions on buying stocks on margin. Buying on margin had encouraged the excessive speculation which preceded the stock market crash of October, 1929.

The National Housing Act of 1934

This act created the Federal Housing Administration (FHA). Designed to promote home building and to revive employment in the construction industry, the FHA insured mortgages made by private lending institutions. By 1941, the FHA had insured $3.5 billion in home mortgages.

The Frazier-Lemke Farm Bankruptcy Act

This law, adopted in 1934, made the foreclosure of farm mortgages more difficult. Postponing farm foreclosures for five years, the law made it possible for a farmer who was behind in his mortgage payments to repurchase his land at a reappraised price, based on depressed land values. Declared unconstitutional by the Supreme Court in 1935, the law was rewritten that year. The revised law established a three-year postponement of foreclosures and made it possible for farmers threatened with foreclosure to keep their land by paying a fair rental determined by a court.

The Communications Act of 1934

This law established the Federal Communications Commission (FCC) to regulate radio broadcasting and telegraph and cable communications.

The Second New Deal

Following the congressional elections of 1934, which gave the Democrats increased majorities in both houses of Congress, President Roosevelt launched what historians have come to call the Second New Deal.

After two years of New Deal policies, the American economy remained sluggish. In an effort to relieve continuing distress and to promote recovery, the President initiated new relief and recovery programs. In addition, he moved to promote some fundamental reforms.

The Second New Deal expanded earlier efforts to put people to work in government-supported jobs until more employment became available in the private sector. Federal aid to the farmers continued, and the government moved to provide more help to organized labor. Legislation was enacted to regulate holding companies more strictly. And the Social Security system was created.

Major Programs of the Second New Deal (1935)

The Emergency Relief Appropriation Act
The National Youth Administration
The Rural Electrification Administration
The Social Security Act
The Banking Act of 1935

The Wheeler-Rayburn Public Utility Holding Company Act
The Resettlement Administration
The Revenue Act of 1935
The National Labor Relations Act (Wagner Act)

The Emergency Relief Appropriation Act

This law, passed in April, 1935, created the Works Progress Administration (WPA), headed by Harry Hopkins. WPA-sponsored work projects put some 3.5 million people to work during the following year. Continuing until 1943, the WPA spent some $11 billion and provided temporary employment for 8.5 million people.

Most WPA jobs involved manual labor, building and repairing roads, bridges, airports, parks, and public buildings. The WPA also sponsored projects which employed artists, writers, actors, and musicians.

Alongside the WPA, the Public Works Administration (PWA) continued its activities with increased funding. PWA projects constructed dams in the valleys of the Tennessee, Missouri, Columbia, and Colorado Rivers.

The National Youth Administration

Established in 1935, the National Youth Administration (NYA) provided opportunities for part-time employment for young people, aged 16 to 25, who were enrolled in high school and college. Designed to help students continue their education, the NYA aided some 4 million students up to the time it was disbanded in 1943.

The Rural Electrification Administration

The Rural Electrification Administration (REA), created in 1935, extended electric power lines into areas which previously had been without electricity. The REA assisted the establishment of electric cooperatives and made loans to these cooperatives so they could build facilities for the distribution of power. Bringing electric power into the countryside helped reduce some of the differences between rural and urban life.

The Social Security Act

The Social Security Act of 1935 proved to be one of the most enduring measures of the New Deal. Drafted under the direction of Secretary of Labor Frances Perkins, the Social Security Act established a program of government-sponsored old age pensions, unemployment compensation, and benefits to dependent persons.

A payroll tax paid by both employers and employees supported pensions paid to retired workers beginning at age 65. This tax also supported the payment of benefits to the dependent survivors of deceased workers.

A tax levied on employers supported a program of unemployment compensation administered by the states.

The Social Security system also provided aid to the states to assist crippled children and the blind and for maternity and infant care services.

The Banking Act of 1935

This law increased the authority of the Federal Reserve Board to buy and sell government securities on the open market. This strengthened the Federal Reserve Board's control of the monetary system.

The Wheeler-Rayburn Public Utility Holding Company Act

This 1935 law prohibited the pyramiding of holding companies by making it illegal for public utility holding companies to own other holding companies or to control operating companies that were engaged in different lines of business or widely separated in locations.

The Resettlement Administration

Established in 1935, the Resettlement Administration (RA)

aided farm families in moving to more fertile land by providing low interest loans for the purchase of land and equipment. The RA assisted about 800,000 families.

The Revenue Act of 1935

Denounced by the wealthy as the "soak the rich" tax law, this act provided for sharply increased taxes on large incomes and on corporate profits and estates.

The Wagner Act

In 1933, when Roosevelt became President, fewer than three million American workers belonged to labor unions. Section 7a of the National Industrial Recovery Act (NIRA) of 1933, which guaranteed workers the right to organize and to bargain collectively, encouraged the growth of labor unions. When the Supreme Court invalidated the NIRA, Congress adopted the National Labor Relations Act of 1935, better known as the Wagner Act. Sponsored by Senator Robert F. Wagner of New York, this law banned unfair labor practices. Such practices included employer discrimination against workers because of union membership or activity and employer refusal to bargain with any union selected by the workers in an election to represent them. The Wagner Act created the National Labor Relations Board to enforce the law's provisions. Hailed as the Magna Carta of labor, the Wagner Act was declared constitutional by the Supreme Court in the 1937 decision in the case of *NLRB v. Jones and Laughlin Steel Co.*

The Development of the Congress of Industrial Organizations

The Wagner Act encouraged the further growth of organized labor. The American Federation of Labor (AFL), headed by William Green, continued to emphasize the organization of workers primarily on the basis of the crafts in which they were engaged. A dissident minority in the AFL favored industry-wide organizing, which would bring both skilled and unskilled workers into the same union.

In 1935, these advocates of industrial unionism (as opposed to craft unionism) organized the Committee for Industrial Organization (CIO). Chief among the CIO's leaders were John L. Lewis of the United Mine Workers (UMW), David Dubinsky of the International Ladies Garment Workers Union (ILGWU), and Sidney Hillman of the Amalgamated Clothing Workers (ACW). The CIO set out to organize the millions of workers in still largely nonunionized industries such as automobiles, steel, rubber, and textiles.

In 1937, the AFL expelled the unions which supported the Committee for Industrial Organization. The following year, the CIO renamed itself the Congress of Industrial Organizations.

Some hard, fought battles were waged in the struggle to organize American industry. At the end of December, 1936, the United Automobile Workers (UAW), an affiliate of the CIO, launched a sit-down strike against General Motors (GM), which lasted until mid-February, 1937.

The GM workers occupied their factories, and the company could not break the strike as long as workers remained in the plants. Governor Frank Murphy of Michigan refused to use the National Guard to drive them out and urged GM to recognize the UAW. In February, 1937, GM gave way and Chrysler soon followed suit. Ford held out against the UAW until 1941, using its security force in the battle with the union.

In March, 1937, the United States Steel Corporation, the largest American steel producer, signed a contract with the United Steelworkers. So-called little steel, the smaller manufacturers resisted unionization until 1941.

In 1937, there were somewhat over 7 million unionized workers. By 1941, union membership reached 10.5 million.

Roosevelt's Critics

While some criticized the President for doing too much, others condemned him for not doing enough.

Dr. Francis Townsend, a physician from Long Beach, California, gained the support of many older Americans for his Old Age Revolving Pensions Plan, popularly known as the Townsend Plan. This plan proposed the enactment of a national sales tax. The money raised would provide every retired person 60 years of age or older with a pension of $200 a month, with the proviso that the recipient would have to spend the money within 30 days. The plan was designed both to aid the elderly and to encourage economic activity. Several million people joined Townsend Clubs which were organized to support the doctor's plan.

Father Charles Coughlin, the radio priest from Royal Oak, Michigan, demanded a living annual wage for Americans and denounced President Roosevelt, international bankers, Communists, and Jews. Coughlin organized his followers in the National Union for Social Justice.

The flamboyant Senator Huey P. Long of Louisiana promoted his Share the Wealth scheme which, he said, would make "every man a king." Long, known as the Kingfish, called for an outright grant of $5,000 to every family and a guaranteed annual income of $2,000. The money to support this program would come from heavy taxes imposed on the wealthy. The virtual dictator of Louisiana, Long won a large following. His effort to become a powerful national figure came to an end when he was assassinated in September, 1935.

Roosevelt's New Deal evoked much alarm and resentment from conservatives, both Republicans and Democrats. These conservatives charged that Roosevelt represented a threat to the American tradition of rugged individualism and free enterprise. Wealthy conservatives organized the American Liberty League and spent millions of dollars in an anti-New Deal campaign. Even Al Smith, whom Roosevelt had nominated for President in 1928, backed the Liberty League. Smith was evidently embittered because Roosevelt had succeeded where he had not.

The 1936 Election

As their presidential candidate, the Republicans nominated Alfred M. Landon, the Governor of Kansas. Landon charged Roosevelt with being a spendthrift who had wasted public money. The Republicans also contended that Roosevelt had usurped the powers of Congress. Acknowledging that the New Deal had made some positive accomplishments, the Republicans promised to continue the New Deal's worthwhile features and to administer them more effectively and with less cost than the Democrats had.

Roosevelt had earlier sought to win the cooperation and support of the leaders of business and industry for his plans to combat the depression. But they had turned against him and denounced the President as "a traitor to his class." Roosevelt now campaigned against what he called the "economic royalists" and promised to continue his New Deal program of relief, recovery, and reform.

James A. Farley, the Postmaster General and a key Democratic political operative, predicted that Roosevelt would carry every state except Maine and Vermont. Farley's prediction proved correct. Roosevelt won an overwhelming victory, polling over 60 percent of the popular vote. Almost 28 million Americans voted for Roosevelt, who won 523 electoral votes. The Democratic majority was based on the support of the Solid South, Catholics and Jews in the nation's urban centers, blacks, and many farmers.

Landon polled almost 17 million votes and won 8 electoral votes—those of Maine and Vermont.

The Democrats' majority in Congress was more overwhelming than ever. There were now only 19 Republican Senators, and the Republicans held only 107 seats in the House of Representatives.

Third party candidates fared poorly in 1936. The Socialist Norman Thomas won fewer than 200,000 votes, less than a quarter of the votes he had polled in 1932. William Lemke, a congressman from North Dakota, ran as the candidate of the radical anti-New Deal Union party. Backed by Townsend and Father Coughlin, Lemke won only 900,000 votes.

Roosevelt and Court Packing

During 1935 and 1936, the Supreme Court angered Roosevelt by declaring several New Deal acts unconstitutional, including the National Industrial Recovery Act and the Agricultural Adjustment Act.

Following his overwhelming reelection victory, Roosevelt took the offensive against the Supreme Court, which he regarded as reactionary and excessively rigid in its interpretation of the Constitution.

In February, 1937, the President proposed a plan to appoint additional federal judges, including one additional Supreme Court justice—up to a total of six—for every sitting justice who had reached the age of seventy.

Roosevelt's plan encountered heavy opposition in Congress, and his opponents charged him with an attempt at court packing. The plan was defeated.

While the President did not succeed in packing the court, New Deal legislation fared better in the Supreme Court during 1937. In March, 1937, the Supreme Court held, in the case of *West Coast Hotel Co. v. Parrish*, that it was constitutional for states to establish minimum wage laws. In an earlier case, the court had ruled that such laws were unconstitutional. In the case of *NLRB v. Jones and Laughlin Steel Co.*, decided two weeks later, the Supreme Court ruled that the Wagner Act was constitutional.

In May, 1937, one of the more conservative justices retired, and Roosevelt appointed his successor. The Supreme Court then decided two cases, both by votes of five to four, upholding the constitutionality of the Social Security law.

A series of retirements and deaths of Supreme Court justices between 1937 and 1939 made it possible to appoint four new justices who strongly supported the New Deal. By 1941, Roosevelt had appointed a total of seven justices. In that year, the moderate Chief Justice Charles Evans Hughes retired, and Roosevelt appointed Associate Justice Harlan F. Stone as his successor.

The Recession of 1937

By mid-1936, production, profits, and wages had made a considerable recovery, although unemployment remained high. This recovery resulted, at least in part, from government spending. Roosevelt had grown concerned about continuing budget deficits and the increasing national debt and had acted to tighten credit and reduce spending. In particular, funds for the WPA were cut.

By late 1936 to early 1937, an economic downturn became evident. Farm prices declined once again, and unemployment mounted as two million additional workers lost their jobs.

The federal government responded quickly, increasing expenditures to promote an economic upturn. By mid-1938, a considerable recovery had been accomplished. But the economy continued to show signs of weakness, and unemployment remained high until World War II restored prosperity to the nation.

Later New Deal Measures

1937	The Bankhead-Jones Farm Tenancy Act
1938	The Second Agricultural Adjustment Act
1938	The Fair Labor Standards Act
1938	The Food, Drug, and Cosmetic Act

The Bankhead-Jones Farm Tenancy Act

This law, passed in July, 1937, established the Farm Security Administration (FSA). Replacing the Resettlement Administration, the FSA provided tenants with loans to help them purchase the farms they were working. Operating with a small budget, the FSA had only limited impact. Its major effect was as a relief program which helped some poor white families survive difficult times.

The Second Agricultural Adjustment Act

In 1938, Congress approved a new Agricultural Adjustment Act. It resembled the Agricultural Adjustment Act of 1933, except that it did not provide for the processing tax which had been declared unconstitutional by the Supreme Court. Instead, payments made to farmers came from general treasury funds. The second Agricultural Adjustment Act represented another attempt to reduce agricultural surpluses in order to raise the prices of agricultural products and increase farm incomes. The act authorized the Secretary of Agriculture to establish acreage allotments for staple crops. Subsidies would be paid to farmers who planted soil-conservation crops rather than staple crops.

The act did not substantially reduce agricultural surpluses, and the subsidy program proved to be expensive. American agriculture remained troubled until World War II brought an increased demand for agricultural products, absorbing the surpluses produced by the nation's farmers and restoring prosperity to agriculture.

The Fair Labor Standards Act

Adopted in 1938, the Fair Labor Standards Act set a minimum wage of 25 cents per hour for workers engaged in interstate and foreign commerce and placed severe restrictions on work by children under the age of 16. The basic work week of 44 hours would be continued for three years and would then be reduced to 40 hours. The law also mandated time-and-a-half for overtime work. The Supreme Court upheld the constitutionality of the act in 1941.

The Food, Drug, and Cosmetic Act

This law, also adopted in 1938, expanded the provisions of the Pure Food and Drug Act enacted in 1906. The new law banned false or misleading advertising of covered products. In addition, it prohibited the misbranding of these products and required the listing of ingredients on product labels. The Federal Trade Commission (FTC) had the responsibility of enforcing this law.

The Elections of 1938

Despite congressional approval of this New Deal legislation, a coalition of conservative Democrats, mainly southerners, and Republicans blocked the enactment of other programs favored by the President. In response to this opposition, Roosevelt intervened in several Democratic primaries in 1938 in an attempt to defeat the renomination of anti-New Deal Democrats. All but one survived. This set back dealt a severe blow to the President's political prestige and provided a clear indication of a decline in his authority.

In the congressional elections of 1938, the Republicans gained 7 seats in the Senate and 76 in the House of Representatives, although the Democrats continued to hold a substantial majority of seats in both houses. Nevertheless, the coalition of conservative Democrats and Republicans dominated the Congress for most of the next quarter century.

By late 1938, the New Deal was clearly losing momentum. This resulted in part from the increased power of conservatives in Congress. It also resulted from the intensifying international crisis, which drew people's attention away from domestic problems.

Women and the New Deal

During the New Deal years, there was no active women's movement and little emphasis was placed on women's rights.

It was a common attitude that women who worked outside the home were depriving men of jobs that were properly theirs. A Gallup poll revealed that 82 percent of the people polled disapproved of working wives, and three-quarters of the women agreed with this opinion. Federal civil service regulations prohibited the employment of more than one member of a family. School districts frequently discriminated against women teachers who were married, refusing to employ married women and often firing women teachers who got married.

Relatively few women found jobs in the projects of the Civil Works Administration or the Public Works Administration. Employment on the construction projects of these agencies was regarded as unsuitable for women. Women were excluded entirely from the Civilian Conservation Corps, although women found more opportunities for employment on projects sponsored by the Works Progress Administration. By 1940, the percentage of women in the American work force was about what it had been in 1910. The increased demand for labor during World War II brought the first really dramatic increase in the number of women employed outside the home.

Women's wages continued to be lower than those of men. A number of National Recovery Administration codes approved lower wages for women. Both the Social Security Act and the Fair Labor Standards Act failed to cover areas, such as domestic service, which employed many women.

Nevertheless, women did make some gains during the New Deal years. Eleanor Roosevelt became the most active First Lady up to that point in American history. Mrs. Roosevelt traveled several hundred thousand miles, making thousands of speeches and public appearances. In 1935, she began to write a newspaper column, "My Day," which appeared in hundreds of newspapers. Mrs. Roosevelt was, in particular, a strong advocate for the oppressed, the poor, blacks, and other minorities.

President Roosevelt appointed Frances Perkins as Secretary of Labor, the first woman ever to hold a cabinet post. The President named women to diplomatic positions and to the federal judiciary, although no woman served on the Supreme Court.

In 1934, Hattie W. Caraway of Arkansas became the first woman ever elected to the United States Senate. The same year, six women won terms in the House of Representatives. While women could find opportunities in public service, law schools and medical schools continued to discriminate against women in their admissions policies.

Blacks and the New Deal

Although the Roosevelt administration never directly confronted the issue of racial inequality in American society, New Deal relief programs provided considerable assistance to black Americans during the depression, which hit blacks particularly hard. Southern sharecroppers and tenant farmers, who were mostly black, suffered from the catastrophic drop in the price of cotton from 18 cents to 6 cents a pound. For black workers in industry, the old saying "Last hired, first fired" proved to be true.

By 1933, more than half of urban blacks were unemployed, about double the rate of white unemployment.

The National Recovery Administration did little to help blacks. NRA codes generally permitted lower wages for black workers, and jobs held mainly by blacks were not frequently covered by NRA wage and hours agreements. For many blacks, NRA meant "Negroes Ruined Again." The Social Security Act and the Fair Labor Standards Act provided few benefits for blacks, since farmers and domestic workers were not covered by these laws. About two-thirds of black workers, in fact, worked in uncovered occupations.

New Deal relief programs, however, did provide assistance to about 40 percent of the country's black population. Two hundred thousand black young men served in the Civilian Conservation Corps. They were placed in segregated units. Thousands more young blacks received help from the National Youth Administration to continue their education. By 1939, over a million blacks had found employment on projects of the Works Progress Administration.

Eleanor Roosevelt was a strong advocate of racial equality and worked closely with Mary McLeod Bethune, the president of the National Council of Negro Women, in bringing more attention to the problems of black Americans. Bethune became the head of the Division of Negro Affairs of the National Youth Administration and headed the so-called black cabinet, composed of blacks who held important positions in the Roosevelt administration. The black cabinet received considerable encouragement and support from Mrs. Roosevelt in its efforts to promote the interests of blacks.

President Roosevelt appointed a number of blacks to second-level positions in a number of agencies, but none were named to the cabinet or the Supreme Court. While the President denounced lynching, he refused to support the enactment of a federal antilynching law, nor would he endorse legislation to eliminate the poll tax. Neither of these proposals became law. Roosevelt was reluctant to get directly involved in civil rights efforts of this nature because he was afraid of antagonizing his white southern supporters.

In 1939, the Daughters of the American Revolution refused to permit a concert by the black contralto, Marian Anderson, to be held in the DAR's Constitution Hall in Washington. President Roosevelt responded to this refusal by arranging for Secretary of the Interior Harold Ickes to invite Miss Anderson to present an Easter Sunday concert at the Lincoln Memorial. About 75,000 people attended. Mrs. Roosevelt protested the DAR's action by publicly resigning from the organization.

While the record of the New Deal was clearly mixed, Roosevelt did more for the cause of American blacks than any President since Lincoln. Blacks responded by supporting Roosevelt and the Democrats, abandoning their traditional ties to the Republican party. In 1936, about three-quarters of the black voters supported Roosevelt.

Indians and the New Deal

In the late 1920s, government investigations revealed widespread official corruption in the administration of the Dawes Severalty Act of 1887. This law had provided for the break up of Indian tribal lands into individual farms.

When Roosevelt became President, he appointed John Collier, a social worker from Georgia and an ardent advocate of Indian rights, to the position of Commissioner of the Bureau of Indian Affairs. Collier encouraged instruction in Indian languages and culture in reservation schools and recognized the Indians' right to perform their traditional religious ceremonies. He also promoted the Indians' production of handicrafts, such as jewelry and blankets, in order to increase their incomes.

In the Wheeler-Howard Act of 1934, the government abandoned the policy established in the Dawes Severalty Act. Instead of breaking up tribal lands, this law emphasized tribal unity and enabled the Indian tribes to reassert tribal control over their lands. The law also provided aid for the development of tribal self-sufficiency, loans for Indian-owned businesses, and support for education.

Mexican-Americans and the New Deal

Mexican-Americans received few benefits from the New Deal. Most Mexican-Americans worked as migrant agricultural laborers on cotton, vegetable, and fruit farms in California and the Southwest. In the California fields, wages dropped from 35 cents to 14 cents an hour by 1933. The migrant workers were seldom reached by New Deal programs, although the Works Progress Administration did provide employment for some. After 1937, however, WPA jobs could not be held by aliens.

When dust bowl conditions resulting from an extended drought in the Great Plains during the mid-1930s drove many farmers westward, competition for migrant labor jobs grew. The Roosevelt administration attempted to reduce the size of the work force by restricting further immigration from Mexico, denying entry to any person found "likely to become a public charge." Many Mexican-Americans were forced to return to Mexico. It proved to be less expensive to deport them than it was to provide them with support from relief programs.

Coming only a few months following Herbert Hoover's inauguration in March, 1929, the stock market crash in October signaled the beginning of the Great Depression. Hoover believed that the economy was basically sound and hoped that action undertaken by business leaders would lead to a quick recovery. When it became clear that private activity would not suffice, he supported a limited program of action by the federal government. As the depression deepened, the American people chose a new leader in 1932.

When Franklin D. Roosevelt took the oath of office in 1933, he confronted an American system in danger of collapse. Roosevelt moved vigorously to deal with the crisis within the framework of the Constitution and the American political tradition, without a revolutionary upheaval.

The New Deal did not succeed in completely overcoming the Great Depression. While government programs put millions of Americans to work, 10 million people were still unemployed in 1938. Government spending seemed to offer the only way to promote recovery and provide jobs. Paying federal subsidies to farmers seemed to be the only way to prevent a virtual collapse of American agriculture.

The New Deal did succeed in initiating some important reforms, including the Social Security system, maximum hours and minimum wage legislation, and the recognition of labor's right to organize and bargain collectively.

The New Deal also did much to revive a spirit of confidence and hope among the American people. And the New Deal established powerful precedents for an expanding role for the federal government in the life of the nation.

Recommended Reading

Frederick Lewis Allen, *Since Yesterday: The Nineteen-Thirties in America* (1940).

Leonard Baker, *Back to Back: The Duel Between FDR and the Supreme Court* (1967).

Irving Bernstein, *The Turbulent Years: A History of the American Worker, 1933–1941* (1970).

Alan Brinkley, *Voices of Protest: Huey Long, Father Coughlin, and the Great Depression* (1982).

James MacGregor Burns, *Roosevelt: The Lion and the Fox* (1956).

Paul K. Conkin, *The New Deal* (2nd ed., 1975).

Sidney Fine, *Sit-Down: The General Motors Strike of 1936–1937* (1969).

Frank Freidel, *Franklin D. Roosevelt* (4 vols., 1952–73).

Frank Freidel, *F.D.R. and the South* (1965).

Walter Galenson, *The C.I.O. Challenge to the A. F. L.: A History of the American Labor Movement, 1935–1941* (1960).

John A. Garraty, *The Great Depression* (1986).

Otis L. Graham, Jr., *An Encore for Reform: The Old Progressives and the New Deal* (1967).

Josep P. Lash, *Eleanor and Franklin: The Story of Their Relationship* (1971).

William E. Leuchtenberg, *Franklin D. Roosevelt and the New Deal, 1932–1940* (1963).

Jane DeHart Mathews, *The Federal Theatre, 1935–1939: Plays, Relief, and Politics* (1967).

Donald R. McCoy, *Angry Voices: Left of Center Politics in the New Deal Era* (1958).

George McJimsey, *Harry Hopkins: Ally of the Poor and Defender of Democracy* (1987).

Raymond Moley, *After Seven Years* (1939).

James T. Patterson, *Congressional Conservatism and the New Deal: The Growth of the Conservative Coalition in Congress, 1933–1939* (1967).

James T. Patterson, *The New Deal and the States: Federalism in Transition* (1969).

Arthur M. Schlesinger, Jr., *The Age of Roosevelt* (3 vols., 1957–60).

Studs Terkel, *Hard Times: An Oral History of the Great Depression* (1970).

Charles J. Tull, *Father Coughlin and the New Deal* (1965).

Susan Ware, *Beyond Suffrage: Women in the New Deal* (1981).

T. Harry Williams, *Huey Long* (1969).

Raymond Wolters, *Negroes and the Great Depression: The Problem of Economic Recovery* (1970).

CHAPTER 11

American Foreign Relations Between Two World Wars, 1920–1941

Time Line

1921–1922	The Washington Conference seeks to achieve naval arms limitation and political stability in the Pacific
1923	France occupies the Ruhr
1924	The Dawes Plan for German reparations wins approval
1928	The Kellogg-Briand Pact outlaws war

1929	The Young Plan reduces German reparations
1931	Hoover proposes a one-year moratorium on intergovernmental payments
	Japanese forces invade Manchuria
1933	Roosevelt becomes President
	Hitler comes to power in Germany
	The United States launches the Good Neighbor policy
	The United States recognizes the Soviet Union
	The London Economic Conference fails to reach agreement on the international stabilization of currency
1934	The United States inaugurates the reciprocal trade policy
1935	Germany introduces military conscription
	Italy invades Ethiopia
	Congress adopts the First Neutrality Act
1936	Hitler remilitarizes the Rhineland
	The Spanish Civil War begins
	Hitler and Mussolini form the Rome-Berlin Axis
	Congress adopts the Second Neutrality Act
	The Pan-American Union begins efforts to promote western hemisphere collective security

1937	Japan attacks China
	Germany, Italy, and Japan sign the Anti-Comintern Pact
	Roosevelt calls for quarantining the aggressors
	Congress adopts the Third Neutrality Act
1938	Germany annexes Austria
	The Munich Conference awards the Sudetenland to Germany
1939	Germany and the Soviet Union sign a Non-Aggression Pact
	Germany invades Poland; World War II begins in Europe
1940	The America First Committee promotes American isolationism
	Roosevelt wins a third term as President
	Congress enacts a peacetime draft
1941	Congress passes the Lend-Lease Act
	Germany invades the Soviet Union
	Japan attacks Pearl Harbor

Following World War I, the United States sought to reduce its involvement in world affairs. But American isolationism was far from complete. The United States continued to play its traditionally active role in Latin America and remained committed to the promotion of political stability in East Asia and the maintenance of the economic Open Door policy in China. American financial and economic interests led to an ongoing involvement in European affairs.

During the depression years of the 1930s, Americans became increasingly more isolationist in their attitudes as they focused their attention on domestic problems. The United States recognized the Soviet Union in 1933, and the Good Neighbor policy of the Roosevelt administration improved relations between the United States and Latin America. At the same time, the United States strove to avoid entanglement in the developing conflicts in Europe and Asia which resulted from the aggressive policies of Germany, Italy, and Japan. In the end, the United States could not avoid involvement. American aid, short of war with Great Britain, brought the United States to the brink of war with Germany. And American efforts to restrain Japanese expansion in Asia led to Japan's decision to attack Pearl Harbor.

War Debts and Reparations

The tangled problem of war debts and reparations proved to be one of the most troubling issues in American foreign relations in the years following World War I.

In 1914, when war broke out in Europe, the United States had been a debtor nation, owing $2 billion to other countries. By the early 1920s, the United States was a creditor nation, owed $16 billion by others. During the war, the United States had lent some $10 billion to its allies. The United States wanted the debt paid, while the Allies called on Washington to write off the debt as a cost of the war. When the United States continued to insist on repayment, the Allies began to speak of America as "Uncle Shylock."

Under the terms of the Treaty of Versailles, Germany was

obliged to pay approximately $33 billion in reparations to the French and other Allies as compensation for damage caused by the war. The Allies expected to use the reparations received from Germany to pay their debt to the United States. Although the American government refused to concede any connection between war debts and reparations, the two issues were obviously related.

By 1923, the Germans had fallen behind in their reparations payments. In response, the French occupied the industrialized Ruhr valley of western Germany. If the Germans would not pay what they owed, the French were prepared to take it. The Germans now encouraged a catastrophic inflation of their currency, which threw Germany into financial and economic chaos.

Some urged that the only way out of the impasse was a general cancellation, or at least a substantial reduction, of both reparations and war debts. President Calvin Coolidge reacted to this proposal by remarking: "They hired the money, didn't they? Let them pay it."

In 1924, a commission headed by Charles G. Dawes, a Chicago banker, produced a plan to ease the reparations crisis. The Dawes Plan provided for lower reparations payments over a longer period of time, without reducing Germany's total reparations obligation. In addition, the Dawes Plan provided for more private American loans to Germany to promote that country's economic recovery.

For the next several years, American bankers lent money to Germany, the Germans paid their reparations on schedule, and the Allies made payments on their war debt to the United States.

In 1929, a commission headed by the American industrialist Owen D. Young produced a new reparations plan. The Young Plan reduced Germany's total reparations debt to $8 billion and extended the term for its payment.

The depression brought an end to the circuit flow of capital. American loans to Germany ceased, the Germans stopped paying reparations, and the Allies fell behind in their debt repayments to the United States. In 1931, President Hoover proposed a one-year moratorium on all intergovernmental payments. Following the expiration of the moratorium in 1932, a meeting at Lausanne, Switzerland, agreed to a virtual cancellation of German reparations. While Germany ceased all reparations payments, the United States refused to cancel the Allied war debts. During 1932, several nations, including France, failed to make any debt payments to the United States. After 1932, Great Britain paid only a minimal amount. Only Finland paid its debt to the United States in full. The Allies' default on the debts owed to the United States helped intensify the isolationist attitudes of Americans during the depression years.

American Relations with the League of Nations and the World Court

While the United States never joined the League of Nations, American observers did attend meetings at the League head-quarters in Geneva, Switzerland, and elsewhere dealing with such matters as cultural affairs, economic relations, drug trafficking, public health, and prostitution.

During the 1920s, both Presidents Coolidge and Hoover endorsed American membership in the World Court, which met in The Hague, the Dutch capital. In 1926, the Senate approved U.S. membership, but added five reservations. The members of the World Court rejected the American reservation regarding advisory opinions. In 1929, Hoover renewed efforts to join the World Court, but he failed to win Senate approval for the measure.

The Kellogg-Briand Pact

The popular movement to outlaw war reached a culmination in the signing of the Kellogg-Briand Pact of 1928, officially known as the Pact of Paris. It bore the names of Frank B. Kellogg, the Secretary of State in the Coolidge administration, and French Foreign Minister Aristide Briand. Those signing the pact renounced war as an instrument of national policy. There was no ban on defensive wars, and the pact did not contain any provisions for action to be taken against violators. Some 62 nations ultimately ratified the pact.

The United States and Latin America

The United States had traditionally exercised considerable political and economic domination over Latin America. Following World War I, the U.S. began to move away from the interventionist policies carried out by the administrations of Theodore Roosevelt, Taft, and Wilson. At the same time, the United States wished to retain a powerful political influence in Latin America and to expand its trade and investment in the area.

American marines were withdrawn from the Dominican Republic in 1924. In the same year, the marines left Nicaragua, ending an intervention that began in 1909. However, the outbreak of a civil war led to a new American intervention in Nicaragua in 1926; the marines remained until 1933.

In December, 1928, Undersecretary of State J. Reuben Clark drafted a statement repudiating the Roosevelt Corollary to the Monroe Doctrine. According to the Clark Memorandum, the Monroe Doctrine did not give the United States the right to intervene in the domestic affairs of Latin American countries, although the memorandum did repeat the traditional U.S. claim to a right to protect endangered American lives and property. American policy toward Latin America in the 1920s thus revealed that while the United States wanted to move away from interventionism, it found it difficult to abandon that approach entirely.

By the time Franklin D. Roosevelt became President in 1933,

American relations with Latin America showed some signs of improvement. Roosevelt wanted to continue that improvement and in his inaugural address called for a Good Neighbor policy.

At the Pan-American Conference held in Montevideo, Uruguay, in December, 1933, Secretary of State Cordell Hull officially committed the United States to a policy of nonintervention in the internal affairs of Latin American states. American marines left Nicaragua in 1933, and the marines pulled out of Haiti in 1934, ending an intervention that had begun in 1915.

In 1934, the United States renounced the Platt Amendment, which had given the U.S. the right to intervene in Cuba, although the U.S. retained its naval base at Guantanamo Bay.

Under the terms of a treaty negotiated with Panama in 1936, the United States reduced its control over that country and agreed to an increase in Panama's share of the income from the Panama Canal. Controversy over this treaty delayed its ratification by the Senate until 1939.

In 1938, a crisis developed when the revolutionary government of Mexico nationalized foreign-owned property, including oil resources owned by American companies. Roosevelt resisted demands for intervention made by American investors. Negotiations produced a settlement on terms favorable to Mexico in 1941.

As the international situation became more unsettled, Roosevelt began to push for collective security agreements among the states of the western hemisphere. At the Pan-American Conference held in Buenos Aires, Argentina, in 1936, the American states agreed to consult in the event an action, taken by a non-American state, endangered the maintenance of peace in the Americas.

The Pan-American Conference held in Lima, Peru, in 1938 approved the Declaration of Lima. In this declaration, the American republics committed themselves to resist "all foreign intervention or activities that may threaten them."

Subsequent Pan-American conferences resulted in further steps toward collective security. In the Declaration of Panama of 1939, the American states established a security zone around the Western Hemisphere, south of Canada, and warned warring states to refrain from naval action in this area.

The Act of Havana of 1940 declared that an act of aggression committed against one American republic would be regarded as an attack on all of them. In addition, the act authorized the American states, acting individually or collectively, to occupy any European possession in the Western Hemisphere which was threatened by aggression. This was intended to keep the Germans from moving into European colonies in the New World.

By promoting inter-American collective security, Roosevelt was, in effect, internationalizing the Monroe Doctrine. The rights and responsibilities that the United States had once claimed for itself were now to be shared by the American republics collectively.

The Reciprocal Trade Policy

The New Deal's reciprocal trade policy was closely related to Roosevelt's Good Neighbor policy, since the President was anxious to increase trade with Latin America.

The Trade Agreements Act, passed in 1934, authorized the President to reduce tariff rates by as much as 50 percent if the trading partner involved responded with similar tariff reductions. These reciprocal trade agreements would become effective without Senate ratification.

By the end of 1939, the United States had negotiated reciprocal trade agreements with 21 countries, most of them in Latin America. During these years, America's foreign trade registered a substantial increase.

Relations with the Soviet Union

In the years following the Bolshevik Revolution of 1917, the United States refused to establish diplomatic relations with the Soviet government. Despite the absence of formal relations, in the early 1920s, then-Secretary of Commerce Herbert Hoover organized a famine relief program to aid Soviet Russia. In addition, a number of American firms entered into trade and technical assistance agreements with the Soviets during the 1920s.

During these years, the Soviet government became more firmly established and won recognition from other major world powers, despite their opposition to Communism.

In late 1933, the Roosevelt administration established full diplomatic relations with Moscow. The Soviets promised to stop revolutionary propaganda in the United States and agreed to a future discussion of the tsarist debts which the Soviets had repudiated. In fact, Soviet revolutionary propaganda did not cease, and the issue of the tsarist debts was never resolved.

While the two countries now exchanged ambassadors, relations between Moscow and Washington remained decidedly cool. The increase in U.S.-Soviet trade, which many Americans hoped would help ease the impact of the depression, did not materialize.

The United States and Asia

During the period following World War I, tension increased between the United States and Japan. While Japan was developing its industry, the country lacked essential raw materials which it hoped to acquire by expanding its power on the Asian mainland. The prospect of Japanese expansion challenged the American-sponsored Open Door policy in China. Ultimately, the United States would confront the choice of either abandoning its support of China or resisting Japan's expansion.

The Washington Conference of 1921–22 sought to find a settlement of the situation in Asia. The American government invited countries with interests in East Asia to attend. The conference had two major objectives: to reach a political settlement and to end the developing naval rivalry between the United States and Japan.

In the past, Great Britain had been the world's leading naval power. It now appeared, however, that both the United States and Japan would soon overtake Britain. The considerable cost of naval expansion caused the major naval powers to seek limits to the naval arms race.

When the conference opened, Secretary of State Charles Evans Hughes proposed a comprehensive plan for naval arms limitation. The Five Power Treaty, signed in 1922, embodied much of Hughes' proposal. This treaty limited capital ships (battleships) in a tonnage ratio of 5–5–3 for Great Britain, the United States, and Japan and 1.67–1.67 for France and Italy. Japan agreed to accept a lower tonnage ratio in return for American and British pledges not to fortify their bases in the Pacific, including the Philippines and Singapore. The Five Power Treaty slowed down the naval race, even though it did not place any limits on lesser categories of ships.

The Washington Conference produced two other treaties. In the Four Power Treaty of 1922, which replaced the Anglo-Japanese Alliance of 1902, the United States, Great Britain, France, and Japan promised to maintain the status quo in the Pacific. The Nine Power Treaty of 1922 contained a pledge to respect China's sovereignty and territorial integrity and to maintain the economic Open Door policy in China.

The agreements reached in 1922 endured until 1931, when Japanese forces overran Manchuria. At this point, the attention of Americans was focused on the depression, and the U.S. government offered only a weak response to Japan's aggression. In January, 1932, Henry L. Stimson, Hoover's Secretary of State, declared that the United States would not recognize any territorial acquisitions which resulted from aggression. Neither this Stimson Doctrine nor the League of Nation's condemnation of Japan as an aggressor deterred the Japanese. Japan simply withdrew from the League and proceeded to reorganize Manchuria as the Japanese-controlled puppet state of Manchukuo. Many observers later regarded the Japanese conquest of Manchuria as the opening round of World War II.

The Roosevelt Administration and the Philippines

The depression served to make Americans more aware of the Philippines as a financial liability. Not only was it costly to administer the Philippines, but American producers of sugar and other products were growing more concerned about competition from the Philippines. American labor leaders wanted to keep Filipinos out of the American labor market in a time of heavy unemployment.

In 1934, Congress adopted the Tydings-McDuffie Act, providing for Philippine independence after a ten-year period of political and economic preparation. The Philippines actually became independent on July 4, 1946, following World War II.

The London Economic Conference

During the depression years of the 1930s, the United States sought more than ever to focus on its own economic and social problems and to avoid international complications.

In the summer of 1933, some 66 nations gathered at the London Economic Conference. The conference hoped to initiate a coordinated international effort to overcome the depression. In particular, it hoped to achieve monetary stabilization in order to provide a solid foundation for economic recovery. While the United States had seemed prepared to support this effort, President Roosevelt concluded that an international agreement on currency stabilization would hinder his efforts to promote an

American economic recovery. He refused to commit the United States to currency stabilization, and the London Economic Conference ended with no agreement.

The Rise of the Aggressors

The international crises of the 1930s resulted primarily from the actions of three discontented nations: Germany, Italy, and Japan.

In Germany, Adolf Hitler came to power in January, 1933, and proceeded quickly to establish his National Socialist (Nazi) dictatorship. At first, the Nazi Führer pursued a cautious foreign policy, since Germany was not yet strong enough militarily to take risks. In late 1933, Hitler pulled Germany out of the Disarmament Conference and the League of Nations, charging that Germany was not being treated as an equal. He declared his support of the maintenance of peace and pledged his cooperation once Germany received equal treatment.

By 1935, Hitler was becoming more daring. He openly violated the Treaty of Versailles by reintroducing military conscription and announcing that Germany had an air force. A year later, in March, 1936, Hitler sent German forces into the demilitarized Rhineland in western Germany, once again violating the Treaty of Versailles. The Führer was proved correct in his belief that the demoralized French and British would not oppose his actions with force.

In Italy, the Fascist dictator Benito Mussolini had come to power in 1922. By the mid-1930s, Mussolini began to pursue a more actively aggressive policy. In 1935, Italy invaded Ethiopia in East Africa. Ethiopia's Emperor Haile Selassie appealed to the League of Nations, which condemned Italy as an aggressor. The League failed, however, to place an embargo on the sale of oil to Italy and thus did little to halt Italy's conquest of Ethiopia. Mussolini responded to the League's condemnation by pulling

Italy out of the international organization. In 1936, the Italian Duce joined with Hitler to create the Rome-Berlin Axis.

In Asia, Japan continued the expansionist course it had begun with the seizure of Manchuria in 1931. In 1934, the Japanese announced that they would no longer observe the naval limitations imposed by the Five Power Treaty of 1922. The following year, Japan's delegates walked out of the London Naval Disarmament Conference of 1935, ending all hopes for achieving any further agreements on the limitation of naval arms. In 1937, Japan began an undeclared war against China that did not end until August, 1945.

In Europe, Great Britain and France seemed incapable of developing an effective counterforce to the aggressive policies of Germany and Italy. In Asia, China was too weak to overcome the Japanese threat.

In 1937, Germany, Italy, and Japan signed the Anti-Comintern Pact, creating what was called the Rome-Berlin-Tokyo Axis. While the pact was officially directed against the Soviet Union, it actually presented a much broader threat.

American Isolationism

As the international situation worsened, Americans became determined to do everything in their power to avoid becoming embroiled in another war.

In April, 1934, Congress passed the Johnson Debt Default Act which banned any further American loans to countries which had defaulted on the repayment of debts to American lenders.

Also in 1934, Senator Gerald P. Nye, a Republican from North Dakota, became chairman of a special Senate committee which conducted a two-year investigation of the role munitions makers played in America's entry into the First World War. The Nye Committee produced evidence revealing the munitions' makers huge profits. With little evidence to support its conclusion, the committee also charged that munitions makers and bankers had formed a conspiracy to promote American intervention in the war so they could make more money.

The Neutrality Acts

The findings of the Nye Committee helped encourage the adoption of neutrality legislation.

The First Neutrality Act, adopted in August, 1935, banned the sale of American arms to warring nations and authorized the President to warn Americans not to sail on ships belonging to belligerent powers.

The Second Neutrality Act, passed in February, 1936, extended the 1935 act and banned American loans to warring nations.

The Third Neutrality Act, adopted in May, 1937, retained the bans on the loans and the sale of arms and authorized the President to list nonmilitary goods which belligerents would have to pay cash for on delivery. This act also banned travel by Americans on ships of warring countries.

President Roosevelt signed the neutrality acts although he privately shared the view of critics who argued that these laws prevented the American government from making any distinctions between aggressor states and their victims.

The United States and the Spanish Civil War

In July, 1936, a civil war broke out in Spain, as Nationalist rebels, led by General Francisco Franco, attempted to overthrow the left-wing government of the Spanish republic. Great Britain and France advocated a policy of nonintervention by foreign powers. Nevertheless, Hitler and Mussolini aided the Nationalists, while the Soviet Union provided help to the Loyalists, as the republican government was known.

The United States continued to maintain diplomatic relations with the Loyalist government. Traditional American practice would have permitted the Spanish government to purchase arms from the United States, since the neutrality acts did not apply to civil wars. In January, 1937, however, Congress banned the sale of arms to either side in Spain. Like Great Britain and France, the United States wished to avoid any direct involvement in the Spanish conflict.

Franco and the Nationalists finally succeeded in defeating the Loyalists in the spring of 1939. The failure of the democracies to support the Loyalist cause provided Hitler and Mussolini with further evidence that they would go to extreme lengths to avoid involvement in war. This encouraged the European dictators in their aggressive course.

President Roosevelt and the Intensifying International Crisis

While President Roosevelt had doubts about the wisdom of the neutrality acts, he signed them without protest. On occasion, the President attempted to restrict their impact.

When Japan invaded China in 1937, the President did not invoke the Third Neutrality Act, since the so-called China Incident was not an officially declared war. China was able to continue to buy arms in the United States.

Concerned about the aggressive actions of Germany, Italy, and Japan, Roosevelt, in an October, 1937, address, called for "positive endeavors" to "quarantine the aggressors." When this speech evoked strong protests from isolationists, the President insisted that he did not intend to propose a repeal of the neutrality acts. It was evident that Roosevelt, who was a realistic politician, recognized the strength of isolationist sentiment. Any attempt to challenge it directly at this point would fail, he believed, and an acrimonious national debate over isolationism might well endanger the enactment of additional New Deal programs.

The *Panay* Incident

In December, 1937, Japanese aircraft sank the *Panay*, an American gunboat, in the Yangtze River of China. Two Americans were killed and 30 were wounded. To the relief of Americans, the crisis passed when Japan apologized and offered to pay compensation.

The Coming of War in Europe

In March, 1938, Hitler annexed Austria, the land of his birth. By summer, Hitler was demanding possession of the Sudetenland, an area of Czechoslovakia with a large German-speaking population. Hitler insisted that the Sudetenland was the last territorial demand he had to make in Europe.

British Prime Minister Neville Chamberlain and French Premier Edouard Daladier met with Hitler and Mussolini at the Munich Conference in September, 1938. The four leaders agreed that Czechoslovakia should cede the Sudetenland to Germany.

The Anglo-French policy at Munich is known as appeasement. The supporters of appeasement believed that if Hitler's desires were satisfied, he would become a reasonable and cooperative statesman. The error of appeasement was that Hitler could not be satisfied. Acceding to one of his demands would serve only to encourage him to make additional demands.

In March, 1939, Hitler destroyed what was left of Czechoslovakia. Recognizing that Hitler could not be trusted, Great Britain and France now guaranteed Poland, promising to aid that country in the event of a German attack.

During the summer of 1939, the British and French attempted to get the Soviet Union to agree to a mutual defense treaty. Negotiations conducted at the same time by the Soviets and Germans resulted in the signing of the Nazi-Soviet Non-Aggression Pact on August 23, 1939. In exchange for Soviet neutrality, Germany conceded the Soviets a large sphere of influence in Eastern Europe. Joseph Stalin, the Soviet dictator, evidently hoped that Hitler and the Western democracies would exhaust one another in war, leaving him the master of Europe.

On September 1, 1939, Germany invaded Poland. On September 3, Great Britain and France went to war. Within three weeks, the Nazi Blitzkrieg (lightning war) smashed Poland. While the Germans occupied western Poland, the Soviets annexed the eastern half of the country.

The Revision of the Neutrality Act

When the European war began, President Roosevelt proclaimed American neutrality. At the same time, the President and the great majority of the American people were sympathetic to the Allies, but most Americans continued to hope that the United States could remain at peace.

In September, 1939, two weeks after the outbreak of the European war, Roosevelt called Congress into special session and proposed a revision of the Third Neutrality Act, passed in 1937. The President's proposal called for a repeal of the embargo on the sale of arms and placing all trade with belligerents on a cash-and-carry basis. This would require purchasers to pay for American arms and other goods in cash and then to transport them on their own ships. Since Great Britain and France controlled the North Atlantic, this proposal favored them. The Neutrality Act of 1939 won congressional approval in November.

The War in Europe (1939–40)

Following the German defeat of Poland, the European front remained quiet during the so-called Phony War in the winter of 1939–40.

In November, 1939, however, the Soviets attacked Finland,

beginning the Winter War. Americans sympathized with Finland, the only European country which had repaid in full its debt to the United States. Congress voted $30 million in nonmilitary aid to Finland. Although the Finns offered vigorous resistance, by March, 1940, they had to admit defeat. The Soviets annexed some Finnish territory near Leningrad. Also during the spring of 1940, the Soviets annexed the three Baltic republics of Estonia, Latvia, and Lithuania and seized the province of Bessarabia from Romania.

In the West, the Phony War ended in April 1940, when the Germans overran Denmark and Norway. Sweden, however, succeeded in remaining neutral. On May 10, the Germans launched their long-awaited assault on western Europe. Luxembourg was overrun immediately. The Netherlands fell after five days. At the end of May, Belgium surrendered. On June 22, France signed an armistice with Germany. As France stood on the brink of defeat, Mussolini joined his ally Hitler in the war on June 10.

After the fall of France, Great Britain stood alone in the struggle against Hitler's Germany. If Britain fell, the Germans might gain control of the British navy. Hitler would then be able to move against the Western Hemisphere.

Aid Short of War

President Roosevelt believed that the United States should provide the British with aid, while at the same time attempting to avoid direct American involvement in the war. In June, 1940, in an effort to win broader national support, Roosevelt named two Republicans to his cabinet. Henry L. Stimson became Secretary of War, and Frank Knox became Secretary of the Navy.

In September, 1940, Roosevelt made the destroyers-for-bases deal. The President gave 50 old American destroyers to the British in exchange for leases which allowed the United

German Conquests, 1939–1940

States to build naval and air bases in eight British possessions in the Western Hemisphere, reaching from Newfoundland to British Guiana in South America.

Also in September, 1940, Congress approved the Selective Service and Training Act (also known as the Burke-Wadsworth Act). This established the first peacetime draft in American history, providing for the training of 1.2 million troops each year, along with 800,000 reservists.

The America First Committee

In mid-1940, isolationist opponents of the President's policy established the America First Committee. Its diverse group of leaders included Robert E. Wood, a Sears, Roebuck executive; Senator Robert A. Taft, a conservative Republican from Ohio; Norman Thomas, the leader of the American Socialist party; and Colonel Charles A. Lindbergh, the greatest American hero of the interwar years who had made the first solo transatlantic flight, from New York to Paris, in 1927. The America First Committee hoped to mobilize American opinion against Roosevelt's policy of aid short of war.

The White Committee

Supporters of the President's policy organized the Committee to Defend America By Aiding the Allies. Led by William Allen White, a Republican newspaper editor from Emporia, Kansas, the group became known as the White Committee. These interventionists rejected the argument of the isolationists that the war in Europe would have no impact on the security of the United States.

The 1940 Election

In 1940, Roosevelt ran for an unprecedented third term as

President. He replaced Vice President John Nance Garner with Secretary of Agriculture Henry A. Wallace as his running mate.

Senator Taft of Ohio and Thomas E. Dewey, a successful New York prosecutor, were the leading candidates for the Republican presidential nomination. However, the Republican national convention gave the nomination to Wendell L. Willkie, a businessman and former Democrat.

Willkie supported most of Roosevelt's New Deal program, although he criticized the Democratic administration for its extravagance and inefficiency and condemned the President for violating tradition and seeking a third term. Willkie agreed with Roosevelt's efforts to strengthen national defense and supported aid to Great Britain.

Although Willkie lost the election, he polled more popular votes than any Republican presidential candidate up to that point in American history. Roosevelt won over 27 million popular votes and 449 electoral votes, while Willkie polled over 22 million popular votes and took 82 electoral votes.

The Lend-Lease Act

By early 1941, Great Britain was running short of money to buy arms from America. Roosevelt wished to avoid the development of a future controversy over the repayment of American debts like the one which had done so much to poison the United States' relations with its World War I allies. The President proposed a program to lend or lease American arms to countries fighting against aggression, declaring that the United States should become an "arsenal of democracy." Following an intense national debate, Congress approved the Lend-Lease Act in March, 1941, appropriating $7 billion to support the program. During World War II, the United States provided $50 billion in lend-lease aid to its allies. The British received over $31 billion of the total.

The German Invasion of the Soviet Union

World War II entered a new stage on June 22, 1941, when Hitler, by invading the Soviet Union, began the war he had always wanted to fight. Several months later, the United States agreed to provide $1 billion in lend-lease aid to the Soviets. During the war, the Soviet Union received $11 billion in American assistance.

The Atlantic Charter

In August 1941, President Roosevelt met with British Prime Minister Winston Churchill in Argentia Bay, off the coast of Newfoundland. This was the first meeting of the two wartime leaders. The meeting produced the Atlantic Charter, which expressed the plans and hopes of the Americans and British for the postwar world. The Atlantic Charter endorsed the principle of freedom of the seas and opposed imperialist annexations. It supported the principle of national self-determination, declaring that there should be no territorial changes against the wishes of the people involved and endorsing the right of people to choose their own governments. The Atlantic Charter called for international economic cooperation and greater freedom of trade. It called for the disarmament of the aggressor nations and for the creation of a new international association to replace the League of Nations.

On January 1, 1942, 42 nations signed the Declaration of the United Nations, endorsing the principles set forth in the Atlantic Charter.

The Undeclared War

The Lend-Lease Act enabled the British to acquire American arms without having to pay cash for them. But the British still had to transport these arms across the submarine-infested Atlantic Ocean.

During the summer of 1941, ships of the American navy began to convoy British merchant vessels in the North Atlantic. This unneutral act soon led to an undeclared naval war between Germany and the United States.

On September 4, 1941, a German submarine attacked the American destroyer *Greer*, which suffered no damage. Roosevelt responded to this attack by ordering American destroyers to open fire on German submarines on sight.

On October 17, a German submarine damaged the destroyer *Kearney*, killing 11 Americans. On October 30, another German submarine sank the destroyer *Reuben James*, with the loss of about 100 lives.

In November, 1941, Congress approved an amendment of the Neutrality Act of 1939, authorizing the arming of American merchant ships and permitting them to enter combat zones carrying arms being shipped to Great Britain.

As the undeclared war in the North Atlantic intensified, it seemed likely that formal declarations of war by Germany and the United States would not be long in coming.

Mounting Tension with Japan

It was conflict with Japan, however, rather than with Germany, which ultimately brought the United States into World War II.

The Japanese had succeeded in conquering most of the coastal areas of China, but their efforts to overrun the interior had bogged down. Chinese resistance continued under the leadership of Chiang Kai-shek.

In early September, 1940, Japanese forces occupied bases in the northern part of French Indochina. In the same month, Japan signed the Tripartite Pact, allying itself more closely with Germany and Italy.

In an attempt to contain the Japanese threat and to aid China, the United States began to apply economic pressure on Japan, which depended heavily on American sources of scrap iron, steel, petroleum, and aviation gasoline. In late September, 1940, President Roosevelt imposed an embargo on the shipment of scrap iron and steel to Japan.

In July, 1941, the Japanese occupied the rest of French Indochina, which suggested that they were pressing forward in their efforts to create what they called the Greater East Asia Co-Prosperity Sphere. Roosevelt responded to Japan's action by freezing Japanese assets in the United States. This action brought an almost complete stop to American trade with Japan.

The United States had, by Operation Magic, broken the Japanese diplomatic code. American intelligence regularly intercepted messages from Tokyo to the Japanese embassy in Washington and thus learned of many Japanese actions before they were carried out.

American economic sanctions against Japan confronted the Japanese with a dilemma. In order to get what it needed from the United States, especially petroleum and aviation gasoline, Japan would have to cease its aggression. The alternative was for Japan to seize the oil resources of the Dutch East Indies, an action likely to evoke a strong American response.

In September, 1941, Prince Fumimaro Konoye, Japan's prime minister and a relative moderate, offered a compromise to the United States. Japan would withdraw from French Indochina and pledge no further moves into Southeast Asia if the United States agreed to accept the Japanese presence in China and end the trade embargo. The United States rejected the offer and renewed its call for a Japanese withdrawal from China.

In October, Konoye resigned and was succeeded by General Hideki Tojo, a militant. Japan now began to prepare for what it regarded as a virtually inevitable war with the United States.

In late November, talks resumed in Washington between Secretary of State Cordell Hull and two Japanese negotiators,

Ambassador Kichisaburo Nomura and special envoy Saburo Kurusu. The Japanese demanded a free hand in China, the unfreezing of Japanese assets in the United States, a resumption of trade, and an end to the American naval build-up in the western Pacific.

In his reply to the Japanese, Hull called for a Japanese withdrawal from China and Indochina, promising to free Japanese assets and to resume trade if they complied. There did not appear to be any possibility of finding a compromise between the American and Japanese positions.

War with Japan

On November 26, the Japanese carrier force that attacked Pearl Harbor set sail. On December 1, Japan publicly rejected Hull's proposals.

On the evening of December 6, the first parts of the official Japanese reply to Hull's proposals arrived in Washington. U.S. naval intelligence decoded the message from Tokyo faster than the clerks in the Japanese embassy. When Roosevelt saw the text of the Japanese response late on the night of December 6, he declared: "This means war."

While the American government expected war, it thought that the Japanese would probably attack the Philippines, the Dutch East Indies or British Malaya. It evidently did not believe that the Japanese had the ability to attack Hawaii. Washington sent warnings to American bases in the Pacific, but they did not arrive in time.

At 7:55 a.m. Hawaiian time on December 7, 1941, Japanese aircraft attacked the American naval base at Pearl Harbor. It was just after noon in Washington. In the Pearl Harbor attack, the Japanese crippled the American Pacific fleet, sinking eight battleships and a number of other ships and killing over 2,400

Americans. Luckily for the United States, its three aircraft carriers were not in port.

In Washington, the Japanese envoys had an appointment with Secretary of State Hull at 1 p.m. When they appeared at about 2 p.m., Hull had just received the news of the attack on Pearl Harbor.

On December 8, Roosevelt asked Congress for a declaration of war. Congress quickly complied with only one dissenting vote, that of pacifist congresswoman Jeannette Rankin of Montana, who had also voted against war in April, 1917. On December 11, Germany and Italy declared war on the United States.

While the United States attempted to avoid entanglement in European affairs, American isolationism during the 1920s was far from complete. The United States remained involved in the thorny issues of Allied war debts and German reparations and joined with France in promoting the Kellogg-Briand Pact of 1928.

In Latin America, the United States sought to reduce its interventionism while maintaining its political influence and expanding its economic interests. During the 1930s, Roosevelt promoted his Good Neighbor policy in an effort to improve relations with the countries of Latin America.

In Asia, the United States attempted to restrain Japanese expansion. While the treaties negotiated at the Washington Conference of 1921–22 represented a step toward that end, Japan nevertheless overran Manchuria in 1931.

As the international situation deteriorated during the 1930s, the determination of Americans to avoid involvement in another world war increased. Congress became more isolationist in its attitudes and adopted the Neutrality Acts.

Nazi Germany's victories in Europe in 1939–40 presented a threat to American interests, and the Roosevelt administration moved to provide assistance to Great Britain and then to the

*Soviet Union. While American relations with Germany wor-
sened, Japan's expansion in Asia led to increasing conflict with
the United States.*

*The Japanese attack on Pearl Harbor brought an end to the
domestic political debate between the isolationists and interventionists. Americans united to fight their enemies.*

Recommended Reading

Selig Adler, *The Uncertain Giant, 1921–1941* (1965).

Thomas A. Bailey and Paul B. Ryan, *Hitler vs. Roosevelt: The Undeclared
Naval War* (1979).

Dorothy Borg, *The United States and the Far Eastern Crisis of 1933–1938*
(1964).

Thomas H. Buckley, *The United States and the Washington Conference, 1921–
1922* (1970).

Warren I. Cohen, *America's Response to China* (2nd ed., 1980).

Wayne S. Cole, *America First: The Battle Against Intervention, 1940–41*
(1953).

Robert Dallek, *Franklin D. Roosevelt and American Foreign Policy, 1932–
1945* (1979).

Charles de Benedetti, *Origins of the Modern American Peace Movement, 1915–
1929* (1978).

Robert A. Divine, *The Illusion of Neutrality* (1962).

Robert A. Divine, *The Reluctant Belligerent: American Entry into World War
II* (1965).

L. Ethan Ellis, *Republican Foreign Policy, 1921–1933* (1971).

Herbert Feis, *The Road to Pearl Harbor: The Coming of the War Between the
United States and Japan* (1950).

Robert H. Ferrell, *American Diplomacy in the Great Depression: Hoover-Stim-
son Foreign Policy, 1924–1933* (1957).

Robert H. Ferrell, *Peace in Their Time: The Origins of the Kellogg-Briand Pact*
(1952).

Peter G. Filene, *Americans and the Soviet Experiment, 1917–1933* (1967).

Lloyd Gardner, *Economic Aspects of New Deal Diplomacy* (1964).

Irwin F. Gellman, *Good Neighbor Diplomacy: United States Policies in Latin America* (1979).

Allen Guttmann, *The Wound in the Heart: America and the Spanish Civil War* (1962).

William S. Langer and S. Everett Gleason, *The Challenge to Isolation, 1937–1940* (1952).

William S. Langer and S. Everett Gleason, *The Undeclared War, 1940–1941* (1953).

Thomas R. Maddux, *Years of Estrangement: American Relations with the Soviet Union, 1933–1941* (1980).

Charles E. Neu, *The Troubled Encounter: The United States and Japan* (1975).

Gary B. Ostrower, *Collective Insecurity: The United States and the League of Nations During the Early Thirties* (1979).

Gordon W. Prange, *At Dawn We Slept: The Untold Story of Pearl Harbor* (1981).

Gordon W. Prange, *Pearl Harbor: The Verdict of History* (1986).

Christopher Thorne, *The Limits of Foreign Policy: The West, the League, and the Far Eastern Crisis of 1931–1933* (1973).

Jonathan G. Utley, *Going to War with Japan, 1937–1941* (1985).

John E. Wiltz, *From Isolation to War, 1931–1941* (1968).

Bryce Wood, *The Making of the Good Neighbor Policy* (1961).

CHAPTER 12

The Era of the
Second World War

Time Line

1941	Japan attacks Pearl Harbor
	The Red Army successfully defends Moscow
1942	Japan conquers the Philippines and most of Southeast Asia
	Japanese-Americans are sent to relocation camps

The U.S. Navy halts the Japanese advance in the Battles of the Coral Sea and Midway

American marines take Guadalcanal in the Solomon Islands

The Republicans make gains in the congressional elections

Anglo-American forces invade North Africa

1943
Roosevelt and Churchill meet at Casablanca and call for the unconditional surrender of the Axis

The Red Army defeats the Germans at Stalingrad

Anglo-American forces invade Sicily and Italy

The United Mine Workers union calls a strike

Roosevelt, Churchill, and Stalin meet at Teheran

1944
American, British, and Canadian forces invade Normandy

Congress adopts the G. I. Bill of Rights

American forces return to the Philippines

Roosevelt wins a fourth term

The Germans launch their last major counterattack on the western front in the Battle of the Bulge

1945	Roosevelt, Churchill, and Stalin confer at Yalta
	American troops take Iwo Jima and Okinawa
	Roosevelt dies; Truman becomes President
	Germany surrenders
	Atomic bombs are dropped on Hiroshima and Nagasaki
	The Soviet Union declares war on Japan
	Japan surrenders

During World War II, the United States played a central role in the grand alliance which defeated the Axis powers—Germany, Italy, and Japan—and the war made the United States one of the world's two superpowers with major international responsibilities.

Organizing to fight a two-front war required a massive mobilization of manpower and the economy, resulting in an unprecedented expansion of the federal government. The shortage of labor provided new employment opportunities for women and for blacks and other minorities. World War II began a process of change that would transform American society in the postwar era.

Mobilization for Victory

The requirements of total war compelled the United States to carry out a more complete mobilization than had ever occurred in American history.

Military Mobilization

When the United States went to war in December, 1941, some 1.5 million Americans were already in uniform. By the time the war ended in 1945, almost 16 million Americans had served in the armed forces.

To direct the American war effort, President Roosevelt created the Joint Chiefs of Staff in January, 1942. Chaired by Admiral William D. Leahy, the Joint Chiefs also included General George C. Marshall, Admiral Ernest J. King, and General Henry H. Arnold, the Chiefs of Staff of the Army, Navy, and Air Force respectively.

The U.S. Army Air Force had been only an air corps until June 1941. During the war, the air force experienced a massive expansion and became the equal of the ground forces in the army's organizational structure.

Intelligence Operations

An executive order issued in June, 1942, created the Office of Strategic Services (OSS), headed by Colonel William J. Donovan. The OSS carried out intelligence gathering and covert actions and even sponsored the writing of a psychological analysis of Adolf Hitler. The OSS was the wartime predecessor of the Central Intelligence Agency (CIA), established in 1947.

Economic Mobilization

Economic mobilization proved to be a complex task. Civilian industry had to be converted to war production. A rapid expansion of production had to be achieved. Materials in short supply had to be allocated, a labor force had to be recruited. Housing had to be provided for workers in defense industries. Reasonable living standards had to be maintained. Inflation had to be kept under control.

In order to mobilize the economy more effectively, the government established a number of new alphabet agencies. In January, 1942, Roosevelt appointed Donald M. Nelson, a Sears, Roebuck executive, to head the War Production Board (WPB), with the task of mobilizing the resources of the United States to meet the demands of total war.

In October, 1942, the President persuaded James F. Byrnes to step down from the Supreme Court to become what was called the assistant president to supervise economic mobilization. In May, 1943, Byrnes became head of the new Office of War Mobilization (OWM), which supervised the activities of the federal agencies directing the war economy.

William S. Knudsen, the president of the industrial giant General Motors, headed the War Resources Board, established to develop plans to convert factories to military production.

The productive might of the American economy quickly produced a mass of supplies for the armed forces of the United States and its allies. Between 1939 and 1942, the United States' production of airplanes rose by 2,400 percent, and it doubled again by 1945. By 1944, the United States was producing war planes at the rate of almost 100,000 a year.

Industrialist Henry J. Kaiser adapted assembly line techniques to the production of merchant ships, called Liberty ships and Victory ships. This massive production of ships replaced the ships lost to German submarines and made it possible for the output of American industry to reach the troops in the field.

The Office of Price Administration

In order to combat inflation, the Office of Price Administration (OPA) was created in January, 1942, with the authority to establish ceiling prices and to regulate rents. Rationing programs limited civilian consumption of tires, gasoline, coffee, sugar, meat, butter, cheese, some canned goods, shoes, and goods made of rayon and nylon. The OPA achieved some success in controlling inflation. From 1941 to 1945, consumer prices rose by 31 percent, compared with an increase of 62 percent during World War I. In the face of shortages, black markets developed to provide consumers with an illegal source of scarce goods at inflated prices.

The Cost of the War

It cost the United States about $300 billion to fight World War II. As the federal budget increased, taxes rose. The Revenue Act of 1942 quadrupled the number of Americans who had to pay income taxes. Tax rates on personal income were increased, and corporation taxes were raised. The practice of withholding income tax payments from employees' paychecks began in July, 1943.

Despite tax increases, the federal government had to borrow to cover part of the war's costs. During the war, the national debt increased from about $48 billion in 1941 to approximately $247 billion in 1945.

Most of the money spent by the government went to about 100 of the 18,000 companies which received contracts from the government. General Motors alone received about 8 percent of the government contracts, and other major corporations also received a sizable share.

The Truman Committee

Senator Harry S Truman of Missouri headed the Senate's War Investigating Committee, which sought to make certain that the government got value for it s money by exposing waste, corruption, and excess profits.

Censorship and Propaganda

Shortly after Pearl Harbor, Roosevelt established the Office of Censorship, headed by Byron Price of the Associated Press. Wartime censorship placed some restrictions on freedom of expression, although war correspondents often voluntarily held back information which might endanger the nation's war effort.

In order to stimulate public support for the war effort and promote the government's viewpoint, Roosevelt established the Office of War Information (OWI) in June, 1942. Elmer Davis, a professional correspondent, headed the OWI.

Organized Labor and the War

During the war, union membership increased considerably, from 10.5 million in 1941 to 14.7 million in 1945.

Shortly after Pearl Harbor, the unions responded to an appeal of the President by giving a no strike pledge. In January, 1942, the National War Labor Board (NWLB) was established, with representatives from management, labor, and the public. The NWLB had the task of mediating labor disputes and keeping wage increases within limits set by the government.

There were relatively few strikes during the war. In 1943, however, a major coal strike occurred, involving 450,000 soft coal and 80,000 hard coal miners. Under heavy pressure from the President, John L. Lewis, the head of the United Mine Workers (UMW), agreed to halt the strike.

Following the coal strike, Congress passed the Smith-Connally Anti-Strike Act, also known as the War Labor Disputes Act, over the President's veto in June, 1943. This act required that unions give 30 days' notice of any intention to strike in war industries (the 30-day cooling-off period) and authorized the President to seize plants where a strike would endanger war production. Strikes were made illegal in plants seized by the government.

In order to prevent a railroad strike in December, 1943, Roosevelt ordered the army to take temporary control of the nation's railroads. In December, 1944, the army took control of Montgomery Ward headquarters in Chicago when the company refused to obey the NLWB's orders to observe the right of its employees to organize. Soldiers carried protesting Montgomery Ward head Sewell L. Avery—still sitting in his desk chair—from his office.

Politics During Wartime

Although Americans united to fight their enemies, partisan politics were not abandoned. The Republicans made gains in the congressional elections of 1942, gaining 9 seats in the Senate and 46 in the House of Representatives. The Democrats, however, continued to control both houses of Congress.

The Election of 1944

In 1944, Roosevelt decided to seek a fourth term as President. As his vice presidential running mate, he chose the moderate Senator Harry S Truman of Missouri in place of liberal Vice President Henry A. Wallace.

As their presidential candidate the Republicans nominated Governor Thomas E. Dewey of New York. During the campaign, Dewey indicated his acceptance of most of Roosevelt's domestic and foreign policies, but he promised the voters that he and the Republicans could carry out these policies more effectively than the Democrats.

Roosevelt polled 25.6 million popular votes to Dewey's 22 million. Roosevelt's plurality of 3.6 million votes was smaller than that received by any successful presidential candidate since World War I. The electoral vote count was 432 for Roosevelt, 99 for Dewey.

Roosevelt's Death

Roosevelt lived less than three months after his fourth inauguration on January 20, 1945. He died at Warm Springs, Georgia on April 12 of that year. Vice President Truman succeeded to the Presidency.

The War During 1942 and 1943

When the United States entered the war, the Allies decided to pursue a Germany first policy; that is, the war would be pressed against Germany, while the Allies would remain on the defensive in regard to Japan. The war against Japan got off to a bad start and quickly got worse. Only three days after the devastating assault on Pearl Harbor, the Japanese sank the British battleship *Prince of Wales* and the battle cruiser *Repulse* on December 10, 1941. This action crippled the British fleet in Southeast Asia.

The Japanese moved quickly to conquer Hong Kong, British Malaya with its great port at Singapore, British Burma, and the Dutch East Indies. Advancing into New Guinea, the Japanese moved toward Port Moresby and threatened Australia. In addition, the Japanese seized the American possessions of Guam and Wake islands in the Central Pacific and occupied two of the westernmost Aleutian Islands in the Bering Sea off Alaska.

The American Loss of the Philippines

The Japanese conquest of the Philippines left 20,000 Americans desperately resisting the enemy in the Bataan Peninsula on the island of Luzon. Roosevelt ordered General Douglas

MacArthur, the American commander, to go to Australia to assume command of the Allied forces in the Southwest Pacific. Bataan fell in early April 1942, and the remaining American defenders withdrew to Corregidor Island in Manila Bay. In early May, General Jonathan Wainwright surrendered Corregidor to the Japanese.

The Bombing of Tokyo

American carrier-based B-25 bombers under the command of Major General James H. Doolittle hit Tokyo, Japan's capital, for the first time on April 18, 1942. This air raid had little military significance, but it gave a tremendous boost to American morale.

The Battles of the Coral Sea and Midway

Two important naval battles took place in the Pacific in the spring of 1942. The Battle of the Coral Sea, fought on May 7 and 8, was the first naval battle in history in which the ships did not directly engage one another; all of the fighting was done by carrier-based airplanes. The American aircraft carrier *Lexington* was sunk, and the Japanese also lost a carrier. While the battle itself ended in a draw, it served to halt the Japanese advance on Port Moresby in New Guinea and to eliminate the threat to Australia.

The Battle of Midway, fought in the Central Pacific from June 3 to 6, resulted in an American victory over the Japanese fleet commanded by Admiral Yamamoto. The United States lost the carrier *Yorktown*, while four Japanese carriers were sunk. The American victory at Midway ended the Japanese advance in the Central Pacific and eliminated the threat to Hawaii.

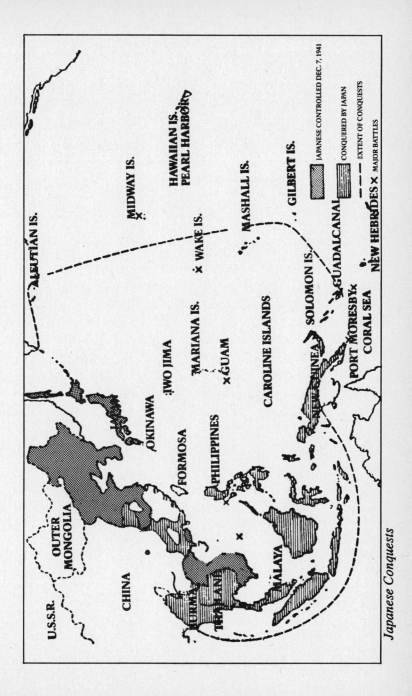

U.S.S.R.

OUTER
MONGOLIA

CHINA

BURMA

THAILAND

MALAYA

FORMOSA

PHILIPPINES

OKINAWA

IWO JIMA

MARIANA IS.
×GUAM

CAROLINE ISLANDS

NEW GUINEA

SOLOMON IS.

PORT MORESBY×

CORAL SEA

GUADALCANAL

LEUTIAN IS.

ALEUTIAN IS.

MIDWAY IS.
×

× WAKE IS.

HAWAIIAN IS.
PEARL HARBOR×

MASHALL IS.

·· GILBERT IS.

NEW HEBRIDES ×

JAPANESE CONTROLLED DEC. 7, 1941

CONQUERED BY JAPAN

EXTENT OF CONQUESTS

× MAJOR BATTLES

Japanese Conquests

Guadalcanal

On August 7, 1942, American marines landed on Guadalcanal in the Solomon Islands east of New Guinea. The battle for Guadalcanal lasted for several months until the remaining Japanese defenders abandoned the island in early 1943.

The War Against Japan During 1943

During the second half of 1943, the Americans succeeded in gaining control of the Solomon Islands, thereby securing General MacArthur's flank in his drive toward the Philippines.

In the Central Pacific, the commander of the American Pacific fleet, Admiral Chester W. Nimitz, began his campaign of island hopping to acquire bases for launching air raids against Japan. The taking of Tarawa in the Gilbert Islands cost the Second Marine Division almost 1,000 men.

The Battle of the Atlantic

The German submarine threat in the Atlantic remained serious, as U-boats sank Allied ships faster than they could be replaced. By June, 1942, German submarines were sinking an average of five Allied ships daily. The Allies gradually began to win the Battle of the Atlantic with the help of convoys, radar and sonar, and increased production of ships. There were two turning points in the Battle of the Atlantic. The first came in November, 1942, the last month in which Allied ships' losses exceeded new construction, and the second was in May, 1943, the first time the Germans lost more submarines than they constructed.

The War in North Africa

During early 1942, the German Afrika Korps, commanded by Field Marshal Erwin Rommel, pushed from the Italian colony of Libya deeply into Egypt. By summer, Rommel reached El Alamein, about 60 miles west of Alexandria, posing a threat to the Suez Canal.

In November, Field Marshal Bernard Montgomery's British Eighth Army counterattacked and began to push Rommel's forces back.

At the same time, on November 8, 1942, Anglo-American forces, commanded by General Dwight D. Eisenhower, carried out Operation Torch, the invasion of Morocco and Algeria in French North Africa.

The North African invasion came as a substitute for an invasion of Western Europe, which was beyond the ability of the Americans and British in 1942. The Soviets, who continued to face powerful German armies, were unhappy with the decision to invade North Africa and continued to press for a Second Front in France.

In North Africa, the German defenders and their Italian allies were caught in a squeeze as Eisenhower's forces advanced from the west and the Eighth Army pressed forward from the east. In May, 1943, the remaining 250,000 Axis defenders surrendered in Tunisia.

The Invasion of Sicily and Italy

Victory in North Africa in the spring of 1943 led almost inevitably to the Anglo-American decision to invade Sicily and Italy.

The invasion of Sicily in July, 1943, was followed by the Italians' overthrow of Benito Mussolini the same month. Conquering Sicily, Anglo-American forces invaded Italy in September. The new Italian government, headed by Marshal Pietro Badoglio, surrendered to the Allies. The Germans had anticipated an Italian surrender and quickly took control of about two-thirds of the country.

For the Allies, the Italian campaign proved long and frustrating. The American and British troops had to fight their way through the rugged Italian terrain which gave most of the advantages to the German defenders. The Allies did not take Rome until June 4, 1944, only two days before the invasion of Normandy, and the war in Italy lasted until the spring of 1945, coming to an end only a few days before the final German surrender.

The Russo-German War

At the time of the Japanese attack on Pearl Harbor in December, 1941, the Soviets were engaged in a desperate struggle to keep Hitler's forces from taking Moscow. Succeeding in that effort, the Soviets forced the Germans to retreat some distance from Moscow before they succeeded in stabilizing the front.

In the spring of 1942, the Germans launched a new offensive directed toward two objectives: the oil-rich Caucasus, lying between the Black and Caspian seas, and the city of Stalingrad on the Volga River. While the Germans advanced into the Caucasus, they did not succeed in reaching the oil fields. At Stalingrad, the German attackers and Soviet defenders became engaged in one of the war's bloodiest battles. In early 1943, Field Marshal Friedrich von Paulus surrendered what remained of his army, the first German army to surrender in the field since the Napoleonic wars. That summer, the Germans launched their final offensive in the Soviet Union. A few days later, the Soviets counterattacked and began a push forward that did not end until the Red Army reached Berlin in April, 1945.

The War in Europe During 1944 and 1945

By 1944, an Allied victory was in sight. In Italy, the American and British troops continued their slow advance, while the Red Army pushed into the Baltic States, Poland, and the Balkans.

The Normandy Invasion

On June 6, 1944 (D-Day), American, British, and Canadian forces commanded by General Dwight D. Eisenhower began the Second Front in France. Operation Overlord, the invasion of Normandy, was the largest amphibious operation in history.

As Eisenhower's troops began to push beyond Normandy toward Paris, other Allied forces carried out Operation Dragoon (earlier called Operation Anvil), landing August 15 on the coast of southern France between Marseilles and Nice.

Following the liberation of Paris on August 25, Allied troops advanced into the Low Countries. By September, the Allied forces were approaching Germany, and it seemed that the European war might be over by the end of 1944. This assessment proved to be overly optimistic; it discounted both the determination and the ability of the Germans to continue their resistance.

V-1 and V-2 Rocket Bombs

German V-1 rocket bombs first hit London on June 12, 1944, six days after D-Day. These V-1 rocket attacks on England reached their peak during July and August. On September 7, the first V-2 rocket bomb struck London. The V-2's flew faster than sound. Although these German rocket bombs did some damage and killed several thousand people, they were not particularly effective weapons, since they could not be directed against specific targets.

The Air War Against Germany

By 1944, increased American aircraft production made it possible for the United States Army Air Force to put thousands of heavy bombers and escort fighters into the skies over Germany. The Americans specialized in daylight high altitude precision bombing, hitting at key targets, including facilities for the production of synthetic gasoline and rubber, aircraft factories, ball bearing works, submarine bases, railroads, and electric power stations. The British Royal Air Force (RAF) concentrated on night area bombing.

Allied bombing did heavy damage to Germany's cities and the German economy. In particular, the bombing made it difficult for the Germans to concentrate their efforts on important weapons programs. The bombing was not decisive, however. Victory over the Germans was not won by air raids but rather by victories on the fields of battle.

The Battle of the Bulge

The Germans displayed their determination and ability to resist in the Battle of the Bulge, fought in the Ardennes Forest in Belgium in December, 1944. For about ten days, this German counterattack pushed the Americans back and inflicted about 27,000 casualties. The Germans failed, however, to achieve a breakthrough. That failure helped bring home to the Germans the fact that victory now lay beyond their grasp.

The End of the European War

With American and British forces moving from the west and the Red Army pressing forward from the east, General Eisenhower decided not to attempt to beat the Russians to Berlin. Several factors influenced this decision. Eisenhower was concerned about the possibility of a Nazi stronghold in southern Germany that might have to be dealt with. In addition, the Allies had already agreed on the zones of occupation in Germany. Although Berlin would be under four-power control, the area surrounding the city had been assigned to the Soviet zone. If the American army sought to beat the Soviets to Berlin, it would suffer heavy casualties and would then have to withdraw to the zone assigned to the United States.

With the Red Army in Berlin, Adolf Hitler committed suicide in his bunker beneath the city on April 30, 1945. His successor, Grand Admiral Karl Doenitz, surrendered to the Allies on May 7.

The War Against Japan (1944–1945)

Although the Allies had intially decided on a "Germany First" strategy, the American success in mobilizing manpower and the economy made it possible to press the war against Japan before Germany was defeated.

American Aid to China

When the Japanese occupied Burma, the route for sending supplies to China via the Burma Road was cut. Supplies were then flown in from India, "over the hump" of the Himalaya Mountains.

The Kuomintang (Nationalist) government of Chiang Kai-shek was ineffective and corrupt. Chiang was as busy trying to limit the power of the Chinese Communists, led by Mao Tse-tung, as he was fighting the Japanese.

Island Hopping During 1944

In the Central Pacific, American forces moved into the Marshall Islands, taking Kwajalein and Eniwetok in February. Saipan in the Mariana Islands was taken in July and Guam was reoccupied in August.

The Retaking of the Philippines

On August 20, 1944, troops commanded by General MacArthur landed in the Philippines. In late October, the Battle of Leyte Gulf was fought. Actually three separate engagements, this was the last and greatest of the naval battles of the Pacific war. The battle resulted in the destruction of most of what was left of Japan's naval power and left the United States in full control of the sea around the Philippines.

The campaign in the Philippines ended with the fall of Manila to the Americans in February, 1945.

The Taking of Iwo Jima

American marines landed on Iwo Jima, in the Bonin Islands some 750 miles from Tokyo, on February 19, 1945. Mount Suribachi was taken after heavy fighting on February 23. Over 4,000 marines died before the battle for Iwo Jima ended on March 17.

The Taking of Okinawa

On April 1, 1945, the United States Tenth Army landed on Okinawa in the Ryukyu Islands southwest of Japan. During this brutal battle, Japanese kamikaze (suicide) pilots crashed their planes into American ships. The battle for Okinawa ended on June 21. At that time, 110,000 Japanese lost their lives, and the Americans took 8,000 prisoners. Over 11,000 Americans died during the battle, and almost 44,000 were wounded in the last major engagement in the Pacific.

The End of the War Against Japan

Possession of these island bases enabled the United States to step up the air war against the Japanese home islands. American military planners believed, however, that Japan could be defeated only by an invasion, which was scheduled to begin about November 1, 1945. It was estimated that this invasion would cost about one million American lives.

Concern about heavy casualties was a major factor contributing to the American decision to use the atomic bomb against Japan. On August 6, 1945, the first atomic bomb was dropped on Hiroshima. On August 9, a second atomic bomb hit Nagasaki. The following day, Emperor Hirohito decided that Japan had no choice other than to surrender. He set one condition: He must be permitted to keep his throne.

Though they had earlier insisted on the unconditional surrender of Japan, the Allies agreed to accept Hirohito's condition, and the news of Japan's surrender became public on August 14. The formal surrender documents were signed on September 2 on board the American battleship *Missouri* anchored in Tokyo Bay. The Second World War had ended.

The Development of the Atomic Bomb

The atomic bomb was the greatest achievement of American science and technology harnessed to the war effort. Brigadier General Leslie R. Groves headed the Manhattan Project, which Roosevelt established to develop the atomic bomb. The first nuclear chain reaction took place at the University of Chicago on December 2, 1942. Major atomic research and development centers were located at Hanford, Washington; Oak Ridge, Tennessee; and Los Alamos, New Mexico. The first successful test of the atomic bomb took place at Alamogordo, New Mexico on July 16, 1945.

American Losses in the War

Some 290,000 Americans lost their lives in World War II, about two-thirds of them in the European theater of operations. About 670,000 Americans were wounded. In comparison, the Soviet Union lost approximately 20 million military and civilian people.

Allied Wartime Diplomacy

The Arcadia Conference

Two weeks after the attack on Pearl Harbor in December, 1941, British Prime Minister Winston Churchill traveled to Washington to meet with President Roosevelt in a conference code-named Arcadia. The two leaders agreed on the Germany First strategy and established the Combined Chiefs of Staff, consisting of British and American military officers.

The First Moscow Conference

In August, 1942, Churchill and W. Averell Harriman, who represented Roosevelt, met in Moscow with Joseph Stalin, the Soviet leader. Churchill and Harriman informed Stalin that it would not be possible for the western Allies to open a Second Front in France during 1942. The Soviets were fighting a desperate struggle against the German armies advancing into the Caucasus and toward Stalingrad and had called on their American and British allies to ease the pressure on them by invading western Europe. The Soviets were unhappy with the Anglo-American decision to invade French North Africa instead.

The Casablanca Conference

Roosevelt and Churchill met at Casablanca in French Morocco in January, 1943. The two leaders agreed to demand the unconditional surrender of the Axis powers. In part, this decision resulted from a desire to reassure the Soviets that the western powers would not attempt to make a separate peace with Hitler.

Roosevelt and Churchill disagreed on the matter of the Second Front. While Roosevelt favored an invasion of France, Churchill called for on assault an what he called the "soft underbelly" of Europe; that is, Italy and especially the Balkans. Churchill believed that an invasion of the Balkans by the western Allies would contain the expansion of Soviet power in the area. While Churchill's phrase was catchy, it was also misleading. Both Italy and the Balkans are mountainous areas, very far from being "soft" geographically. Launching an invasion in these areas would be difficult, as the subsequent Italian campaign demonstrated.

With victory in North Africa in sight, the two leaders agreed to move forward with an invasion of Sicily and Italy but not to abandon plans for the cross-Channel invasion of France favored by Roosevelt. At the Trident Conference held in Washington in March, 1943, Roosevelt and Churchill agreed to carry out the invasion of Normandy in the spring of 1944.

The First Quebec Conference

The First Quebec Conference, code-named Quadrant, was held in August, 1943. Roosevelt and Churchill agreed to increase the pace of the war against Japan.

The Cairo Conference

In November, 1943, en route to the meeting with Stalin at Teheran, Iran, Roosevelt and Churchill conferred in Cairo, Egypt, with the Chinese leader, Chiang Kai-shek. Roosevelt strongly supported China's desire to be counted among the great powers, since he hoped that China would be able to fill the power vacuum that would be created in East Asia by the defeat of Japan.

In the Cairo Declaration, Roosevelt, Churchill, and Chiang Kai- shek agreed to pursue the war in the Pacific until Japan surrendered unconditionally. They agreed that Japan should lose all the Pacific islands which Japan had acquired since 1914 and that China should regain Manchuria, Formosa, and the Pescadores Islands. They also agreed that Korea should, "in due course," become independent.

The Teheran Conference

From November 28 to December 1, 1943, Roosevelt and Churchill met with Stalin in Teheran. The three leaders discussed the plans for the Second Front in Western Europe, scheduled for the spring, and the Soviets agreed to launch a simultaneous offensive against the Germans.

At Teheran, Stalin made clear his determination to extend Soviet power in Eastern Europe following the war. Roosevelt sought to overcome Stalin's suspicions of the West in an effort to win Soviet cooperation in the postwar world.

The Second Quebec Conference

Roosevelt and Churchill held their second meeting in Quebec in September, 1944, considering the plans for winning the war against both Germany and Japan.

The two leaders also discussed the postwar treatment of Germany and tentatively endorsed the Morgenthau Plan, developed by Roosevelt's Secretary of the Treasury, Henry Morgenthau, Jr. The Morgenthau Plan called for the deindustrialization of Germany, making that country's economy primarily agricultural. A month later, Roosevelt decided that the Morgenthau Plan was impractical and, unwise and abandoned it.

The Yalta Conference

In February 1945, Roosevelt, Churchill, and Stalin met at Yalta in the Soviet Crimea in the most important of the wartime conferences.

The atomic bomb had not yet been developed, and Roosevelt was concerned about the number of casualties the United States might suffer in an invasion of Japan, as well as about the inability of China to deal with the large Japanese army in Manchuria. In response to Roosevelt's appeal, Stalin agreed to enter the war against Japan within three months following the defeat of Germany. In return, the Soviet Union would acquire the southern half of Sakhalin Island, which Russia had lost to Japan in 1905, the Kurile Islands, and a sphere of influence in Manchuria. In addition, the Soviets would receive a zone of occupation in northern Korea.

At Yalta, the three leaders agreed to add France as an occupying power in Germany, dividing that country into four zones of occupation instead of three. Churchill was anxious to encourage France's recovery of its status as a great power, hoping that France would contribute to the reestablishment of a balance of power in Europe.

Agreement was reached on voting procedures in the Security Council of the new United Nations organization, with each of the Security Council's five permanent members (the United States, Great Britain, the Soviet Union, France, and China) to have veto power. The Soviet Union would acquire two additional seats in the UN's General Assembly for the Soviet republics of the Ukraine and Belorussia. Stalin insisted on this concession since he believed that the representation accorded the British dominions would mean additional votes for Great Britain.

The Yalta Conference could not reach agreement on the Soviet demand for reparations from Germany. The issue was submitted to a special reparations commission, which failed to produce an accord.

The question of Poland was the most difficult issue considered at Yalta. The United States and Great Britain maintained relations with the Polish government-in-exile located in London (the London Poles). The Soviets had broken relations with the London Poles after that government refused to accept Moscow's demand that it be allowed to annex eastern Poland. When the Red Army entered Poland in 1944, the Soviets had established a pro-Soviet, Communist-dominated government at Lublin which agreed to Moscow's territorial demands.

At Yalta, Stalin agreed to permit a broadening of the Lublin government by adding to it representatives of the London Poles. While the Polish government was reorganized, it continued to be dominated by pro-Soviet Communists, and the non-Communist representatives found themselves outnumbered and out-maneuvered. Stalin also promised to permit free elections in Poland, but these elections were never held.

While the Soviets annexed eastern Poland, the Poles were to be compensated by territory taken from Germany. No final commitments on this territorial compensation were made at Yalta, but the Soviets ultimately gave Poland the southern part of East Prussia—the Soviets annexed the northern part of the province—and German territory lying east of the line formed by the Oder and Neisse rivers (the Oder-Neisse Line).

The Big Three also agreed on the text of the Declaration on Liberated Europe, pledging that postwar governments in the liberated countries of Europe would be established on the basis of free elections.

There was a basic incompatibility between the Soviet demand for friendly governments in Poland and other Eastern European countries and the western Allies' demand for free elections. In most of Eastern Europe, and certainly in Poland, free elections would almost inevitably have led to the establishment of governments hostile to the Soviet Union. Stalin therefore got the friendly governments he wanted by imposing Communist-dominated regimes on countries occupied by Red Army troops. The Western powers protested Soviet actions, but Moscow ignored the protests.

Following the war, charges were made that a tired and ill Roosevelt had either been duped by Stalin or had simply sold out to the Soviets. This view ignored the realities of power which prevailed in Eastern Europe in 1945. The Red Army occupied Poland and other Eastern European countries—Romania, Bulgaria, Hungary—and the Soviets were thus in a position to enforce their will. There was no way to restrict Soviet influence in Eastern Europe without embarking on a new war.

It is also worth remembering that the Americans and British held the preponderance of power in Western Europe. In France, Italy, and other Western European countries, as well as in Greece, the Americans and British could—and did—use their power to shape politics and the course of events to their liking.

The American Home Front

The End of the Depression

The entry of the United States into World War II brought an end to the depression. There were plenty of jobs and, instead of unemployment, there were serious labor shortages in many areas of the country. As a result of wage increases and overtime pay, real weekly wages of American workers before taxes were 50 percent higher in 1945 than they had been in 1939. Family income rose even more, since women and young people were working in larger numbers than before the war. Increased demand for the products of American agriculture meant that prosperity also returned to the nation's farms. While incomes increased, price controls resulted in only moderate price increases during the war years.

Civilian Contributions to the War Effort

In addition to working in jobs related to the war effort, American civilians contributed to the cause by planting victory gardens in their back yards and in vacant lots. Millions of American kids supplemented their allowances by selling scrap metal and waste paper they collected from their neighbors to junk dealers.

Americans, who were earning more than ever before and had

less to buy because of wartime shortages and restrictions, piled up savings and invested in war bonds and victory bonds sold by the government. Of the almost $100 billion in bonds sold during the war, more than three-quarters of the total were bought by banks, insurance companies, and corporations. But American families bought billions of dollars worth of bonds, as well. These savings helped fuel the tremendous growth of the economy following the war as Americans rushed to buy automobiles, homes, home appliances, and other things they had done without.

Population Mobility

During the war, the American population became more mobile than ever. From 1941 to 1945, 15.3 million people changed their county of residence. Of these, 7.7 million changed their state of residence. The biggest increases in population were registered in the Far West—in California, Oregon, and Washington—and in the Atlantic coast states of Maryland, Virginia, and Florida. California's population increased from 6.9 million in 1940 to 10.5 million in 1950.

The number of Americans engaged in agriculture declined by 17 percent during the war. At the same time, technology and the consolidation of small farms into larger ones made American agriculture more productive than ever.

The G.I. Bill of Rights

In 1944, Congress passed the Servicemen's Readjustment Act, popularly known as the G.I. Bill of Rights. (The term G.I., standing for "government issue," was applied to armed services personnel during the war.) This act was an expression of the nation's gratitude to the veterans for a job well done. In addition, the G.I. Bill was designed to stimulate the economy and to provide more time for the economy to absorb the increase in the work force which demobilization would create.

The G.I. Bill provided a number of benefits to discharged service personnel. They would, first of all, be entitled to a maximum of 52 weeks of payments of $20 per week while seeking civilian employment. Those veterans receiving this benefit were referred to as members of the 52–20 Club.

More important was the G.I. Bill's provision of education benefits for veterans, including tuition, books, and a living allowance for individuals and their dependents. These educational benefits helped increase enrollment in American colleges by 50 percent between 1944 and 1946. The G.I. Bill also provided guaranteed low interest loans to veterans who wanted to buy homes or start businesses.

The Internment of Japanese-Americans

The surprise attack on Pearl Harbor served to increase American hostility to Japanese-Americans, who had long been the victims of racial antagonism and discrimination. The situation of Japanese-Americans grew worse as Japanese successes in early 1942 increased American fears, especially on the west coast, of a Japanese invasion. In fact, the Japanese had never planned an invasion of either Hawaii or the west coast of the United States, since they did not have the means to carry out such an invasion. There were also fears of possible Japanese-American acts of sabotage.

Japanese-Americans living on the Pacific coast became the victims of this hysteria. The army recommended, and the President approved, the moving of Japanese-Americans to ten relocation centers located in seven states. These relocation centers could more accurately be described as concentration camps. Some 110,000 Japanese-Americans were moved to the camps. They had to give up their homes and businesses. Most failed to regain their possessions: The Japanese-Americans lost about $350 million worth of property as a consequence of the relocation. In the case of *Korematsu v. United States*, decided in 1944, the Supreme Court by a vote of 6 to 3, held that relocation was a legitimate exercise of the war powers.

Japanese-Americans, in fact, posed no threat. Some 17,000 Japanese-American troops fought the Germans during the Italian campaign, performing with outstanding bravery.

Blacks and World War II

The war brought many changes to black Americans. The demand for labor increased the opportunities for blacks to find employment in industry and other sectors of the economy. By 1944, more than two million blacks were working in war plants. The war also brought a significant black migration, as more than a million blacks left the South and moved to cities in the North and West.

Black migration made the issue of race more national than sectional in scope. Some serious racial tensions developed, and race riots occurred in a number of cities. In June, 1943, a race riot in Detroit took the lives of 25 blacks and 9 whites.

Black activism intensified during the war. A. Philip Randolph, the president of the Brotherhood of Sleeping Car Porters, threatened to lead a march on Washington on July 1, 1941, to demand greater employment opportunities for blacks. This threat forced President Roosevelt to act. On June 25, only a few days before the planned march, Roosevelt established the Fair Employment Practices Commission (FEPC) with the task of combatting discrimination in employment. Responding to the President's action, Randolph agreed to call off the march. In 1943, Randolph joined with several other black leaders to form the Congress of Racial Equality (CORE), which promoted a more active resistance to racial discrimination than older, more conservative black organizations.

About 700,000 blacks served in the still largely racially segregated armed forces, and several thousand became officers.

In an important 1944 decision in the case of *Smith v. Allwright*, the Supreme Court held that the all-white primary in Texas was unconstitutional. In northern cities, the growing number of blacks created important voting blocs which politicians could not easily ignore. The growing significance of the black electorate had an impact on the growth of the civil rights movement in the years following the war.

Hispanics and World War II

While Hispanics suffered from discrimination and remained a largely overlooked minority, they were not segregated in the armed forces.

Tensions between Hispanics and Anglos became serious in southern California, resulting in the so-called zoot suit riots in Los Angeles in July, 1943. Anglo servicemen clashed with young Hispanics dressed in zoot suits, which featured long, loosely cut jackets and fully cut pants tightly pegged around the ankles.

Women and World War II

The war provided American women with more opportunities in the work force, especially in industry, than ever before. Rosie the Riveter became a symbol of the women who found jobs in war plants. Many other women joined women's branches of the armed forces such as the WACS (Army) and WAVES (Navy). At the same time, old attitudes persisted. Many evidently believed that it was all right for women to work because of necessity, but their proper place was really at home caring for their husbands and children. At war's end, while many women quit their jobs, about two million remained in the work force.

While the war produced no real feminist movement and few demands for complete equality, the war did begin the process of making major changes in the status of American women.

During the Second World War, the United States fought on two fronts: against Japan in the Pacific and against Germany and Italy in the Atlantic, North Africa, and Europe. The two-front war required the greatest military and economic mobilization in American history. Wartime mobilization brought an end to the depression, resulted in a substantial increase in the power of the federal government, and did much to change the position of women and blacks in American life. As the armed might of the United States increased, the Allies were able to abandon their Germany First strategy and to pursue the offensives against Germany and Japan simultaneously.

Victory in the Second World War required cooperation among the United States, Great Britain, the Soviet Union and their allies. When the defeat of the enemy seemed certain, the major allies felt less compulsion to maintain their unity. Differences among the Big Three became evident at the Yalta Conference in 1945. As these differences mounted, the East-West Cold War began.

Recommended Reading

Stephen E. Ambrose, *Eisenhower: Soldier, General of the Army, President-Elect, 1890–1952* (1983).

Karen Anderson, *Wartime Women: Sex Roles, Family Relations, and the Status of Women During World War II* (1981).

Robert Beitzell, *The Uneasy Alliance: America, Britain, and Russia, 1941–1943* (1972).

John M. Blum, *V Was for Victory: Politics and American Culture During World War II* (1976).

A. Russell Buchanan, *Black Americans in World War II* (1977).

A. Russell Buchanan, *The United States and World War II* (2 vols.,   1964).

James MacGregor Burns, *Roosevelt: The Soldier of Freedom* (1970).

Diane Shaver Clemens, *Yalta* (1970).

Roger Daniels, *Concentration Camps USA: Japanese-Americans and World War II* (1971).

Robert A. Divine, *Roosevelt and World War II* (1969).

David Eisenhower, *Eisenhower: At War, 1943–1945* (1986).

Dwight D. Eisenhower, *Crusade in Europe* (1948).

Herbert Feis, *The Atomic Bomb and the End of World War II* (1966).

Herbert Feis, *The China Tangle: The American Effort in China from Pearl Harbor to the Marshall Mission* (1953).

Herbert Feis, *Churchill, Roosevelt, Stalin: The War They Waged and the Peace They Sought* (1957).

Susan M. Hartmann, *The Home Front and Beyond: American Women in the 1940s* (1982).

Patrick J. Hearden, *Roosevelt Confronts Hitler: America's Entry into World War II* (1987).

Trumbull Higgins, *Soft Underbelly: The Anglo-American Controversy over the Italian Campaign, 1939–1945* (1968).

Gabriel Kolko, *The Politics of War: The World and United States Foreign Policy, 1943–1945* (1968).

Deborah E. Lipstadt, *Beyond Belief: The American Press and the Coming of the Holocaust, 1933–1945* (1986).

William Manchester, *American Caesar: Douglas MacArthur, 1880–1964* (1978).

Samuel Eliot Morrison, *The Two Ocean War: A Short History of the United States Navy in the Second World War* (1963).

Forrest C. Pogue, *George C. Marshall* (3 vols., 1963–73).

Richard Polenberg, *War and Society: The United States, 1941–1945* (1972).

Cornelius Ryan, *The Last Battle* (1966).

Cornelius Ryan, *The Longest Day: June 6, 1944* (1959).

Martin J. Sherwin, *A World Destroyed: The Atomic Bomb and the Grand Alliance* (1975).

Gaddis Smith, *American Diplomacy During the Second World War, 1941–1945* (1965).

John L. Snell, *Illusion and Necessity: The Diplomacy of Global War, 1939–1945* (1963).

John L. Snell, ed., *The Meaning of Yalta: Big Three Diplomacy and the New Balance of Power* (1956).

Louis L. Snyder, *The War: A Concise History, 1939–1945* (1960).

Ronald H. Spector, *Eagle Against the Sun: The American War with Japan* (1985).

Studs Terkel, *"The Good War": An Oral History of World War II* (1984).

John Toland, *The Rising Sun: The Decline and Fall of the Japanese Empire, 1936–1945* (1970).

Gordon Wright, *The Ordeal of Total War, 1939–1945* (1968).

David S. Wyman, *The Abandonment of the Jews: America and the Holocaust, 1941–1945* (1984).

Neil A. Wynn, *The Afro-American and the Second World War* (1976).

CHAPTER 13

The Truman Era: Containment and the Fair Deal

Time Line

1945   Roosevelt, Churchill, and Stalin meet in the Yalta Conference

Roosevelt dies; Truman succeeds to the Presidency

World War II ends in Europe; controversy develops over Soviet policy in Eastern Europe

The United Nations is established

The Allied leaders meet in the Potsdam Conference

The atomic bomb is dropped on Hiroshima and Nagasaki

World War II ends in the Pacific

Truman proposes his 21-point domestic program

1946   Winston Churchill warns of the "Iron Curtain" dividing Europe

The Atomic Energy Commission is established

Congress passes the Employment Act of 1946

Truman fires Secretary of Commerce Henry A. Wallace

The Republicans recapture control of both houses of Congress

1947   Congress passes the Taft-Hartley Act

The President's Commission on Civil Rights releases its report

Truman calls for aid to Greece and Turkey and sets forth the Truman Doctrine

The Marshall Plan to promote European recovery is proposed

The National Security Act creates the Department of Defense and reorganizes the armed services

Congress passes the Presidential Succession Act

Truman orders loyalty checks of government workers

1948   The Communists seize power in Czechoslovakia

The Soviets launch the Berlin Blockade

Congress establishes a peacetime draft

Truman ends segregation in the armed forces

Truman wins reelection to the Presidency

1949   The North Atlantic Treaty Organization (NATO) is established

The Chinese Civil War ends with a Communist victory

The Soviet Union explodes an atomic bomb

1950   Congress passes the McCarren Act

Senator Joseph R. McCarthy makes his first charges about Communists in the government

Alger Hiss is convicted of perjury

War breaks out in Korea

1951   The Twenty-Second Amendment is ratified

Truman removes MacArthur as commander in Korea

The United States concludes a peace treaty
with Japan

---

*In 1945, the American people welcomed the return of peace. But
the transition from wartime to peacetime conditions proved difficult. The nation's new President, Harry S Truman, was an unknown quantity, although it soon became evident that he stood
in the reform tradition of earlier Presidents like Wilson and the
two Roosevelts. Truman believed, as they had, that the federal
government had a major responsibility to perform in dealing
with the problems of a complex society.*

*The ending of wartime controls unleashed a soaring infla-
tion, and labor-management conflict intensified in the immediate
postwar period. At the same time, however, the nation moved
into one of the greatest eras of prosperity in its history.*

*World War II had made the United States the world's
greatest power, but it was unable to dictate the shape of the
postwar world. Even before the end of the war, tension with the
Soviet Union had begun to mount, and soon the United States
and its wartime ally would find themselves engaged in a new
world conflict, the Cold War. As the Cold War intensified, the
United States found itself compelled to assume greater world
responsibilities than ever before in its history. American
isolationism was a thing of the past.*

Truman as President

As President, Harry S Truman faced a host of serious
problems, both domestic and foreign. He was handicapped in
dealing with them by his relative lack of experience, although he
had a solid understanding of American political processes. After
serving in the army during World War I, Truman became involved in politics in his home state of Missouri. A protégé of

Tom Pendergast, the Democratic boss of Kansas City, Truman represented Missouri in the United States Senate from 1935 until he became Vice President ten years later.   In 1945, most Americans regarded Truman at best as a rather uncertain successor to Roosevelt.

The Founding of the United Nations

One of Truman's first acts as President was to preside over the convening of the San Francisco Conference on April 25, 1945. Delegates from 50 nations met to draft the Charter of the United Nations.

While most of the details of the Charter had already been worked out, one important issue remained unsettled: the veto power in the Security Council. The Soviets insisted that the great power veto should apply even to the discussion of an issue; i.e., procedural questions; while the Americans, British, and others contended that the veto should apply only to recommendations of actions to be taken by UN members, i.e., substantive questions. After several days of debate, the Soviets gave way.

The United Nations closely resembled the League of Nations in its basic organization. All members of the UN were represented in the General Assembly, while the Security Council consisted of 11 members. The five great powers—the United States, the Soviet Union, Great Britain, France, and China—were permanent members with the right of veto; the other six members were elected for two-year terms by the General Assembly. The Secretariat, headed by the Secretary General, dealt with administrative matters. These UN agencies had their headquarters in New York, while the International Court of Justice met in The Hague, the capital of the Netherlands. The UN Charter also established a number of councils and committees to deal with various political, economic, and social matters.

American opinion, believing that the American refusal to

join the League of Nations contributed to the coming of World War II, strongly favored membership in the United Nations, and the Senate ratified the UN Charter by the overwhelming vote of 89 to 2.

Truman's 21-Point Program

Less than two weeks after the formal signing of the Japanese surrender in early September, 1945, Truman submitted his 21-point domestic program to Congress. In this program, the President proposed a continuation and extension of the New Deal. Truman called for an expansion of unemployment insurance, an increase in the minimum wage, an expansion of Social Security, the enactment of a full employment program, the creation of a national health insurance program, federal aid to education, slum clearance and low rent housing programs, the establishment of a permanent Fair Employment Practices Commission (FEPC), and programs for the development of the nation's river valleys, patterned after the Tennessee Valley Authority (TVA).

Congress was dominated by a conservative coalition of Southern Democrats and Republicans and did not offer a positive response to Truman's proposals.

Demobilization

For a great many Americans, the most pressing issue in the fall of 1945 was demobilization. In September, 1944, the government had established a point system, providing that service personnel who had served the longest would be discharged first.

When the war ended in 1945, the American armed forces totaled over 12 million. By mid-1946, the army numbered 1.5 million and the navy 700,000. By 1947, the size of the armed forces had been reduced to less than 1.6 million, and Congress wanted further cuts.

Truman believed that the United States required a strong military establishment to support the country's responsibilities throughout the world. In October, 1945, he proposed the establishment of universal military training (UMT). Congress turned down this proposal, however, and allowed the military draft to expire at the end of March, 1946. The armed forces depended on volunteer enlistments until Congress reestablished the draft in 1948.

The National Security Act of 1947

Truman did succeed in winning congressional support for a reorganization of the armed services. The National Security Act of 1947 established a new cabinet-level Department of Defense and subcabinet level Departments of the Army, Navy, and Air Force. The Air Force thus became an independent branch of the armed services, instead of being part of the Army. Truman named James V. Forrestal as the first Secretary of Defense. The act also established the Joint Chiefs of Staff (JCS), the National Security Council (NSC), and the Central Intelligence Agency (CIA), which became the successor to the wartime Office of Strategic Services (OSS).

Control of Atomic Energy

The Atomic Energy Act of 1946 established civilian control over atomic energy. A five-member Atomic Energy Commission (AEC) would supervise further atomic development. Truman appointed David E. Lilienthal, the former head of the Tennessee Valley Authority, to direct the work of the AEC.

Reconversion of the Economy

At war's end, there was considerable uncertainty about what the economy had in store for Americans. Pessimists predicted a postwar recession like the one which had followed World War I and feared that unemployment might rise to eight million by 1946.

Some urged an early end to controls over prices, wages, and rents. While this would lead to price increases, advocates of removing controls insisted on the need to give industry incentives to produce more goods more quickly to meet consumer demand. When demand was met, they anticipated, prices would decline.

Others, including the President, argued that it was necessary to retain some controls until production caught up with demand. If controls were not retained, they feared, the consequence would be runaway inflation. In August, 1945, the President ended rationing of gasoline, fuel oil, tires, processed food, and some other goods. Within a few weeks after the Japanese surrender, the government cancelled $35 billion worth of war contracts and removed a number of other controls on industry, thereby enabling industry to convert to peacetime production. In October, the construction industry was freed from most restrictions. At the same time, however, the wartime Office of Price Administration (OPA) retained its authority to exercise control over prices until its scheduled expiration on June 30, 1946, and Truman reminded the country that some controls were still needed over prices, wages, and rents.

Price Controls and Inflation

While demands for the removal of price controls increased, prices remained relatively stable until the spring of 1946. By that time, the OPA had permitted a number of price increases, and some inflationary pressures were becoming evident. With the OPA's authority scheduled to expire on June 30, Truman called for its extension.

In late June, Congress passed a bill continuing OPA, but in

such a way as to permit general price increases. Truman vetoed the bill, and Congress did not pass a new law until late July. As a result, no price controls were in effect from July 1 to July 25. During this period, the wholesale prices of farm products jumped 24 percent, and retail food prices increased almost 14 percent. The price index of 900 commodities rose more than 10 percent.

This experience made it clear that the removal of controls would lead to serious inflation, but demands continued for the end of price controls. Taking matters into their own hands, cattle raisers withheld beef from the market. As consumer anger increased, Truman ended price controls on meat in October. In November, most other price and wage controls were removed, with the exception of rent controls and controls on the price of sugar and rice. During the last half of 1946, food prices rose by about 30 percent, and consumer prices generally increased by 15 percent.

Labor-Management Conflict

Following the end of the war, conflict between labor and management mounted. During the winter of 1945–46, this conflict resulted in a number of strikes. While labor demanded wage increases with no increase in prices, business sought wage stability and higher prices.

The United Automobile Workers (UAW), led by Walter Reuther, went into negotiations with General Motors (GM) demanding a 30 percent wage increase. The union insisted that GM could pay the raise without having to increase car prices. Negotiations broke down, and the GM workers went on strike in November, 1945.

A strike also occurred in the steel industry, when 750,000 steel workers went on strike in January, 1946, after the steel companies refused the demand of the United Steel Workers (USW) for a $2 a day wage increase. The steel companies insisted that they could not afford to raise wages unless the Office of Price Administration (OPA) allowed them to increase steel prices. The OPA relented and agreed to permit the steel companies to increase prices by as much as $5 a ton. The strike was settled with the steel workers receiving a wage increase of 18.5 cents an hour. The 18.5 cents an hour formula was also used to settle the General Motors strike, which ended in March, 1946.

John L. Lewis, the colorful head of the United Mine Workers (UMW), was not willing to settle for 18.5 cents an hour and also demanded stronger safety regulations and a welfare fund. The coal strike, which began in April, 1946, threatened the economy with coal shortages. After 40 days, the government seized the mines. Secretary of the Interior Julius A. Krug accepted most of the UMW's demands. The government retained control of the mines when the operators refused to accept the new contract terms. In November, Lewis took the coal miners out on strike for the second time in a year, acting in defiance of a government injunction. Lewis was held in contempt of court, and both he and the union were required to pay heavy fines.

While most of the railroad brotherhoods reached accords with management without strikes, the trainmen and locomotive engineers did not and went on strike. In May, 1946, the government seized the railroads, and pressure from the White House forced the brotherhoods and management to reach a settlement.

New union contracts providing for wage increases contributed to mounting inflationary pressures.

Postwar Prosperity

While some pessimists had anticipated a postwar recession, the economy continued to prosper. During 1946, civilian employment increased to over 55 million, which was almost 7 million higher than in 1940. Unemployment was only 2.3 million, less than it had been in 1942, the first year of the war. In 1946, annual per capita income was about $500 higher than it had been in 1929. The gross national product (GNP) had regained the level of 1929 for the first time in 1940, when it reached $100.6 billion. By 1952, it had grown to $347 billion.

America's farmers shared in the postwar prosperity. With high demand for agricultural products in both domestic and foreign markets, farm prices rose considerably. In 1947, farm income totaled $15.5 billion, the highest it had ever been.

A number of factors helped fuel prosperity. First of all, there was a tremendous consumer demand for goods and services that could not be met during the war. This demand was supported by some $37 billion in savings that people had available to buy what they wanted. No automobiles for civilian use had been manufactured during the war. Automobiles were produced in 1946 and 1947, but even the 4 million cars which rolled off the assembly lines in 1948 were not enough to meet the demand. In 1950, 6.6 million cars were produced.

Demand for housing was also high. In 1949, over one million nonfarm housing units were under construction. The Federal Housing Administration (FHA) helped sustain the boom in housing construction by guaranteeing long-term loans to home buyers.

Industry's expenditures for new plants and equipment and a continued high level of government spending also contributed to the prosperity. In 1948, industry spent about $22 billion in capital outlays, an increase of 250 percent over 1945. The federal budget of $33 billion in 1948 was substantially less than the wartime peak of $98 billion but considerably more than the approximately $9 billion budget of 1940. Government commitments at home and abroad pushed federal expenditures to higher levels after 1948.

The Baby Boom

The surge in population, the so-called baby boom, provided another powerful stimulus for the economy. During the 1930s, the United States experienced a modest population growth of 8.9 million. During the 1940s, the population increased by 19 million. The birth rate, which stood at 19.4 per 1,000 in 1940, rose to more than 24 per 1,000 in 1946 and did not begin to decline until the 1960s.

The Employment Act of 1946

During the New Deal era and World War II, the role of the federal government in the nations' economy had expanded considerably. This expansion continued following the war.

The 1944 Democratic platform had called for a program of "full employment." In the Employment Act of 1946, the federal government assumed a major role for maintaining a high level of employment and economic prosperity. The act declared that the federal government had a responsibility for making available "useful employment opportunities, including self-employment, for those able, willing, and seeking to work, and to promote maximum employment, production, and purchasing power." Although the act did not specify how these goals would be reached, it was clear that the government would use its taxing, spending, and other fiscal powers to influence the business cycle. The act created the three-member Council of Economic Advisers to advise the President on economic policy.

The 1946 Congressional Elections

An increasing number of Americans blamed the Democrats for the country's postwar problems, including inflation and labor-management conflict. Truman became more unpopular, and a poll taken in April, 1946, revealed that a third of the people believed that the President was incapable of handling his job.

The Republicans scored major gains in the 1946 congressional elections, winning 246 seats in the House of Representatives, while the Democrats held 188, and taking the Senate by a margin of 51 seats to 45. For the first time since 1930, the Republicans controlled both houses of Congress. The conservative 80th Congress and the liberal Truman seemed to be on a collision course.

The Taft-Hartley Act

Conservatives had long contended that the Wagner Act (National Labor Relations Act) of 1935 unduly favored organized labor, and during the postwar period there had been a growth of antiunion sentiment in much of American opinion. The Republican-controlled 80th Congress was determined to enact a new law.

In 1947, Congress passed the Taft-Hartley Act over Truman's veto. The law prohibited the closed shop (only workers who were union members could be hired) but permitted the union shop (a worker, once hired, would be required to join the union), unless the union shop was banned by state law. Unions were required to observe a 60-day cooling off period before calling a strike. Employers were permitted to sue unions to recover losses suffered as a result of broken contracts or for damages incurred during strikes. Employers gained more freedom to campaign against union organizing efforts. Restrictions were imposed on jurisdictional disputes between unions. Unions were barred from making political contributions, and union officials had to take an oath that they were not Communists.

The Taft-Hartley Act had little negative impact on strong unions, but it served to weaken other unions and made it more difficult for unions to organize nonunion workers. Within a decade after the act's passage, 19 states had enacted "right-to-work" laws, banning the union shop.

The Conflict Over Tax Cuts

While the 80th Congress favored tax cuts, Truman believed that tax revenues should be sufficient both to cover current expenditures and to provide a surplus which could be used to reduce the national debt. In 1930, the national debt had amounted to $16 billion and had increased to $43 billion in 1940. When World War II ended in 1945, the national debt exceeded $258 billion. At the end of 1946, the national debt stood at $269 billion.

Truman vetoed tax reduction bills passed by Congress in May and July, 1947. Congress then passed a third tax bill in April, 1948, providing for a $5 billion tax cut. The bill removed over 7 million low-income taxpayers from any income tax liability and raised the personal exemption from $500 to $600. Truman also vetoed this bill, but Congress overrode the veto.

Presidential Succession

The Presidential Succession Act of 1947 revised the line of succession to the Presidency. Under its terms, the succession would pass from the Vice President to the Speaker of the House to the President Pro Tempore of the Senate and then to the Secretary of State and other members of the cabinet in the order of their rank. Underlying this act was the belief that elected officials should take precedence over appointed officials in the line of succession. Previously, the succession passed from the Vice President to the Secretary of State and then to the other members of the cabinet in the chronological order of the creation of their departments.

Civil Rights

Truman emerged as a strong advocate of civil rights for black Americans and other minorities. In 1946, Truman appointed the President's Commission on Civil Rights, a panel of distinguished citizens, both black and white. In its report *To Secure These Rights*, issued in 1947, the commission called for the "elimination of segregation based on race, color, creed, or national origin from American life."

In 1948, Truman urged congressional enactment of laws against lynching and the poll tax and also called for the establishment of a Fair Employment Practices Commission (FEPC). The President's proposals encountered strong opposition, especially from southerners. Although Congress refused to enact civil rights legislation, Truman used his executive authority to eliminate segregation in the armed forces and to ban discrimination in federal employment policies.

In its 1948 decision in the case of *Shelley v. Kramer*, the Supreme Court ruled that private restrictive covenants designed to prevent blacks from moving into white residential neighborhoods could not be legally enforced.

In the late 1940s, Ralph Bunche, a black, emerged as an important American figure at the United Nations, directing its trusteeship division. Bunche won the Nobel Peace Prize for his work in negotiating the 1949 Arab-Israeli truce. Later, in 1960, he supervised the UN peacekeeping force in the Congo.

Blacks made advances in other areas, as well. In 1947, Jackie Robinson signed a contract with the Brooklyn Dodgers, becoming the first black to play major league baseball. Within a few years, blacks became prominent in virtually all professional sports.

Divided Europe

One of the first major problems confronting Truman when

he became President was increasing tension in American-Soviet relations. As a consequence of its advance against Germany, the Red Army had come to dominate much of Eastern Europe. Joseph Stalin, the Soviet dictator, used the power his army gave him to establish Communist dictatorships in Poland, Romania, Bulgaria, and—slightly later—Hungary. By the end of the war, local Communists had established themselves in power in Yugoslavia and Albania. At the same time, a legitimate coalition government was established in Czechoslovakia, although Communists held most of the important positions. Stalin had thus accomplished his goal of making certain that the countries along the western frontier of the Soviet Union would have friendly governments.

American officials became increasingly concerned about Soviet actions in Eastern Europe and encouraged Truman to take a firm stand against Moscow. As American-Soviet tensions increased, Truman sent Harry Hopkins, who had been one of Roosevelt's closest advisers, to Moscow to confer with Stalin. When Hopkins warned Stalin that Soviet actions in Poland were having a negative impact on American opinion, Stalin remained adamant, reminding Hopkins of the importance of Poland for the security of the Soviet Union.

The Occupation of Germany

In the aftermath of the defeat of Germany, the Americans, British, and French took control of their occupation zones. Berlin, the former German capital lying within the Soviet zone in eastern Germany some 100 miles from the western zones, was divided into four occupation sectors. The western powers had access to their sectors in Berlin by highway, railroad, and air routes through the Soviet zone. Moscow maintained that the western powers' use of these routes was a privilege, not a right. With no

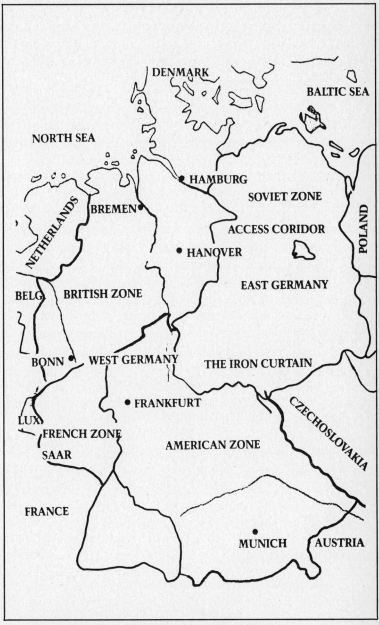

The Occupation of Germany after World War II

specific treaty guarantees of their use of these routes, the western powers had to rely on the Soviets' willingness to cooperate.

The Potsdam Conference

In mid-July 1945, Truman met with Stalin and British Prime Minister Winston Churchill in Potsdam, near Berlin. During the conference, Churchill was replaced by the newly elected British Prime Minister, Clement Attlee, the leader of the Labor party. The wartime Allies agreed to establish a Council of Foreign Ministers to draft peace treaties with Germany's allies.

Focusing much of its attention on Germany, the Potsdam Conference agreed that the occupation authorities should promote demilitarization, denazification, and democratization in Germany. On the controversial issue of reparations, it was agreed that each power should be permitted to remove property from its own zone, while the Soviets would also receive a percentage of useful capital equipment from the western zones. Although the question of the future border between Poland and Germany was deferred to the final peace conference, the Soviets unilaterally transferred part of their zone to Poland, thereby establishing the frontier along the so-called Oder-Neisse line. In addition, the Soviets gave Poland the southern part of the German province of East Prussia and annexed the northern part to the Soviet Union.

The Potsdam Conference agreed to establish a four-power Allied Control Council to determine the policies to be executed in all of the four zones in Germany. In practice, however, the four powers failed to reach agreement on common policies and thus each power proceeded to determine policy for its own zone.

The War Crimes Trials

The Potsdam Conference gave final approval for holding trials of war criminals. In the fall of 1945, 22 major German war criminals were brought to trial before the International Military Tribunal in Nuremberg, Germany. In October, 1946, almost a year later, the verdicts were reached. Of the defendents, 12 were sentenced to death, 3 to life imprisonment, and 4 to shorter prison terms, while 3 were acquitted. (One defendant, Robert Ley, had committed suicide during the trial; another, Hermann Goering, took his own life before his death sentence could be carried out.) Other trials of less important German and other Axis war criminals continued for several years. A trial of 25 major Japanese war criminals took place in Tokyo during 1946.

The Onset of the Cold War

During late 1945 and early 1946, American-Soviet relations continued to deteriorate. In a speech at Fulton, Missouri, in March, 1946, former British Prime Minister Churchill introduced a new term to the political vocabulary when he declared: "From Stettin in the Baltic to Trieste in the Adriatic, an iron curtain has descended across the continent."

Secretary of State James F. Byrnes continued his efforts to reach agreement with Moscow on a host of issues, but to no avail. Despairing of ever establishing common four-power policies for Germany, Byrnes proposed in September, 1946, the merger of the American zone with the other western zones for economic purposes, in order to make it possible for the Germans to support themselves. The British accepted Byrnes' offer and in early 1947 Bizonia came into being. The French joined their zone several months later. The western powers thus took the first steps toward the establishment of a separate West German state.

The Containment Policy

In 1947, Truman and his new Secretary of State, General George C. Marshall, began the process of developing a more vigorous policy to counter Soviet actions. In this effort, major roles were played by Undersecretary of State Dean Acheson and George F. Kennan. In early 1946, while serving on the staff of the American embassy in Moscow, Kennan had drafted a lengthy analysis of the Soviet Union and its expansionist policies. Recalled to Washington to head the State Department's new Policy Planning Staff, Kennan played a central role in designing a policy to halt Soviet expansion, the policy he called containment. Kennan believed that only a policy of determined and continuing resistance could stop the advance of Soviet power.

The Truman Doctrine

The first major step in implementing the policy of containment came in response to an urgent appeal from the British. Great Britain had assumed a major responsibility in the eastern Mediterranean, providing assistance to the Greek government in its war against Communist rebels and to Turkey in its efforts to resist Soviet demands for a larger voice in the control of the Dardanelles. In February, 1947, the British informed Washington that they no longer had the financial strength to continue this role. The United States would have to take over.

Marshall and Acheson met with the leaders of the Republican-controlled Congress to explain the seriousness of the situation. Acheson, in particular, made a powerful impression as he explained how the Soviets were "playing one of the greatest gambles in history" and how "we and we alone were in a position to break up the play." Senator Arthur Vandenberg of Michigan, one of the leading Republican foreign policy spokesmen, pledged his support. In so doing, Vandenberg made an important contribution to the emerging bipartisan foreign policy.

Appearing before a joint session of Congress on March 12, 1947, Truman called for the appropriation of $400 million for military and economic assistance to Greece and Turkey. The President also expressed what came to be known as the Truman

Doctrine: "I believe that it must be the policy of the United States to support free peoples who are resisting attempted subjugation by armed minorities or by outside pressure." Congress quickly approved the President's appeal for aid to Greece and Turkey.

The Marshall Plan

By early 1947, it was evident that Europe was in dire economic straits. If Europe's economy collapsed, the Soviets might be able to extend their power over the entire continent.

Speaking at Harvard University in June, 1947, Secretary of State Marshall proposed a broad program of American assistance to help all of Europe recover economically. The Soviets refused to participate, evidently believing that the Marshall Plan was designed to weaken their hold on Eastern Europe, and Moscow also prohibited its Eastern European satellites from participating. The Western European countries estimated that they would need between $16 and $22 billion in American aid over the next four years.

Congress initially showed considerable reluctance about undertaking such an extensive commitment, and the debate dragged on for several months. Then, in February, 1948, a Soviet-inspired coup in Czechoslovakia overthrew that country's coalition government and established a Communist dictatorship. Believing that the Marshall Plan would help stop the advance of Soviet power in Europe, Congress approved it in April, 1948, establishing the European Cooperation Administration (ECA) to administer the program. Between 1948 and 1952, the European Recovery Program (ERP), as the Marshall Plan was officially known, provided about $13 billion in American assistance for the economic revival of Western Europe. Truman had originally requested a total appropriation of $17 billion to support the Marshall Plan.

The Peacetime Draft

Increasing fears about Soviet intentions convinced Congress of the necessity to increase the size of the American armed forces. Congress approved the enactment of a peacetime military draft in 1948.

The Berlin Blockade

As the western powers proceeded with their plans for creating a separate West German state, the Soviets decided to apply pressure on the West where they could do so with the greatest ease, at Berlin.

On June 20, 1948, the Soviets cut off the highway and railroad routes between the western occupation zones and Berlin, thereby initiating the Berlin Blockade. In response, the United States moved to establish the Berlin airlift, designed to provide the three western sectors of the city with food, fuel, and other supplies. It was a calculated risk. No one knew if the airlift would be able to provide for the needs of the Berliners. And no one knew if the Soviets would attempt to interfere with the airlift.

The Berlin airlift achieved a remarkable success in meeting the needs of the western sectors, and the Soviets decided against escalating the crisis. In May, 1949, the Soviets ended the blockade, and the western powers proceeded with their plans to establish the Federal Republic of Germany, which came into being in mid-1949. The Soviets responded by creating an East German state, the German Democratic Republic, in their zone.

The Establishment of NATO

Mounting East-West tension gradually led the western powers to join in a military alliance. In March, 1948, Great Britain, France, and the Benelux states (Belgium, the Netherlands, and Luxembourg) signed a treaty of alliance, the Brussels Pact.

A year later, in April, 1949, representatives of 12 nations met in Washington to sign the North Atlantic Pact. The 12 signers included the five Brussels Pact states plus the United States, Canada, Iceland, Denmark, Norway, Italy, and Portugal. Greece and Turkey joined in 1952, and West Germany was added in 1955. The North Atlantic Pact established the North Atlantic Treaty Organization (NATO) to coordinate the activities of the alliance.

The North Atlantic Treaty won Senate ratification in July, 1949, by a vote of 82 to 13. This was the first formal military alliance entered into by the United States since 1778.

The establishment of NATO served to intensify the Cold War. In reality, there was little real likelihood of a Soviet attempt to use military force to win control of Western Europe, and the creation of NATO increased Soviet fears of the West. At the same time, however, the West had, at best, an imprecise understanding of Soviet intentions. Western fears of the Soviets were real, and these fears increased following the Soviets' development of the atomic bomb, which Truman announced to the American public in September, 1949.

In 1950, the State Department's Policy Planning Staff, now headed by Paul Nitze following Kennan's resignation, prepared a new statement of American defense policy. This statement, known as NSC–68, declared that the Soviet Union "mortally challenged" the United States because of Moscow's desire "to impose its absolute authority over the rest of the world." To meet this perceived challenge, NSC–68 proposed a vast expansion of the nation's military establishment.

The 1948 Election

With the Democrats and Republicans united in support of the

bipartisan foreign policy, domestic issues were of central importance in the hotly contested 1948 presidential election. In early
1948, Truman's chances of winning reelection seemed slight.
The President appeared to be unpopular with many voters. Many
southern Democrats opposed Truman's support of civil rights,
while many liberal Democrats believed that Truman had abandoned Roosevelt's policies in both domestic and foreign affairs.
Some Democrats hoped that a strong candidate could be found
to replace Truman as their party's standard-bearer. General
Dwight D. Eisenhower and Supreme Court Justice William O.
Douglas were approached, but neither was interested in seeking
the nomination.

In December, 1947, Henry A. Wallace announced that he
would seek the Presidency as the candidate of a new Progressive
party and hoped he would win the support of New Deal
Democrats. Truman had fired Wallace as Secretary of Commerce in September, 1946, because of Wallace's dissent from
the President's anti-Soviet foreign policy.

The Democratic national convention nominated Truman on
the first ballot and gave its vice presidential nod to Senator Alben
W. Barkley of Kentucky, who was expected to give the ticket
added strength in the South. The strongly liberal Democratic
platform called for the repeal of the Taft-Hartley Act, an increase
in the minimum wage, the expansion of Social Security, and
flexible farm price supports. A bitter debate over civil rights saw
liberal Democrats, led by Mayor Hubert H. Humphrey of Minneapolis, win the adoption of a platform plank calling for strong
civil rights legislation.

Anti-Truman southern Democrats split from the national
party. The States' Rights Democrats, who quickly became
known as Dixiecrats, picked Governor J. Strom Thurmond of
South Carolina as their presidential nominee and chose Governor Fielding Wright of Mississippi as his running mate.

Henry Wallace's Progressive party selected Senator Glen H.

Taylor of Idaho as its vice presidential candidate. The Progressives endorsed a strongly liberal domestic program and called for improved relations with the Soviet Union.

The Democratic party seemed hopelessly split into three groups, and the Republicans were supremely confident of recapturing the White House. For President the Republicans nominated Governor Thomas E. Dewey of New York, their 1944 standard-bearer, and chose Governor Earl Warren of California as their vice presidential nominee. In the contest for the nomination, Dewey defeated several other contenders, including Senator Robert A. Taft of Ohio, former Governor Harold E. Stassen of Minnesota, and Governor Warren. The Republican platform called for lower taxes, greater efficiency and honesty in government, and a more active campaign against the alleged threat of domestic Communism.

Most observers were convinced that Dewey was a sure winner, but Truman conducted a vigorous campaign, undertaking a 31,000 mile whistle-stop tour of the country denouncing the "do-nothing Republican 80th Congress." In contrast, the confident Dewey ran a cautious, noncommittal campaign.

Truman won reelection with 24 million popular votes and 303 electoral votes to Dewey's 22 million popular votes and 189 electoral votes. Truman owed his victory to his success in holding together the New Deal coalition, winning the votes of most of the South, as well as those of industrial workers, many farmers, minority groups, and intellectuals. The President benefitted both from the nation's prosperity and from the fear of many that the Republicans might endanger this prosperity and attempt to undo some of the economic and social reforms enacted since 1933.

Wallace and Thurmond each won slightly over one million popular votes. Wallace carried no states, while Thurmond captured the 39 electoral votes of South Carolina, Alabama, Mississippi, and Louisiana. The Democrats regained control of both houses of Congress.

The Fair Deal

In his State of the Union message, presented to Congress in January, 1949, Truman repeated his earlier calls for a broad program of economic and social reform, which became known as the Fair Deal. Truman proposed the repeal of the Taft-Hartley Act, increasing the minimum wage to 75 cents an hour, higher taxes on corporations and on the wealthy, an expansion of Social Security, slum clearance and low-cost housing programs, federal aid to education, national health insurance, and civil rights legislation.

Congress and the Fair Deal

While the Democrats held a majority of seats in both houses, Congress was in fact controlled by a conservative coalition of southern Democrats and Republicans. Congressional conservatives generally opposed any new initiatives in domestic policy. Congress refused to repeal the Taft-Hartley Act and rejected proposals for federal aid to education, national health insurance, and antilynching and antipoll tax legislation, as well as a Fair Employment Practices Commission.

Congress was more willing, however, to extend already existing programs. In 1949, Congress passed legislation increasing the minimum wage from 40 cents to 75 cents an hour.

The National Housing Act of 1949 established a national goal of providing "a decent home and a suitable living environment for every American family." The law provided more federal aid for slum clearance programs and for the construction of 800,000 units of low-income housing during the next six years. In practice, however, this objective was not met.

In 1950, Congress approved substantial increases in Social

Security benefits and extended Social Security coverage to more than ten million additional workers, including the self-employed, domestic servants, and farm laborers.

The Brannan Plan

While farmers had enjoyed a considerable prosperity during the war and immediate postwar years, agricultural income declined considerably in 1949.

Secretary of Agriculture Charles F. Brannan proposed a new approach to the farm problem. The Brannan Plan was designed to reduce the production of nonperishable commodities such as wheat and cotton which were flooding government storage facilities and to increase consumption of milk, meat, fruit, vegetables and other perishable goods. Brannan proposed to continue high, fixed price supports for only a limited portion of a farmer's production of nonperishable commodities. Perishable commodities would be sold at the market price, and the government would pay the farmer the difference between the sale price and the higher support price. Brannan insisted that his plan would assure farmers of a good income and, at the same time, provide low prices for consumers. Congressional conservatives opposed the Brannan Plan, however, charging that it would be too expensive and that it involved excessive governmental control over agriculture. Congress kept in place the existing program of high, fixed agricultural price supports.

Following the outbreak of the Korean War in 1950, prices of agricultural products increased. Net farm income, which had been $13 billion in 1949, rose to $16.3 billion in 1951. The return of prosperity to the nation's farms reduced the pressure on Congress to produce new farm legislation.

Government Reorganization

Congress undertook efforts to reform both the legislative and executive branches of the federal government. The Legislative Reorganization Act of 1946 was designed to improve the efficiency of congressional operations. The act reduced the number of standing committees in both the House of Representatives and Senate and required lobbyists to register and report their expenses.

Congress established the Commission on the Organization of the Executive Branch, headed by former President Herbert Hoover. The Hoover Commission's report led to the adoption of the Reorganization Act of 1949 which enabled the President to make changes in the organization of the executive branch, subject to congressional veto.

Congress also adopted the Twenty-Second Amendment to the Constitution, which limited future Presidents to two terms. The amendment was ratified in 1951.

The Loyalty Issue

Stung by continuing criticism that his administration was "soft on Communism," Truman, in 1947, created the Loyalty Review Board to screen federal employees. He also instructed the Attorney General to draw up a list of subversive organizations. This came to be known as the Attorney General's List.

The President's actions did not satisfy those who were convinced that Communist subversion was the major cause of the nation's problems at home and abroad. In 1947, the House Unamerican Activities Committee (HUAC) began investigating allegations of Communist influence in the government and in other aspects of national life, including the movie industry.

The Hiss Case

Of all the witnesses who appeared before HUAC, the most sensational was Whittaker Chambers, a former Soviet agent and an editor of *Time* magazine. Chambers charged that Alger Hiss, a former official of the State Department who had gone on to become the head of the Carnegie Endowment for International Peace, had provided him with classified State Department documents in 1937 and 1938. When Hiss denied the charges under oath, Chambers provided evidence further implicating Hiss. Since the statute of limitations had expired, Hiss could not be charged with espionage. He was, however, indicted on charges of perjury. The first Hiss trial ended in July, 1949, with a hung jury. The second trial ended in January, 1950, with a guilty verdict, and Hiss received a prison sentence. The development of the Hiss case before the House Unamerican Activities Committee brought a young Republican congressman from California, Richard M. Nixon, into national prominence for the first time.

The Rosenberg Case

In 1950, an Anglo-American spy ring which had provided the Soviets with information about the development of the atomic bomb was revealed. In Great Britain, authorities arrested Klaus Fuchs. In the United States, Julius and Ethel Rosenberg were arrested, tried, and convicted of espionage during wartime. The Rosenbergs were executed in 1953. The Hiss and Rosenberg cases both helped to add fuel to the flames of anti-Communist hysteria and contributed to the growth of McCarthyism.

Senator Joseph R. McCarthy

In February, 1950, shortly after the Hiss conviction, Republican Senator Joseph R. McCarthy of Wisconsin charged in a speech delivered in Wheeling, West Virginia, that he had a list of Communists and Communist sympathizers in the State Department. McCarthy repeated this charge and leveled others about Communist influence in government but never produced any evidence to substantiate them. Nevertheless, McCarthy gained many supporters as fear of Communist subversion mounted.

The McCarran Act

Fear of Communist subversion was becoming more intense as the United States moved from the 1940s into the 1950s. In September, 1950, Congress passed, over Truman's veto, the Internal Security Act (McCarran Act). This act required Communist and Communist-front organizations to register with the government and barred from entry into the United States any alien who had been a member of a totalitarian organization.

The American Occupation of Japan

Although the Truman administration's most immediate foreign policy concerns were in Europe, Asia increasingly became a focus of American interest and involvement. When the war against Japan ended in 1945, the United States quickly established its dominant position in the military occupation of the defeated island empire. In particular, General Douglas MacArthur, the Supreme Commander of the Allied Powers (SCAP) in Japan, refused to allow the Soviet Union to have any voice in Japan's reconstruction. Under MacArthur's supervision, the Japanese drafted a new constitution, transforming their government into a Western-style democracy.

The Communist Victory in China

Following the end of the war against Japan, China was torn apart in the civil war between Chiang Kai-shek's Nationalists (the Kuomintang) and the Communists, led by Mao Tse-tung. The United States provided Chiang with considerable economic, financial, and military assistance. But the Nationalist cause was weakened by widespread corruption and a devastating inflation.

The United States sought to mediate between the contending sides in China. General George C. Marshall, prior to becoming Truman's Secretary of State, went to China in late 1945 and attempted to create a coalition government between Chiang and Mao. Marshall's effort was virtually doomed to failure, and the Chinese civil war intensified. Mao's Red Army gradually extended its control over more and more of China. In October, 1949, Mao proclaimed the establishment of the People's Republic of China, formed an alliance with the Soviet Union, and initiated a campaign against American influence and power in East Asia. In December, 1949, Chiang withdrew the remnant of his forces to the island of Taiwan.

In a *White Paper*, the American State Department presented a defense of American policy in China and insisted that there was nothing the United States could have done to reverse the course of the Chinese civil war, apart from all-out intervention. Republican critics of American policy charged that Truman was responsible for the loss of China to Communism. The United States refused to recognize the Communist government on the Chinese mainland and instead maintained diplomatic relations with Chiang Kai-shek's government on Taiwan. In addition, the United States began to emphasize the development of Japan as America's main ally in Asia. In 1951, the United States concluded a peace treaty with Japan. The American occupation of Japan ended in 1952, and the two nations signed a security treaty.

The Korean War

The Japanese had annexed Korea in 1910, but at the end of World War II, the country was occupied by American and Soviet forces, with the line between the zones of occupation established at the 38th parallel. In the south, the United States supported the establishment of a Korean government headed by Syngman Rhee, a conservative nationalist. In the north, the Soviets

created a Communist government, led by Kim Il-Sung. Both occupying powers withdrew in 1949.

On June 25, 1950, the army of North Korea attacked South
Korea. The North Koreans may have been acting on the orders
of the Soviets, although it is possible that Kim Il-Sung may have
taken the initiative, certain that Moscow would have to support
him.

Truman moved promptly to support South Korea. The
United States took advantage of a temporary Soviet absence
from the UN Security Council to win that body's condemnation
of North Korea as an aggressor and endorsement of American
intervention. The Security Council's action made the Korean
war officially a United Nations police action, although the bulk
of the fighting was done by the Americans and South Koreans.

At first, the Korean War went badly as North Koreans poured
across the 38th parallel. In August, the North Korean advance
was halted at Pusan in the southeast corner of the country. In
September, General Douglas MacArthur, the commander of the
UN forces, carried out a brilliant landing at Inchon, behind the
North Korean lines. Most of the North Korean army in the south
was cut off and destroyed.

Although the United States had originally intervened in
Korea in order to restore the dividing line of the 38th parallel,
MacArthur's victory presented the prospect of using military
force to unite all of Korea. The Chinese warned that they would
intervene if the UN forces approached the Yalu River, the border between North Korea and China. The United States dis-
regarded the warnings.

In October, MacArthur's army crossed the 38th parallel and,
by November, was approaching the Yalu. The Chinese then advanced in force and drove the UN forces entirely out of North
Korea by December. MacArthur finally succeeded in stabilizing the front near the 38th parallel.

When the Truman administration decided to wage a limited

war in Korea and not to attempt to reunify the country, Mac-Arthur protested, declaring: "There is no substitute for victory." In April, 1951, Truman relieved MacArthur of his command. While the President's action initially evoked a storm of protest, Congress and the public soon accepted the decision. Under the command of General Matthew Ridgway, UN armies smashed the Chinese, who lost over a million men in Korea, and advanced northwards, establishing a line roughly along the 38th parallel. Armistice talks were initiated at Panmunjom in October, 1951, but no settlement was reached during the remainder of Truman's term.

Truman continued the New Deal program of expanding the welfare state, winning congressional approval for the Employment Act of 1946, the National Housing Act of 1949, an increase in the minimum wage, and an expansion of Social Security. Nevertheless, the Republicans and conservative southern Democrats who controlled Congress refused to approve new programs, such as federal aid to education, national health insurance, and the Brannan Plan for agriculture. Congress also rejected the President's civil rights proposals, including antilynching and antipoll tax legislation and a federal Fair Employment Practices Commission. Postwar labor-management conflict increased antilabor sentiment in Congress, leading to the adoption of the Taft-Hartley Act in 1947. The loyalty issue also became a center of controversy in domestic politics.

In foreign affairs, the United States did not attempt to revert to the isolationism of the past. Instead, the United States played a leading role in the establishment of the United Nations and in opposing the expansion of Soviet power. The containment policy led to the adoption of the Truman Doctrine program of aid to Greece and Turkey and the Marshall Plan, as well as the creation of the North Atlantic Treaty Organization. In 1950, the

United States went to war in Asia to prevent a takeover of South Korea by Communist North Korea.

Recommended Reading

Herbert Agar, *The Price of Power: America Since 1945* (1957).

Stephen E. Ambrose, *Rise to Globalism: American Foreign Policy Since 1938* (rev. ed., 1985).

William C. Berman, *The Politics of Civil Rights in the Truman Administration* (1970).

Paul S. Boyer, *By the Bomb's Early Light: American Thought and Culture at the Dawn of the Atomic Age* (1985).

Richard M. Dalfiume, *Desegregation of the U.S. Armed Forces: Fighting on Two Fronts, 1939–1953* (1969).

Robert J. Donovan, *Conflict and Crisis: The Presidency of Harry S Truman, 1945–1948* (1977).

Robert J. Donovan, *Tumultuous Years: The Presidency of Harry S Truman* (1982).

Herbert Feis, *Between War and Peace: The Potsdam Conference* (1960).

Herbert Feis, *From Trust to Terror: The Onset of the Cold War, 1945–1950* (1970).

Robert H. Ferrell, *Harry S. Truman and the Modern American Presidency* (1983).

Rosemary Foot, *The Wrong War: American Policy and the Dimensions of the Korean Conflict, 1950–1953* (1985).

John Lewis Gaddis, *The United States and the Origins of the Cold War, 1941–1947* (1972).

Lloyd C. Gardner, *Architects of Illusion: Men and Ideas in American Foreign Policy, 1941–1949* (1970).

Robert Griffith, *The Politics of Fear: Joseph R. McCarthy and the Senate* (1970).

Alonzo L. Hamby, *Beyond the New Deal: Harry S Truman and American Liberalism* (1973).

Fraser J. Harbutt, *The Iron Curtain: Churchill, America, and the Origins of the Cold War* (1986).

Susan M. Hartmann, *Truman and the 80th Congress* (1971).

Michael J. Hogan, *The Marshall Plan: America, Britain, and the Reconstruction of Western Europe, 1947–1952* (1987).

Joyce Kolko and Gabriel Kolko, *The Limits of Power: The World and United States Foreign Policy, 1945–1954* (1972).

Bruce R. Kuniholm, *The Origins of the Cold War in the Near East: Great Power Conflict and Diplomacy in Iran, Turkey, and Greece* (1980).

Walter LaFeber, *America, Russia, and the Cold War, 1945–1980* (1980).

Donald R. McCoy, *The Presidency of Harry S Truman* (1984).

Merle Miller, *Plain Speaking: An Oral Biography of Harry S Truman* (1974).

Thomas G. Paterson, *Soviet-American Confrontation: Postwar Reconstruction and the Origins of the Cold War* (1973).

Thomas C. Reeves, *The Life and Times of Joe McCarthy: A Biography* (1982).

Richard H. Rovere, *Senator Joe McCarthy* (1959).

Leila J. Rupp and Verta Taylor, *Survival in the Doldrums: The American Women's Rights Movement, 1945 to the 1960s* (1987).

Michael Schaller, *The American Occupation of Japan: The Origins of the Cold War in Asia* (1985).

Richard N. Smith, *Thomas E. Dewey and His Times* (1982).

Athan G. Theoharis, *Seeds of Repression: Harry S Truman and the Origins of McCarthyism* (1971).

Hugh Thomas, *Armed Truce: The Beginnings of the Cold War, 1945–1946* (1987).

Harry S Truman, *Memoirs,* (2 vols. 1955–56).

Allen Weinstein, *Perjury: The Hiss-Chambers Case* (1978).

Daniel Yergin, *Shattered Peace: The Origins of the Cold War and the National Security State* (1977).

CHAPTER 14

The Eisenhower Era: Affluent America

Time Line

1952	Republican Dwight D. Eisenhower wins the Presidency; the Republicans take control of both houses of Congress
1953	The signing of an armistice ends the Korean War
	Eisenhower appoints Earl Warren as Chief Justice of the United States
	The Submerged Lands Act recognizes state ownership of the off-shore oil lands

The Department of Health, Education, and Welfare is established

Joseph Stalin dies; the Soviets establish a collective leadership

The United States helps restore the Shah to power in Iran

1954   The Supreme Court outlaws school segregation in *Brown v. Board of Education of Topeka*

The Senate votes to condemn Senator Joseph McCarthy

The United States takes the lead in forming the South East Asia Treaty Organization (SEATO)

The Democrats regain control of Congress

The United States helps overthrow the Arbenz government in Guatemala

The Geneva Accords divide Vietnam at the 17th parallel

1955   Dr. Martin Luther King, Jr., leads the Montgomery bus boycott

The AFL and the CIO reunite

Eisenhower meets Khrushchev and Bulganin at a summit meeting in Geneva

West Germany enters NATO

The United States takes the lead in forming the Baghdad Pact (CENTO)

1956   The Federal Highway Act begins the construction of the interstate highway system

The Suez Crisis and Soviet intervention in Hungary intensify international tension

Eisenhower wins reelection to the Presidency

1957   Federal troops force the integration of Central High School in Little Rock, Arkansas

Congress passes the Civil Rights Act of 1957

The Soviets launch Sputnik I, the first artificial earth satellite

1958   The National Aeronautics and Space Agency (NASA) is established

The National Defense Education Act provides extensive federal aid to education

The Democrats win an overwhelming victory in the congressional elections

American troops intervene in Lebanon

1959   Hawaii and Alaska become states

Fidel Castro takes power in Cuba

Nikita Khrushchev visits the United States

The gross national product (GNP) reaches $500 billion

| 1960 | The U-2 incident leads to a collapse of the Paris summit |

By 1952, the limited war in Korea had driven a large segment of the American people to frustration and anger. For the first time in 20 years, the American electorate denied the Presidency to a Democrat and turned instead to the Republican candidate, the war hero General Dwight D. Eisenhower, known to his countrymen as "Ike."

Although Eisenhower was basically conservative and denounced the danger of "creeping socialism," the American welfare state continued to expand. The Eisenhower administration did much to consolidate the reforms of Roosevelt's New Deal and Truman's Fair Deal. While the country was not entirely free of economic problems, there was considerable growth of the gross national product (GNP) and the standard of living. The United States came to experience greater affluence than ever before in its history. Civil rights for black Americans became a major issue, as the Supreme Court outlawed racial segregation in public education and blacks themselves took the lead against segregation in other areas of national life.

During the 1950's, American-Soviet relations remained troubled, and the United States experienced a decline in its ability to exercise a controlling influence in world affairs. This decline resulted from the growth of Soviet power, the recovery of Europe, and the development of nationalism in Asia, the Middle East, and Latin America.

The 1952 Election

By 1952, Truman's popularity had sunk to a low point and, following a poor showing in the New Hampshire primary, he decided not to seek reelection.

Senator Robert A. Taft, an Ohio conservative, made a strong bid for the Republican presidential nomination, but the party's convention chose General Dwight D. Eisenhower. Respected as a war hero, "Ike" was also genuinely liked for his warm and sincere personality. As his running mate, Eisenhower selected Senator Richard M. Nixon of California. The Republican platform denounced Roosevelt and Truman for giving way in the face of the advance of Soviet power. The Republicans also promised to combat inflation and to promote honesty in government. And Eisenhower pledged that, if he won the election, he would go to Korea to seek an end of the war.

The Democrats nominated Governor Adlai E. Stevenson of Illinois, who defeated Senator Estes Kefauver of Tennessee in the contest for the nomination. Stevenson chose Senator John J. Sparkman of Alabama as his vice presidential running mate, expecting that Sparkman would strengthen the ticket in the South. Stevenson's eloquence and wit appealed especially to intellectuals, and his campaign caused many young people to become active in support of the Democratic party. At the same time, Stevenson suffered from the unpopularity of the Korean War and from the widespread belief that the Democrats had been in power too long.

Eisenhower won a sweeping victory, capturing 41 states and winning almost 34 million popular votes and 442 electoral votes. He made inroads into the traditionally Democratic South, carrying Virginia, Tennessee, Florida, Oklahoma, and Texas. Stevenson polled slightly more than 27 million popular votes and won 89 electoral votes. Eisenhower was clearly more popular than his party, since the Republicans won control of both houses of Congress only by very narrow margins.

Eisenhower as President

Eisenhower had spent virtually his entire career in the

military, although he served as president of New York's Columbia University from 1948 to 1950. He left that position to become the first Supreme Commander of NATO. Entering politics for the first time as a presidential candidate, Eisenhower declared his support of what he called "dynamic conservatism" and "modern Republicanism." While he did not favor a wholesale abolition of the economic and social legislation enacted by the New Deal and Fair Deal, he warned about the danger of the expanding federal bureaucracy, budget deficits, and "creeping socialism."

As his Secretary of State, Eisenhower chose John Foster Dulles, a Wall Street corporation lawyer and a major Republican spokesman on foreign policy. George Humphrey, the head of a major financial firm and a fiscal conservative, became Secretary of the Treasury. The president of General Motors, Charles E. Wilson, became Secretary of Defense. The liberal journal, the *New Republic*, described the Eisenhower cabinet as "eight millionaires and a plumber." Martin Durkin, the head of the plumbers' union, served as Secretary of Labor but resigned in less than a year.

Sherman Adams, a former Governor of New Hampshire, played a key role in the administration as Eisenhower's personal assistant. Like a chief of staff in the military, Adams controlled the access of persons and the flow of information to the President.

Eisenhower named Clare Boothe Luce, a former Republican congresswoman from Connecticut, as ambassador to Italy. Luce was the first woman ever to head the American embassy in a major foreign capital.

In 1953, following the death of Fred Vinson, Eisenhower named Earl Warren, the liberal Republican Governor of California, as Chief Justice of the United States. The Warren appointment would prove to be one of the most important of Eisenhower's eight years in the White House.

The Eisenhower administration proved to be probusiness in domestic affairs. This probusiness orientation became evident in policy toward taxes, off-shore oil, and electric power.

Eisenhower's Tax Policy

Although most Republicans favored tax cuts, Eisenhower insisted that federal expenditures should be reduced first. The budget for 1954 contained cuts in both civilian and military spending and reduced the deficit to slightly more than $3 billion. Congress then passed tax cuts of over $7 billion, with the benefits going mainly to high-income taxpayers and business. In an effort to prevent inflation, the Federal Reserve Board placed restrictions on credit and raised interest rates. The resulting slowdown in the economy led to a recession during the winter of 1953–54. By the late spring of 1954, the economy began to recover as a result of increases in private investment and consumer spending, as well as increased federal expenditures for Social Security and unemployment insurance.

Private Power vs. Public Power

In 1953, Congress angered supporters of public power when it rejected a proposal to build a new Tennessee Valley Authority (TVA) steam plant to provide electric power to Memphis, Tennessee. Eisenhower, who believed in private economic initiative, supported a plan proposed by the Dixon-Yates utility syndicate to build a privately owned plant. Following a two-year debate, the Dixon-Yates project collapsed in the midst of conflict of interest charges. The problem was resolved when Memphis agreed to build a municipal power plant.

In another dispute involving private vs. public power, the Idaho Power Company won a license to build three dams on the

Snake River. This private project replaced the plan to construct a huge federal dam at Hell's Canyon.

The Atomic Energy Act of 1954 also benefitted private power interests by providing for the construction of privately owned nuclear power plants regulated by the Atomic Energy Commission (AEC).

Off-Shore Oil

The Submerged Lands Act of 1953 ended a long conflict between the federal government and the states—especially California, Texas, and Louisiana—over the control of off-shore lands rich in oil. The act transferred the ownership of some $40 billion worth of off-shore oil lands along the California and Gulf of Mexico coasts to the states. Opponents of this act argued that these oil resources should belong to the American people as a whole. Transferring ownership to the states, they contended, would result in a giveaway to a few favored oil companies.

Expansion of Federal Activities

In some areas, the Eisenhower administration expanded the activities of the federal government. In 1953, the administration won congressional approval for the establishment of a cabinet-level Department of Health, Education, and Welfare (HEW). Oveta Culp Hobby became the first Secretary of HEW; she was the second woman ever to be a member of the cabinet.

In 1954, Congress approved American participation with Canada in the development of the St. Lawrence Seaway. This project, which was completed in 1959, made the Great Lakes accessible to oceangoing ships.

The Federal Highway Act, passed in 1956, provided for federal government payment of 90 percent of the cost of building some 42,500 miles of interstate highways.

The Downfall of McCarthy

Senator Joseph R. McCarthy of Wisconsin continued his charges of Communist subversion in the federal government even after his fellow Republican Eisenhower became President. Eisenhower disappointed many by refusing to attack McCarthy directly, although he worked against him behind the scenes.

In the summer of 1953, McCarthy sent his two young assistants, Roy M. Cohn and G. David Schine, to Europe to purge supposedly subversive books from libraries operated by the International Information Agency.

In 1954, McCarthy, as chairman of the Senate's Permanent Investigation Subcommittee, accused the army of protecting and promoting Communists, centering his attention on the case of Major Irving Peress, a dentist. The televised Army-McCarthy hearings in the spring of 1954 made millions of Americans aware of McCarthy as an arrogant bully, standing in marked contrast to Joseph Welch, the dignified Boston attorney who represented the Army.

In December, 1954, the Senate passed a resolution by a vote of 67 to 22 condemning McCarthy for "conduct unbecoming a senator," and McCarthy's influence came to an abrupt end. The heavy-drinking Senator died of cirrhosis of the liver in 1957 at the age of 48.

The Fear of Subversion

While fear of domestic Communism declined, it did not entirely disappear. Eisenhower broadened Truman's loyalty program by permitting the dismissal of federal employees found to be security risks, instead of restricting firings to those who were deemed guilty of disloyalty. The new "Red Scare" led to the dismissal of thousands of government employees. The American government lost, for example, the expertise of old China hands such as John Paton Davies and John Carter Vincent, who had shown insufficient enthusiasm for Chiang Kai-shek and had defied the conventional wisdom by suggesting that the alliance between the Soviet Union and the People's Republic of China would not necessarily prove to be permanent.

One of the most famous cases occurred in 1953, when the Atomic Energy Commission withdrew the security clearance of the noted nuclear physicist and father of the atomic bomb, J. Robert Oppenheimer, who was charged with being insufficiently sensitive to the needs of security.

The 1956 Elections

Although Eisenhower continued to enjoy overwhelming popular support among the American people, some elements of uncertainty clouded the domestic political picture. First of all, the Democrats regained control of both houses of Congress in the 1954 congressional elections, even though the President campaigned actively for Republican candidates. Then, in September, 1955, Eisenhower suffered a serious heart attack. He made an excellent recovery, however, and announced in February, 1956, that he would seek a second term.

In 1956, the Republican team of Eisenhower and Nixon benefitted from the President's personal popularity, the end of the Korean War, and economic prosperity. Despite the recession of 1953–54, the gross national product (GNP) and per capita income had increased significantly, and in 1956 the unemployed numbered only slightly over two million.

The Democrats again nominated Adlai Stevenson for the Presidency. Stevenson allowed the Democratic National Convention to select his running mate. A hard-fought contest saw Senator Estes Kefauver of Tennessee defeat Senator John F. Kennedy of Massachusetts for the vice presidential nomination.

In 1956, Eisenhower won an even more overwhelming victory than in 1952, winning 36 million popular votes and 457 electoral votes. Stevenson polled 26 million popular votes and won 73 electoral votes.

The Democrats continued to control both houses of Congress, and two powerful Democrats from Texas became increasingly more prominent in national affairs: Speaker of the House Sam Rayburn and Lyndon B. Johnson, the Senate majority leader.

Eisenhower and Labor

During the Eisenhower years, Congress refused to respond to organized labor's continuing call for a repeal of the Taft-Hartley Act. In other areas, however, Congress proved to be more responsive to the needs and interests of labor. In 1954, eligibility for unemployment compensation benefits was extended to about four million additional workers. In 1955, Eisenhower called for an increase in the minimum wage from 75 cents to 90 cents an hour. Congress raised it to $1.00. Social Security reforms extended the program's benefits to professional people, members of the armed forces, and other previously uncovered workers. Social Security benefits were increased in 1959.

In 1957, hearings conducted by a Senate Select Committee, chaired by Senator John F. McClellan of Arkansas, revealed the abuses of some labor union leaders, including illegal expense accounts, racketeering, and bribery. In response to calls for more regulation of unions, Congress passed the Welfare and Pension Plans Disclosure Act in 1958. This law provided for public access to the records of union welfare and pension funds in order to protect the workers' rights.

The Labor Management Reporting and Disclosure Act (the Landrum-Griffin Act) of 1959 established further regulation of labor unions. Unions were required to file financial reports with the Secretary of Labor. Persons convicted of felonies were barred from holding union office, and additional controls were placed on picketing and secondary boycotts.

In 1955, the long-standing split in the ranks of organized labor was healed when the American Federation of Labor (AFL) and the Congress of Industrial Organizations (CIO) agreed to merge to form a single union federation with 15 million members. George Meany became the first president of the AFL-CIO.

Eisenhower and Agriculture

Charging that farmers had become dependent on the federal government's maintaining the prices of agricultural products and farm incomes, Secretary of Agriculture Ezra Taft Benson called for the establishment of flexible price supports. A law passed in 1954 authorized the Secretary of Agriculture to set price supports in relation to production, with increases in agricultural production leading to lower support prices. The administration hoped that this system would encourage farmers to reduce production.

Surpluses of agricultural products continued to increase, however. As commodities flowed into storage facilities, the government's cost of operating the farm program increased. The Agricultural Trade Development and Assistance Act of 1954, frequently referred to as P.L. 480, provided that surplus agricultural products could be sold overseas for foreign currencies instead of dollars. Surplus commodities could also be bartered or even given away to poor countries. In addition, the act encouraged increased domestic consumption through government-supported school lunch and welfare programs.

Agricultural surpluses continued to be a problem and, to compound matters, farm income declined from $15.3 billion in 1952 to $12.6 billion in 1954 and dropped even more in 1955 and 1956. Concerned about the political repercussions of falling farm income, Congress approved the administration-supported soil bank program in April, 1956. In a renewed effort to reduce agricultural surpluses, this program provided direct payments to farmers who removed land from production.

The Space Race

The Soviet launching of Sputnik I, the first artificial earth satellite, on October 4, 1957, stunned Americans. The United States now began a major effort to catch up with the Soviets, placing its first satellite in orbit on January 31, 1958. The National Aeronautics and Space Act of 1958 placed the nonmilitary aspects of the space program under the control of the National Aeronautics and Space Agency (NASA).

The widespread belief that the Soviets had a substantial lead in the space race became a domestic political issue as Democrats charged the Republicans with responsibility for the missile gap. The alleged missile gap became an issue in the 1960 presidential election, although no gap existed in reality.

The National Defense Education Act

Reacting to Soviet space achievements, Congress moved to provide federal aid to education. The National Defense Education Act, passed in 1958, provided assistance for the improvement of instruction in the critical areas of science, mathematics, and foreign languages at all levels. Loan programs for college students were established, and graduate fellowships were provided for students interested in college-teaching careers.

The Recession of 1957–58

Declines in consumer spending, private investment, and industrial production produced the recession of 1957–58, the second of three recessions during the Eisenhower years. (The first had occurred in 1953–54. The third, in 1960–61, helped the

Democrats regain the Presidency in 1960.) By December, 1957, unemployment had hit 5.2 percent and would rise even higher in early 1958.

In principle, Eisenhower opposed increasing federal spending to stimulate the economy (referred to as pump priming). Faced with the 1957–58 recession, however, the President agreed to increase the pace of military procurement by the Defense Department, which also stepped up work on military construction projects. In addition, the government increased spending for interstate highway construction and for the construction of hospitals and other public facilities. The Federal Reserve Board reduced interest rates in order to stimulate the economy, while the Federal Housing Administration (FHA) reduced down payments for FHA-insured home mortgages in an attempt to encourage private construction. These pump-priming measures helped pull the nation out of the recession.

The 1957–58 recession stymied Eisenhower's efforts to get federal spending under control. The President did reach his objective of a balanced budget in fiscal years 1956 and 1957. But for the fiscal year ending in June, 1958, the deficit reached $2.8 billion, and for the 1959 fiscal year it increased to $12.4 billion. The national debt, which had been $260 billion in 1953, rose to $286 billion in 1960.

The 1958 Congressional Elections

While Eisenhower remained personally popular, the recession hurt the Republicans. In addition, the administration was damaged by a scandal involving presidential assistant Sherman Adams, who had to resign after admitting that he had accepted gifts from a Boston textile firm seeking government favors. Farmers, too, were unhappy with the administration's farm programs.

In the 1958 congressional elections, the Democrats had big

gains. Gaining 48 seats in the House of Representatives, the Democrats increased their majority to 282 seats compared to 154 for the Republicans. In the Senate, the Democrats picked up 15 seats and outnumbered the Republicans 64 seats to 34.

The Mass-Consumption Society

Increasingly, during the 1950s, the United States became an affluent society, to use the term popularized by economist John Kenneth Galbraith. More Americans than ever before could afford material goods far beyond the mere necessities of life: cars, clothing, jewelry, furniture, appliances, vacation and leisure time activities, etc. Between 1945 and 1960, the gross national product (GNP) increased more than 250 percent, from $200 billion to over $500 billion. From 1946 to 1960, the purchasing power of Americans rose by 22 percent. Although about one-fifth of the nation's families continued to be affected by poverty, discretionary spending increased from $40 billion in 1940 to $100 billion in 1950. By 1959, discretionary spending reached $200 billion. By the mid-1960s, the United States—with 5 percent of the world's population—produced and consumed more than one-third of the world's goods and services.

Consumer Credit

The ready availability of credit helped bolster the consumer spirit of the American people. Before World War II, consumer credit was used primarily for major purchases, such as homes and cars. In 1946, short- and intermediate-term loans totaled only $8 billion but increased to $127 billion in 1970. Department stores introduced revolving charge accounts with the then-unheard-of annual interest rate of 12 percent. American Express, Diner's Club, and Carte Blanche cards became a familiar aspect of American life, although bank credit cards such as Visa (originally BankAmericard) and MasterCard (originally

Master Charge) did not come into widespread use until the 1960s.

Advertising

The expansion of advertising helped encourage people's desires to consume. In *The Hidden Persuaders* (1957), Vance Packard praised advertising for its promotion of continued economic growth and for being "a colorful, diverting aspect of American life."

The Automobile

More than ever, America was a nation on wheels. During the 1950s, the number of privately owned cars doubled, and about 70,000 to 80,000 miles of new highways were built each year. In 1950, the federal government spent $429 million for highway construction. With the commitment to construct the interstate highway system, federal spending for highways rose to $2.9 billion in 1960.

The automobile also encouraged the development of national franchise operations like Holiday Inn, Kentucky Fried Chicken, Burger King, and McDonald's. By 1962, McDonald's total sales had reached $76 million. In 1974, they hit $2 billion.

Television

During the 1950s, television swept across the country. In 1946, only 8,000 households in major cities had television sets, while 34 million households had radios. By 1947, 66 commercial television stations were on the air. In 1950, almost 4 million households had television sets. During the 1950s, manufacturers produced from 6 to 7 million sets a year, and by the end of the decade 500 television stations were operating. In

1960, close to 46 million American households had television sets, while just over 50 million had radios.

The Computer

During the 1950s, many Americans became aware of computers for the first time. Although they had been developed during World War II, computers were not marketed commercially until the early 1950s. In 1953, computer sales totaled $25 million. By 1960, they had reached $1 billion.

International Business Machines (IBM), headed by Thomas J. Watson, was a major pioneer in computer technology. The Mark I computer, built in 1943, stood 8 feet high and was 55 feet long and contained about a million parts. A big breakthrough came in 1948 when the transistor was developed. Transistors would quickly replace electronic tubes.

Corporate Consolidation

Corporate consolidation, which had long been a major feature of American business, continued through the post-World War II years. By 1960, the fewer than 100 corporations with assets of more than $1 billion owned almost half the nation's corporate wealth. The American Telephone and Telegraph Company (AT & T) was the nation's largest corporation, with assets in excess of $24 billion. General Motors, the largest manufacturing corporation, had assets of almost $13 billion. In the automobile industry, three firms—General Motors, Ford, and Chrysler—were more dominant than ever. Small competitors had either disappeared completely or had merged to form American Motors.

American corporate activity also began increasingly to involve conglomerates and multinational corporations. Conglomerates developed as corporations sought to gain protection against market shifts by taking over companies which were engaged in completely unrelated activities. Multinational corporations expanded considerably as a result of growing operations in foreign countries.

Agricultural Consolidation

Just as American business expanded during the years after 1945, so too did American agriculture. Between 1945 and 1970, the value of agricultural production in constant dollars increased by 120 percent. While the productivity of farm labor tripled, the size of the farm labor force decreased by over 50 percent. New machinery was introduced, and the use of fertilizers and pesticides increased. The value of farm land rose from $69 billion in 1945 to $168 billion in 1960 and to $266 billion in 1970. Consolidation led to an increase in the size of the average farm from 195 acres in 1945 to 373 acres in 1970. Agribusiness expanded as more farms came to be owned by corporations and financial institutions rather than by independent farmers.

The Baby Boom

The postwar baby boom continued through the 1950s. In 1940, there had been 2.5 million births in the United States. In 1950, there were 3.5 million births, and in 1957, the baby boom peaked with 4.3 million births. At the same time, life expectancy rose. In 1920, the average life expectancy was 55 years for whites and 45 years for blacks. By the mid 1950s, it had increased to 70 years and 64 years, respectively. While the American population grew by 19 million in the 1940s, it increased by 29 million in the 1950s, reaching 179 million in 1960.

During the 1950s, large families became more common than they had been in the depression decade of the 1930s. There was a reemphasis of the traditional role of women as wives and mothers and an emphasis on family "togetherness." In 1946, Dr. Benjamin Spock published *Baby and Child Care*, which appeared in repeated new editions during the following years. With its emphasis on a child-centered approach to raising children, Spock's book had a powerful influence on the lives of millions of American families and still sells actively today.

The baby boom led to a great expansion of the American school system. During the decade from 1946 to 1956, enrollments in grades one through eight increased from 20 million to 30 million and spurred a great boom in school construction.

The baby boom also produced a growing number of young consumers who had their own tastes in both clothing and music and the money to satisfy these tastes. The 1950s and 1960s became increasingly an age of blue jeans, T-shirts, and rock 'n' roll. In 1951, Allen Freed, a white disk jockey in Cleveland, began to play rhythm and blues for a primarily white audience. Freed claimed he was the inventor of the term rock 'n' roll. In 1954, Freed moved to WINS, a major AM station in New York, and by the mid-1950s, rock 'n' roll was changing the sound of American pop music. In 1953, "Crazy Man Crazy" by Bill Haley and the Comets became the first rock 'n' roll record to make the *Billboard* pop charts. Haley's other hits included "Shake, Rattle and Roll," which made the top ten in both the United States and Great Britain, and "Rock Around the Clock," which hit number one in the United States and was featured in *Blackboard Jungle*, a 1955 movie about juvenile delinquents. In the summer of 1956, Elvis Presley made his first appearance on national television on the "Tommy and Jimmy Dorsey Show." Rock 'n' roll performers increased their audiences and record sales by making frequent tours and appearing on television shows such as Dick Clark's "American Bandstand."

While the introduction of rock 'n' roll revolutionized the music business, it was aided by technology, with the introduction of 45 rpm records for singles and 33 rpm long-playing discs for albums. The youth culture also brought great changes to the movie industry. With the advent of television, adults tended to stay home more, and during the 1950s, over 70 percent of those who bought movie tickets were under 30 years of age.

Cultural Dissent

While the 1950s appeared to be a time of conformity in American society, there were some who questioned its values. Holden Caulfield, the central figure in J. D. Salinger's novel *The Catcher in the Rye* (1951) became a symbol for sensitive young people who were striving to define and maintain their individuality and independence. Similar themes were reflected in movies—among them *Rebel Without a Cause*, starring James Dean, and *The Wild One*, Marlon Brando.

The writers and poets of the "beat" generation, often known as beatniks, were in open revolt against the self-satisfaction of the affluent society. In his novel *On the Road* (1957), Jack Kerouac wrote of a cross-country trip by car and extolled a life free of the restraints imposed by conventional middle-class society. The flamboyant Allen Ginsberg published his poem "Howl" in 1956, and it quickly became a sensation, especially after Ginsberg was charged with violating laws against obscenity. These and other "beat" writers, such as Lawrence Ferlinghetti and William Burroughs, were precursors of the counterculture which emerged in the 1960s.

Population Mobility

While Americans grew in numbers, they also became more mobile. The country's rural population continued to decline, and during the 1950s more than a million people a year left the nation's farms in search of employment elsewhere. The westward shift of population, which had become pronounced during World War II, continued. Between 1940 and 1950, the southwestern and western states of Texas, New Mexico, Arizona, Utah, Nevada, California, Oregon, and Washington all experienced a population growth of more than 20 percent. California led the way with a population increase of over 53 percent and by 1963 became the nation's most populous state. During the 1950s, Los Angeles replaced Philadelphia as the nation's third largest city. The westward movement of the American people was symbolized by the granting of statehood to Alaska and Hawaii in 1959.

The Growth of the Suburbs

In 1940, just over half of the American people lived in areas defined by the Census Bureau as metropolitan. By 1960, about 63 percent did. At the same time, within these metropolitan areas, the population was shifting from the central cities to suburbs located outside the city limits. As a result, some cities, including Boston, New York, Philadelphia, Detroit, and Chicago, actually lost population during the 1950s. By the end of the decade, about a third of the American people lived in suburbs.

Religion

Religion shared in the general expansion of the postwar years. Between 1945 and 1970, church membership almost doubled, and well over 90 percent of adult Americans identified themselves with a religious denomination.

Eisenhower expressed the national mood in many ways during the 1950s, and he did so in his support of the importance of religion in national life. During the decade the words "under God" were added to the Pledge of Allegiance, and the motto "In God We Trust" was placed on all currency. The evangelist the Rev. Billy Graham became a national figure, and *The Power of Positive Thinking* (1952), by Dr. Norman Vincent Peale, became one of the best sellers of the 1950s. Roman Catholic Bishop Fulton J. Sheen won a large audience for his regularly-scheduled primetime television program, "Life Is Worth Living."

Women in the 1950s

During the 1950s, there was a reemphasis of traditional male-female roles and family "togetherness." Popular television situation comedy series, such as "I Love Lucy," "Father Knows Best," "Ozzie and Harriet," and "Leave It to Beaver," both reflected and intensified this trend. Nevertheless, more married women entered the labor force than ever before. In 1940, only 15 percent of married women worked outside the home. By 1950, 21 percent did, and by 1960 the figure had risen to 30 percent. Married women came to account for more than half of all working women; this represented a dramatic change. Many working-class families found that the wives' incomes were necessary for survival, while middle-class women sought second incomes in order to help their families achieve a higher standard of living or to pay for the college education of their children.

Black women had fewer opportunities for employment than white women. At the end of the 1940s, the median income of black women was less than half that earned by white women. During the 1950s, black women gradually found more opportunities to move into white collar jobs, and by 1960 over a third of black working women had professional, clerical, sales or service jobs. Black working women now had an income that amounted to about 70 percent of that earned by white women.

Blacks in the 1950s

During the 1940s, over 1.5 million blacks left the rural South. While some moved to southern cities, most migrated to cities in the Northeast and upper Midwest. A comparable number went West. Almost as many blacks moved from the rural South in the 1950s with the migration following the general pattern of the 1940s.

While Truman's civil rights program had not won congressional enactment, blacks could not be as readily ignored or oppressed as in the past. In 1932, only about 100,000 blacks had been registered voters in the South. By 1952, the number had increased to over one million, even though many southern states continued to restrict black voting rights. By the early 1950s, blacks had made some gains in winning admission to the professional schools of southern universities, and black graduate students had enrolled in the previously segregated universities of Oklahoma, Texas, Missouri, and North Carolina.

The May, 1954, Supreme Court decision in the case of *Brown v. Board of Education of Topeka* marked the beginning of the end of segregation in American public education. In a unanimous decision drafted by Chief Justice Earl Warren, the Supreme Court rejected the doctrine of "separate but equal" in public education. "Separate educational facilities," the court declared, "are inherently unequal." The decision had far-reaching implications, since schools in 21 states and the District of Columbia were segregated on the basis of race. A year later, in the spring of 1955, the Supreme Court ordered the implementation of the Brown decision "with all deliberate speed."

In the South, the Brown decision evoked shock and anger. In many communities, White Citizens Councils were established to organize resistance to school integration, and several state governments called for "massive resistance" campaigns. Some states enacted pupil placement laws which authorized school officials to assign children to schools on the basis of their academic ability and social behavior. These laws provided a means to maintain school segregation in defiance of the Supreme Court decision. Other forms of resistance to school desegregation involved the closing of public schools when court orders made integration inevitable and withholding state funds from integrated schools. In March, 1956, over 100 southern members of Congress, led by North Carolina's Senator Sam Ervin, issued the "Southern Manifesto." This statement criticized the Supreme Court's interference in local affairs and pledged to use all lawful means to reverse this trend. In a 1958 decision in the case of *Shuttlesworth v. Birmingham Board of Education,* the Supreme Court ruled pupil placement laws unconstitutional.

The Eisenhower administration was reluctant to promote desegregation, but the President recognized his obligation to carry out the law of the land. While Eisenhower ordered the desegregation of the schools in the District of Columbia, he showed considerable sympathy for the South in a time of transition.

In September, 1957, the court-ordered integration of Central High School in Little Rock, Arkansas, provoked a crisis. White resistance to integration was intensified by the attitude of Governor Orval Faubus, a determined segregationist. In the face of continuing white defiance of a federal court order, Eisenhower federalized the Arkansas National Guard and sent paratroopers to Little Rock to protect the black students attending Central High School.

In 1955, the Interstate Commerce Commission (ICC) barred segregation on interstate trains and buses and in passenger waiting rooms. At the same time, local transit systems throughout the South remained segregated.

In December, 1955, blacks launched a boycott of the bus system in Montgomery, Alabama. Mrs. Rosa Parks sat down in the front section of a city bus where the seats were reserved for whites and refused to move. She was arrested for violating Montgomery's Jim Crow (segregation) laws. Blacks responded to Mrs. Parks' arrest by organizing a bus boycott. The Rev. Martin Luther King, Jr., a 27-year-old Baptist minister, played a leading role in the bus boycott and quickly became a major figure in the growing civil rights movement. The year-long boycott ended segregation on Montgomery's buses, and the idea spread to other southern cities. In late 1956, the Supreme Court barred segregation on city transit systems.

The Montgomery bus boycott helped spur the creation of the

Southern Christian Leadership Conference (SCLC), led by King. Mounting black activism also encouraged the revitalization of older black organizations such as the National Association for the Advancement of Colored People (NAACP), the Congress of Racial Equality (CORE), and the Urban League. In addition, more radical black groups emerged, including the Black Muslims which had about about 100,000 members by 1960.

In 1957, Congress passed the first Civil Rights Act in 82 years. Steered through Congress by Senator Lyndon B. Johnson, the Democratic majority leader, the Civil Rights Act of 1957 established the Civil Rights Commission, as well as the Civil Rights Division in the Justice Department. The law authorized the Justice Department to take legal action in cases where blacks were denied the right to vote. Continuing efforts to bar blacks from voting led to the enactment of the Civil Rights Act of 1960, which authorized federal judges to appoint referees who would assist blacks in voter registration and voting.

Hispanics in the 1950s

Most Hispanics in the United States were of Mexican, Central American, Cuban or Puerto Rican birth or descent. The most numerous were the Mexican-Americans or Chicanos. Under the terms of the Migratory Labor Agreement with Mexico, millions of Mexicans came to the United States for temporary work, with most providing labor for the harvest of crops in the Southwest and West. The braceros, as these farm laborers were known, were supposed to return to Mexico when their work ended, but many remained. In addition, several million other Mexicans entered the United States illegally.

The Chicanos and other Hispanics suffered from patterns of discrimination similar to those experienced by blacks, and during the 1950s Hispanics made few breakthroughs.

American Indians in the 1950s

Following World War II, Congress established the Indian Claims Commission to review Indian claims that tribal lands had been taken from them in violation of federal treaties. In a number of cases, the Indians received substantial financial settlements and, in a few instances, land was restored to Indian ownership.

During the 1950s, the Eisenhower administration abandoned the Indian policy of the New Deal which had supported the maintenance of tribal identity and autonomy. The federal government began to promote the so-called termination policy which was designed to eliminate Indian reservations and to encourage Indians to assimilate into American society. The new policy led to considerable disruption of Indian life and was abandoned by the Kennedy administration in 1961.

Foreign Trade and Aid

When Eisenhower became President, there were some demands for a more protectionist trade policy, but Eisenhower continued the policies of Roosevelt and Truman which were designed to reduce barriers to trade. Congress voted extensions of the Trade Agreements Act of 1934 which provided for reciprocal trade agreements involving reductions in tariffs and other restrictions on trade.

Balance of payments deficits proved to be an increasing problem and, by the late 1950s, caused a serious drain on American gold reserves. These deficits resulted from private investments and military expenditures abroad, imports, spending by tourists, and foreign aid. Eisenhower hoped that a growth of international trade would lead to an increase in American exports and reduce the outflow of gold. While the surplus of exports over imports generally ranged from $4 to $6 billion a year during the 1950s, this surplus was not large enough to cover other American expenditures and investments overseas.

American foreign aid programs were designed to assist overseas economies in recovering from the damage suffered during World War II, to promote the development of underdeveloped countries, and to reduce the appeal of Communism and restrict Soviet expansion. Foreign aid took various forms: economic and military assistance, technical and educational assistance, and long-term loans that were intended mainly to promote economic development. During the Eisenhower years, annual expenditures for foreign aid ranged from a low of $2.7 billion to a high of $6 billion.

Defense Policy

During the 1950s, the arms race between the United States and the Soviet Union intensified. The United States tested its first hydrogen bomb in 1952, and the Soviets followed suit two years later.

During the 1952 campaign, the Republicans promised a "New Look" in defense policy, pledging a stronger defense at less expense. After taking office, Eisenhower and Secretary of Defense Wilson sought to reduce spending by emphasizing air power and atomic weapons, which would provide maximum destructive power at the lowest cost. In the words of one observer, there would be "more bang for a buck."

Explaining this policy in January, 1954, Secretary of State Dulles created a furor by declaring that the United States would "depend primarily upon a great capacity to retaliate, instantly, by means and at places of our own choosing." Dulles' remark began a national debate over this policy, which became know as "massive retaliation." Dulles' critics, which included the frightened allies of the United States, insisted that "massive retaliation" meant that in any conflict the United States would have to respond either by launching a nuclear war or doing nothing. In fact, however, despite Dulles' rhetoric, there was no decisive change in American defense policy. American conventional forces remained substantially larger than they had been in 1950. The military budget had averaged $12 billion a year in the late 1940s, rising to close to $50 billion in 1953, the year the Korean War ended. In 1955, military spending dropped to about $40 billion and then began to increase once again, reaching $45 billion by the end of the decade.

The Liberation Policy

The Republicans had criticized the containment policy of the Truman administration as a negative policy and had urged a policy of liberation designed to promote a rollback of Soviet power in Europe. In practice, however, there was no way to liberate the "captive nations" of Eastern Europe without a war, and Eisenhower's foreign policy did not differ dramatically from Truman's.

The 1953 East German Uprising

In July, 1953, East Germans demonstrated against their own government and the Soviet occupation authorities. While the United States expressed sympathy for the East Germans, it did not intervene. This demonstrated the Eisenhower administration's continued practice of the policy of containment rather than an attempt to implement the policy of liberation.

The 1956 Hungarian Revolt

In the fall of 1956, the Soviet Union intervened militarily in Hungary to suppress an anti-Soviet revolt. While the United States protested, it took no action to come to the aid of the Hungarian rebels, which would have created the possibility of a general war. Once again, the Eisenhower administration did not attempt to practice liberation, and the Soviets imposed a pro-Soviet regime on Hungary.

The American reaction to the revolts in both East Germany and Hungary indicated that the United States acknowledged its inability to influence events in Eastern Europe. At the same time, the East German and Hungarian revolts provided evidence of a gradual erosion of the Soviets' ability to dominate Eastern Europe as totally as they had in the years immediately following the end of the war in 1945.

West German Rearmament

The Eisenhower administration continued the policy, initiated by Truman, which sought to reach an agreement among the Western allies to rearm West Germany and bring that country into the Western defense system. France's fear of a rearmed Germany stood as the main obstacle in the path of achieving this objective.

In an effort to win French agreement, the United States applied pressure on France. In December, 1953, Secretary of State Dulles warned the French that their refusal to agree to West Germany's rearmament "would compel an agonizing reappraisal of basic United States policy." Despite Dulles' threat of an "agonizing reappraisal," the French rejected the treaty for the creation of the European Defense Community (EDC) in the summer of 1954. The EDC proposed the creation of an integrated Western European army including West German troops.

Following the collapse of the EDC, negotiations among the Western allies resulted in a British commitment to maintain several divisions on the European continent in order to provide reassurance to the French. The Western powers then agreed to permit the rearmament of West Germany, and the Federal Republic of Germany became a member of NATO in 1955.

The Middle East and the Suez Crisis of 1956

In 1947, Truman expressed American support of the establishment of an independent Jewish state in Palestine, which was then a British mandate. In May, 1948, when the state of Israel was proclaimed, Truman immediately recognized the new country. Although the Arab states went to war against Israel, the Israelis made good their claim to independence.

In the early 1950s, a revolt in Egypt resulted in the overthrow of King Farouk and the gradual emergence of Gamal Abdel Nasser, an ardent nationalist, as Egypt's leader. An advocate of both Egyptian nationalism and Pan-Arabism, Nasser initiated a campaign against British influence and Western influence generally in the Middle East. Nasser developed an ambitious plan for Egypt's economic development, which was centered on the construction of a high dam at Aswan on the Nile River. Egypt received pledges of loans to help build the dam from the United States, Great Britain, and the World Bank.

When Nasser tried to play the two sides in the Cold War off against one another and secured arms and a loan from the Soviets, the United States responded in July, 1956, by canceling American support for the Aswan high dam. Great Britain and the World Bank did the same. At the end of July, Nasser retaliated by seizing the privately-owned Suez Canal Company. Although Nasser agreed to compensate the company's owners, the British and French were troubled by Egyptian control of the strategically important canal.

Great Britain and France entered into a plan with Israel, which feared an Egyptian attack. Acting in accord with London and Paris, Israel launched a preemptive strike against Egypt on October 29, 1956. Britain and France quickly moved into the canal zone, ostensibly to separate the antagonists but in reality to retake control of the canal.

World opinion joined in condemnation of the British,

French, and Israelis. The United States and the Soviet Union cooperated in supporting a United Nations resolution calling on the invaders to withdraw. Isolated diplomatically, the British, French, and Israelis complied. Egypt paid the Suez Canal Company's stockholders $81 million for the canal, and the Soviets helped the Egyptians build the Aswan high dam. The Soviets benefitted from the crisis since they were able to present themselves as strong defenders of Arab nationalism.

The Middle East After the Suez Crisis

In the aftermath of the Suez crisis, the United States had to reassess its policy in the Middle East. In the Eisenhower Doctrine, set forth in 1957, the United States expressed its readiness to intervene in the Middle East if any government, threatened by "international Communism," requested American assistance. In its emphasis on international Communism, the Eisenhower Doctrine paid insufficient attention to the role of Arab nationalism in promoting instability in the Middle East. In addition, the United States was committing itself to promote stability in a region where there were few stable states.

The Middle East continued to be beset by troubles in the late 1950s. An arms race intensified between Israel and the Arab states, while the Arabs remained embroiled in disputes among themselves. In 1958, Nasser united Egypt with Syria to form the United Arab Republic (UAR) under his leadership. While Nasser remained strongly antagonistic toward the West, Turkey, Iraq, and Iran were generally pro-Western.

Saudi Arabia, Lebanon, and Jordan sought to steer a middle course, but faced growing pressure from elements sympathetic to Nasser. In 1957, Jordan's King Hussein survived an attempted coup and began to draw closer to the United States and Great Britain. In 1958, anti-Western elements seized power in Iraq. Threatened by Nasser partisans, Lebanon and Jordan appealed to the Western powers for help. In mid-1958, American forces intervened in Lebanon, while British paratroopers landed in Jordan. In both countries, pro-Western governments remained in power.

Korea

Korea stood at the top of the Eisenhower administration's agenda for Asia. In December, 1952, Eisenhower fulfilled his campaign promise to go to Korea, although his trip did more to boost the morale of American troops in the field and civilians at home than it did to break the stalemate in the armistice negotiations.

The negotiations had been stalled by the prisoner of war issue, with the North Koreans and Chinese insisting on repatriation of all prisoners without regard for their own desires. In March, 1953, the North Koreans and Chinese unexpectedly agreed to accept the principle of voluntary repatriation. It remains unclear whether this shift came as a result of a thinly veiled American threat to use nuclear weapons or as a consequence of changes in Soviet policy following Stalin's death in early March. With the logjam broken, negotiations moved forward. On July 27, 1953, an armistice was signed at Panmunjom. Under its terms, Korea remained divided at the 38th parallel. During the Korean War, over 33,000 Americans were killed in action, while more than 20,000 died of other causes. Over 103,000 were wounded.

Indochina

Although the war in Korea had ended, the United States gradually became involved in Indochina in opposition to what it regarded as an expansion of Communist power.

In Indochina, nationalist elements had begun a guerrilla war in an effort to prevent the reestablishment of French imperialist

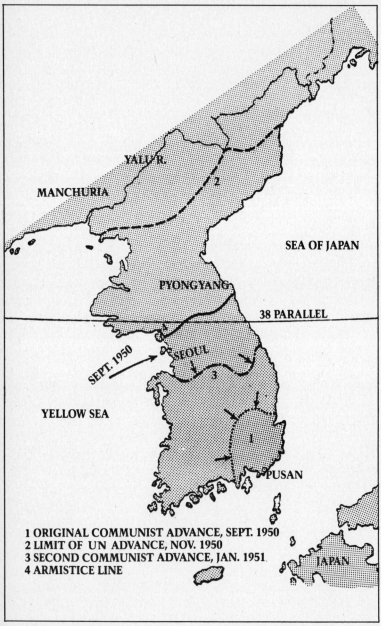

YALU R.

MANCHURIA

2

SEA OF JAPAN

PYONGYANG

38 PARALLEL

SEPT. 1950 → SEOUL

3

YELLOW SEA

1

PUSAN

1 ORIGINAL COMMUNIST ADVANCE, SEPT. 1950
2 LIMIT OF UN ADVANCE, NOV. 1950
3 SECOND COMMUNIST ADVANCE, JAN. 1951
4 ARMISTICE LINE

JAPAN

The Korean War

control following World War II. What made Indochinese nationalism different from nationalism elsewhere in Asia was the fact that Ho Chi Minh, the leading Indochinese nationalist, was a Communist. Because Ho Chi Minh bore that label, the conflict in Indochina became a part of the Cold War.

By 1950, Ho Chi Minh had united the nationalists in the part of Indochina that would become known as Vietnam into a movement called the Viet Minh. Ho Chi Minh's forces succeeded in inflicting a series of defeats on the French, and the United States provided an increasing level of support for the French cause. Despite this aid, the French stronghold of Dienbienphu fell to the Viet Minh in May, 1954, and the French decided to withdraw from Indochina.

Eisenhower compared the situation in Southeast Asia to a row of dominoes. According to this "domino theory," if one country fell to the Communists, the others would quickly topple over like a row of dominoes standing on end. At the same time, Eisenhower resisted pressure for direct American military intervention in Indochina to take France's place in the war against the Viet Minh.

An international conference held in Geneva, Switzerland, in the summer of 1954 reached agreement on the Geneva Accords, which divided Indochina into the three separate and independent states of Laos, Cambodia, and Vietnam and then further divided Vietnam at the 17th parallel. This separation of North and South Vietnam was supposed to be temporary, pending elections scheduled for 1956 which would determine the nature of Vietnam's government. Ho Chi Minh, who was in control of North Vietnam, expected that these elections would give him control of the South, as well.

While the United States did not sign the Geneva Accords, it declared that it would refrain from the threat or use of force to disrupt them. The United States began to provide assistance to South Vietnam and selected Ngo Dinh Diem, a Catholic and fervent anti-Communist, to lead the country. With American support, Diem refused to carry out the agreement to hold elections in 1956. In response, Ho Chi Minh renewed the war in Vietnam. The United States increased its support of Diem's government and came in time to be directly involved in the conflict.

SEATO

In September, 1954, following the conclusion of the Geneva Accords, the United States sponsored the creation of the Southeast Asia Treaty Organization (SEATO), which was intended to be the Asian equivalent of NATO. SEATO's members included the United States, Great Britain, France, Australia, New Zealand, the Philippines, Thailand, and Pakistan. A number of SEATO's members were obviously not Asian states, and the membership did not include several important ones, among them Indonesia and India.

The Baghdad Pact

The Eisenhower administration completed the American alliance system by creating the Baghdad Pact in 1955. Consisting of Great Britain, Turkey, Iraq, Iran, and Pakistan, the Baghdad Pact joined NATO and SEATO. Turkey, the easternmost member of NATO, was the westernmost member of the Baghdad Pact, while Pakistan, the westernmost member of SEATO, was the easternmost member of the Baghdad Pact.

In 1958, Iraq dropped out of the Baghdad Pact in the wake of an anti-Western coup. Since Baghdad was Iraq's capital, the alliance was renamed the Central Treaty Organization (CENTO).

China

The Eisenhower administration maintained an implacable

hostility toward the Communist government of the People's Republic of China (PRC) and supported Chiang Kai-shek's Nationalist government on Taiwan. There was even some talk of "unleashing Chiang Kai-shek," although there was little realistic possibility of his returning to the mainland. While the United States clearly did not want to become embroiled in a conflict with the PRC, the Eisenhower administration backed the Nationalists in their desire to hold onto the two small off-shore islands of Quemoy and Matsu. In the Formosa Resolution of 1955, Congress authorized the President to defend the two islands if an attack on them appeared to be a step toward an attack on Taiwan (Formosa).

American Interventionism

The United States actively intervened in the domestic affairs of Iran and Guatemala.

By 1953, there was growing concern that Mohammed Mossadegh's government in oil-rich Iran might draw closer to the Soviet Union. In response to this threat, the United States provided aid—including the assistance of CIA operatives—to conservative elements in Iran. Mossadegh was overthrown, and Shah Mohammed Reza Pahlevi was restored to power. Mossadegh had earlier nationalized the British-controlled Anglo-Iranian Oil Company, and the Shah now agreed to the creation of an international consortium which gave substantial control of Iran's oil to the Western powers. The Shah's government remained closely tied to the United States for the next 25 years.

In 1951, the leftist government of Jacobo Arbenz Guzmán came to power in Guatemala. The Arbenz government then seized the property of the American-owned United Fruit Company, the country's largest landowner. The Eisenhower administration brought American influence to bear in the Organization of American States (OAS) to secure the adoption of a resolution which identified the Arbenz government with "international Communism." In June, 1954, American CIA agents collaborated with Guatemalan rebels led by Col. Carlos Castillo Armas in overthrowing Arbenz.

The intervention in Guatemala strengthened anti-American sentiment in much of Latin America. When Vice President Richard M. Nixon visited Lima, Peru, and Caracas, Venzuela, in 1958, he encountered angry mobs and had to cancel the balance of his trip.

The United States and the New Soviet Leadership

Following Joseph Stalin's death in March, 1953, the Soviet government passed into the hands of a more moderate collective leadership. Communist party chief Nikita Khrushchev and Premier Nikolai Bulganin spoke of the "noninevitability of war" and "peaceful coexistence" between the Soviet Union and the West.

In 1955, the Soviet Union and the major Western allies, the United States, Great Britain, and France, reached agreement on the Austrian State Treaty. This accord ended the four-power occupation of Austria, which became a fully independent state committed to neutrality.

The Geneva Summit

In July, 1955, Eisenhower, British Prime Minister Anthony Eden, and French Premier Edgar Faure met with Khrushchev and Bulganin in Geneva. This was the first meeting in a decade of the heads of the four governments, who conducted their talks in a cordial atmosphere. Following this summit meeting, there was talk of the "Spirit of Geneva," even though East and West had not reached any agreements on the major issues which divided them, especially the reunification of Germany and arms limitation.

The Berlin Crisis of 1958

During 1957, Khrushchev established his dominant position among the Soviet leadership and ended his partnership with Bulganin. By 1958, Khrushchev was prepared to initiate action in an effort to solve the German question on terms favorable to the Soviet Union.

In November, 1958, Khrushchev demanded that the West agree to accept the neutralization and demilitarization of West Berlin within six months. If they did not, the Soviets would sign a separate peace treaty with East Germany and turn all of their rights in Berlin over, the East Germans. This would force the Americans, British, and French to deal with a government they did not recognize.

The Soviets wanted to act in Berlin because West Berlin provided an easy escape route for dissatisfied East Germans. The flight of a large number of East Germans to the West was creating a crisis situation for the East German economy, which could not continue to sustain the loss of so much skilled labor.

When the Western powers refused to give way, Khrushchev let the six-month deadline pass. It remained apparent, however, that the Soviet leader was not prepared to accept the Berlin situation as it stood.

Nevertheless, the immediate crisis had passed by the spring of 1959, and in September Khrushchev paid a generally cordial visit to the United States. Eisenhower and Khrushchev agreed to discuss Germany and other outstanding issues at a summit meeting to be held in Paris in the spring of 1960. A visit by Eisenhower to the Soviet Union was also planned.

The U-2 Incident and the Collapse of the Paris Summit

Since 1955, American high-altitude U-2 spy planes had been carrying out surveillance operations over Soviet territory. On May 1, 1960, the Soviets succeeded in downing a U-2 and capturing its pilot, Francis Gary Powers. A Soviet court convicted Powers of spying and sentenced him to a prison term of ten years. In 1962, Powers was exchanged for Col. Rudolf Abel, a Soviet agent held by the United States.

Khrushchev used the U-2 incident to break up the Paris summit meeting as it was about to convene in June. He also canceled Eisenhower's planned visit to the Soviet Union. In all probability, Khrushchev was pleased to have a pretext for calling off the summit, since it was evident that neither side was prepared to give way on any of its established positions.

The U-2 incident and the collapse of the Paris summit created an atmosphere of uncertainty in American-Soviet relations on the eve of the 1960 presidential election.

As President, Eisenhower sought to pursue a traditional Republican policy of reducing the role of the federal government. Despite this intention, the activities of the federal government continued to expand. The establishment of the cabinet-level Department of Health, Education, and Welfare in 1953 served as a symbol of this expanding role of the federal government in the lives of the American people.

The Supreme Court's 1954 decision banning racial segregation in the public schools and the Montgomery bus boycott of 1955 marked the beginning of a concerted effort to assure the civil rights of black Americans following years of inconclusive debate. The Eisenhower administration was reluctant, however, to undertake vigorous action to promote civil rights.

In foreign affairs, the Eisenhower administration continued to practice the policy of containment, which had been developed under Truman, despite earlier Republican calls for a more active policy of liberation. The armistice of 1953 brought an end to the Korean War, but serious tension continued in American-Soviet relations. Although the Geneva summit meeting of 1954 brought a temporary easing of the Cold War, the Eisenhower ad-

ministration found it difficult to find new approaches to American-Soviet relations in its dealings with the new Kremlin leadership which took power following Stalin's death in 1953.

Recommended Reading

Sherman Adams, *Firsthand Report: The Story of the Eisenhower Administration* (1961).

Charles C. Alexander, *Holding the Line: The Eisenhower Era, 1952–1961* (1975).

Richard A. Aliano, *American Defense Policy from Eisenhower to Kennedy: The Politics of Changing Military Requirements, 1957–1961* (1975).

Stephen E. Ambrose, *Eisenhower: President and Elder Statesman, 1952–1969* (1984).

Stephen E. Ambrose, *Eisenhower: Soldier, General of the Army, President-Elect, 1890–1952* (1983).

Stephen E. Ambrose, *Rise to Globalism: American Foreign Policy Since 1938* (rev. ed., 1985).

John W. Anderson, *Eisenhower, Brownell, and the Congress: The Tangled Origins of the Civil Rights Bill of 1956–1957* (1964).

Numan V. Bartley, *The Rise of Massive Resistance: Race and Politics in the South During the 1950s* (1969).

Daniel Bell, *The End of Ideology: On the Exhaustion of Political Ideas in the Fifties* (1960).

Alexander M. Bickel, *Politics and the Warren Court* (1965).

Robert L. Branyan and Lawrence H. Larson, eds., *The Eisenhower Administration, 1953–1961: A Documentary History* (2 vols., 1971).

Piers Brendon, *Ike: His Life and Times* (1986).

John Brooks, *The Great Leap: The Past Twenty-Five Years in America* (1966).

Robert F. Burk, *Dwight D. Eisenhower: Hero and Politician* (1986).

Robert F. Burk, *The Eisenhower Administration and Black Civil Rights* (1984).

James Cable, *The Geneva Conference of 1954 on Indochina* (1986).

Chester L. Cooper, *The Lion's Last Roar: Suez 1956* (1978).

Carl N. Degler, *Affluence and Anxiety, 1945–Present* (1968).

Robert A. Divine, *Eisenhower and the Cold War* (1981).

Dwight D. Eisenhower, *Mandate for Change, 1953–1956* (1963).

Dwight D. Eisenhower, *Waging Peace, 1956–1961* (1965).

John Kenneth Galbraith, *The Affluent Society* (1958).

Eric F. Goldman, *The Crucial Decade—and After: America, 1945–1960* (1961).

Michael A. Guhin, *John Foster Dulles: A Statesman and His Times* (1972).

Alonzo L. Hamby, *Liberalism and Its Challengers: F.D.R. to Reagan* (1985).

Kenneth T. Jackson, *Crabgrass Frontier: The Suburbanization of the United States* (1985).

Eli J. Kahn, Jr., *The China Hands: America's Foreign Service Officers and What Befell Them* (1975).

Richard Kluger, *Simple Justice: The History of Brown v. Board of Education* and Black America's Struggle for Equality (1977).

William Leuchtenberg, *A Troubled Feast: American Society Since 1945* (rev. ed., 1983).

John Bartlow Martin, *Adlai E. Stevenson of Illinois* (1976).

John Bartlow Martin, *Adlai E. Stevenson and the World* (1977).

Douglas T. Miller and Marion Nowak, *The Fifties: The Way We Really Were* (1977).

James T. Patterson, *Mr. Republican: A Biography of Robert A. Taft* (1972).

Gary W. Reichard, *The Reaffirmation of Republicanism: Eisenhower and the Eighty-Third Congress* (1975).

Andrew J. Rotter, *The Path to Vietnam: Origins of the American Commitment to Southeast Asia* (1987).

Harvard Sitkoff, *A New Deal for Blacks: The Emergence of Civil Rights as a National Issue* (1978).

G. Edward White, *Earl Warren: A Public Life* (1982).

CHAPTER 15

The New Frontier and the Great Society: The Era of Kennedy and Johnson

Time Line

1960	Democrat John F. Kennedy wins the Presidency
	Civil rights activists conduct sit-ins
1961	Retiring President Eisenhower warns the nation about the "military-industrial complex"

Civil rights activists conduct freedom rides

The Bay of Pigs invasion fails

Kennedy and Khrushchev meet in Vienna

The Berlin Wall is erected

The Peace Corps is established

The United States launches the Alliance for Progress

The Twenty-Third Amendment is ratified

1962   Kennedy protests increases in the price of steel

John Glenn orbits the earth

The University of Mississippi is integrated

The *Baker v. Carr* decision establishes the one-person, one-vote rule

The Cuban missile crisis threatens world peace

Michael Harrington publishes *The Other America*

1963   Martin Luther King, Jr., leads the march on Washington

The University of Alabama is integrated

Betty Friedan authors *The Feminine Mystique*

The U.S. and the Soviet Union sign the Nuclear Test Ban Treaty

A coup in Vietnam overthrows the government of Ngo Dinh Diem

Kennedy is assassinated; Vice President Lyndon B. Johnson succeeds to the Presidency

1964   Johnson wins congressional approval for a tax cut

Johnson begins the war on poverty

Congress passes the Civil Rights Act of 1964

The Twenty-Fourth Amendment is ratified

Civil rights activists launch the Freedom Summer campaign

Congress adopts the Gulf of Tonkin Resolution

Johnson wins an overwhelming victory in the presidential election

1965   Johnson proposes his Great Society program

Congress passes Medicare and Medicaid

Martin Luther King, Jr., leads a march from Selma to Birmingham, Alabama

Congress passes the Voting Rights Act

The Watts riot occurs in Los Angeles

The Department of Housing and Urban Development is created

The United States sends combat troops to Vietnam

The United States intervenes in the Dominican Republic

1966   The Department of Transportation is created

1967   The Corporation for Public Broadcasting is established

The Twenty-Fifth Amendment is ratified

Johnson appoints Thurgood Marshall to the Supreme Court

1968   Martin Luther King, Jr., is assassinated

The Viet Cong launch the Tet offensive

Johnson withdraws from the presidential race

In his farewell address to the nation, delivered three days before he left the Presidency in January, 1961, President Eisenhower warned about the "acquisition of unwarranted influence by the military-industrial complex. This conjunction of an immense military establishment and a large arms industry is new in the American experience," he declared.

Despite Eisenhower's cautions, most Americans entered the 1960s with a sense of optimism and a resolution to put forth greater efforts to solve their domestic and foreign problems. During the decade of the 1950s, the American economy had experienced remarkable expansion, and Americans had come to enjoy a higher standard of living than ever before in the nation's history. Americans had no reason to doubt that economic ex-

pansion and prosperity would continue, and they were confident of their ability to solve the problems which accompanied the growth of an affluent society. The only real danger, it seemed, came from abroad in the form of "international Communism."

The 1960s, however, became a time of turmoil for the American people. A struggle developed over the achievement of civil rights for black Americans. President Kennedy was assassinated. Lyndon Johnson's attempt to build the Great Society was met with obstacles as the United States sank deeper into the quagmire of Vietnam. A significant portion of the nation's youth rebelled against the attitudes and values of American society. As the decade drew to a close, the nation faced a major political and social crisis. The events of the 1960s introduced a powerful element of pessimism into American life, as many people began to doubt the nation's ability to deal effectively with the problems confronting it at home and abroad.

The 1960 Election

Vice President Richard M. Nixon won the Republican presidential nomination in 1960 without major opposition. In the race for the Democratic nomination, Senator John F. Kennedy succeeded in defeating Senator Hubert H. Humphrey of Minnesota and Senator Lyndon B. Johnson of Texas. Having won the nomination, Kennedy selected Johnson as his vice presidential running mate.

Kennedy was a Roman Catholic, and in the wake of Al Smith's defeat in 1928, many had become convinced that a Catholic could never win the Presidency. During the race for the Democratic nomination, however, Kennedy defeated Humphrey in the West Virginia primary. Kennedy's victory in this heavily Protestant state helped defuse the Catholic issue, and he defused it further during the campaign in a forthright speech to the Houston Ministerial Association in September, when he expressed his strong support of the absolute separation of church and state.

When Kennedy and Nixon faced one another in the first televised debates ever held with presidential candidates, the Democrat benefited. The debates made Kennedy better known to the American people and favorably presented his personality, wit, and knowledge of the issues.

While Kennedy polled 303 electoral votes to Nixon's 219, the popular vote was extremely close. With Kennedy winning 34,227,000 votes and Nixon polling 34,109,000, the Democrat's margin of victory was only slightly over 118,000. The Democrats continued to control both houses of Congress but by reduced margins.

Kennedy as President

The 43-year-old Kennedy was the youngest man ever elected to the Presidency. In contrast with Eisenhower, he wanted to be an activist President. In his inaugural address, he spoke of the "New Frontier" as he called on his fellow citizens to "ask not what your country can do for you. Ask what you can do for your country."

As his Secretary of State, Kennedy selected Dean Rusk, a career diplomat and more recently head of the Rockefeller Foundation. Robert S. McNamara, a former president of the Ford Motor Co., became Secretary of Defense, while C. Douglas Dillon, a banker and Republican, was named Secretary of the Treasury. In defiance of convention, Kennedy appointed his younger brother, Robert F. Kennedy, as Attorney General. Adlai Stevenson, the Democrats' 1952 and 1956 standard-bearer, became Ambassador to the United Nations.

Kennedy proposed a substantial legislative program, including an increase in the minimum wage, federal aid to education, medical insurance for the elderly, and increased appropriations for housing and urban renewal programs. However, a coalition of conservative southern Democrats and Republicans dominated Congress, which refused to approve most of Kennedy's legislative proposals.

Kennedy and the Economy

During the 1950s, the American gross national product (GNP) had increased considerably, although at a lower rate than experienced by other highly industrialized countries. In addition, the inflation rate had begun to increase in the late 1950s, and during the decade there had been three recessions. In the 1958–61 recession, the unemployment rate reached 7 percent.

While Kennedy wanted to revitalize the economy, he was concerned about controlling inflation. Thus, he hesitated to propose tax cuts to provide a boost to the economy, fearing that decreased revenues would lead to increased budget deficits. These, in turn, might promote inflation. When the economy failed to revive as much as he had hoped, Kennedy responded favorably to a tax cut proposal advanced by Walter Heller, the Chairman of the Council of Economic Advisers.

In early 1963, Kennedy called for a $13.5 billion reduction in corporation taxes over a three-year period. While this tax cut would produce increased budget deficits, it would also make more capital available for investment in the economy. The expectation was that economic recovery and growth would ultimately lead to substantial increases in tax revenues. This was the first time that an American President deliberately used Keynesian theory in the area of finance policy.

The tax cut proposal encountered strong resistance from congressional conservatives, who could not accept the idea that deficits might help to encourage economic growth.

Kennedy and the Steel Companies

In an effort to control inflation, the Kennedy administration persuaded the steelworkers' union to agree to a contract providing only modest increases in wages and benefits. In return, it was expected that the steel companies would refrain from increasing prices.

In April, 1962, however, several steel companies led by United States Steel announced a substantial price increase of $6 a ton. Kennedy was furious and charged that the increase was unjustified. Heavy pressure from the President, including threats of antitrust suits, forced the steel companies to cancel the increase.

Kennedy's Legislative Achievements

While much of Kennedy's legislative program remained bogged down in Congress, some of his proposals won congressional approval.

The Area Redevelopment Act of 1961 authorized $400 million in grants and loans to promote the development of depressed areas.

In 1961, Congress approved an increase in the minimum wage from $1.00 to $1.25 an hour and extended the coverage of the minimum wage law to 3.6 million additional workers.

The Housing Act of 1961 provided $5 billion over a period of five years to support programs of urban renewal.

The Trade Expansion Act of 1962 was one of Kennedy's most important achievements. This act gave the President extensive authority to adjust tariff rates and led to the Kennedy round of trade negotiations which produced tariff cuts of about 35 percent in trade between the United States and the European Common Market.

The Higher Education Facilities Act of 1963 established a

five-year program of grants and loans for construction projects at public and private colleges and universities.

In addition, the Twenty-Third Amendment to the Constitution, submitted to the states in 1960 prior to Kennedy's inauguration, was ratified in 1961. This amendment enabled residents of the District of Columbia to vote in presidential elections.

The Space Race

In April, 1961, Soviet cosmonaut Yuri Gagarin orbited the earth, and in August another Soviet cosmonaut made a space flight of 17 orbits. On February 20, 1962, Marine Lt. Col. John Glenn, one of the original American astronauts, orbited the earth three times.

In a message to Congress in May, 1961, Kennedy proposed a commitment to the goal of putting an American on the moon by the end of the decade. On July 20, 1969, astronaut Neil Armstrong of the Apollo II crew took the first step on the moon at 10:56:20 PM, EDT.

Kennedy and Civil Rights

The Montgomery bus boycott of 1955 helped initiate a grassroots campaign against racial segregation by American blacks. The black activists encouraged a campaign of nonviolent direct action and civil disobedience.

On February 1, 1960, four black college students sat at a lunch counter in a Woolworth store in Greensboro, North Carolina in violation of local custom and refused to leave when they were denied service. The sit-in movement spread to dozens of other cities and towns and won the attention of the media. By the end of 1960, over 70,000 persons had participated in sit-ins.

Black college students created the Student Nonviolent Coordinating Committee (SNCC) to promote the sit-in movement and to conduct voter registration drives. SNCC worked in cooperation with the Southern Christian Leadership Conference (SCLC), headed by Martin Luther King, Jr., to promote the cause of civil rights.

In May, 1961, black and white opponents of segregation joined on the first freedom ride from Washington, DC, to New Orleans. Traveling by bus, the freedom riders sought to test the court-ordered desegregation of public transportation facilities in the South. Angry white mobs attacked the freedom riders in Anniston, Alabama, and in Birmingham and Montgomery, as well. This and subsequent freedom rides were organized by SNCC and the Congress of Racial Equality (CORE).

Although the black vote had played an important part in Kennedy's election to the Presidency, once in office he took a cautious approach to civil rights. The President did not want to antagonize southern representatives and senators whose votes he needed for the passage of his legislative program.

Black activism gradually forced the administration to act more vigorously in support of civil rights.

James Meredith, a black air force veteran, secured a court order affirming his right to be admitted to the University of Mississippi, which had rejected his application on the basis of race. Governor Ross Barnett, an ardent racist, declared that Meredith would never be admitted. When violence erupted on the campus, Kennedy federalized the Mississippi National Guard and sent federal troops to Oxford, Mississippi, to restore order and to compel Meredith's admission to the university. A year later, in September, 1963, Governor George Wallace of Alabama sought to block the enrollment of several black students at the University of Alabama. Wallace gave way when Kennedy dispatched federal marshals to the campus and federalized the Alabama National Guard.

Following the congressional elections in November, 1962, Kennedy issued a long-promised executive order barring segregation in federally financed housing. The Justice Department, headed by Attorney General Robert Kennedy, moved to enforce the desegregation of public transportation in the South, to compel southern officials to enable blacks to register and vote, and to reduce resistance to school integration.

In April, 1963, Martin Luther King, Jr. began a campaign against segregation in Birmingham, Alabama. When blacks began their nonviolent protest, city officials moved against the demonstrators, charging them with parading without a license. Some 2,200 blacks were arrested over a five-week period. Police Commissioner Eugene "Bull" Connor used police dogs, tear gas, electric cattle prods, and high pressure fire hoses against the demonstrators. The events in Birmingham were reported nationally on television, and images of police violence were etched on the minds of the American people.

Arrested during the demonstrations, King wrote his "Letter from the Birmingham Jail," a powerful statement of his philosophy of nonviolence in the struggle for civil rights. The crisis in Birmingham ended with an agreement to desegregate municipal facilities, to establish more equitable hiring practices, and to create a biracial committee that would seek to resolve differences and promote racial harmony.

Violence against blacks was not restricted to Birmingham. On June 12, 1963, Medgar Evers, an official of the NAACP, was fatally shot outside his home in Jackson, Mississippi.

Kennedy proposed a strong civil rights bill that prohibited segregation in restaurants, hotels, and other places of public accommodation and authorized withholding federal funds from programs discriminating against blacks. It also authorized the Justice Department to bring suits in order to promote school integration.

Black leaders planned a great march on Washington to demonstrate support of the civil rights bill. On August 28, 1963, more than 200,000 people gathered on the Mall in front of the

Lincoln Memorial. The high point of the day came when King delivered his memorable "I Have a Dream" speech.

Despite powerful public support for civil rights, Kennedy's civil rights bill remained bottled up in congressional committees.

The Kennedy Assassination

In November, 1963, Kennedy went to Texas in an effort to promote unity among the state's Democrats in preparation for his 1964 reelection campaign. On November 22, while riding in a motorcade in Dallas, he was assassinated by Lee Harvey Oswald. Two days later, Jack Ruby, a Dallas nightclub operator, shot and killed Oswald as he was being moved from the Dallas jail where he had been held.

An investigation by a special Presidential Commission, headed by Chief Justice Earl Warren, concluded that Oswald had acted alone. Many people continue to believe, however, that Oswald had been part of some sort of conspiracy.

Johnson as President

When Vice President Lyndon B. Johnson succeeded to the Presidency, he became the first southerner to hold that office since Woodrow Wilson. Johnson brought with him to the White House close to thirty years' experience in Washington and a powerful reputation for his ability to get things done.

Johnson was determined to use his formidable skills to push Kennedy's legislative program through Congress. He worked first for action on a tax cut and civil rights and then moved on to federal aid to education, Medicare, and the war on poverty. The Johnson legislative program proved to be the most extensive since the New Deal, and the President began to speak of creating the "Great Society."

The Tax Reduction Act

To gain conservative support for a tax cut, Johnson promised to reduce spending and submitted a proposed budget for the next fiscal year of approximately $98 billion, which reduced the projected deficit considerably.

The Tax Reduction Act of 1964 reduced personal income tax rates, resulting in a tax cut of some $10 billion. This tax cut helped promote a major economic boom. The gross national product (GNP) registered a steady increase: 7.1 percent in 1964, 8.1 percent in 1965, and 9.5 percent in 1966. Unemployment fell, and inflation remained under control in the mid-1960s. The budget deficit declined, since a booming economy produced increases in tax revenues.

At the same time, the cost of Johnson's Great Society programs, combined with the cost of the Vietnam War, pushed the federal budget upwards. In 1961, the federal government spent $94.4 billion. In 1970, federal expenditures totaled $196.6 billion. While 1969 produced a small surplus, there were budget deficits in other years. In 1968, the deficit reached $25 billion, the highest in American history up to that point.

The War on Poverty

In 1960, about 40 million Americans, in a total population of 179 million, lived below the officially established poverty level. Michael Harrington did much to bring the nation's attention to the reality of poverty in the midst of plenty through his book *The Other America* (1962).

In his 1964 State of the Union message, Johnson called for the inauguration of a "war on poverty." The Economic Opportunity Act of 1964 established the Office of Economic Opportunity (OEO) to carry out antipoverty programs established by this act and other legislation. The VISTA (Volunteers in Service to America) program was designed to provide educational and social programs in poor communities. The Job Corps was created to provide vocational training for young people. The Head Start program was initiated to prepare preschool children from disadvantaged backgrounds for entry into elementary school, while Upward Bound was designed for disadvantaged high school students who hoped to attend college. The work-study program for college students was created. Various community action programs were established to give the poor "maximum feasible participation" in the areas of housing, education, and health care in their own communities.

Other Early Johnson Legislation

The Urban Mass Transportation Act of 1964 provided $375 million in assistance for the nation's financially troubled urban transit systems.

The Wilderness Preservation Act of 1964 protected some 9 million acres of national forest lands against commercial use and the construction of permanent roads and buildings. The law provided for the addition of other lands, and by 1973 almost 2 million acres had been added.

The 1964 Election

A resurgence of conservative forces in the Republican party made Senator Barry Goldwater of Arizona a prime contender for the party's presidential nomination in 1964. Goldwater had set forth his ultraconservative views in *The Conscience of a Conservative* (1960). In the race for the nomination, Goldwater easily defeated Governor Nelson Rockefeller of New York, a liberal Republican.

Winning the Democratic nomination, Johnson chose Senator Hubert Humphrey of Minnesota as his running mate.

During the campaign, a large number of Americans found Goldwater's views on domestic policy excessively conservative and his views on foreign policy dangerously aggressive. Goldwater proposed an abolition of social security and raised the question of using nuclear weapons in Vietnam.

Winning 43 million popular votes and 486 electoral votes, Johnson trounced Goldwater, who polled 27 million popular votes and won the 52 electoral votes of six states—his home state of Arizona and five southern states where race was the overriding issue.

The Democrats won huge majorities in both houses of Congress, controlling the Senate by a margin of 68 seats to 32 and the House of Representatives by 295 seats to 140. Johnson could now overcome the conservative coalition of Republicans and southern Democrats which had blocked reform in the past.

Johnson's Legislative Accomplishments During 1965

The first session of the 89th Congress in 1965 produced a flood of legislation in response to the President's proposals. The Elementary and Secondary School Act of 1965 was the first large-scale program of federal aid to elementary and secondary schools. The act provided $1.3 billion to school districts to improve the education of disadvantaged children. The act permitted the granting of funds to benefit pupils attending nonpublic schools.

The Higher Education Act of 1965 provided federal scholarships for college undergraduates, as well as other assistance to colleges and universities.

The Medicare program was adopted to help elderly Americans pay the increasing cost of health care. Operating through the Social Security system, the Medicare program provided a basic hospital insurance program and a voluntary medical insurance program covering physicians' fees and other services. In addition, the Medicaid program was established to help meet the medical needs of those under the age of 65 who could not afford private insurance. The federal government and the states shared the cost of the Medicaid program. By January, 1968, 30 states were participating in Medicaid.

The Omnibus Housing Act of 1965 established a program of rent supplements for low-income families.

The Department of Housing and Urban Development (HUD) was established to administer federal programs related to housing and to develop programs for community improvement. Robert C. Weaver was named the first Secretary of Housing and Urban Development, becoming the first black ever to serve in the cabinet.

The National Endowment for the Arts (NEA) and the National Endowment for the Humanities (NEH) were created to channel federal grants to artists and scholars.

The Water Quality Act of 1965 required states to establish and enforce water quality standards for all interstate waterways located within their boundaries.

The Immigration Act of 1965 reformed the restrictive immigration policy based on national quotas which had been established in the 1920s. The 1965 act provided that a total of 290,000 persons a year would be admitted to the United States, with priorities based on such things as skills and the need for political asylum. A maximum of 20,000 immigrants would be permitted to enter from any one nation, and an annual quota of 120,000 was established for immigrants from Western Hemisphere countries.

Other Legislation of the Johnson Administration

While a remarkable amount of important Great Society legislation emerged from Congress in 1965, the remaining years of the Johnson administration also witnessed the passage of significant legislation.

The National Traffic and Motor Vehicle Safety Act of 1966 provided for the establishment of federal safety standards for motor vehicles and tires, while the Highway Safety Act of 1966 required states to establish highway safety programs. The influence of consumer advocate Ralph Nader was apparent in both of these laws.

In 1966, the minimum wage was raised from $1.25 an hour to $1.40, effective February 1, 1967, and to $1.60, effective February 1, 1968. Coverage was extended to 9 million additional workers.

Also in 1966, the cabinet-level Department of Transportation was created, bringing together federal agencies dealing with air, rail, and highway transportation.

In 1967, the Corporation for Public Broadcasting was created to provide support for noncommercial television and radio broadcasting. This brought into being the Public Broadcasting System (PBS).

The Open Housing Act of 1968 prohibited discrimination in the sale or rental of most of the nation's housing.

The Truth-in-Lending Act of 1968 required lenders to disclose information about the annual rate of interest charged borrowers.

Other legislation adopted in 1968 furthered the cause of conservation. This legislation included the Scenic Rivers Act, designed to preserve wild and scenic rivers in their natural state, and laws establishing two new national parks.

In 1967, the Twenty-Fifth Amendment to the Constitution was ratified. Proposed by Congress in 1965, this amendment enabled the President to fill a vacancy in the Vice Presidency, with the President's nominee subject to confirmation by a majority vote of both houses of Congress. The amendment also established procedures to be followed in the event of the disability of the President.

Johnson and Civil Rights

When he became President, Johnson decided to press for the enactment of a civil rights bill. The Civil Rights Act of 1964 was the most far-reaching piece of civil rights legislation ever enacted by Congress. In addition to outlawing segregation in all public accommodations, the law authorized the Attorney General to bring suits to force school desegregation. It further sought to reduce barriers to voting by blacks by providing that completion of the sixth-grade was evidence of literacy. The law also prohibited discrimination in employment on the basis of race, religion, sex or national origin. The Equal Employment Opportunity Commission (EEOC) was established to enforce this provision.

In January, 1964, the Twenty-Fourth Amendment to the Constitution was ratified. Proposed by Congress in August, 1962, the amendment eliminated the poll tax as a prerequisite for voting in federal elections.

The Student Nonviolent Coordinating Committee (SNCC), the Congress of Racial Equality (CORE), and other civil rights groups joined in the 1964 Freedom Summer Campaign in Mississippi. Black and white students established freedom schools and carried out other activities to promote black rights. There was an upsurge of white violence against civil rights workers. In Philadelphia, Mississippi, whites murdered three civil rights workers—Andrew Goodman and Michael Schwerner, who were white, and James Chaney, a black. Other civil rights activists were beaten, and several hundred were arrested. A number of black churches, which served as centers for civil rights activities, were bombed or burned.

Black Mississippians organized the Mississippi Freedom Democratic Party (MFDP) which sent a delegation to the Democratic national convention to challenge the regular delegation from Mississippi. The MFDP finally received only token representation: two at-large seats in the convention.

In March, 1965, Martin Luther King, Jr., led a 54-mile march from Selma to Montgomery, Alabama, as part of a campaign to compel state officials to permit blacks to register as voters. Jim Clark, the Selma sheriff, received national notoriety for leading the police in violent attacks on the demonstrators.

On the eve of the Selma march, Johnson made a powerful appeal to Congress for a stronger voting rights act. The Voting Rights Act of 1965 banned literacy tests and other devices which had traditionally been used in the South to prevent blacks from voting. The Attorney General was authorized to appoint federal voting registrars in areas where less than half of the voting-age blacks were registered to vote. When Johnson became President, about a quarter of the South's blacks were registered voters. When he left office in early 1969, about two-thirds were. The Voting Rights Act of 1965 is widely regarded as one of the most important pieces of legislation adopted during the 1960s.

To underline his commitment to civil rights, Johnson appointed Thurgood Marshall to the Supreme Court in 1967. A former attorney for the NAACP and a federal judge, Marshall was the first black ever to serve on the nation's highest court.

In addition to supporting efforts to eliminate segregation and to promote civil rights, Johnson also endorsed the concept of affirmative action. In addition to eliminating overtly racist practices that denied employment opportunities to blacks, advocates of affirmative action believed that employers should adopt positive measures to recruit more black employees. In 1968, the Department of Labor ruled that all contractors doing business with the federal government had to develop affirmative action programs. Requirements for affirmative action policies were gradually extended to all institutions doing business with the federal government or receiving federal funds. The concept of affirmative action also came to be extended to other racial and ethnic minorities and to women, as well.

Urban Violence

In the mid-1960s, outbreaks of violence began to occur in the nation's urban ghettos. The civil rights movement had focused primarily on legally imposed and enforced segregation and discrimination in the South. At the same time, the campaign for civil rights did not have a direct impact on other problems facing the nation's blacks. Many blacks, for example, lived in deep poverty. The median income for black workers was only slightly more than half that of whites. Black unemployment was about twice that of whites, and for black males between the ages of 18 and 25 unemployment was about five times higher than that of whites. About 60 percent of the nation's black children lived in poverty. In the nation's urban ghettos, both North and South, housing, schools, and health facilities were substandard.

In the mid-1960s, urban blacks expressed their discontent in riots. During the summer of 1964, disturbances occurred in the ghettos of New York City, Rochester, New York, and several northern New Jersey cities. In August, 1965, a huge riot broke out in the Watts section of Los Angeles. The riot left close to three dozen dead, and several hundred were injured. Property damage was substantial. Other riots took place in 1965, and additional disturbances occurred in the summers of 1966 and 1967. Detroit experienced what was perhaps the worst race riot since the Civil War in the summer of 1967. Forty-three people were killed.

Then in April, 1968, James Earl Ray, a white racist, assassinated Martin Luther King, Jr. In the aftermath of King's assassination, enraged blacks rioted in over 100 cities, with the most serious disturbances occurring in Chicago and Washington, D.C.

Johnson responded to the urban violence by appointing the Commission on Civil Disorders, headed by Governor Otto Kerner of Illinois. In its report, the Kerner Commission noted that the riots of the 1960s had been started by blacks, while earlier race riots had been caused by whites whose violence then provoked black counterattacks. The riots resulted from a black sense of frustration, despair, and anger. The basic cause of these attitudes, the Kerner Commission concluded, was "white racism" which denied blacks good jobs, restricted them to ghettos, and left them without hope of improving their lives. The commission urged the creation of federal programs to improve conditions of life and work in the ghettos.

Black Power

Increasingly frustrated by the slow pace of change and by the persistence of racism, some black leaders began to promote the idea of Black Power. In 1966, Stokely Carmichael, a vocal advocate of Black Power, became head of the Student Nonviolent Coordinating Committee (SNCC) and moved the organization in a more radical direction. Whites were expelled from SNCC, which now advocated a policy of separation of the races. Integration, Carmichael charged, was "a subterfuge for the maintenance of white supremacy." Carmichael's policies were continued by his successor, H. Rap Brown, who took over the leadership of SNCC in 1967.

In 1966, Huey P. Newton, Bobby Seale, and Eldridge Cleaver founded the Black Panther party in Oakland, California. The Black Panthers proclaimed themselves to be "urban revolutionaries" and denounced both racism and capitalism. In 1968, the Black Panthers nominated Cleaver, a paroled convict and the author of an articulate autobiography, *Soul on Ice* (1967), for President.

Black separatism was also advocated by the Black Muslims,

led by Elijah Muhammad. In the early 1960s, Malcolm X emerged as a major spokesman for the Black Muslims and in his *Autobiography* (1965) presented a powerful account of the black experience in America. In 1964, Malcolm X broke with the Black Muslims and established the Organization of Afro-American Unity. He now viewed the struggle for black rights in America as part of a worldwide struggle for human rights. Malcolm X was assassinated by Black Muslim fanatics in 1965.

The Supreme Court and Reform

During the 1960s, the Supreme Court, headed by Chief Justice Earl Warren, became an important instrument of reform. The court quickly upheld the constitutionality of the Civil Rights Act of 1964 and the Voting Rights Act of 1965. In the case of *Loving v. Virginia,* decided in 1967, the court invalidated a state law which prohibited interracial marriages.

The Supreme Court's 1962 decision in the case of *Baker v. Carr* opened the way to the reapportionment of legislative bodies on the basis of the one person, one vote principle.

In other cases, the Supreme Court declared that prayer and Bible reading in the public schools were unconstitutional and that obscenity laws could not be invoked against allegedly pornographic material which had some "redeeming social value."

The Supreme Court acted to protect the rights of criminal suspects. In a 1963 decision in the case of *Gideon v. Wainwright,* the court held that poor suspects had the right to court-appointed legal counsel. In 1964, in the case of *Escobedo v. Illinois,* the court ruled that a suspect had to be allowed access to an attorney during police questioning. In the case of *Miranda v. Arizona,* decided in 1966, the court held that suspects had to be warned that statements they made to the police could be used against them and that they had the right to remain silent and to consult an attorney.

Women in the 1960s

The increased number of women in the American work force helped spur the development of a more active women's movement. Between 1940 and 1960, the proportion of women in the work force doubled, and by 1963 over a third of married women were working outside the home. Women faced widespread job discrimination, and in nearly every occupation they earned less than men who did the same work. In 1963, the average working woman earned about 63 percent of what a man earned. By 1973, the figure had declined to 57 percent. Many jobs were closed to women for no particular reason, and in many fields women were barred from promotion to higher level managerial positions. These conditions, which affected the overwhelming majority of women workers, were resented especially by the growing number of college-educated women. In 1950, women earned about a quarter of the BA degrees awarded. By 1970, the figure had increased to 41 percent. Educated young women had growing expectations and increasingly came to support the women's movement.

Betty Friedan emerged as one of the leaders of the new women's movement. In *The Feminine Mystique* (1963), Friedan maintained that the traditional woman's role had the effect of "burying millions of women alive. The only way for a woman . . . to know herself as a person," Friedan wrote, "is by creative work of her own."

In 1966, Friedan joined with other feminists to establish the National Organization of Women (NOW). In addition to calling for equal employment opportunities and equal pay for equal work, NOW advocated an equal rights amendment to the Constitution, which had originally been proposed in 1923. In addition, NOW called for changes in the divorce laws and the repeal of laws against abortion. In 1967, NOW's members totaled 1,000. By 1971, the membership rolls had swelled to 15,000.

Action by the federal government also served to advance the cause of women's rights. In the early 1960s, Kennedy appointed a Commission on the Status of Women, headed by Esther Peterson. The Civil Rights Act of 1964 banned discrimination on the basis of sex. In practice, however, the Equal Employment Opportunity Commission (EEOC) focused its attention primarily on cases of discrimination against blacks. Gradually, however, both federal agencies and the courts stepped up the pressure on employers to observe the legal prohibition against discrimination on the basis of sex.

Hispanics in the 1960s

By the 1960s, Hispanics had become the fastest-growing minority group in the United States. In 1960, there were about 3.5 million Hispanics in the country. By 1970, they had increased to 9 million, of whom 7 million were of Mexican background. As their numbers grew, Hispanics began to have a greater impact on American politics. For example, Chicanos (Mexican-Americans) strongly supported Kennedy in 1960, and their votes helped put Texas in the Democratic column.

One of the most influential Chicano leaders was César Chavez, who organized the United Farm Workers to represent the cause of the migrant farm workers in the West. Primarily Chicanos, these farm workers worked long hours for very low wages. In 1965, Chavez began a prolonged strike against the California grape growers. The union demanded higher wages and improved benefits, better working conditions, and recognition of the union by the growers. When the growers refused the union's demands, Chavez organized a national consumer boycott of grapes and grape products. While several wine companies reached an agreement with the union, a bitter conflict developed with the DiGiorgio Corporation. In 1966, DiGiorgio agreed to hold a union election but was then charged with rigging the results. California's Governor Edmund G. "Pat" Brown ordered an investigation resulting in a new election, won by the union. Brown was the first major public official to champion the cause of the Chicano farm workers. By 1970, the United Farm Workers had signed contracts with about half of California's growers of table grapes.

Indians in the 1960s

The American Indian population remained relatively small, growing from about 550,000 in 1969 to 790,000 in 1970. More than half of the Indians lived on reservations. The Indians experienced widespread poverty, high unemployment, a life expectancy that was more than 20 years lower than the national average, and a suicide rate for young Indian men that was 100 times higher than that of whites.

In 1961, representatives of 67 tribes met in Chicago and adopted a Declaration of Indian Purpose in which the Indians asserted their right to choose their own way of life. The Kennedy and Johnson administrations sought to give the Indians a larger voice in their own affairs. In particular, Johnson promised federal programs that would eliminate old attitudes of paternalism and emphasize self-determination. Federal aid to the Indian tribes was increased substantially, and the governments of the Indian reservations were recognized as sponsoring agencies for federal poverty programs.

American Indians—many of whom now preferred the term Native Americans—brought a series of lawsuits charging violations of their treaty rights. In one such case, the Court of Claims ruled in 1967 that the government had forced the Seminole Indians of Florida to give up their land in 1823 for an unreasonably low price. The government was ordered to make an additional payment to the Seminoles.

Foreign Policy in the 1960s

Both Kennedy and Johnson continued to view international affairs in terms of the Cold War conflict between the United States and the Soviet Union. The central issue for them, as it had been for Truman and Eisenhower, was the threat of "international Communism," directed by the Soviet Union. The task of the United States was to combat this threat wherever it might appear in the world.

Kennedy's Military Policy

During the 1960 campaign, Kennedy had contended that the missile gap was real and that the Soviets had surpassed the United States in the number of missiles and warheads it had available. Although the missile gap did not, in fact, exist, President Kennedy pushed for substantial increases in the nation's nuclear arsenal. Kennedy also stressed the need to strengthen the conventional forces of the United States and the other members of NATO. Having both effective nuclear and conventional forces at their disposal, the western allies could make a "flexible response" to any Soviet pressure in Europe.

Kennedy also sought to develop counterinsurgency units, the Special Forces or the Green Berets, as they were popularly known. These units would be available to fight "brush fire" wars or guerrilla wars in the Third World.

Kennedy and the Third World

Kennedy developed his most creative approach to foreign policy in regard to the world's underdeveloped nations, the Third World. The President stressed the importance of programs designed to promote economic development, particularly the increase of agricultural productivity and the development of modern communication and transportation systems. Economic development, he believed, would promote political stability in Asia, Africa, and Latin America and thereby thwart the expansion of international Communism.

The Peace Corps, established in 1961, sent thousands of American volunteers as teachers and agricultural and public health specialists to work on development projects in dozens of Third World nations.

The Agency for International Development (AID) was created for the purpose of coordinating American economic assistance projects throughout the world.

Kennedy initiated the Alliance for Progress to coordinate and support cooperative programs between the United States and the countries of Latin America. These programs were intended to promote land reform and economic development.

The Bay of Pigs Invasion

In 1959, Fidel Castro overthrew the government of Fulgencio Batista, the American-backed dictator of Cuba. Soon after Castro took power, strains developed in Cuban-American relations. Ugly trials and executions of Batista's officials and police created a bad impression in the United States. In February, 1960, Castro concluded a trade treaty with the Soviet Union providing for the exchange of Cuban sugar for Soviet oil and machinery. When American oil companies in Cuba refused to refine Soviet oil, Castro nationalized them. He also seized the property of other American corporations which had long dominated Cuba's economy and indulged in anti-American rhetoric.

In response to Cuba's actions, the United States reduced its imports of Cuban sugar. Shortly before Eisenhower left office in January, 1961, the United States broke diplomatic relations with Cuba.

Anti-Castro Cubans in exile wanted to organize an invasion of Cuba. They were convinced that such an invasion would be greeted by a great uprising of the Cuban people. Under Eisenhower, the Central Intelligence Agency (CIA) had begun training Cuban exiles in Central America for such an invasion.

When Kennedy took office in early 1961, he reluctantly approved the plan for the invasion of Cuba. On April 17, 1961, a Cuban exile force of some 1,500 men landed at the Bay of Pigs on Cuba's southern coast. The expected uprising by the Cuban people failed to materialize. The United States, seeking to avoid direct involvement, did not commit its air force in support of the invaders. Castro's forces crushed the invasion within three days and took 1,200 prisoners. In December, 1961, Castro proclaimed himself a Marxist-Leninist and moved closer to the Soviet Union. In the United States, concern grew about Castro's efforts to export revolution to other Latin American countries.

The Berlin Wall

In June, 1961, Kennedy met with Soviet leader Nikita Khrushchev in Vienna. It proved to be a chilly encounter as Khrushchev renewed his threats regarding Berlin.

Concerned about Soviet intentions, Kennedy called on Congress for over $3 billion in new appropriations for national defense. He also urged an increase in the size of the armed forces and an expanded civil defense program.

On August 13, 1961, the Soviets and East Germans closed the border between East and West Berlin, leaving only a few border crossing points open. The East Germans then began to construct the Berlin Wall around West Berlin. The Berlin Wall prevented the flight of East Germans to the West and thus ended a serious drain on the East German economy. It was now possible for the Soviets and East Germans to live with the continued existence of West Berlin, and the the Berlin crisis gradually eased.

The Cuban Missile Crisis

Concerned about the possibility of American action against Cuba, Castro turned to the Soviet Union for aid. The Soviets provided the Cubans with airplanes and other conventional weapons. During the late summer of 1962, reports began to circulate about Soviet plans to install intermediate range missiles in Cuba. In response to these reports, Kennedy ordered U-2 reconnaissance flights over Cuba. On October 14, these flights provided confirmation of the fact that missile sites were being readied for the installation of Soviet-made missiles. The Cuban missile crisis, the most dangerous East-West confrontation of the Cold War, was about to begin.

Kennedy was determined to force the removal of the missiles. He ruled out both an air strike against the missile sites and a full-scale invasion, at least for the time being, but the American military forces moved to the status of a full alert. American bombers were readied for take-off, and missiles were prepared for firing. The Navy was ready to sail, and troops were prepared to move.

On October 22, Kennedy spoke to the American people on television. He declared that the United States would not shrink from the threat of nuclear war and called on the Soviets to dismantle the missile sites and remove the missiles. Kennedy also announced an American naval quarantine to prevent Soviet ships from bringing additional offensive weapons to Cuba. This quarantine was in fact a blockade, but Kennedy referred to it as a quarantine since in international law a blockade is an act of war.

On October 24, the tension showed signs of easing, as five Soviet ships turned back from the quarantine line. In a message to Kennedy, Khrushchev declared that he would dismantle the missile launching pads and remove the missiles if the United States promised not to invade Cuba. In a second message,

Khrushchev demanded that the United States agree to remove its missiles from Turkey.

Kennedy responded positively to Khrushchev's first message and ignored the second. While the United States had already decided to remove its obsolete missiles from Turkey, the President did not want to act now under pressure from Moscow.

On October 28, the Cuban missile crisis ended. Khrushchev agreed to dismantle the missile launching pads and remove the missiles, and Kennedy pledged not to invade Cuba. The United States agreed informally to pull its missiles out of Turkey, although this commitment was not a formal part of the agreement which ended the crisis.

In the aftermath of the Cuban missile crisis, the Washington-Moscow hot line was established to facilitate speedy communication between the two capitals in the event of another crisis. The hot line was used for the first time during the Arab-Israeli Six-Day War in 1967.

For their part, the Soviets became determined to build up their armed strength, especially in nuclear weapons, so they could never again be made to appear inferior to the United States.

The Nuclear Test Ban Treaty

Following the resolution of the Cuban missile crisis, long-stalled American-Soviet negotiations resumed and resulted in the signing of the Nuclear Test Ban Treaty in July, 1963. The treaty banned the testing of nuclear weapons in the atmosphere. Underground tests could continue. A number of other nations adhered to the treaty, although France and the People's Republic of China did not. These two countries were busy developing their own nuclear weapons.

Intervention in the Dominican Republic

In April and May, 1965, Johnson sent 20,000 American

troops to the Dominican Republic to support that country's government, claiming that American intervention was necessary to turn back the threat of Communism.

In 1961, the longtime dictator of the Dominican Republic, Rafael Trujillo, had been assassinated. For the next four years, several political factions engaged in a struggle for power. In the spring of 1965, supporters of Juan Bosch, a left-wing nationalist, launched a revolt against the conservative military government. The American intervention was designed to help prop up the government. The American troops remained until 1966 when a conservative, Joaquin Balaguer, defeated Bosch in the Dominican presidential elections.

In the so-called Johnson Doctrine, the President declared that domestic revolution in a Western Hemisphere country could not be regarded as merely a local concern when the object was the establishment of a Communist dictatorship.

The Vietnam War

American involvement in Southeast Asia increased during the 1960s. In the spring of 1961, the United States came close to intervention in Laos in an effort to halt the growth of Communist influence. Instead of intervening, however, the United States promoted the establishment of a neutralist coalition in Laos.

In South Vietnam, the United States increased its support of the government headed by Ngo Dinh Diem. Aided by Ho Chi Minh and North Vietnam, guerrillas in South Vietnam, known as the Viet Cong or National Liberation Front, were waging a guerrilla war against the South Vietnamese government. The position of the Diem government was weakened by its failure to carry out economic and social reforms and to win widespread popular support.

Some advocates of American intervention in Vietnam

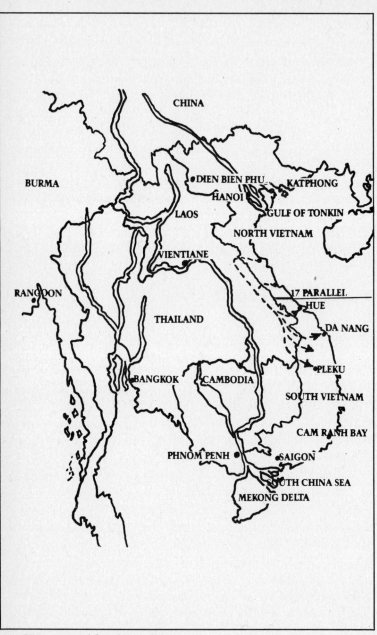

Vietnam and Southeast Asia

recalled the experience of the late 1930s, when the British and French had attempted to appease Hitler. Instead of satisfying the German dictator, the policy of appeasement served only to whet his appetite. Now, proponents of intervention believed, a failure to halt the advance of Communism in Southeast Asia would intensify the Soviet Union's expansionist tendencies. Supporters of intervention in Vietnam also pointed to the domino theory, set forth by Eisenhower in the 1950s. If one Southeast Asian country fell to Communism, they feared, the others would soon topple like a row of dominoes.

At the end of 1960, about 900 American advisers were providing assistance to South Vietnam. While Kennedy rejected recommendations for a major increase in the American military presence, by the end of 1961 the number of advisers had increased to 3,200. At the end of 1962, there were over 11,000. These American advisers did not normally participate directly in combat.

Despite American support, the Diem government found it difficult to hold on, and Diem's repressive policies provoked increasing opposition, especially from South Vietnam's Buddhists. After receiving the tacit consent of the United States, South Vietnamese military leaders overthrew Diem and created a new government in early November, 1963. Diem, his brother, and several associates were killed, something which the United States had not sanctioned. South Vietnam's military men proved to be no more effective in governing the country and fighting the war than Diem had been. The Viet Cong continued to gain ground.

Kennedy believed that the South Vietnamese had to win their own war, and in October, 1963, he had indicated his hope of withdrawing American forces from Vietnam by the end of 1965. Whether he would in fact have done so is a question that cannot be answered.

When Johnson became President in late November, 1963, he

viewed the situation in Vietnam in terms of the Cold War, just as his predecessors had. The war in Vietnam against Ho Chi Minh, Johnson believed, was a part of the worldwide effort to contain the expansion of Communism and Soviet power, which were regarded as the same thing.

In August, 1964, Johnson won congressional approval for increasing American involvement in the war. The President reported to Congress that North Vietnamese torpedo boats had attacked two American destroyers in the Gulf of Tonkin. He described the attack as unprovoked, although in fact the destroyers had violated North Vietnam's territorial waters in order to observe South Vietnamese attacks on two North Vietnamese islands. These attacks had been planned by American advisers.

Congress quickly approved the Gulf of Tonkin Resolution, which authorized the President to "take all necessary measures to repel any armed attack against the forces of the United States and to prevent further aggression." In effect, the resolution empowered the President to expand American involvement in the war whenever he chose to do so. The House of Representatives approved the resolution by a vote of 416 to 0. In the Senate, the vote was 88 to 2. Democrats Wayne Morse of Oregon and Ernest Gruening of Alaska were the two dissenters.

Following Johnson's reelection victory in 1964, the United States increased its involvement in Vietnam. In February, 1965, Viet Cong forces attacked the American base at Pleiku, killing several Americans and wounding over 100. Other attacks on American installations quickly followed. In response, Johnson ordered the first sustained air attacks on North Vietnam. Known as Operation Rolling Thunder, these attacks were designed to cut off the flow of supplies and manpower from North Vietnam to the Viet Cong.

Johnson also sent American ground troops into action under the leadership of the new American commander in South Vietnam, General William C. Westmoreland. The United States now took over the primary military responsibility in South Vietnam. Up to this point, the South Vietnamese army (the ARVN) had done most of the fighting. At the end of 1964, there were slightly more than 23,000 American troops in Vietnam. By the end of 1965, the number had grown to 184,000. The increase continued to 385,000 at the end of 1966, to 485,000 at the end of 1967, and to 536,000 at the end of 1968.

As the ground combat intensified and the bombing of North Vietnam increased, American losses mounted and increasing popular opposition to the war developed in the United States.

At the end of January, 1968, the North Vietnamese and the Viet Cong launched the Tet offensive, named for the Vietnamese New Year. The North Vietnamese and Viet Cong attacked American and South Vietnamese forces throughout South Vietnam. They assaulted the American embassy and presidential palace in Saigon, South Vietnam's capital, and struck at the American military headquarters at Tan Son Nhut airbase.

While the Tet offensive was turned back, the North Vietnamese and Viet Cong won a powerful psychological victory. The Tet offensive forced many Americans to acknowledge the fact that they were involved in a war they might not be able to win.

As the situation in Vietnam deteriorated, Johnson's unpopularity increased. In the New Hampshire Democratic primary in March, 1968, Senator Eugene McCarthy of Minnesota, running as an antiwar candidate, won 42 percent of the vote to Johnson's 48 percent. This was a remarkable showing by a relatively little known senator challenging an incumbent President and prompted Senator Robert F. Kennedy of New York to enter the presidential race as an antiwar candidate.

Shortly thereafter, on March 31, 1968, Johnson announced a limited halt to the bombing of North Vietnam and a renewal of the efforts to reach a negotiated settlement. He also announced that he would not seek reelection to the Presidency. The Vietnam war had claimed another victim.

Student Radicalism and the New Left

The 1960s gave birth to a movement of student radicalism. In 1962, a group of young radicals, meeting in Michigan, established the Students for a Democratic Society (SDS). In the Port Huron Statement, largely written by Tom Hayden of the University of Michigan, the SDS protested against the persistence of poverty, racial bigotry, and the threat of nuclear war. The Port Huron Statement called for a revitalization of democracy by restoring "power to the people," and the SDS pledged to work for the creation of a "New Left." As this New Left developed, it proved to be a broad coalition of mostly white, middle-class, and idealistic young Americans in revolt against the predominant political, economic, and social attitudes of American society.

One of the first major expressions of the growing student radicalism came at the University of California at Berkeley. In September, 1964, the university administration sought to bar student groups from distributing protest materials outside the main campus gate at the head of Telegraph Avenue. The Free Speech Movement, led by Mario Savio and others, insisted that the students' activities should not be subject to restriction by the university.

When the students refused to give way, confrontations developed with the university administration and the police. The conservative Board of Regents of the University of California ordered disciplinary action against student protesters. In response, students occupied Sproul Hall, the main administration building, in December. The police stormed the building and arrested a number of students. A student strike then mobilized additional support for the Free Speech Movement. In the wake of intensifying conflict, Clark Kerr, the university's president, resigned.

Initially the conflict at Berkeley involved a student demand for a traditional right in a democratic society, the right to express one's views on political and social issues. Gradually, at Berkeley and on other campuses, student protesters moved on to broader issues, attacking the impersonality of the university and rules of campus discipline, including drinking and dormitory visitation rules. Student protesters called for a larger student voice in university affairs, curriculum reform, and the admission of larger numbers of minority students.

The Antiwar Movement

When the build-up of American troops in Vietnam began in 1965, over 80 percent of Americans polled indicated their belief that the United States should remain committed to the defeat of the Communist forces in Vietnam. Soon, however, questions began to be raised about the wisdom of the apparent American commitment to combat Communism wherever it might appear in the world. College campuses quickly became a center of antiwar protests.

The first teach-in on the Vietnam war occurred at the University of Michigan in March, 1965, and other teach-ins quickly followed. In May, a teach-in at Berkeley lasted for 36 hours and attracted 12,000 people. The first teach-ins included both supporters and opponents of the American involvement in Vietnam, but soon they became, in effect, antiwar rallies.

Opponents of the war, led by SDS and other student organizations, promoted a wide range of antiwar activities, such as the March on the Pentagon on October 17, 1967, the Spring Mobilization in April, 1968, and the Vietnam Moratorium in the fall of 1969. During these and other antiwar activities, demonstrations occurred on hundreds of college campuses.

One of the most tumultuous student demonstrations of the late 1960s occurred in April, 1968, at Columbia University in New York City. The Columbia SDS chapter, led by Mark Rudd, organized an antiwar protest directed against the university's ties with the Institute of Defense Analysis, while the Afro-American Society initiated a protest against the construction of a new gymnasium, charging that it encroached on the neighboring black community of Harlem. Student demonstrators occupied several buildings. When Grayson Kirk, the university's president, called in the police to clear the buildings, a riot developed. In the midst of turmoil, Columbia University ended its spring semester early, and Kirk resigned the presidency.

Although the student activists remained a minority, they won an increasing audience for their protests against the war and for their more general challenge to the attitudes and values of American society. At the same time, however, the antiwar movement antagonized many highly patriotic blue-collar workers who had traditionally voted Democratic, pushing them in a more conservative direction.

While some protested the war in campus demonstrations, many young Americans who were in immediate danger of being drafted left the United States. By the end of 1972, over 300,000 draft resisters had found refuge in Canada, while another 10,000 had gone to Sweden, Mexico, and other countries. Perhaps as many as another 10,000 were living under cover in the United States. Yet another 250,000 may have avoided the draft by never registering.

The Counterculture

Student activism in the 1960s was closely related to the emergence of a counterculture. This counterculture proved to be an extraordinarily diverse phenomenon, which manifested itself in many ways. Some of the simplest forms of self-expression proved to be extremely disturbing to older Americans. Young men wore their hair long and often grew beards and hung beads around their necks. Young men and women customarily wore blue jeans, and other, less conventional dress styles appeared. What the counterculture promoted above all was a rejection of what its members regarded as the dominant values of American society: an emphasis on middle-class conformity, money, success, and gaining power over others. Some of the background of the counterculture could be traced back to the beat poets and writers of the 1950s.

Before long the counterculture found its intellectual defenders and advocates. In *The Making of a Counter Culture* (1969), Theodore Roszak proclaimed that the counterculture sought to create "a new heaven and a new earth," while Charles Reich, a Yale professor, wrote *The Greening of America* (1970), hailing the emergence of a new consciousness, Consciousness III, which had "emerged out of the wasteland of the corporate state, like flowers pushing up through the concrete pavement."

Sex, Drugs , and Rock'n'Roll

The growth of the counterculture in the 1960s was accompanied by changing attitudes toward sex, an increased use of drugs, and a new music.

Changing attitudes about sex and the availability of effective contraception, especially the "pill" (oral contraceptives) which began to be widely used during the 1960s, went hand in hand to produce a revolution in sexual behavior, especially among young Americans. Premarital and casual sex gained wide acceptance, and the sexual revolution also led to changed attitudes about nudity, pornography, homosexuality, and traditional male-female roles.

During the mid- and late-1960s, a rapidly growing number of young Americans began to smoke marijuana and hashish and to use hallucinogenic drugs, such as LSD (popularly known as acid) and mescaline, as well as amphetamines (uppers or speed) and barbiturates (downers). Timothy Leary, a former professor at Harvard University and founder of the League for Spiritual Discovery, emerged as the guru of the drug culture, urging his followers to "turn on, tune in, and drop out."

In music, a number of influences were at work. Rock'n'roll music, with its roots in the rhythm and blues music of black Americans, had swept the country during the 1950s, and folk music became widely popular at the end of the decade.

During the early 1960s, folk singers like Joan Baez and Peter, Paul, and Mary were active in the civil rights movement. The folk movement also produced Bob Dylan, one of America's most creative folk and rock artists.

In February, 1964, the Beatles arrived in the United States, soon to be followed by others in what came to be called the "British Invasion": among them the Rolling Stones and the Kinks. A revolution in rock music was under way. In June, 1967, the Beatles released "Sgt. Pepper's Lonely Hearts Club Band," probably the greatest and most influential rock album of the generation that began in the 1960s.

The United States produced its share—and more—of rock artists, including Buffalo Springfield; the Doors; Crosby, Stills, and Nash; and the Jefferson Airplane. Berry Gordy, Jr's. Tamla-Motown organization, based in Detroit, produced records by black artists including the Supremes and the Temptations.

San Francisco became a major center of the counterculture. In 1967, the first "Be-In" took place in the city's Golden Gate Park, and in the decaying Haight-Ashbury district, hippies or "flower children" created an urban subculture that was at its height during the fabled "summer of love" in 1967. That year San Francisco also gave birth to *Rolling Stone* magazine, which devoted its pages to rock music and New Left politics.

If San Francisco served as a magnet for the counterculture,

other drop-outs from conventional society withdrew to rural communes, where they sought to create a simpler way of life with less involvement with material concerns.

The counterculture of the 1960s reached a culmination in the Woodstock Festival, held in upstate New York in August, 1969. The festival drew an unexpectedly large crowd of 400,000 for what was billed as "three days of peace and music." A year following the festival, a local newspaper proposed that a historical marker be erected on the site.

For the United States, the Kennedy-Johnson years were a time of tumult and tragedy. The civil rights movement challenged racial segregation and discrimination, and many blacks, frustrated by the depth of racism in American society, promoted Black Power and separatism. John F. Kennedy, his brother, Robert, and Martin Luther King, Jr. were assassinated. The war in Vietnam deepened, giving rise to the antiwar movement. The counterculture challenged many of the assumptions on which American life was based.

Yet there were achievements, too. The nation maintained a high level of economic prosperity. Although his life ended in tragedy, John F. Kennedy inspired a great outpouring of optimism and idealism among many Americans. After years of debate, Congress passed a broad range of civil rights legislation. The nation acknowledged the presence of poverty in the midst of plenty and sought to find remedies. In foreign policy, the Cuban missile crisis gave rise to efforts to achieve a relaxation of tension in relations with the Soviet Union.

Recommended Reading

Rodolfo Acuna, *Occupied America: A History of Chicanos* (1981).

Ronald Berman, *America in the Sixties: An Intellectual History* (1968).

Carl M. Brauer, *John F. Kennedy and the Second Reconstruction* (1977).

James MacGregor Burns, *John Kennedy: A Political Profile* (1960).

Robert A. Caro, *The Years of Lyndon Johnson* (1982).

William H. Chafe, *The American Woman: Her Changing Social, Economic, and Political Roles, 1920–1970 (1972).*

William H. Chafe, *Civilities and Civil Rights: Greensboro, North Carolina and the Black Struggle for Freedom* (1980).

Frances FitzGerald, *Fire in the Lake: The Vietnamese and the Americans in Vietnam* (1972).

Estelle Freedman and John D'Emilio, *Intimate Matters: A History of Sexuality in America* (1988).

David J. Garrow, *Bearing the Cross: Martin Luther King, Jr., and the Southern Christian Leadership Conference, 1955–1968* (1986).

David J. Garrow, *The FBI and Martin Luther King, Jr.: From "Solo" to Memphis* (1981).

David R. Goldfield, *Promised Land: The South Since 1945* (1987).

David Halberstam, *The Best and the Brightest* (1972).

Michael Harrington, *The Other America: Poverty in the United States* (1962).

George C. Herring, *America's Longest War: The United States and Vietnam, 1950–1975* (1979).

Lyndon B. Johnson, *The Vantage Point: Perspectives of the Presidency, 1963–1969* (1971).

Stanley Karnow, *Vietnam: A History* (1983).

Doris Kearns, *Lyndon Johnson and the American Dream* (1976).

Robert F. Kennedy, *Thirteen Days: A Memoir of the Cuban Missile Crisis* (1969).

Juanita Kreps, *Sex in the Marketplace: American Women at Work* (1971).

David L. Lewis, *King: A Critical Biography* (1970).

Oscar Lewis, *La Vida: A Puerto Rican Family in the Culture of Poverty—San Juan and New York* (1966).

C. Eric Lincoln, *The Black Muslims in America* (1961).

Allen J. Matusow, *The Unraveling of America: A History of Liberalism in the 1960s* (1984).

August Meier and Elliott Rudwick, *CORE: A Study in the Civil Rights Movement, 1942–1968* (1973).

Matt S. Meier and Feliciano Rivera, *The Chicanos: A History of Mexican Americans* (1972).

William L. O'Neill, *Coming Apart: An Informal History of America in the 1960s* (1971).

James T. Patterson, *America's Struggle Against Poverty, 1900–1980* (1981).

Arthur M. Schlesinger, Jr., *A Thousand Days: John F. Kennedy in the White House* (1965).

Kathleen J. Turner, *Lyndon Johnson's Dual War: Vietnam and the Press* (1985).

Irwin Unger, *The Movement: A History of the New Left, 1959–1972* (1974).

Lynn Y. Weiner, *From Working Girl to Working Mother: The Female Labor Force in the United States, 1820–1980* (1985).

Theodore H. White, *The Making of the President, 1960* (1962).

Theodore H. White, *The Making of the President, 1964* (1965).

Raymond Wolters, *The Burden of Brown: Thirty Years of School Desegregation* (1984).

David Zarefsky, *President Johnson's War on Poverty: Rhetoric and History* (1986).

CHAPTER 16

The Nixon Era:
Vietnam and Watergate

Time Line

1968   Republican Richard M. Nixon wins the Presidency

1969   Nixon introduces the policy of Vietnamization of the war in Southeast Asia

Nixon appoints Warren E. Burger as Chief Justice of the United States

1970   American forces invade Cambodia

Student protesters are killed at Kent State University and Jackson State University

Congress establishes the Environmental Protection Agency (EPA)

The Occupational Safety and Health Agency (OSHA) is created

1971   The *New York Times* publishes the "Pentagon Papers"

The Twenty-Sixth Amendment is ratified

Nixon orders a freeze on wages and prices in an effort to combat inflation

1972   The United States launches the Christmas bombing of North Vietnam

Nixon visits China

Nixon and Brezhnev sign the SALT I Treaty

Congress approves federal revenue sharing

Democratic National Committee headquarters in the Watergate complex is burglarized

Nixon wins an overwhelming reelection victory

Congress approves the Equal Rights Amendment

1973   The Paris Accords result in the American withdrawal from Vietnam

Congress passes the War Powers Act

Israel and the Arab states fight the Yom Kippur War

The Arab states place an embargo on petroleum sales to the United States and other countries

In *Roe v. Wade*, the Supreme Court overturns state laws against abortion

The armed forces are placed on an all-volunteer basis

The Senate Watergate committee begins its investigation

Vice President Spiro Agnew resigns; Nixon appoints Gerald Ford as his successor

1974   Nixon resigns the Presidency; Vice President Ford succeeds him

---

For the United States, the late 1960s was a time of national turmoil. While student demonstrators demanded an end to the war in Vietnam and black activists pushed for Black Power, more conservative Americans desired a restoration of stability and law and order. Richard M. Nixon benefitted from this mood in his race for the Presidency in 1968, although as the Watergate scandal unfolded following his 1972 reelection victory, it became evident that Nixon had been one of the most lawless Presidents in American history.

For the American economy, the years after 1968 were a time of limited growth and high inflation, pushed even higher by the energy crisis of the mid-1970s.

In the realm of foreign affairs, the American involvement in the Vietnam war ended, and the United States moved to normal-

ize its relations with China and to ease tension with the Soviet Union. Instability continued to prevail in much of the Third World, especially the Middle East.

1968: The Race for the Democratic Nomination

Following Lyndon Johnson's withdrawal in March, 1968, a three-way race developed for the Democratic presidential nomination between Senators Eugene McCarthy of Minnesota and Robert F. Kennedy of New York and Vice President Hubert H. Humphrey. An antiwar candidate, McCarthy made a good showing in the early New Hampshire primary and then won the primaries in Wisconsin and Oregon. Kennedy, the younger brother of the late President, also opposed the Vietnam war and made a strong appeal to minorities. After winning the primaries in Indiana and Nebraska, Kennedy battled McCarthy in the California primary, held on June 5. Shortly after midnight on June 6, following his victory speech in a Los Angeles hotel, Kennedy was shot and killed by Sirhan Sirhan, a young Palestinian who was angered by Kennedy's strong support of Israel.

When the Democratic national convention met in Chicago in August, Humphrey's nomination appeared a certainty. The Vice President had the overwhelming support of the big labor unions and the Democratic party leaders of the major state and city organizations. Humphrey had achieved a strong liberal record as a senator from Minnesota prior to his election to the Vice Presidency in 1964, but he had loyally supported Johnson's policy in the Vietnam war.

While convention delegates debated whether to include an antiwar plank in the party's platform, antiwar protesters demonstrated outside the convention hall and elsewhere in Chicago. The most colorful of the demonstrators were the Yippies, the Youth International Party, led by Abbie Hoffman and

Jerry Rubin. The Yippies promoted what they called a "festival of life" to contrast with the Democrats' "convention of death."

Chicago's Mayor Richard J. Daley surrounded the convention hall with barricades and police, augmented by National Guard units, to prevent demonstrators from disrupting the convention. On the night Humphrey won the nomination, the police attacked the demonstrators in what was later described as a police riot. As live television reported the events, the demonstrators shouted: "The whole world is watching!"

The Election of 1968

Humphrey and his vice presidential running mate, Senator Edmund S. Muskie of Maine, entered the campaign with what appeared to be a decided disadvantage.

The Republicans nominated former Vice President Richard M. Nixon for the Presidency, and Nixon selected Spiro T. Agnew, the relatively obscure Governor of Maryland, as his running mate. Nixon appealed to the conservative mood of much of the American electorate, pledging to work for stability and law and order. He promised peace with honor in Vietnam. Above all, Nixon's campaign was designed to win the support of respectable, middle-class, white "Middle America," which had been frightened by many of the events of the 1960s.

Governor George C. Wallace of Alabama launched a third-party presidential campaign. Running under the banner of the American Independent Party, Wallace denounced protesters and the intrusion of the federal government into local affairs and appealed especially to those who opposed the gains made by blacks during the 1960s. Wallace's vice presidential running mate, retired air force General Curtis LeMay, advocated expanding the war in Vietnam.

As the campaign progressed, Humphrey gained support, particularly from traditional Democrats who distrusted the

Republicans' economic policies, and the election was closer than expected. Humphrey won 31.3 million popular votes, some 500,000 fewer than Nixon's 31.8 million. In the electoral college, however, Nixon won a strong majority, 301 votes to 191. Wallace polled close to 10 million votes and won 46 electoral votes, carrying five states in the deep South. The Democrats retained control of both houses of Congress.

Nixon as President

The Nixon administration was decidedly more conservative than the Kennedy-Johnson administration which had preceded it. Nixon appointed an all-male, all-white cabinet. John N. Mitchell, a member of Nixon's former law firm and a successful bond lawyer, became Attorney General, and a longtime Republican congressman from Wisconsin, Melvin Laird, became Secretary of Defense. Henry Kissinger, a Harvard professor, served as the National Security Adviser, working closely with the President in developing and carrying out foreign policy. In Nixon's second term, beginning in 1973, Kissinger became Secretary of State, replacing William Rogers who had served in that post since 1969.

As his White House chief of staff, Nixon named H. R. Haldeman, an advertising executive, while lawyer John Ehrlichman became the President's chief adviser on domestic affairs.

The Vietnam War

Nixon regarded finding a solution to the problem of the Vietnam war as the main task of his administration. During the presidential campaign, he had claimed that he had a secret plan to end the war, although in fact a specific plan did not exist.

Nixon promoted a policy of Vietnamization of the war: The United States would finance, train, and equip South Vietnamese forces to fight the war, while American combat troops would gradually be withdrawn. In June 1969, Nixon announced plans to withdraw 25,000 American troops, and in September he declared that an additional 35,000 men would be pulled out by December. At the end of 1968, there had been 536,000 American troops in Vietnam. By the end of 1969, the number had dropped to 475,000. By the end of 1970, the total had fallen to slightly less than 335,000, and by the end of 1971 to about 157,000.

As the troop withdrawals continued, American casualties declined. The President insisted that the "silent majority" of Americans supported his policies. Nevertheless, antiwar protests continued. While Nixon referred to the protesters as "bums," Vice President Agnew denounced critics of administration policy as "nattering nabobs of negativism" and an "effete corps of impudent snobs" and criticized the "misleading" news media.

The frustrating war in Vietnam had a clearly dehumanizing effect on the American military. In November, 1969, the story of the My Lai massacre became public. In March, 1968, American infantrymen killed at least 450 unarmed South Vietnamese civilians, including women and children, in the village of My Lai, which the army feared might be hiding Viet Cong guerrillas. A court martial convicted Lt. William F. Calley, Jr. of responsibility for the massacre.

A decline of morale and discipline among American troops led to refusals to obey orders, drug use, and desertion. There were also reports of "fraggings," the killing of unpopular officers by enlisted men.

While Nixon pushed his policy of Vietnamization forward, he also escalated the war by hitting at staging areas in Cambodia used by the North Vietnamese. In March, 1969, Nixon authorized the air force to begin secret bombing attacks on these sanctuaries in Cambodia. These air raids did not become public knowledge until 1973.

In March, 1970, conservative military leaders in Cambodia, headed by General Lon Nol, overthrew the neutralist government of Prince Norodom Sihanouk. Lon Nol asked for American aid against the Communist activities in his country. On April 30, Nixon announced that American and South Vietnamese forces were moving into Cambodia to attack North Vietnamese bases.

The invasion of Cambodia gave new life to the antiwar movement, and a wave of demonstrations, some violent, swept the country in early May, 1970. On May 4, National Guardsmen killed four students and wounded nine others when they fired on demonstrators at Kent State University in Ohio. Ten days later, state highway patrolmen shot and killed two black students at Jackson State University in Mississippi. On May 9, a large antiwar demonstration took place in Washington.

The invasion of Cambodia ended in late June, with the North Vietnamese continuing to control large areas of the country.

At the end of December, 1970, Congress repealed the Gulf of Tonkin Resolution, thereby depriving the President of what had provided the legal basis for the war. Nixon insisted, however, that he had the authority to continue military operations in order to protect American troops in Vietnam.

Events in early 1971 raised doubts about the effectiveness of the Vietnamization program. In February, the United States provided air support for a major South Vietnamese push into Laos, aimed at North Vietnamese supply bases along the Ho Chi Minh Trail. The South Vietnamese suffered heavy losses in the operation, which had to be suspended ahead of schedule.

On July 1, 1971, the *New York Times* began the publication of excerpts from a secret study of the war in Vietnam prepared by the Defense Department during the Johnson administration. Daniel Ellsberg, a former employee of the Defense Department, had leaked these "Pentagon Papers," as the report became known, to the press. The Supreme Court upheld the right of the *New York Times* and other newspapers to publish the Pentagon

Papers, finding that the government had failed to show that publication endangered the national security. The Pentagon Papers revealed the government's dishonesty in reporting its plans for expanding the war and its deceptive reporting of the course of the war. The Vietnam War became increasingly unpopular, and by 1971 polls revealed that close to two-thirds of Americans favored withdrawal from Vietnam.

In March, 1972, the North Vietnamese launched their biggest offensive across the Demilitarized Zone (DMZ) since the Tet offensive of 1968. In response, Nixon ordered massive bombing attacks on Hanoi, North Vietnam's capital; Haiphong, the country's major seaport; and other targets. He also ordered the mining of Haiphong and other major North Vietnamese harbors to impede the flow of supplies from the Soviet Union and China.

Negotiating a Cease Fire in Vietnam

At the same time that Nixon escalated the war against North Vietnam, negotiations were under way between American and North Vietnamese representatives. In an attempt to defuse the issue during the 1972 presidential campaign, these negotiations were stepped up during the summer, as Kissinger held a series of meetings in Paris with Le Duc Tho, North Vietnam's Foreign Minister. On October 26, a few days before the election, Kissinger announced that "peace is at hand."

Although the United States and North Vietnam had agreed on a plan for a cease fire, South Vietnam's President Nguyen Van Thieu refused to accept it, since it did not provide for the withdrawal of North Vietnamese troops from South Vietnam.

When further talks between Kissinger and Le Duc Tho collapsed in mid-December, the United States began the so-called Christmas bombing of North Vietnam. This bombing involved the heaviest air assaults on North Vietnam during the entire war. Both civilian casualties and American losses were high.

The degree to which the bombing forced concessions from the North Vietnamese is debatable at best. When negotiations resumed in January, 1973, the North Vietnamese made few concessions. On January 27, 1973, the United States, South Vietnam, North Vietnam, and the Viet Cong signed the Paris Accords, officially entitled the "Agreement on Ending the War and Restoring Peace in Vietnam." The agreement provided for an immediate cease-fire. The United States would withdraw its 24,000 remaining troops, and the North Vietnamese would release about 600 American prisoners of war. However, there was no provision for a withdrawal of North Vietnamese forces from South Vietnam, and they continued to hold about 30 percent of the country. The North Vietnamese and Viet Cong remained committed to the reunification of Vietnam under one government and were prepared to use force to achieve that goal.

Kissinger and Le Duc Tho received the 1973 Nobel Peace Prize, although Tho refused his share of the prize because the war was not yet over. American involvement had ended, however. More than 46,000 Americans lost their lives in Vietnam, with 15,000 of these deaths occurring after Nixon became President. Another 10,000 Americans died of noncombat related causes. Over 300,000 Americans were wounded. The war cost the American treasury well in excess of $100 billion. South Vietnamese military dead totaled almost 185,000, while 450,000 South Vietnamese civilians lost their lives. North Vietnamese and Viet Cong dead numbered over one million.

The War Powers Act

In an effort to reduce the President's aility to involve the United States in an undeclared war, Congress passed the War Powers Act over Nixon's veto in November 1973. The act required the President to report to Congress within 48 hours after committing American troops to a foreign conflict. The President would be required to withdraw these troops within 60 days unless Congress authorized that they remain.

Nixon's China Policy

With a reputation as a staunch anti-Communist, Nixon could initiate new approaches to Communist China and the Soviet Union more easily than a liberal Democrat could. For some 20 years, the Republicans had been charging the Democrats with being "soft on Communism."

In 1949, the Chinese Communists defeated the Nationalist leader Chiang Kai-shek and established the People's Republic of China (PRC). The United States refused to recognize the PRC and instead continued to regard the exiled Nationalist government on Taiwan as the legitimate government of China.

Nixon and Kissinger wanted to establish an American relationship with the PRC, believing that such a relationship would serve to strengthen China as a counterbalance to the Soviet Union and would also encourage Moscow to develop a more conciliatory attitude toward the United States. In view of the antagonism between China and the Soviet Union, the Chinese desired improved relations with the United States.

In July, 1971, Kissinger went to Peking (Beijing), China's capital, on a secret mission to visit the Chinese leaders. Following this visit, Nixon announced his intention to visit China. In the fall of 1971, the United States ended its opposition to the admission of the PRC to the United Nations. In October, the UN admitted the PRC and unseated the representatives of the government on Taiwan.

During his visit to China in February, 1972, Nixon met with Communist party leader Mao Tse-tung, Premier Chou En-lai, and other officials. No agreement was reached regarding the establishment of formal diplomatic relations, but more than two decades of hostility ended. The United States and China agreed to expand their trade and to develop scientific and cultural relations. In 1973, the two countries established liaison offices in Washington and Beijing which functioned as unofficial embassies.

Detente with the Soviet Union

During the Johnson administration, efforts had been made to ease tension with the Soviet Union. The American-Soviet Consular Treaty, ratified by the Senate in 1967, provided for the establishment of American consulates in the Soviet Union and Soviet consulates in the United States. A consulate deals primarily with trade relations.

In January, 1967, the United States, the Soviet Union, Great Britain, and 57 other countries signed the Outer Space Treaty, banning weapons of mass destruction, as well as military bases, from outer space.

In June, 1967, Johnson met with Soviet Premier Alexei Kosygin at Glassboro State College in New Jersey, following Kosygin's visit to the United Nations in New York. This Glassboro Summit did not result in any specific agreements.

The United States, the Soviet Union, and 60 other nations signed the Nuclear Nonproliferation Treaty in July, 1968. The treaty was designed to prevent the spread of nuclear weapons to nonnuclear countries. France, the People's Republic of China, and several other countries refused to accept the treaty.

These actions represented the beginning of the policy of detente, the easing of tension between the United States and the Soviet Union. Nixon wanted to continue and further the process of detente.

For several years, negotiations had been underway between the United States and the Soviet Union for a strategic arms limitation treaty (SALT). In May, 1972, Nixon went to Moscow to meet with Soviet General Secretary Leonid Brezhnev and sign the SALT I Treaty. In this treaty, the United States and the Soviet Union agreed to freeze the number of intercontinental ballistic missiles (ICBMs) at their existing levels for five years, although no limit was placed on the number of warheads that could be carried by each missile. SALT I thus did little to end the arms race but instead moved it in a new direction, as each superpower sought to put more multiple independent reentry vehicles (MIRVs) on each missile. In addition, the treaty did not place any limits on the creation of new missile systems to replace obsolete ones. Nixon and Brezhnev also signed the Antiballistic Missile Treaty (ABM). In this treaty, the Americans and Soviets agreed to restrict the construction of antiballistic missile systems to two sites in each country.

The Moscow Summit of 1972 also resulted in other agreements dealing with trade, scientific, and cultural exchanges. One important agreement involved the sale of American wheat and other grains to the Soviet Union over a three-year period. Both parties would benefit, since American grain shipments would make up the shortfall in Soviet production and would also reduce the amount of surplus grain stored in the United States. Heavy grain sales to the Soviet Union, however, created shortages in the United States where higher grain prices added to the problem of inflation.

In June, 1973, Brezhnev visited the United States, meeting with Nixon in Washington and at the President's home in San Clemente, California. Further agreements were reached regarding trade, scientific, and cultural exchanges, although the main purpose of the Washington Summit was to demonstrate the progress of detente between the two superpowers.

In late June and early July, 1974, Nixon paid a second visit to Moscow. While this visit emphasized the continuing commitment to detente, the two superpowers had not made any progress in the negotiations aimed at limiting offensive nuclear arms.

Intervention in Chile

In 1970, Salvador Allende, a Marxist, won the presidential election in Chile. The Central Intelligence Agency (CIA) then began to provide assistance to opposition forces in Chile and to take other action in an effort to destabilize the Allende government. In 1973, a military junta took power in Chile, and Allende was killed. The repressive government headed by General Augusto Pinochet received substantial military and economic assistance from the United States.

The Middle East

American involvement in the tangled affairs of the Middle East remained substantial, as the United States continued its support of Israel and sought to maintain harmonious relations with the Arab states which were hostile to Israel.

In October, 1973, on the eve of Yom Kippur, the most sacred of the Jewish high holy days, Egypt and Syria attacked Israel. While the Israelis were initially caught off balance, they soon launched effective counteroffensives. The United States moved quickly to resupply Israel with military equipment and also pushed for a cease-fire.

In response to American support of Israel during the Yom Kippur War, the oil-producing Arab states instituted an embargo on the sale of oil to countries regarded as favorable to Israel. The embargo ended in March, 1974.

In the aftermath of the Yom Kippur War, Kissinger began his shuttle diplomacy, flying between Israel and the Arab capitals. In November, Kissinger and Egypt's President Anwar el-Sadat agreed to reestablish diplomatic relations between the United States and Egypt, which had been broken off during the

Six-Day War of June, 1967. In addition, Kissinger worked out a cease-fire agreement between Egypt and Israel. In January, 1974, Kissinger won Israeli and Egyptian consent to an agreement providing for a pullback of their forces along the Suez Canal. In May, 1974, Kissinger's shuttle diplomacy resulted in a complex cease-fire and troop withdrawal agreement between Israel and Syria.

In June, 1974, Nixon visited Israel, Egypt, Saudi Arabia, Syria, and Jordan. This presidential visit underlined Kissinger's success in promoting stability in the Middle East and achieving an improvement in American relations with the Arab states.

The New Federalism

While Nixon focused much of his attention on foreign affairs, in the domestic sphere he sought to reduce the influence of the federal government over state and local affairs. Nixon declared that his policy of the New Federalism was designed to "start resources and power flowing back from Washington to the people." In October, 1972, Congress approved a five-year revenue sharing program to distribute over $30 billion in federal tax revenue to state and local governments to use for purposes which they determined.

Nixon and Civil Rights

Nixon and Attorney General Mitchell sought to reduce the pace of school desegregation. In 1969, the administration attempted to delay the court-ordered integration of public schools in 33 Mississippi counties. In its decision in the case of *Alexander v. Holmes County Board of Education*, issued in October, 1969, the Supreme Court ordered an immediate end to school segregation. In protest against the administration's policy of trying to slow desegregation, Leon Panetta, the chief of the Civil Rights Office of the Department of Health, Education, and Welfare, resigned in February, 1970.

The Supreme Court also blocked the administration's efforts to prevent the busing of students in order to desegregate urban public schools. In 1971, in the case of *Swann v. Charlotte-Mecklenburg Board of Education,* the Supreme Court decided that busing was a legitimate means for achieving school integration.

The House of Representatives endorsed an administration proposal calling for a moratorium on court-ordered busing, but a filibuster by Senate liberals blocked its passage in the upper house.

When a federal court ordered busing to promote the integration of the public schools of Boston, to begin in the fall of 1974, violence broke out at South Boston High School, and many white students boycotted the school.

Opponents of busing won a partial victory in the 1974 case of *Milliken v. Bradley.* The Supreme Court invalidated a Detroit plan to bus students from inner-city schools to schools in suburban school districts.

In 1970, Nixon vetoed a renewal of the Voting Rights Act of 1965, but Congress overrode the veto.

Nixon's general reluctance to promote the cause of civil rights reflected his support of the so-called southern strategy, designed to win increased support for the Republican party in the South.

Nixon and the Supreme Court

Conservatives had been outspoken in their criticism of the Supreme Court headed by Chief Justice Earl Warren (the Warren Court), charging that it had been too liberal on race, legislative reapportionment, the rights of criminal suspects, and other issues. Nixon wanted to move the Supreme Court in a more conservative direction by appointing strict constructionists.

When Warren retired as Chief Justice in 1969, Nixon appointed Warren E. Burger, a respected federal appeals court judge from Minnesota, as his successor.

In May, 1969, Justice Abe Fortas, a Johnson appointee, resigned in the wake of charges involving alleged financial irregularities. Nixon ran into trouble when he sought to fill this vacancy. The President began by appointing Clement F. Haynsworth, Jr., a federal appeals court judge from South Carolina. Opposed by liberals, black organizations, and labor unions, the Senate refused to confirm Haynsworth when it was revealed that he had failed to disqualify himself from hearing cases involving corporations in which he had a financial interest. The Senate also rejected Nixon's next appointment, G. Harrold Carswell, a federal appeals court judge from Florida, who was accused of having racist attitudes and of having insufficient qualifications for a seat on the high court.

Nixon angrily charged that the Senate had rejected his nominees because of prejudice against the South. He then named Harry A. Blackmun of Minnesota, who easily won Senate confirmation. Nixon was also able to appoint two other associate justices of the Supreme Court. One was a southerner: Lewis F. Powell, Jr., a respected Virginia judge. The other was William Rehnquist, an official of the Justice Department. In 1987, Rehnquist became Chief Justice.

While the Burger Court was less liberal than the Warren Court, it was still far too liberal for conservative tastes.

The Supreme Court's 1972 decision in the case of *Furman v. Georgia* was particularly controversial. The court declared that the death penalty as it was being applied was cruel and unusual punishment and therefore was in violation of the Eighth Amendment to the Constitution. The decision overturned the death sentences of almost 600 prisoners. Chief Justice Burger's dissent suggested that capital punishment laws which did not result in a random and unpredictable application of the death sentence might be ruled constitutional.

Another highly controversial decision came in 1973. In the case of *Roe v. Wade,* the Supreme Court struck down state laws against abortion.

Nixon and Crime

In his appeal to Middle America, Nixon promised to get tough on crime, although criminal prosecutions were primarily a responsibility of the states. The District of Columbia, however, lay within the jurisdiction of the federal government. In 1970, Nixon won congressional approval of a crime bill for the District of Columbia, although opponents criticized it as a violation of civil liberties. The new law provided for preventive detention of up to 60 days for defendants awaiting trial and a no-knock provision, authorizing the police to enter premises without a warrant.

Congress also approved the Omnibus Crime Control Act of 1970 which provided state and local law enforcement agencies with over $3.5 billion in federal aid during a three-year period.

Nixon and Social Welfare

The Nixon administration cut back on some of the social welfare programs of the Kennedy-Johnson administration, particularly the war on poverty.

Nixon focused his attention on the program of Aid to Families with Dependent Children (AFDC). This program was extremely costly, both because of the amount of aid distributed and because of the huge bureaucracy required to administer the program. To replace AFDC, Nixon proposed the Family Assistance Plan, designed in large part by Daniel Patrick Moynihan, the head of the administration's Council on Urban Affairs. The plan would have provided a poor family of four with a minimum guaranteed income of $1600, plus about $800 in food stamps. People participating in this program would be required to register for job training and to accept employment when it was available. The proposal proved to be controversial. While the House of Representatives approved it, the Senate did not.

Social Security benefits for retired workers and for others entitled to benefits increased, but so too did Social Security taxes. In addition, the federal government assumed full responsibility for financing and administering programs of assistance to the blind and disabled, provided through the Social Security system. These programs had previously been a joint federal-state project.

The Twenty-Sixth Amendment

In 1970, Congress approved the Voting Rights Extension Act, which lowered the voting age to 18 in federal, state, and local elections. In the case of *Oregon v. Mitchell,* decided in 1970, the Supreme Court ruled that Congress had exceeded its authority in reducing the voting age in state and local elections, although Congress could set the voting age for federal elections. In March, 1971, Congress approved the Twenty-Sixth Amendment to the Constitution, reducing the voting age to 18 for all elections. The amendment was quickly ratified.

Environmental Legislation

Congress adopted a series of laws establishing a larger role for the federal government in the area of the environment.

The National Environmental Policy Act of 1969 declared that the protection of the environment was a matter of national policy and established a three-member Council on Environmental Quality. Federal agencies were required to include an environmental impact statement as a part of recommendations for legislation or other major activities. Each year, the President was required to submit to Congress an environmental quality report.

In 1970, the Environmental Protection Agency (EPA) was created, joining in a single agency all programs dealing with the environment.

In 1971, the Public Land Law Review Commission published its report entitled *One Third of the Nation's Land.* The report urged the establishment of strict environmental controls over the 755 million acres of land owned by the federal government.

Congress moved to deal with water pollution by passing the Water Quality Improvement Act of 1970 and by adopting, in 1972, a series of amendments to the Water Pollution Control Act of 1948. The Clean Air Act of 1970 established a comprehensive three-year air pollution control program.

Occupational Safety

In 1970, Congress passed the Occupational Safety and Health Act which required employers to provide work places "free from recognized hazards to employees." The Occupational Safety and Health Agency (OSHA) was authorized to establish and enforce health and safety standards.

Minimum Wage Legislation

In 1974, Congress raised the minimum wage from $1.60 an hour to $2.10 on January 1, 1975, and to $2.30 on January 1, 1976. Coverage by the minimum wage law was extended to an additional seven million workers, including state and local government employees and domestic workers. In 1976, however, the Supreme Court ruled that Congress could not regulate the wages of state employees.

The End of the Military Draft

In 1971, Congress extended the military draft for two years and approved increases in pay and benefits for service personnel. When the draft extension expired in 1973, the armed forces were placed on an all-volunteer basis for the first time since 1948.

The Federal Election Campaign Act

Passed by Congress in 1972, the Federal Election Campaign Act placed limits on the amount candidates and their families could spend on campaigns for federal office. Limits were also placed on total campaign expenditures, and the requirements for reporting campaign contributions and expenditures were tightened. In particular, the law required the reporting of the names of all persons who contributed $100 or more to a campaign for federal office.

Nixon and the Economy

The economy proved to be the most persistent domestic problem faced by Nixon. When he became President in 1969, inflation appeared to be the most immediate economic concern. During Johnson's administration, increased spending for domestic social programs and the Vietnam war led to a substantial expansion of the money supply and budget deficits. As a result, prices moved upward.

In an attempt to reduce inflation, Nixon cut government expenditures, while the Federal Reserve Board tightened credit and increased interest rates in an attempt to slow the expansion of the money supply.

These actions resulted in the recession of 1969–70. Unemployment had been 3.3 percent when Nixon took office. In late 1970, it rose to 6 percent. Following Nixon's election in late

1968, the Dow Jones industrial average stood at 985. By late May 1970, it had fallen to 631, the sharpest drop in more than thirty years. In 1970, the gross national product (GNP) declined for the first time since 1958.

Nixon's policy did not end inflation. Instead, prices continued to rise, despite the economic downturn. The cost of living increased by 15 percent during the first two and a half years of Nixon's term.

The United States now faced the new economic problem of stagflation, a combination of general economic stagnation and inflation. Usually in times of economic slowdown, prices declined.

The Economic Stabilization Act of 1970 authorized the President to regulate wages and prices. While Nixon had not favored this legislation, he decided to use it. On August 15, 1971, he ordered a 90-day freeze on wages and prices. This Phase I program, as it was known, was followed in mid-November by Phase II, which established a system of mandatory guidelines to limit increases in wages and prices. The guidelines were administered by a Pay Board and a Price Commission under the general supervision of the Cost of Living Council (CLC).

In January, 1973, Phase III began. The mandatory guidelines were replaced with voluntary guidelines which proved ineffective. Prices moved upward once again. The inflation rate, which had stood at 5.9 percent in 1971, reached 9 percent in 1973, the highest it had been since the Korean War of the early 1950s.

While inflation was the most apparent economic problem, there were others, as well. The most serious involved declines in American exports and increasing prices for raw materials imported by the United States. In 1971, for the first time in 80 years, the United States reported a balance-of-trade deficit; that is, an excess of imports over exports.

Following World War II, the United States held a position

of dominance in world trade. The United States had a large market overseas for its industrial and agricultural products and it had ready access to inexpensive raw materials. In addition, American industry faced relatively little competition in the domestic market.

This situation gradually changed to the disadvantage of the United States, and the changes were becoming evident by the late 1960s. American industry began to face increasing competition from Western European and Japanese manufacturers of steel, automobiles, and other products in both the world and domestic markets. Raw material costs began to increase because of the competition among the industrialized nations for limited supplies and also because the less developed countries which produced the raw materials began to raise their prices.

The Energy Crisis

The most dramatic example of increased prices for raw materials was provided by petroleum.

The American economy and the whole American way of life were based, in large part, on the availability of cheap energy and especially cheap petroleum. Until the end of World War II, the United States produced more petroleum than it consumed. After 1945, however, American consumption of petroleum increased considerably. More than ever, the United States was a nation on wheels, and by the late 1960s American motorists were driving more than a trillion miles a year. Petroleum was also used for a host of other purposes, in the manufacture of nylon and other synthetic fibers, plastics, paint, fertilizers, and insecticides. Oil and natural gas were being used increasingly for the production of electricity and for heating, in place of coal. By the early 1970s, the United States—with 6 percent of the world's population—was consuming about one-third of the world's petroleum production.   And the United States depended on imports for about one-third of its petroleum.

In 1960, several major petroleum producing countries, among them Saudi Arabia, Kuwait, Iraq, Iran, and Venezuela, joined in the creation of a cartel, the Organization of Petroleum Exporting Countries (OPEC). In its early years, OPEC did not succeed in controlling the price of petroleum, which stood at about $3 a barrel when the Yom Kippur War began in October, 1973. During this war, the Arab states placed an embargo on shipments of petroleum to countries which supported Israel, including the United States, Japan, and most of Western Europe. As a result of Kissinger's efforts, the embargo ended in March, 1974.

The members of OPEC also raised the price of petroleum by almost 400 percent, to about $12 a barrel. This price increase caused a shock throughout the industrialized world, raising prices for a wide range of goods. In the United States, gasoline and fuel oil prices quickly doubled and continued to increase, while the general inflation rate shot up, reaching 12 percent in 1974.   Double-digit inflation continued through most of the 1970s, while the value of the dollar declined and the trade imbalance mounted.

In response to the energy crisis, Nixon urged conservation and increased domestic production, as well as increases in the use of coal and nuclear power. He also spoke of restoring the nation's energy independence, although few concrete steps were taken toward achieving that goal. In an attempt to reduce energy consumption, the highway speed limit was reduced to 55 miles per hour and Congress approved an experiment with year-round daylight savings time. In 1973, Congress approved the construction of an Alaskan pipeline to carry petroleum from the oil fields of northern Alaska.

The 1972 Election

In the race for the Democratic presidential nomination in 1972, Senator George McGovern of South Dakota defeated the other major contenders, Senator Edmund S. Muskie of Maine and former Vice President Hubert H. Humphrey. McGovern, a liberal and outspoken opponent of the Vietnam War, benefitted from reforms of the Democratic party's rules for selecting national convention delegates. These reforms provided for the selection of more young people, women, and representatives of minorities.

McGovern's campaign was weakened by divisions among Democrats and was further hurt by revelations that his vice presidential running mate, Senator Thomas F. Eagleton of Missouri, had been hospitalized three times for psychiatric problems. Eagleton was replaced by R. Sargent Shriver, the former head of the Peace Corps and John F. Kennedy's brother-in-law.

George C. Wallace made a new bid for the Presidency in 1972 but had to end his campaign after he was shot by Arthur Bremer in a Maryland shopping center. As a result of the shooting, Wallace was paralyzed from the waist down.

In his campaign for reelection, Nixon won the overwhelming support of what political analysts Richard Scammon and Ben Wattenberg called the "real majority": the "unyoung, unblack, and unpoor." Nixon polled almost 46 million popular votes and 520 electoral votes. McGovern won 28 million popular votes and carried only Massachusetts and the District of Columbia, winning their 17 electoral votes.

Despite Nixon's hopes of gaining a Republican majority in Congress, the Democrats retained control of both houses.

The Beginning of the Watergate Affair

The events which would ultimately lead to Nixon's resignation from the Presidency began on the night of June 16–17, 1972. Shortly after midnight on June 17, the police arrested five men who had broken into the headquarters of the Democratic National Committee, located in the Watergate apartment-office complex in Washington, D.C. Led by James W. McCord, the Watergate burglars had been going through files and installing electronic listening devices. McCord was the chief of security for the Committee to Reelect the President (CRP or, less respectfully, CREEP). Two others—E. Howard Hunt, Jr. and G. Gordon Liddy—were arrested, and charged with supervising the break-in. Hunt was a White House consultant, while Liddy was counsel to CRP.

Although there were implications of a connection between the Watergate burglary and the President's reelection campaign, on June 22 Nixon categorically denied any involvement of his staff or administration in the burglary. The President's denial was generally accepted, and the Watergate affair did not play any major role in the 1972 election campaign.

In early 1973, five of the seven Watergate defendants pleaded guilty, including Hunt. Refusing to plead guilty, McCord and Liddy went to trial and were convicted. Judge John J. Sirica, who presided at the trial, got McCord to agree to cooperate both with the grand jury and a special Senate investigating committee, chaired by Senator Sam J. Ervin of North Carolina. McCord told Sirica that prominent Republican officials had known about the burglary in advance, that they had put pressure on the defendants not to reveal their involvement, and that perjury had been committed during the trial.

The story of Watergate gradually became public, as a result of investigative reporting by Bob Woodward and Carl Bernstein of the *Washington Post* and through testimony presented to the Senate's Watergate committee. This testimony revealed a host of illegal acts relating not only to the Watergate burglary but also to a wide range of activities which associates of the President had engaged in.

Large sums of money from secret campaign funds had been paid to the Watergate burglars to insure their silence, and the CIA had provided, perhaps unknowingly, some of the equipment used in the break-in.

L. Patrick Gray, the Acting Director of the FBI, had destroyed documents related to the Watergate burglary. This revelation led to Gray's resignation in April, 1973.

A number of corporations had violated federal election laws by making large unreported contributions to Nixon's reelection campaign.

E. Howard Hunt had forged State Department documents implicating President Kennedy in the assassination of President Ngo Dinh Diem of South Vietnam.

The White House had established a so-called "plumbers unit" to stop leaks of confidential information. Both Hunt and Liddy had been involved in the plumbers unit, which had illegally tapped the phones of low-level officials of the National Security Council (NSC) and of several journalists who had been critical of the administration.

The most notorious act of the plumbers unit was the September, 1971, burglary of a psychiatrist's office in a search for information about one of his patients, Daniel Ellsberg, who had leaked the Pentagon Papers to the press. The revelation of the burglary of the psychiatrist's office led to the dismissal of the charges against Ellsberg.

White House special counsel Charles W. Colson had drawn up an "enemies list." The Internal Revenue Service (IRS) had been ordered to audit the tax returns of those whose names appeared on the enemies list and to take other action to harass them.

CRP officials had used illegal methods—"dirty tricks"—in an effort to disrupt the 1972 campaigns of a number of leading Democrats.

As the charges mounted, several of Nixon's closest associates resigned in the spring of 1973, including H. R. Haldeman, John Ehrlichman, White House counsel John W. Dean, III, and Attorney General Richard Kleindienst. Nixon named Elliot L. Richardson to succeed Kleindienst.

Nixon continued to deny any direct involvement either in the burglary or the attempted cover-up. While the President promised to push the investigation of the affair and to punish the guilty, he refused to allow investigators access to White House documents, invoking executive privilege.

No evidence was ever presented to show that Nixon had been involved in the original Watergate burglary. Evidently the key figure in authorizing the burglary was John Mitchell, who had resigned as Attorney General to head CRP shortly after the break-in.

Gradually, however, the evidence began to implicate Nixon in the cover-up of the Watergate burglary. In May, 1973, John Dean told the Senate Watergate committee in great detail about the President's participation in the cover-up. At this point, however, it was a matter of Dean's word against the President's. Republican Senator Howard Baker of Tennessee summed up the issue when he asked: "What did the President know and when did he know it?" Nixon insisted: "I am not a crook."

Alexander P. Butterfield, a White House staffer, created a sensation when he revealed to the Watergate committee that Nixon had made secret tape recordings of White House conversations and telephone calls. Citing executive privilege and national security, Nixon refused to allow the committee access to the tapes.

Facing heavy pressure, the President agreed to appoint a special prosecutor to investigate the Watergate affair. Nixon named Archibald Cox of the Harvard University Law School. While he promised to cooperate with Cox, Nixon then became irritated when the special prosecutor pressed his investigation. In October, 1973, Cox secured a court order requiring Nixon to turn over the tapes. Nixon then ordered Attorney General Richardson to fire Cox. Both Richardson and William Ruckelshaus, his deputy, resigned rather than wait to be fired. Solicitor General Robert Bork obeyed Nixon's order and dismissed Cox on October, 20, 1973. These events evoked a public uproar and quickly became known as the Saturday Night Massacre. Some of the President's critics now began to talk of impeachment.

Nixon agreed to appoint another special prosecutor and named Leon Jaworski, a respected lawyer from Texas. When Jaworski continued to press for release of the tapes, Nixon agreed to turn them over to Judge Sirica. Relevant material from the tapes could be presented to the grand jury investigating Watergate, but Nixon insisted that nothing be made public. It soon became evident that some important tapes were missing and that 18 minutes of a conversation between Nixon, Haldeman, and Ehrlichman on June 20, 1972, had been erased.

The Resignation of Vice President Agnew

While the attention of the nation was focused on the Watergate affair, Vice President Agnew was charged with accepting bribes and kickbacks while he was county executive of Baltimore, Governor of Maryland, and Vice President. At first, Agnew denied the charges. Then in October 1973, he pleaded *nolo contendere* (no contest) to tax evasion charges. This was, in effect, an admission of guilt. Agnew resigned the Vice Presidency. He was fined $10,000, placed on probation for three years, and disbarred as a lawyer.

In accordance with the terms of the Twenty-Fifth Amendment to the Constitution, Nixon nominated Republican Representative Gerald R. Ford of Michigan as Vice President. Congress quickly confirmed the appointment.

Nixon's Tax Problems

Revelations about Nixon's income taxes added to his problems. In response to charges that he had paid almost no taxes during his time as President, in 1973 Nixon released his tax returns from 1969 through 1972. During one two-year period, when his income had been over $500,000, he had paid only about $1,600 in income taxes. To reduce his tax liability, the President had claimed a huge deduction for some of the vice presidential papers he had donated to the National Archives.

Both the Internal Revenue Service (IRS) and a joint congressional committee examined the returns and concluded that the deductions had been unjustified. The IRS charged Nixon almost $500,000 in taxes and interest, which he agreed to pay.

Nixon's Resignation

While special prosecutor Jaworski continued his investigation, the Judiciary Committee of the House of Representatives, chaired by Peter W. Rodino, Jr., of New Jersey, began to consider the possibility of impeachment.

In early 1974, the Watergate grand jury indicted Haldeman, Ehrlichman, Mitchell, Colson, and four other White House staff members on charges of conspiracy to obstruct the Watergate investigation. The grand jury named Nixon as an unindicted coconspirator after Jaworski had informed the jurors that he was not certain that they had the constitutional authority to indict an incumbent President. Judge Sirica turned the grand jury's evidence against Nixon over to the House Judiciary Committee.

In late April, 1974, hoping to reduce the pressure on him, Nixon released edited transcripts of the tapes he had turned over to Judge Sirica in November, 1973. The transcripts did little to help the President's cause. Many were shocked by Nixon's use of rough language, indicated in the transcripts by the phrase "expletive deleted." Even more shocking was Nixon's lack of concern for the public interest.

When the Judiciary Committee received the actual tapes, it became evident that the transcripts released by the White House had been inaccurate. Jaworski secured a court order calling on the White House to release 64 additional tapes, but James St. Clair, the President's lawyer, refused to obey the order. The special prosecutor now took the case of *United States v. Richard M. Nixon* to the Supreme Court, which ruled on August 1, 1974, that the President must turn the tapes over to Jaworski.

In the meantime, the 38 members—21 Democrats and 17 Republicans—of the House Judiciary Committee continued its study of the evidence against the President in televised hearings. In the final days of July, 1974, the committee adopted three articles of impeachment, charging Nixon with obstruction of justice in the Watergate cover-up, with abusing the powers of his office in violating the rights of citizens, and with defiance of the authority of Congress by refusing to obey subpoenas to turn over tapes and other materials. A number of Republicans joined the Democrats on the committee in voting in favor of impeachment.

On August 5, 1974, Nixon released three tapes from June 23, 1972, which revealed that he had already become involved in the Watergate cover-up only a few days following the burglary and that he had ordered the FBI to halt its investigation. In the wake of these revelations, the 11 Republicans on the Judiciary Committee who had voted against the first article of impeachment reversed themselves. It was clear that the House of Representatives would vote to impeach the President and that the Senate would convict him.

On August 8, Nixon resigned, effective at noon the following day. He was the first President in American history to resign his office.

Gerald R. Ford now became President. Nixon retired to his home in San Clemente, California, refusing to admit any wrongdoing other than having made some errors of judgment. Twenty-five members of his administration served prison sentences after being convicted of Watergate-related crimes.

The Women's Movement

As the 1960s passed into the 1970s, the women's movement attracted growing support. In 1971, membership in the National Organization of Women (NOW) reached 15,000. NOW and other women's organizations continued to push for equal employment opportunities, equal pay for equal work, the expansion of child care facilities, and reform of the abortion laws.

Feminist writers continued to express sharp criticisms of American society. In *Sexual Politics* (1969), Kate Millet contended that "every avenue of power within the society is entirely within male hands." In Millet's view, women needed to join together to challenge the domination of the male power structure. In *The Dialectic of Sex: The Case for Feminist Revolution* (1970), Shulamith Firestone insisted that women needed to be freed "from the tyranny of their reproductive biology by every means available."

Ms. magazine, founded by Gloria Steinem and other prominent feminists in the early 1970s, became a powerful voice for the women's movement. By 1973, *Ms.* had close to 200,000 subscribers, most of whom were college-educated women under the age of 35 and were employed in professional, technical, and managerial jobs.

The subscribers to *Ms.* reflected the changes occurring among American women. By the mid-1970s, almost half of all married women held jobs, and close to 90 percent of women with college degrees were employed. The two-career family was becoming an increasingly common feature of American life.

In the field of higher education, once all-male colleges began to admit women. Both Yale and Princeton, for example, accepted their first women undergraduates in 1969. On the other hand, a number of women's colleges became coeducational. Many colleges initiated women's studies programs.

In 1971, the federal government extended affirmative action guidelines affecting contracts and employment to include women. Under the terms of Title IX of the Educational Amendments Act of 1972, colleges were required to initiate affirmative action programs designed to provide equal opportunities for women.

In 1972, the women's movement achieved a major victory when Congress approved the Equal Rights Amendment (ERA). Thirty states, of the 38 required, quickly ratified the amendment, but then a major battle over ratification developed. Phyllis Schafly, a conservative activist, led the opposition to the ERA, asserting that the amendment would "take away from women the rights they already have."

Native Americans

By the late 1960s, a sense of anger and frustration among the approximately 800,000 Native Americans (Indians) was intensifying. Nixon showed some sensitivity to the concerns of Native Americans and in 1969 appointed a Native American as Commissioner of Indian Affairs. The following year, the President formally repudiated the so-called termination policy, which had been adopted in the 1950s in an effort to promote the assimilation of the Indians, and endorsed self-determination. The Indian Self-Determination Law of 1974 enabled Indian tribes to acquire greater control over federal programs and educational programs on their reservations. Other federal legislation restored lands in New Mexico to the Taos Pueblo Indians (1970) and in Alaska to the Alaskan Indians, Eskimos, and Aleuts (1971), while an executive order restored land in Washington state to the Yakima Indians (1972).

Growing Native American militancy was manifested in the occupation of Alcatraz Island, the site of an abandoned federal prison in San Francisco Bay, in 1969. The following year, Native American activists organized the American Indian Movement (AIM), led by two Chippewa Indians, George Mitchell and Dennis Banks. In November, 1972, AIM led about 1,000 protesters in a sit-in at the Bureau of Indian Affairs in Washington, D.C. The protesters held the building for six days.

In early 1973, one of the most dramatic Native American protests occurred at Wounded Knee, South Dakota. Protesters, led by AIM, seized the village of Wounded Knee on the Oglala Pine Ridge Reservation where the Seventh Cavalry had massacred about 200 Sioux Indians in 1890. The Wounded Knee protest was designed to bring to public attention the problems of poverty and mismanagement on the reservation, as well as to demand broader reforms of Indian tribal government.

While the Native American protests were dramatic, more tangible gains were won in lawsuits seeking compensation for violations of treaty rights. Indians in Alaska, Maine, Massachusetts, and other states won significant legal victories, gaining recognition of tribal rights and securing financial compensation for treaty violations.

The cause of Native Americans found expression in such books as *Custer Died for Your Sins* (1969), written by Vine Deloria, Jr., and *Bury My Heart at Wounded Knee* (1971), the best-seller written by Dee Brown, as well as in N. Scott Momaday's Pulitzer Prize-winning novel, *House Made of Dawn* (1968).

Vietnam and Watergate dominated the Nixon Presidency. Although Richard Nixon promised "peace with honor" in Vietnam, direct American involvement in the fighting continued until 1973. The nation then became engulfed in the Watergate crisis, which led to Nixon's resignation in August, 1974.

*While the Nixon Presidency ended in disgrace, it had sub-
stantial accomplishments to its credit, particularly in the field of
foreign policy. Relations improved between the United States
and the People's Republic of China. The policy of detente
resulted in an easing of tension with the Soviet Union and the
signing of the SALT I and ABM treaties. Kissinger's shuttle
diplomacy helped restore a degree of stability in the Middle East
following the Yom Kippur War of 1973 and led to improved
American relations with the Arab states.*

Recommended Reading

Stephen E. Ambrose, *Nixon: The Education of a Politician, 1913–1962* (1987).

Carl Bernstein and Bob Woodward, *All the President's Men* (1974).

Richard Cohen and Jules Witcover, *A Heartbeat Away: The Investigation and Resignation of Vice President Spiro T. Agnew* (1974).

John W. Dean, *Blind Ambition: The White House Years* (1976).

Vine Deloria, Jr., *Behind the Trail of Broken Treaties: An Indian Declaration of Independence* (1974).

John P. Diggins, *American Left in the Twentieth Century* (1973).

Carol Felsenthal, *The Sweetheart of the Silent Majority: The Biography of Phyllis Schafly* (1981).

Lloyd C. Gardner, *The Great Nixon Turnaround: America's New Foreign Policy in the Post-Liberal Era* (1975).

Raymond L. Garthoff, *Detente and Confrontation: American-Soviet Relations from Nixon to Reagan* (1985).

Otis L. Graham, Jr., *Toward a Planned Society: From Roosevelt to Nixon* (1976).

Seymour M. Hersh, *The Price of Power: Kissinger in the Nixon White House* (1983).

Arnold R. Isaacs, *Without Honor: Defeat in Vietnam and Cambodia* (1983).

Henry Kissinger, *The White House Years* (1979).

Henry Kissinger, *Years of Upheaval* (1982).

Robert S. Litwak, *Detente and the Nixon Doctrine: American Foreign Policy and the Pursuit of Stability, 1969–1976* (1984).

Norman Mailer, *Miami and the Siege of Chicago: An Informal History of the Republican and Democratic Conventions of 1968* (1968).

Bruce Mazlish, *In Search of Nixon: A Psychohistorical Inquiry* (1972).

Joe McGinniss, *The Selling of the President, 1968* (1969).

Michael Medved and David Wallechinsky, *What Really Happened to the Class of '65* (1976).

Robin Morgan, ed., *Sisterhood is Powerful: An Anthology of Writings From the Women's Liberation Movement* (1970).

Richard M. Nixon, *RN: The Memoirs of Richard Nixon* (1978).

Herbert S. Parmet, *The Democrats: The Years After FDR* (1976).

Arthur M. Schlesinger, Jr., *Robert Kennedy and His Times* (1978).

John J. Sirica, *To Set the Record Straight: The Break-in, the Tapes, the Conspirators, the Pardon* (1979).

Irwin Unger, *The Movement: A History of the American New Left, 1959–1972* (1974).

Theodore H. White, *Breach of Faith: The Fall of Richard Nixon* (1975).

Theodore H. White, *The Making of the President, 1968* (1969).

Garry Wills, *Nixon Agonistes: The Crisis of the Self-Made Man* (1979).

Bob Woodward and Carl Bernstein, *The Final Days* (1976).

CHAPTER 17

Ford, Carter, and the "Reagan Revolution"

Time Line

1974   Nixon resigns; Vice President Gerald R. Ford succeeds to the Presidency

Ford pardons Nixon

The inflation rate increases; a recession begins

Ford launches his WIN (Whip Inflation Now) program

1975	The Cambodians seize the *Mayaguez*; Ford sends marines to rescue the crew
	North Vietnam completes its conquest of South Vietnam
1976	Democrat Jimmy Carter wins the Presidency
1977	The Senate ratifies the Panama Canal treaties
1978	Egypt and Israel sign the Camp David accords
	The Supreme Court upholds affirmative action in the *Bakke v. University of California* decision
1979	Full diplomatic relations are established between the United States and the People's Republic of China
	The Iranian revolution results in the fall of the Shah
	Iranians seize the American embassy in Teheran, taking over 50 hostages
	A nuclear accident occurs at Pennsylvania's Three Mile Island plant
	The Sandinistas take power in Nicaragua
	The United States and the Soviet Union sign the SALT II Treaty
	The Soviet Union invades Afghanistan

1980	The United States leads a boycott of the Moscow Olympics
	The American attempt to rescue the hostages in Iran fails
	Republican Ronald Reagan wins the Presidency; the Republicans take control of the Senate; the Democrats retain their hold on the House of Representatives
1981	Iran releases the American hostages
	Congress approves Reagan's program of tax reductions and budget cuts for domestic programs
	The United States launches a major military spending program
1982	The United States experiences a serious recession
	Israel invades Lebanon
1983	The American economy begins to revive
	The Soviets shoot down a Korean airliner
	The United States invades Grenada
	Terrorists kill American marines in Beirut
1984	Reagan wins reelection to the Presidency
1985	Reagan and Gorbachev meet in Geneva, Switzerland
	Congress passes the Gramm-Rudman-Hollings Act

1986	The United States bombs Libya
	Reagan and Gorbachev meet in Reykjavik, Iceland
	The Democrats regain control of the Senate
1987	The stock market crash leads to fears of a severe economic downturn
	Reagan and Gorbachev sign the INF Treaty
	Congressional committees investigate the Iran-Contra affair
	The United States provides protection for shipping in the Persian Gulf

---

The American people breathed a collective sigh of relief when Gerald Ford became President in August, 1974. Nixon had resigned, and the national agony of Watergate had ended.

During the mid- and late-1970s, however, the nation faced serious difficulties. The economy was troubled by limited growth, declining productivity, high inflation, and unemployment. Then, during the 1980s, the economic picture brightened as inflation subsided and employment increased. But the nation was living on borrowed money, and budget deficits and the national debt soared to unprecedented heights. In late 1987, a substantial collapse of stock prices and a sharp drop in the value of the dollar in international exchange raised serious questions about the nation's economic and financial health.

In the realm of foreign affairs, the United States continued to struggle with uncertainty in the Middle East and instability in Central America. In relations with the Soviet Union, the detente of the 1970s gave way in the following decade to talk of a new

Cold War. Nevertheless, as the Reagan Presidency entered its final months, the two superpowers moved toward agreement on significant reductions in the level of arms and a substantial improvement in relations.

Ford as President

During his long tenure in the House of Representatives, Gerald Ford had achieved a record as a conservative and a staunch Republican partisan. While his fellow congressmen did not find him to be intellectually outstanding, they regarded him as hardworking, decent, and amiable, and elected him to positions of leadership.

As his Vice President, Ford appointed former Governor Nelson Rockefeller of New York, a liberal Republican. He retained Nixon's Secretary of State, Henry Kissinger, but gradually replaced a number of the other members of the Nixon cabinet. Among Ford's notable cabinet appointments were Secretary of Housing and Urban Development Carla A. Hills, the third woman in the nation's history to hold a cabinet post, and Secretary of Transportation William T. Coleman, the second black to serve in the cabinet.

The Nixon Pardon

In September, 1974, a month after Nixon's resignation, Ford granted a pardon to the former President for any crimes he might have committed during his term of office. Ford justified the pardon as necessary to bring the Watergate affair to an end. The pardon hurt Ford's credibility with many Americans, who believed that the new President was guilty of bad judgment. Rumors circulated, although they were never substantiated, that Nixon had arranged a deal with Ford prior to his resignation.

Ford and the Economy

The economy provided Ford with the biggest problem of his Presidency. In mid-1974, inflation was running at an annual rate of about 12 percent.

Declaring that inflation was the major problem facing the economy, Ford encouraged Americans to support his campaign against inflation by wearing WIN (Whip Inflation Now) buttons. The WIN campaign focused on a voluntary program which encouraged business, labor, and consumers to conserve energy and to form grassroots organizations to fight inflation.

The Democrats benefitted from the nation's economic troubles, winning 43 additional seats in the House of Representatives and 4 in the Senate in the congressional elections of 1974.

In his campaign against inflation, Ford opposed efforts to reduce taxes, sought to reduce federal spending, and encouraged the Federal Reserve Board to tighten credit, which would push up interest rates. This policy led to a severe recession in 1975. Industrial production dropped by more than 10 percent in early 1975, while unemployment increased to close to 9 percent. As tax revenues declined, the federal budget deficit mounted to a record $66 billion in 1976. While the inflation rate dropped to under 5 percent in 1976, it soon began to increase once again. In order to combat the recession, Ford was compelled to propose tax cuts and other measures to stimulate the economy.

Ford and Vietnam

Although the Paris Accords of 1973 ended direct American involvement in the Vietnam war, the United States hoped that South Vietnam would be able to survive. In the spring of 1975, the North Vietnamese intensified their attacks on South Vietnam, and South Vietnamese resistance quickly collapsed. Ford, who had always been a hawk on Vietnam, urged Congress to provide more aid to South Vietnam. Congress refused. On April 29,

1975, the last Americans left Saigon and North Vietnamese forces took the city, renaming it Ho Chi Minh City. The long war in Vietnam finally reached its end.

As the North Vietnamese moved to solidify their control over the country they had reunited by force of arms, many Vietnamese fled their homeland. In the immediate aftermath of the fall of South Vietnam, close to 140,000 Vietnamese refugees found new homes in the United States.

The *Mayaguez* Incident

While the North Vietnamese were completing their takeover of the South, the radical Communist Khmer Rouge succeeded in overthrowing the pro-American government of Cambodia. On May 12, 1975, Cambodian patrol boats seized the American cargo ship *Mayaguez* in the Gulf of Siam. Ford demanded that the *Mayaguez* and its crew be set free. Despite the Cambodians' agreement to release the crew, Ford ordered a marine assault on the island where the Mayaguez had been taken. Some three dozen marines died in the attack, most of them in a helicopter accident. Most Americans supported Ford's show of force, however unnecessary and costly it was, at a time when the country's world power and prestige seemed to be on the decline.

American opinion also supported the sharp words which United States Ambassador to the United Nations Daniel Patrick Moynihan directed against Third World nations and the United Nations itself. Moynihan won a United States Senate seat from New York in 1976.

Ford and Detente

Ford and Soviet General Secretary Leonid Brezhnev met in Vladivostok, Siberia in late 1974 and agreed on the framework for a new SALT (strategic arms limitation) agreement. Several years would elapse, however, before a treaty would be ready to be signed.

In the summer of 1975, a European Security Conference met in Helsinki, Finland. The Soviet Union and the West agreed to acknowledge the frontiers that had been established in Europe following World War II, and the Soviets made a commitment to respect human rights.

Ford and the Middle East

In the Middle East, Secretary of State Henry Kissinger's shuttle diplomacy led to an easing of tension, particularly in relations between Egypt and Israel. The two powers agreed not to resort to force in an effort to resolve disputes. At the same time, Kissinger failed in his efforts to achieve more far-reaching accords.

The 1976 Election

In his campaign to win the Republican presidential nomination in 1976, Ford faced the opposition of Ronald Reagan, the former Governor of California. Reagan had the support of ultraconservative Republicans and won several primaries. When the Republican national convention met in August, Ford controlled a slim majority of the delegates and won renomination. As his vice presidential running mate, Ford dumped Rockefeller in favor of the more conservative Senator Robert Dole of Kansas.

A host of Democrats sought their party's nomination. Among them were Senators Henry Jackson of Washington, Frank Church of Idaho, Lloyd Bentsen of Texas, and Birch Bayh of Indiana, as well as Representative Morris Udall of Arizona and Governors George Wallace and Jerry Brown of Alabama and California, respectively. Jimmy Carter, the former Governor of Georgia who had come out of obscurity to become the

Democratic frontrunner, won the nomination. In the aftermath of Watergate, Carter turned to his advantage the fact that he was a Washington outsider and emphasized his integrity and openness. As his running mate, Carter selected Senator Walter Mondale of Minnesota. The choice of Mondale improved Carter's position with northern liberals and the leaders of organized labor.

At the beginning of the campaign, the polls showed Carter with a strong lead, but as the campaign progressed, Ford began to catch up. Both candidates were vague on the issues, although Carter stressed the importance of dealing with the nation's high level of unemployment, while Ford continued to emphasize the need to reduce inflation. Carter won the election with 40.8 million popular votes and 297 electoral votes to Ford's 39.1 million popular votes and 241 electoral votes. Carter recreated the old coalition of the South and major northern industrial states that had been the key to Democratic presidential victories for several generations. Carter's success in winning over 90 percent of the black vote played a significant role in his victory.

Carter as President

As President, Jimmy Carter confronted a series of extremely difficult domestic and foreign problems. The major domestic problems, the recession and inflation, were intensified by the shortage and increasing cost of energy.

In foreign policy, the United States not only had to deal with its relations with the Soviet Union, the Middle East, and Latin America but also faced the problem of reduced respect for American authority in the world.

Carter had campaigned as a Washington outsider, and he remained an outsider in the White House. He did not establish a close working relationship with congressional leaders and with other power centers traditionally important for a Democratic President, such as the leadership of the AFL-CIO. Most of

Carter's closest advisers were people he had worked with in Georgia, although he did name nationally known Democrats to some major offices. Joseph Califano, who had been a close adviser of Lyndon Johnson, became Secretary of Health, Education, and Welfare (HEW), while Cyrus Vance became Secretary of State. Zbigniew Brzezinski, an anti-Soviet hard-liner, became Carter's National Security Adviser.

Carter appointed more blacks and women to office than any previous President. Andrew Young, a close associate of Martin Luther King, Jr., became Ambassador to the United Nations. Juanita Kreps served as Secretary of Commerce, while Patricia Roberts Harris, a black, served first as Secretary of Housing and Urban Development and then succeeded Califano as Secretary of Health, Education, and Welfare. When HEW was divided into two departments, Harris continued as Secretary of Health and Human Services, while Shirley M. Hufstedtler became Secretary of Education.

Carter sought to move away from the "imperial Presidency" of Johnson and Nixon. Dressed in an ordinary business suit at his inauguration, he walked with his wife and daughter from the Capitol to the White House following the ceremony, rather than ride in a limousine. In a televised fireside chat, Carter wore a cardigan sweater as he explained administration policies. He also visited small towns, where he attended community meetings and spent the night in the homes of ordinary citizens.

Carter and Energy

Early in his administration, Carter declared that the nation's effort to solve its energy problem was "the moral equivalent of war" and proposed a broad program to deal with the crisis. He called for the deregulation of the oil industry but urged the adoption of legislation to tax the windfall profits of the oil companies. Deregulation would increase prices, and thereby help reduce consumption, and would also encourage domestic oil exploration. At the same time, however, deregulation would result in large increases in the oil companies' profits. While liberals opposed deregulation, because it would lead to higher prices, conservatives opposed the windfall profits tax. The result of this disagreement was a weak energy bill, which Congress passed in August, 1978. In 1977, Congress established a cabinet-level Department of Energy.

In March, 1979, an accident at the Three Mile Island nuclear plant in Pennsylvania resulted in some 800,000 gallons of radioactive water being spilled from a defective valve. This accident increased doubts about nuclear power providing a ready solution to the energy problem.

Increasing instability in the Middle East resulted in another oil shortage in the summer of 1979, as well as in another substantial price increase by the Organization of Petroleum Exporting Countries (OPEC). Opinion polls showed Carter with an approval rating of 26 percent, which was lower than Nixon's when the Watergate crisis was at its height.

Carter gathered his advisers at Camp David, Maryland, for a series of meetings to discuss the problems of the administration and the country. Emerging ten days later, the President addressed the country on television, speaking of a "crisis of confidence" and calling for "a rebirth of the American spirit." He also proposed a stronger energy program. Carter failed to win much of a positive public response, and Congress voted only modest funding to the new Synthetic Fuels Corporation established to promote the development of new energy sources.

Carter and the Economy

Like Nixon and Ford, Carter faced the problem of stagflation in the economy, but he decided to focus his attention on efforts to reduce unemployment rather than inflation. A tax cut and increased spending for public works and public services produced a modest decline in unemployment, from 8 percent in late 1976 to 7 percent in 1977. At the same time, inflation rose from an annual rate of about 5 percent when Carter took office to 7 percent in late 1977. During 1978, the inflation rate increased to nearly 10 percent and kept on mounting.

In an effort to combat inflation, Carter had to reverse gears on his economic policy. He delayed tax reductions and pushed for cuts in government spending. The economic situation continued to deteriorate, however. During 1980, unemployment reached 7.5 percent, while inflation reached an annual rate of close to 13 percent. In fact, during one month in 1980, inflation hit an annual rate of 18 percent. In an attempt to curb inflation, the Federal Reserve Board raised interest rates. Mortgage rates reached 15 percent, while the prime interest rate mounted to 20 percent, an all-time high.

Carter had hoped to restore a balanced budget, but continuing economic problems made that impossible. The lowest deficit of the Carter years—almost $28 billion—came in 1979, while the highest deficit, in 1980, totaled close to $60 billion.

Other Measures of the Carter Administration

Carter deregulated the airline, railroad, and trucking industries and reformed the civil service in an effort to make career officials more responsive to public needs. In 1979, the Department of Health, Education, and Welfare was divided into two departments, the Department of Education and the Department of Health and Human Services.

Carter established a task force to consider the problem of those who had evaded the draft during the Vietnam War. Most of the evaders had fled the country. On the basis of the task force's recommendations, an amnesty was offered to the evaders.

Carter succeeded in winning congressional approval for legislation dealing with the environment. Controls were established over strip mining, and a $1.6 billion superfund was created to clean up chemical waste sites. Over 100 million acres of land in Alaska were set aside as national parks, national forests, and wildlife refuges.

Affirmative Action and the Bakke Decision

The question of implementing affirmative action policies to achieve racial and sexual balance became one of the most controversial issues of the late 1970s. White males complained of reverse discrimination as affirmative action came to be applied more extensively in employment and college admissions.

Allen Bakke, a white male, filed suit against the University of California at Davis, charging that affirmative action quotas had resulted in his being denied admission to the university's medical school. In the case of *Bakke v. University of California,* decided in 1978, the Supreme Court ruled by a vote of five to four that the use of strict affirmative action quotas was illegal and, therefore, that Bakke should be admitted. At the same time, the court upheld, also by a vote of five to four, the principle of affirmative action, ruling that racial factors could legitimately be considered in making decisions about college admissions or employment.

The Human Rights Campaign

Carter believed that efforts to promote human rights should be a central feature of American foreign policy, and he established an Office of Human Rights in the State Department. The President criticized the Soviet Union's repression of dissidents and its denial to Soviet Jews of the right to emigrate. He also withdrew American military and economic aid from several non-Communist countries, including Argentina and Chile, which were guilty of human rights violations. At the same time, Carter refrained from criticizing violations of human rights in countries allied with the United States, such as South Korea, the Philippines, and the Shah's Iran.

The SALT II Treaty

In March, 1977, Carter introduced an entirely new set of proposals into the American-Soviet strategic arms limitation talks. Carter hoped that these proposals would lead to a more extensive arms limitation agreement, but instead they interrupted the progress of the negotiations.

Finally, in mid-1979, Carter and Brezhnev met in Vienna to sign the SALT II Treaty placing limits on long-range missiles, bombers, and nuclear warheads. The treaty encountered strong opposition from conservatives, who charged that the treaty favored the Soviets. The intensity of the opposition made Senate ratification of the treaty doubtful.

The Soviet Invasion of Afghanistan

In December, 1979, the Soviet Union invaded Afghanistan in an effort to defend the pro-Soviet government against insurgents. Carter was furious. He imposed economic sanctions on the Soviet Union, including an embargo on American grain sales to the Soviets. He also organized a boycott of the 1980 Moscow Summer Olympic Games and withdrew the SALT II Treaty from Senate consideration. Both sides continued to observe the obligations of the treaty, however.

By 1980, detente appeared to be at an end, and there was talk of a new Cold War.

The Panama Canal Treaties

In Panama, protests against continued American control of

the Panama Canal Zone had been underway for several years. Negotiations between the United States and Panama resulted in two treaties, providing for the transfer of sovereignty over the Canal Zone to Panama by the year 2000, a guarantee of the permanent neutrality of the canal, and assurances of access to the canal by American ships. Conservatives denounced the treaties as a retreat by the United States from the assertion of its power in the world.

In 1978, the Senate ratified the Panama Canal Treaties by a vote of 68 to 32, a margin of only one vote more than the required two-thirds.

The Camp David Accords

Carter's greatest success in foreign policy came in the achievement of a peace settlement between Israel and Egypt.

In November, 1977, Egyptian President Anwar el-Sadat addressed Israel's parliament, declaring that Egypt was prepared to recognize Israel. Israel's Prime Minister Menachem Begin was reluctant, however, to make concessions to match Sadat's bold gesture.

In September, 1978, Sadat and Begin met with Carter at Camp David, Maryland. The negotiations proved to be extremely difficult, but Carter succeeded in inducing the two leaders to sign the Camp David Accords, which established a framework for a peace treaty between Egypt and Israel. In March, 1979, Sadat and Begin returned to Washington to sign a formal peace treaty, in which Israel agreed to return the occupied Sinai peninsula to Egypt. No agreement was reached, however, on an Israeli withdrawal from the West Bank of the Jordan River or the troublesome issue of the Palestinian refugees.

Diplomatic Relations with China

The improvement of relations between the United States and

the People's Republic of China, which had begun with Nixon, continued under Carter. The United States ended its official recognition of the rival Chinese government on Taiwan, and full diplomatic relations between the United States and the People's Republic of China were established in January, 1979.

The Iranian Hostage Crisis

The Carter administration continued the United States' close relationship with the arbitrary government of Reza Pahlavi, the Shah of Iran. By the late 1970s, however, Iranian opposition to the Shah's government was mounting. Several months of revolt led to the Shah's decision to go into exile in January, 1979. Ayatollah Ruhollah Khomeini, a Muslim zealot, took power at the head of a fundamentalist Islamic regime. Khomeini was hostile toward the West and, in particular, the United States.

In October, 1979, Carter allowed the Shah, who was fatally ill with cancer, to come to the United States for treatment. On November 4, militant Iranian students seized the American embassy in Teheran and took hostages. Several hostages were released after a few days, but 53 remained as prisoners in the embassy.

In April, 1980, a raid by American commandos failed to secure the release of the hostages. Secretary of State Cyrus Vance, who had opposed the commando raid, resigned. Carter named Senator Edmund S. Muskie of Maine as his successor. While Muskie proved to be a capable Secretary of State, he was unable to win the release of the hostages.

After spending 444 days in captivity, the hostages were released on January 20, 1981, the day that Carter left the Presidency.

The Iranian hostage crisis served as a painful symbol of the inability of the United States to exercise control over world affairs.

The Election of 1980

As Carter's popularity declined in 1979, Senator Edward M. Kennedy decided to challenge the President for the 1980 Democratic nomination. Carter turned back Kennedy's threat, winning renomination on the first ballot at the Democratic national convention.

Ronald Reagan, a former movie actor and two-term Governor of California, defeated George Bush, a former congressman and CIA director, for the Republican presidential nomination. At the age of 69, Reagan was the oldest candidate ever nominated for the Presidency by a major party. Reagan selected Bush as his running mate.

Representative John Anderson, a liberal Republican from Illinois, launched an independent campaign for the White House.

An ultraconservative, Reagan denounced big government and promised to "get the government off the backs of the people." He called for reducing government spending, cutting taxes, balancing the budget, and strengthening national defense. In foreign affairs, Reagan pledged to pursue a tough line in relations with the Soviet Union and to restore America's sagging prestige in the world.

Reagan benefitted from the country's growing conservative mood. In particular, he won strong support from religious conservatives, many of whom joined under the banner of the Moral Majority, led by the Reverend Jerry Falwell, a Baptist pastor from Virginia. These religious conservatives opposed pornography, the Equal Rights Amendment, and homosexual rights. They also urged the adoption of constitutional amendments to allow prayer in the public schools and to ban abortions.

Winning 44 million popular votes and 489 electoral votes, Reagan defeated Carter, who polled 35 million popular votes and won the 49 electoral votes of only six states. Anderson won 5.6 million popular votes. Reagan made inroads into groups which had strongly supported Democratic candidates in the past: blue-collar workers, Catholics, Jews, and white southerners. Only black voters remained overwhelmingly Democratic.

The Republicans won control of the Senate for the first time since the election of Eisenhower in 1952. The Democrats held on to their majority in the House of Representatives, although Republicans and conservative southern Democrats—the so-called boll weevils—had effective control of the lower house.

Reagan as President

Reagan was the most conservative President in more than half a century. His critics contended that he lacked the knowledge to be an effective President, and he sometimes seemed befuddled at press conferences, which he held as infrequently as possible. At the same time, Reagan quickly became known as the "Great Communicator" because of his effectiveness in delivering prepared texts with confidence and charm. He also gained a reputation as the "Teflon President" because of his ability to emerge unscathed, with his popularity intact, in the wake of his public misstatements, policy failures, and charges of wrongdoing by members of his administration.

As his Secretary of State, Reagan named General Alexander Haig, a retired NATO commander and White House Chief of Staff during Nixon's final months in office. When Haig stepped down in 1982, he was succeeded by George Shultz, who favored a more moderate policy toward the Soviet Union. Caspar Weinberger, a staunch advocate of a major military build-up, became Secretary of Defense. Secretary of the Treasury Donald Regan and Budget Director David Stockman played central roles in Reagan's push for tax cuts and budget reductions.

James Edwards, the former Governor of South Carolina who served as Secretary of Energy in Reagan's cabinet, denied that there was any energy problem, advocated the further development of nuclear power, and urged the abolition of his own department.

Edwin Meese, III, who served as a White House adviser before becoming Attorney General in 1984, became one of the most controversial figures in the Reagan administration. Criticized by liberals for his tough law and order stance, Meese also faced charges of questionable financial dealings. With the support of the President, Meese rebuffed demands for his resignation.

The controversies involving Edwin Meese's ethics in office reflected what came to be called the "sleaze factor" in the Reagan administration.   By the end of 1987, several dozen of the President's appointees had been investigated on various charges of wrongdoing. A number had been tried and convicted, while the cases of several others had not yet gone to trial.

Deregulation

As a part of his campaign to reduce the role of the federal government in national life, Reagan pushed for deregulation in such areas as consumer protection, the workplace, and the environment. This deregulation involved limiting the activities of the Consumer Product Safety Commission, the Occupational Safety and Health Administration (OSHA), and the Environmental Protection Agency (EPA).

Secretary of the Interior James Watt became a center of controversy because of his efforts to undo the conservationist policies of previous administrations. Watt was a leader of the so-called Sagebrush Rebellion of western businessmen who wanted federally owned lands opened to development by cattle, lumber, and mining interests. Watt believed that giving private business control over public lands would spur economic development and promote national security. He leased public lands to coal and oil companies, relaxed controls on strip-mining, and permitted drilling for oil and natural gas in ecologically sensitive off-shore areas. Conservation organizations like the Sierra Club fought Watt's policies and breathed a sigh of relief when he resigned toward the end of Reagan's first term.

Reaganomics

Reagan entered office determined to reduce the activities of the federal government and especially to cut back on the government's responsibility for the economic and social well-being of individuals. Shortly after taking office, he ended all price and allocation controls on petroleum. A few weeks later, in March, 1981, he eliminated 37,000 federal jobs.

In his approach to economic policy, Reagan generally supported the doctrine known as supply-side economics, which maintained that excessive taxation was responsible for most of the nation's economic problems. Economic recovery and expansion could best be promoted by reducing taxes. Substantial tax cuts, the supply siders believed, would lead to greater investment in the economy. This investment would promote economic growth which, in turn, would lead to increased tax revenues.

The tax bill proposed by the Reagan administration in 1981 provided tax cuts for people in every tax bracket, although the greatest benefits would go to the wealthy. Wealthy taxpayers, the administration believed, would be more likely to invest their tax savings, while poorer taxpayers would simply spend their extra income, thereby fueling inflation. In August, 1981, Congress approved the Economic Recovery Tax Act (ERTA) providing for a $749 billion tax cut spread over a five-year period. The wealthy benefitted not only from income tax reductions but also from cuts in capital gains, gift, and inheritance taxes. As an added incentive to investment, the tax bill provided that anyone with earned income could invest up to $2,000 a year in an Individual Retirement Account (IRA). The amount invested and any interest it earned would be free from taxation until the person retired and would presumably be in a lower tax bracket.

In addition to tax cuts, Reagan's economic policy—dubbed Reaganomics—also called for reductions in federal spending. With spending for the military being increased, budget cutting focused on domestic spending, especially social programs such as job training, legal aid, food stamps, Medicaid, and school lunch programs. From 1980 to 1982, domestic spending was cut by over $100 billion. These reductions in spending had their greatest impact on families earning less than $10,000 a year. Despite administration promises to provide a safety net to protect the poor against serious deprivation, the number of Americans with incomes below the poverty line increased from 29.3 million in 1980 to 35.3 million in 1983.

Although Reagan called for reducing the scope of the federal government's activities, the number of civilians employed by the federal government rose from 2.75 million in 1981 to 2.9 million in 1987.

Budget Deficits and the National Debt

In his campaign for the Republican nomination in 1980, Bush had denounced supply-side economics as "voodoo economics." While Bush as Vice President loyally supported Reagan, critics of Reaganomics insisted that it was impossible to simultaneously reduce taxes, increase military spending substantially, and balance the budget, as the President expected to do. The 1980 budget deficit of $59 billion increased to $110 billion in 1982 and $195 billion in 1983. The 1984 deficit totaled $175 billion, and the deficit in 1985 amounted to $212 billion. In 1986, the deficit hit a record $221 billion. These were the largest budget deficits in American history. The largest deficit before the 1980s was the $66 billion deficit of 1976.

As deficits mounted, so did the national debt. In 1980, the

national debt stood at $907 billion. By the end of Reagan's first term, it had increased to $1.2 trillion. By the end of 1987, the national debt had doubled, reaching an astounding $2.4 trillion.

In an attempt to control deficits, Congress passed the Gramm-Rudman-Hollings Act in 1985. This act provided for mandatory across-the-board budget cuts if the President and Congress could not agree on reducing expenditures. The enforcement of the act was designed to produce a balanced budget by 1991.

Recession and Recovery

A serious recession began in 1981 and continued through 1982. By late 1982, unemployment exceeded 10 percent, and more people were out of work than at any time since the Great Depression of the early 1930s. At the same time, the recession did lead to a drop in the rate of inflation.

In late 1982, the Federal Reserve Board relaxed restrictions on credit in order to put more money into the economy in an effort to spur a recovery. Heavy government borrowing to finance the national debt also increased the amount of money in circulation. By mid-1983, unemployment declined to slightly over 8 percent. As the recovery continued, unemployment fell below 7 percent in early 1986. Inflation remained relatively low, in the range of 4 or 5 percent through the mid-1980s.

By late 1987, however, signs of economic trouble were appearing once again. On "Black Monday," October 19, the New York Stock Exchange experienced a collapse in stock prices, and the Dow Jones industrial average dropped by 508 points in the trading frenzy. For the balance of the year, uncertainty and volatility continued, as stock prices rose and fell in a relatively narrow range. During October, unemployment increased slightly to 6 percent.

Other problems confronting the economy involved the unfavorable balance of trade and a decline in the value of the dollar in international exchange. In the mid-1980s, high American interest rates, caused in part by heavy American borrowing to finance the budget deficits, had attracted foreign investment in the United States and increased the value of the dollar. As the value of the dollar rose, the price paid for American goods by foreign buyers increased, while it became cheaper for Americans to buy foreign products. As a result, the balance of trade became increasingly unfavorable, as Americans imported more and exported less. The 1980 trade deficit of $20 billion increased to over $100 billion by 1986. This increased dependence on imports damaged basic American industries, including steel, automobiles, and textiles, and also injured agriculture. In 1985, for the first time since 1914, the United States became a debtor nation, with the amount of private foreign investment in the United States exceeding the amount of private American investment abroad. In other words, Americans owed foreigners more than they owed Americans.

The changing position of the United States in the world economy was also reflected in the fact that in 1986 West Germany led the world in exports. For the first time since World War II, the United States fell to second place. Indeed, the United States, with $217 billion in exports, only narrowly surpassed Japan, whose exports totaled $211 billion.

In an effort to reduce the trade deficit, the Reagan administration began, in late 1985, to promote a decline in the value of the dollar. This decline was then accelerated by a loss of confidence, particularly in Western Europe and Japan, in the ability of the American government to reduce the budget deficit substantially. Between mid-1985 and the end of 1987, the dollar fell by an average of about 37 percent against the currencies of 15 major industrialized countries. The drop in the value of the dollar did not reduce the trade deficit as rapidly as the government hoped, while the higher cost of imported goods was expected to increase the rate of inflation.

In December, 1987, the Reagan administration scaled back its earlier optimistic economic forecasts for 1988. The Council of Economic Advisers reduced its prediction of an economic growth rate of 3.5 percent in 1988 to 2.4 percent. In 1989, it was predicted, the growth rate would bounce back to 3.5 percent. Unemployment was expected to remain at the November, 1987, level of 5.9 percent. The government's predictions stood in contrast to the expectations of nongovernment economic forecasters who predicted slower growth in 1988 and either a recession or very weak growth in 1989. These forecasters also anticipated a drop in the number of new jobs created in 1988 to approximately 1.5 million, down from 1987's almost 2.5 million new jobs. Economists expected that the quality of the new jobs would also decline, with many of them being part-time service positions offering low wages, few benefits, and no long-term job security.

Defense Spending

The budget deficits of the 1980s were fueled by increased spending for national defense. The Reagan administration claimed that the United States had fallen behind the Soviet Union in military power and proposed the largest peacetime arms build-up in history, costing $1.7 trillion over a five-year period.

The Reagan administration began, in 1983, to push for the development of the Strategic Defense Initiative (SDI), quickly nicknamed "Star Wars." SDI involved the use of satellites and lasers in the effort to destroy enemy missiles in outer space. Ambitious claims of the supposed effectiveness of SDI were greeted with skepticism in much of the scientific community, but the administration remained determined to press forward with the program.

The Oil Glut

The recovery of the American economy in the mid-1980s was encouraged by ample supplies of petroleum which led to reduced prices. While the Organization of Petroleum Exporting Countries (OPEC) sought to restrict production in order to keep prices high, unanimity among the OPEC countries collapsed. In addition to increased production by OPEC members, more petroleum was being produced by non-OPEC countries, including Mexico, Great Britain, and Norway.

The oil glut had a negative impact on the economies of oil-producing states like Texas, Oklahoma, and Louisiana. In addition, oil producing countries had to reduce their imports of manufactured goods. Mexico was particularly hard hit and could not afford to pay even the interest on its large foreign debt.

Problems in Agriculture

The 1970s had been a time of general prosperity for American agriculture. In their optimism, many farmers expanded their operations, borrowing money to buy more land and equipment. Between 1975 and 1983, farm mortgage loans increased from less than $50 billion to more than $112 billion. By the 1980s, the prices of agricultural products were declining, as was the value of farm land. For many farmers, the recession in agriculture led to bankruptcy.

The Assassination Attempt

On March 31, 1981, as he was leaving the Washington Hilton Hotel, Reagan was shot in the chest by John Hinckley, Jr. Two security officers and James Brady, the President's press secretary, were also wounded. Although seriously wounded, Reagan reacted calmly and even joked with the emergency room doctors at George Washington University Hospital.

The Air Controllers' Strike

In August, 1981, the nation's air controllers went on strike in violation of a law prohibiting them from striking. Acting with determination, Reagan ordered the air controllers to return to work. When they refused to do so, Reagan ordered that all 11,000 be fired. Replacements were quickly trained, and the air controllers' union was destroyed.

The Space Program

Between 1969 and 1972, the National Aeronautics and Space Agency (NASA) scored a spectacular success with its Apollo program, sending six missions to the moon. In July, 1975, Apollo 18 linked in space with Soyuz 19, a Soviet space vehicle. The Apollo 18 mission was the last manned American space flight of the 1970s. During 1973–74, the orbiting space station program (Skylab) achieved a success equaling that of the Apollo program.

In the early 1980s, shortly after Reagan became President, flights began by Columbia, a manned space shuttle. Columbia and other space shuttles put satellites in orbit to carry out both scientific and military research.

The space program suffered a tragic setback in February, 1986, when the space shuttle Challenger exploded shortly after its take off from the Kennedy Space Center in Florida. All seven members of the Challenger crew died.

The 1984 Election

In 1984, the Democrats nominated former Vice President Walter Mondale for the Presidency. In the race for the nomination, Mondale defeated Senators Gary Hart of Colorado and John Glenn of Ohio, as well as the Reverend Jesse Jackson, a black activist. As his running mate, Mondale selected Representative

Geraldine Ferraro of New York, the first woman ever to run on the national ticket of a major party.

Reagan remained an overwhelmingly popular President and campaigned with the upbeat slogan "It's Morning in America." He easily defeated Mondale, polling over 53 million popular votes and winning 523 electoral votes. With under 37 million popular votes, Mondale captured only the 13 electoral votes of his home state of Minnesota and the District of Columbia. While 85 percent of black voters supported Mondale, only 35 percent of white voters did.

The Republicans retained control of the Senate. The Democrats held on to their majority in the House of Representatives and recaptured the Senate in the 1986 midterm elections.

Reagan and the Supreme Court

Reagan began his effort to turn the Supreme Court in a more conservative direction in 1981, when he appointed Sandra Day O'Connor, a judge from Arizona, as an associate justice.

In 1986, Chief Justice Warren Burger retired, and Reagan named Associate Justice William H. Rehnquist as his successor. He then appointed Antonin Scalia to fill Rehnquist's slot.

In 1987, when Associate Justice Lewis F. Powell, Jr. retired, Reagan ran into trouble trying to find a successor. His first nominee, Robert Bork, withdrew when it became evident that the Senate would not confirm his appointment. Reagan's second nominee, Douglas Ginsburg, also withdrew after admitting that he had smoked marijuana as a student and young law professor. Reagan then named Anthony Kennedy, a federal judge from California. Kennedy easily won Senate confirmation.

Income Tax Reform

For some years, there had been discussion of simplifying the nation's income tax laws. Reagan endorsed tax reform but he opposed any tax increase, despite the large budget deficits. The President insisted that any new income tax law would have to be revenue neutral and not increase the government's total tax revenues.

The Income Tax Act of 1986 reduced the maximum tax rate on incomes and doubled the personal exemption. At the same time, many tax shelters were eliminated and many deductions allowed in the past were either eliminated or reduced. Some six million low income people would no longer have to pay income taxes.

The tax rate for corporations was also reduced, although it was expected that the elimination of loopholes and exemptions would produce more revenue from corporations than had been collected in the past.

Reagan and the New Cold War

Reagan pursued a hard line toward the Soviet Union, which he denounced as "the evil empire." He charged that the "Soviet Union underlies all the unrest that is going on" in the world.

The President advocated a major American arms build-up in the belief that if the United States expanded both its nuclear and conventional forces, the Soviets would be forced to adopt a more conciliatory policy. He was convinced that the Soviets' serious economic problems would make it impossible for them to sustain the cost of an arms race with the United States.

Reagan criticized the SALT II Treaty negotiated by the Carter administration. While the treaty was never submitted to the Senate for ratification, both sides observed its terms.

In April, 1981, Reagan lifted the embargo on sales of American grain to the Soviet Union which Carter had imposed following the Soviet invasion of Afghanistan. The President contended that this embargo hurt American farmers more than it did the Soviets, since they were able to purchase grain elsewhere.

Reagan did attempt to prevent the sale to the Soviet Union of heavy equipment needed for the construction of a pipeline to carry natural gas to Western Europe. The Western Europeans were determined to carry out the project, however, and Reagan decided to allow the sale to take place.

American-Soviet relations were also strained by events in Poland. In 1981, under pressure from Moscow, the Polish government imposed martial law in an attempt to destroy the challenge to its authority presented by Solidarity, an independent labor organization. In protest, the United States imposed economic sanctions on Poland.

The atmosphere of the new Cold War was further intensified in September, 1983, when a Soviet fighter shot down a Korean Airlines 747 which had strayed over Soviet territory on a flight from Alaska to Seoul, South Korea. All 269 persons aboard the plane died. The Soviets insisted that the plane had been engaged in spying. Evidently they had mistaken the jetliner for an American reconnaissance plane they had been tracking earlier.

Negotiations for Arms Limitation

Changes in the Soviet leadership also served to complicate relations between the two superpowers. In November, 1982, General Secretary Leonid Brezhnev died following a long illness. His successor, Yuri Andropov, died in 1984. General Secretary Konstantin Chernenko was clearly in failing health when he took office and died in 1985. Following Chernenko's death, the Soviets turned to a younger generation of leaders. In March, 1985, Mikhail Gorbachev became General Secretary. Gorbachev combined ability and toughness with an attractive public personality and appeared to be more moderate and flexible than his predecessors. In late 1985, Reagan and Gorbachev held a cordial meeting in Geneva, Switzerland, agreeing to resume arms limitation negotiations.

The two leaders held their second summit meeting in Reykjavik, Iceland in October, 1986. Some progress was made in negotiations on arms limitation, although no agreements were reached because of continuing discord over Reagan's determination to press ahead with efforts to develop the Strategic Defense Initiative (SDI).

Continuing American-Soviet negotiations resulted in the drafting of a treaty to eliminate intermediate-range nuclear missiles. Reagan and Gorbachev signed the Intermediate Range Nuclear Forces (INF) Treaty in Washington on December 8, 1987. The treaty called for the scrapping, over a three-year period, of all American and Soviet missiles with a range of 315 to 3,125 miles. The United States would destroy 364 cruise and Pershing II missiles deployed in Western Europe, while the Soviets would destroy 683 missiles. The INF Treaty was the first American-Soviet agreement to reduce the level of arms.

Reagan and Gorbachev promised to work toward a reduction of other nuclear weapons, particularly long-range missiles, although the disagreement over SDI continued. In addition, the Americans and the Soviets remained at odds over human rights in the Soviet Union and the Soviet intervention in Afghanistan. By 1987, American covert aid to the anti-Soviet rebels in Afghanistan reached a level of about $1 billion a year.

The Reagan Administration and Human Rights

The Reagan administration reduced the emphasis the Carter administration had placed on human rights, particularly in authoritarian countries which supported the United States. Secretary of State Haig reaffirmed the view of Jeane Kirkpatrick, the American Ambassador to the United Nations, that the United States should "distinguish between the so-called totalitarian and authoritarian regimes" and take a strong position on denials of human rights by totalitarian states such as the Soviet Union and its allies.

In 1986, the United States played an active role in deposing two anti-Communist dictators whose ability to hold onto power had evidently evaporated. In Haiti, a military regime replaced dictator Jean-Paul Duvalier. In the Philippines, President Ferdinand Marcos was succeeded by Corazón Aquino, the widow of a murdered opponent of Marcos. Aquino strove to establish a viable democratic political system in the Philippines in the face of grave economic troubles and the uncertain loyalty of some of the country's military leaders.

The Grenada Invasion

In October, 1983, Reagan used American marines and soldiers to overthrow the Cuban-backed Marxist government of the small Caribbean island republic of Grenada. The invasion was popular among the American public, who viewed it as a reassertion of national power, and was welcomed by the Grenadans themselves and by neighboring Caribbean countries.

Central America

In El Salvador, the United States supported the democratically-elected government of President José Napoleon Duarte, who had to contend with opposition from both leftist guerrillas and reactionaries in the country's power elite. The United States sent military advisers to help train the Salvadoran army and provided substantial military and economic assistance to the Duarte government.

In Nicaragua, the Sandinista revolutionaries had taken power in 1979, overthrowing the dictatorship of the Somoza family which had dominated the country for forty years. The Sandinista government, headed by Daniel Ortega, embraced a Marxist-Leninist ideology and received aid from the Soviet Union and Castro's Cuba. The Reagan administration charged that the Sandinistas were supplying weapons to the rebel forces in El Salvador.

In an effort to destabilize the Sandinista government and promote its overthrow, the United States applied economic pressure. Then, in late 1981, Reagan directed the Central Intelligence Agency (CIA) to assist in organizing and arming Nicaraguan rebels, known as the Contras. The President found it difficult to win congressional approval of financial support for the Contras, although in June, 1986, Congress appropriated $100 million in Contra aid.

The power of the Sandinistas was threatened both by the Contras and by the near-collapse of the country's economy. From 1979 to 1986, Nicaraguan exports declined from $660 million to $249 million. During the same period, the gross national product (GNP) dropped by 50 percent. It remained uncertain to what extent the economic decline resulted from pressures applied by the United States and to what extent it was a result of the mismanagement of the Sandinistas.

Many Americans opposed the President's policy toward Nicaragua. Some opponents romanticized the Sandinistas and overlooked the totalitarian features of the regime. Others believed in the principle of nonintervention in the domestic affairs of Latin American countries. Opponents of American intervention feared that the United States might become involved in "another Vietnam" in Central America.

Critics of administration policy urged American collaboration with the Contadora Group—Mexico, Panama, Colombia, and Venezuela—in its efforts to find a compromise solution to conflict in Central America and encouraged support of the peace efforts of President Oscar Arias of Costa Rica.

The Iran-Contra Affair

Congressional hearings in 1986 revealed that the administration had sold American arms to Iran, in the vain hope of cultivating favor with moderate elements in that country's government and winning the release of American hostages taken by Middle Eastern extremists, and then had used the profits from the arms sales to provide aid to the Contras, at a time when Congress had prohibited such aid. The Senate and House committees investigating the Iran-Contra Affair concluded that a "cabal of zealots" had taken control of foreign policy, both in selling the weapons to Iran and aiding the Contras. These zealots included Rear Admiral John Poindexter, the President's National Security Adviser, and his deputy, Lt. Col. Oliver North, as well as the late William Casey, the director of the CIA. While the President approved the sale of arms to Iran, he denied any involvement in providing illegal aid to the Contras.

South Africa

In the Republic of South Africa, the system of Apartheid enforced the separation of the races in order to maintain the dominance of the white minority. By the mid-1980s, opposition to this denial of the basic political and social rights of the black majority was increasing among South African blacks and white liberals, as well as in the world community.

Some American opponents of Apartheid favored the imposition of economic sanctions against South Africa and disinvestment by American firms doing business there. Reagan believed instead that diplomatic pressure should be applied in an effort to induce the South African government to reform its policies. The President feared, in particular, that a collapse of the white government might lead to the creation of a Communist dictatorship.

The Middle East

In the 1980s, the Middle East remained a region of conflict. In October, 1981, Egyptian nationalist extremists assassinated President Anwar el-Sadat. Egypt's new leader, Hosni Mubarak, continued the moderate foreign policy of his predecessor, and the peace settlement between Israel and Egypt remained intact.

In June, 1982, Israel invaded Lebanon to strike at Palestine Liberation Organization (PLO) bases, which had been used for launching terrorist raids across the Israeli border. A cease-fire was arranged, and the United Nations organized an international peacekeeping force with American, British, French, and Italian troops to establish a buffer zone between contending elements in Lebanon. Although the Israelis withdrew to southern Lebanon, conflict intensified between Lebanese Christians and various Muslim groups, some of which were backed by Syria.

American marines were stationed in Beirut, Lebanon's capital, to help prop up the weak Lebanese government headed by Amin Gemayel, who represented the Christian minority. The Reagan administration hoped that the Gemayel government might succeed in stabilizing the situation in Lebanon. In October, 1983, a Muslim extremist carried out a suicide mission, driving a truck loaded with explosives into the marine barracks near the Beirut airport. Over 200 marines died in the attack. Reagan's critics blamed the President for sending the marines to Lebanon and charged him with failing to protect them once they were there. In early 1984, Reagan withdrew the marines from Lebanon.

In the early and mid-1980s, terrorist activities increased in the Middle East and elsewhere, with American diplomats, service personnel, and businessmen being frequent targets. Arab terrorists were hostile toward the United States because of its support of Israel. In the summer of 1985, Arab terrorists hijacked an American passenger jet, murdered a sailor, and terrorized the other passengers. In October, terrorists seized the *Achille Lauro*, an Italian cruise liner, in the eastern Mediterranean and killed a handicapped American tourist. The hijackers surrendered to the Egyptians on condition that they be provided with safe transit to Libya. U.S. Navy jets succeeded in intercepting the Egyptian airliner and forced it to land in Italy, where the terrorists were arrested.

The Reagan administration believed that Muammar al-Qaddafi, the Libyan dictator, was actively supporting international terrorism. In the spring of 1986, the United States claimed it had evidence implicating Qaddafi's government in the bombing of a nightclub in West Berlin frequented by American service personnel. Two servicemen died in the bombing. In retaliation against this and other acts of state-sponsored terrorism, American planes based in Great Britain struck at several targets in Libya.

Elsewhere in the Middle East, a war between Iraq and Iran entered its eighth year in 1987. The United States became more deeply involved in policing the Persian Gulf, where a mistaken attack by an Iraqi fighter on an American destroyer, the *USS Stark*, killed 37 sailors on May 17. Reagan offered protection against Iranian attacks to Kuwaiti tankers that flew the American flag. Nevertheless, attacks on shipping in the Persian Gulf continued, and more than 150 occurred during the year.

Blacks in the 1980s

In 1980, the black population numbered 26.5 million, and, for many black Americans, poverty remained a major problem. In late 1983, the national unemployment rate stood at slightly over 8 percent. Black unemployment was almost 18 percent, and for black teenagers the unemployment rate was close to 50 percent. While blacks amounted to about 12 percent of the population, they accounted for 28 percent of those living below the poverty line.

One major factor contributing to the persistence of poverty among blacks was the increase in the number of black families headed by women. In 1940, 18 percent of black families had a woman at their head. By 1980, 49 percent did. The figures for whites were 10 percent and 13 percent, respectively. Over half of the black families headed by women lived below the poverty line.

Other blacks were moving into the middle class, however. In 1950, black college students totaled 83,000. By 1966, the number had increased to 282,000, and in 1976 over 1 million black students were attending college. By 1980, about one-third of black high school graduates entered college, about the same proportion as whites. By the mid-1980s, between one-third and one-half of blacks had achieved middle-class status. There were increasing signs of a growing split in black society between middle-class blacks and those who remained poor. William Julius Wilson examined this situation in his controversial book *The Declining Significance of Race* (1978). Wilson contended that middle-class blacks were coming to have more in common with middle-class whites than with the poor blacks who comprised what threatened to become a permanent underclass.

In the 1980 election, relatively few blacks voted for Reagan, and the Reagan administration placed little emphasis on black concerns. Enforcement of the civil rights laws was relaxed. The President appointed conservative whites to the Civil Rights Commission and named very few blacks to significant positions in his administration, although Samuel R. Pierce, Jr. became Secretary of Housing and Urban Development.

Hispanics in the 1980s

Although the census of 1980 counted about 15 million

Hispanics, many observers believed the Hispanic population to-taled closer to 20 million. Many Hispanics were illegal im-migrants and had not been counted in the census. The prospect was that Hispanics would soon come to outnumber blacks as the nation's largest minority.

The Hispanics were a diverse group. The Chicanos (Mexicans) were the most numerous of the Hispanics, living primarily in California and the Southwest. The Cubans were concentrated in Miami and elsewhere in South Florida, while the Puerto Rican population was centered in New York City and the Northeast.

Poverty was a problem for many Hispanics, and about 28 percent lived below the poverty line in 1984, compared with al-most 34 percent of blacks and 11.5 percent of whites. Only about 30 percent of Hispanic students graduated from high school, and less than 7 percent graduated from college.

During the 1980s, there was a growing national debate over bilingual education. Advocates of bilingual education believed that Spanish-speaking children were entitled to schooling in their own language and that bilingual education made learning easier for students whose first language was Spanish. Opponents of bilingual education insisted that it served to restrict the assimila-tion of Hispanics into American society. Opponents of bilin-gualism promoted the adoption of English-only laws, which required government and education to conduct their affairs en-tirely in English.

Women in the 1980s

At the beginning of the 1980s, the national debate over the ratification of the Equal Rights Amendment (ERA) continued. As the 1979 deadline for the completion of the ratification process approached, only 35 of the necessary 38 states had ratified the ERA. Congress granted a three-year extension of the deadline. When this extension ran out in 1982, the ERA died.

Although Reagan opposed the ERA, he named a number of women to high positions in his administration. Jeane Kirkpatrick became Ambassador to the United Nations, and Sandra Day O'Connor was appointed to the Supreme Court. Reagan appointed two women to his cabinet: Margaret Heckler became Secretary of Health and Human Services and Elizabeth Dole served as Secretary of Transportation.

Women made other advances in politics, as well. In 1980, Republican Paula Hawkins of Florida won election to the U.S. Senate, joining Nancy Kassebaum of Kansas, another Republican, in the upper house. Although two women had served simultaneously in the Senate in the past, this was the first time that both had won seats in their own rights rather than succeeding husbands who had died in office. Nineteen women gained seats in the House of Representatives in 1980. Fifteen were reelected, and there were four newcomers. Jane Byrne became Richard J. Daley's successor as mayor of Chicago, and women won mayoral elections in other major American cities, including San Francisco and Houston. In 1984, the Democratic party nominated Representative Geraldine Ferraro of New York for the Vice Presidency.

Women became more numerous in the medical, legal, and academic professions, as well as in corporate management. In 1983, Sally Ride became the first woman astronaut to fly in space. And on December 27, 1987, sportscaster Gayle Sierens became the first woman to do the play-by-play broadcast of a National Football League game, the contest between the Kansas City Chiefs and the Seattle Seahawks, televised by NBC.

More women than ever were employed outside the home. In 1940, women comprised 24 percent of the work force. By 1960, this had increased to 33 percent and by 1970, to 38 percent. In 1980, 42 percent of the work force consisted of women, and by

1984, the figure had grown to 45 percent. Women continued to earn less money than men, however. In 1982, women earned an average of 62 cents for every dollar earned by men. During the 1980s, demands for equal pay for equal work continued, and a new demand began to be made for equal pay for different jobs requiring analogous training and skills (comparable worth).

The American People in the 1980s

In 1980, the American population totaled 226.5 million, an increase of more than 23 million (11.5 percent) over the 1970 population of 203.2 million. During the 1980s, the population continued to increase and by 1987, the population had grown to 243.4 million.

Immigration accounted for close to 20 percent of the nation's population growth during the 1970s. Of the 4 million immigrants during the decade, most came from Asia and Latin America, rather than from Europe and Canada, which had been the pattern in the past. This trend continued in the 1980s. In 1985, for example, there were 570,000 immigrants. About 50 percent came from Asia, while some 40 percent were from Latin America. In addition, there was a growing number of illegal immigrants, most of whom came from Latin America, impelled by worsening economic conditions in their homelands.

During the 1970s and 1980s, the American population grew at a slower rate than during the "baby boom" years from the 1940s to the mid-1960s. While the birth rate declined, the death rate fell, as well. In 1970, the birth rate stood at 18.4 births per 1,000 people. The birth rate of 14.6 per 1,000 in 1975 was the lowest in the twentieth century. In the early 1980s, the birth rate increased slightly, although in 1984 it remained below 16 births per 1,000. The death rate declined from 9.5 per 1,000 in 1970 to 8.6 per 1,000 in 1983. Life expectancy at birth increased from 67.1 years for males and 74.7 years for females in 1970 to 71 years for males and 78.3 for females in 1983. In 1970, 8 percent of Americans were over the age of 65. In 1983, 12 percent were, and that was expected to grow to 20 percent by the year 2000. The American population was aging, and the median age of 28 in 1970 increased to 30 in 1980.

Higher expenditures for Social Security and Medicare were one consequence of the aging population, while at the same time the number of people paying taxes to support the Social Security system was growing smaller.

The drop in the birth rate meant that fewer children were attending school. School enrollment totaled 60 million in 1970; by 1983 it had declined to under 58 million. At the same time, a growing number of people were attending school longer. In 1940, only 38 percent of those from 25 to 29 years of age had graduated from high school. In 1980, almost 86 percent of those in the same age group were high school graduates. The percentage of the same age group who were college graduates increased from 5.9 percent in 1940 to 24.3 percent in 1980.

American households were growing smaller, while the divorce rate remained high. In 1920, the average household consisted of 4.34 persons. By 1960, the size of the average household had shrunk to 3.3 persons and by 1980, to only 2.75. By 1980, single people living alone made up about one-quarter of the households.

During the 1980s, there were an average of 1.1 million divorces annually. By 1980, the percentage of households headed by women increased to 17.5 percent from slightly over 10 percent in 1970. And by 1980, close to 25 percent of all children under the age of 17 lived in single-parent households.

The American population was increasingly urban, and by 1980 three-quarters of the people were classified as urban dwellers, living in towns and cities with a population of 2,500 or more.

During the 1980s, the migration of Americans from the

Frostbelt of the Northeast and Midwest to the Sunbelt of the South and West continued. The southern and western states of the Sunbelt accounted for 15 million of the nation's population increase of 17 million from 1980 to 1987. In 1987, Florida replaced Pennsylvania as the nation's fourth most populous state, ranking behind California, New York, and Texas.

Between 1980 and 1987, California's population grew by 4 million to 27.7 million, while the population of Texas increased by 2.6 million to 16.8 million. Texas was hard-hit by the decline of world oil prices, however, and registered a population growth of only 100,000 between mid-1986 and mid-1987. Florida's population grew by 2.3 million from 1980 to 1987, reaching 12 million. Florida's 23 percent population increase was surpassed by Alaska's 31 percent, Nevada's 26 percent, and Arizona's 25 percent. These three states had considerably smaller populations than Florida, however. New York, which held on to second place, experienced a population growth of only 200,000 between 1980 and 1987, from 17.6 million to 17.8 million.

Five Midwest farm states experienced losses of population in the 1980s: Iowa, Nebraska, North Dakota, Montana, and Idaho. The decline of oil prices led to depressed economies and population declines in Louisiana, Oklahoma, and Wyoming, while West Virginia also lost population. In 1980, Alaska had been the least populous state. With a 1987 population of 525,000, Alaska came to surpass Wyoming, the least populous state, with 490,000 inhabitants.

An atmosphere of uncertainty prevailed as 1988, the final year of the Reagan administration, began. Continuing federal budget deficits, an immense national debt, the decline in the dollar's value, the unfavorable trade balance, and a nervous stock market caused concern about the nation's economic and

*financial strength. While the signing of the INF Treaty marked
an improvement in American-Soviet relations, conflict continued
in the Middle East and Central America, threatening international stability. Americans were becoming increasingly aware of the
inability of the United States to control events beyond its borders
and were seeking to adjust to the reality of a multipolar global
balance of power which had come to replace the superpower
bipolarity of the post-World War II years.*

*Advances in medicine, including the CAT scan, laser
surgery, improvements in chemotherapy and radiation therapy,
and organ transplantation, made possible longer and healthier
lives but also resulted in rapidly increasing costs for medical services. Heart disease and cancer continued to take a heavy toll,
and AIDS (acquired immune deficiency syndrome) presented a
threat of unknown dimensions to public health. U.S. Surgeon
General C. Everett Koop cautioned in January 1988 that a cure
for AIDS might never be found and that a vaccine might not be
developed until sometime in the next century.*

*While more Americans were receiving more schooling than
ever before in the nation's history, critics of the educational system pointed to its inadequacies, and Allan Bloom's* The Closing
of the American Mind *hit the best-seller lists in 1987.*

*The nation faced other challenges as well: the persistence of
poverty and homelessness in the midst of plenty, the struggle of
women and minorities to achieve equal rights and opportunities,
and preserving the solvency of the Social Security system, among
them.*

*In the midst of uncertainty, the American people retained
both a spirit of optimism and a sense of national purpose. In his
State of the Union address, delivered to a joint session of Congress in January, 1988, President Reagan reminded the nation
of its responsibility to protect and pass on "lovingly this place
called America, this shining city on a hill, this government of, by
and for the people." If the nation faced problems, the American*

people possessed the ability to confront them. Their effectiveness in doing so remained for the future to reveal.

Recommended Reading

Lawrence I. Barrett, *Gambling with History: Ronald Reagan in the White House* (1984).

Jack Bass and Walter DeVries, *The Transformation of Southern Politics: Social Change and Political Consequence Since 1945* (1976).

Bill Boyarsky, *Ronald Reagan: His Life and Rise to the Presidency* (1981).

Peter N. Carroll, *It Seemed Like Nothing Happened: The Tragedy and Promise of America in the 1970s* (1982).

Jimmy Carter, *Keeping Faith: Memories of a President* (1982).

Peter Clecak, *America's Quest for the Ideal Self: Dissent and Fulfillment in the 60s and 70s* (1983).

Alan Crawford, *Thunder on the Right: The "New Right" and the Politics of Resentment* (1980).

Robert Dallek, *Ronald Reagan: The Politics of Symbolism* (1984).

Ronnie Dugger, *On Reagan: The Man and His Presidency* (1983).

J. Wayne Flynt, *Dixie's Forgotten People: The South's Poor Whites* (1979).

Gerald R. Ford, *A Time to Heal: The Autobiography of Gerald R. Ford* (1979).

Betty Glad, *Jimmy Carter: In Search of the Great White House* (1980).

Douglas G. Glasgow, *The Black Underclass: Poverty, Unemployment, and Entrapment of Ghetto Youth* (1980).

Michael Goldfield, *The Decline of Organized Labor in the United States* (1987).

Charles O. Jones, *The Trusteeship Presidency: Jimmy Carter and the United States Congress* (1988).

Susan Estabrook Kennedy, *If All We Did Was to Weep at Home: A History of White Working-Class Women in America* (1979).

Walter LaFeber, *Inevitable Revolutions: The United States and Central America* (1983).

Michael Ledeen and William Lewis, *Debacle: The American Failure in Iran* (1981).

Michael Novak, *The Rise of the Unmeltable Ethnics: Politics and Culture in the 70s* (1972).

Richard Reeves, *A Ford, Not a Lincoln* (1975).

Richard Reeves, *The Reagan Detour* (1985).

David W. Reinhard, *The Republican Right Since 1945* (1983).

Gaddis Smith, *Morality, Reason, and Power: American Diplomacy in the Carter Years* (1986).

Theodore H. White, *America in Search of Itself: The Making of the President, 1956–1980* (1982).

J. Harvie Wilkinson, III, *From Brown to Bakke: The Supreme Court and School Integration, 1954–1978* (1979).

Bob Woodward, *Veil: The Secret Wars of the CIA* (1987).

APPENDIX 1

The Declaration of Independence

The original spelling, capitalization, and punctuation have been retained in this version.

In Congess, July 4, 1776, the unanimous Declaration of the thirteen United States of America.

When, in the Course of human events, it becomes necessary for one people to dissolve the political bands which have connected them with another, and to assume, among the Powers of the earth, the separate and equal station to which the Laws of Nature and of Nature's God entitle them, a decent respect to the opinions of mankind requires that they should declare the causes which impel them to the separation.

We hold these truths to be self-evident, that all men are created equal, that they are endowed by their Creator with certain unalienable Rights, that among these, are Life, Liberty, and the pursuit of Happiness. That, to secure these rights, Governments are instituted among Men, deriving their just Powers from the consent of the governed. That, whenever any form of Government becomes destructive of these ends, it is the Right of the People to alter or to abolish it, and to institute new Government, laying its foundation on such Principles, and organizing its Powers in such form, as to them shall seem most likely to effect their Safety and Happiness. Prudence, indeed, will dictate that Governments long established should not be changed for light and transient causes; and, accordingly, all experience hath shewn, that mankind are more disposed to suffer, while evils are sufferable, than to right themselves by abolishing the forms to which they are accustomed. But, when a long train of abuses and usurpations, pursuing invariably the same Object, evinces a design to reduce them under absolute Despotism, it is their right, it is their duty, to throw off such Government, and to provide new Guards for their future Security. Such has been the patient sufferance of these Colonies; and such is now the necessity which constrains them to alter their former Systems of Government. The history of the present King of Great Britain is a history of repeated injuries and usurpations, all having in direct object the establishment of an absolute Tyranny over these States. To prove this, let Facts be submitted to a candid world.

He has refused his Assent to Laws, the most wholesome and necessary for the public good.

He has forbidden his Governors to pass Laws of immediate and pressing importance, unless suspended in their operation till his Assent should be obtained; and when so suspended, he has utterly neglected to attend to them.

He has refused to pass other Laws for the accommodation of large districts of People, unless those people would relinquish the right of Representation in the legislature; a right inestimable to them and formidable to tyrants only.

He has called together legislative bodies at places unusual, uncomfortable, and distant from the depository of their Public Records, for the sole Purpose of fatiguing them into compliance with his measures.

He has dissolved Representative Houses repeatedly, for opposing, with manly firmness, his invasions on the rights of the People.

He has refused for a long time, after such dissolutions, to cause others to be elected; whereby the Legislative Powers, incapable of Annihilation, have returned to the People at large for their exercise; the

State remaining in the mean time exposed to all dangers of invasion from without, and convulsions within.

He has endeavoured to prevent the Population of these States; for that purpose obstructing the Laws for Naturalization of Foreigners; refusing to pass others to encourage their migrations hither, and raising the conditions of new Appropriations of Lands.

He has obstructed the Administration of Justice, by refusing his Assent to Laws for establishing judiciary Powers.

He has made Judges dependent on his Will alone, for the tenure of their offices, and the amount and payment of their salaries.

He has erected a multitude of New Offices, and sent hither swarms of Officers to harrass our People, and eat out their substance.

He has kept among us, in times of Peace, Standing Armies, without the Consent of our legislatures.

He has affected to render the Military independent of and superior to the Civil Power.

He has combined with others to subject us to a jurisdiction foreign to our constitution, and unacknowledged by our laws; giving his Assent to their Acts of pretended Legislation;

For quartering large bodies of armed troops among us:

For protecting them, by a mock Trial, from Punishment for any Murders which they should commit on the Inhabitants of these States:

For cutting off our Trade with all parts of the world:

For imposing Taxes on us without our Consent:

For depriving us, in many cases, of the benefits of Trial by Jury:

For transporting us beyond Seas to be tried for pretended offences:

For abolishing the free System of English Laws in a neighbouring province, establishing therein an Arbitrary government, and enlarging its Boundaries, so as to render it at once an example and fit instrument for introducing the same absolute rule into these Colonies:

For taking away our Charters, abolishing our most valuable Laws, and altering fundamentally the Forms of our Governments:

For suspending our own Legislatures, and declaring themselves invested with Power to legislate for us in all cases whatsoever.

He has abdicated Government here, by declaring us out of his protection, and waging War against us.

He plundered our seas, ravaged our Coasts, burnt our towns, and destroyed the Lives of our People.

He is at this time transporting large Armies of foreign Mercenaries to compleat the works of death, desolation and tyranny, already begun with circumstances of Cruelty and perfidy scarcely paralleled in the most barbarous ages, and totally unworthy the Head of a civilized nation.

He has constrained our fellow Citizens, taken Captive on the high Seas, to bear Arms against their Country, to become the executioners of their friends and Brethren, or to fall themselves by their Hands.

He has excited domestic insurrections amongst us, and has endeavoured to bring on the inhabitants of our frontiers, the merciless Indian Savages, whose known rule of warfare, is an undistinguished destruction of all ages, sexes, and conditions.

In every stage of these Oppressions, We have Petitioned for Redress, in the most humble terms: Our repeated Petitions have been answered only by repeated injury. A Prince, whose character is thus marked by every act which may define a Tyrant, is unfit to be the ruler of a free People.

Nor have We been wanting in attentions to our British brethren. We have warned them from time to time of attempts by their legislature to extend an unwarrantable jurisdiction over us. We have reminded them of the circumstances of our emigration and settlement here. We have appealed to their native justice and magnanimity, and we have conjured them, by the ties of our common kindred, to disavow these usurpations, which, would inevitably interrupt our connexions and correspondence. They too have been deaf to the voice of justice and consanguinity. We must, therefore, acquiesce in the necessity, which denounces our Separation, and hold them, as we hold the rest of mankind, Enemies in War, in Peace Friends.

WE, THEREFORE, the Representatives of the UNITED STATES OF AMERICA, in GENERAL CONGRESS assembled, appealing to the Supreme Judge of the World for the rectitude of our intentions, DO, in the Name, and by Authority of the good People of these Colonies, solemnly PUBLISH and DECLARE, That these United Colonies are, and of Right ought to be FREE AND INDEPENDENT STATES; that they are Absolved from all Allegiance to the British Crown, and that all political connexion between them and the State of Great Britain, is and ought to be totally dissolved; and that, as FREE and INDEPENDENT STATES, they have full Power to levy War, conclude Peace, contract Alliances, establish Commerce, and to do all other Acts and Things which INDEPENDENT STATES may of right do. AND for the support of this Declaration, with a firm reliance on the protection of divine Providence, we mutually pledge to each other our Lives, our Fortunes, and our sacred Honour.

APPENDIX 2

The Constitution of the United States of America

The original spelling, capitalization, and punctuation have been retained in this version.

We the People of the United States, in Order to form a more perfect Union, establish Justice, insure domestic Tranquility, provide for the common defence, promote the general Welfare, and secure the Blessings of Liberty to ourselves and our Posterity, do ordain and establish this CONSTITUTION for the United States of America.

Article I

Section 1. All legislative Powers herein granted shall be vested in a Congress of the United States, which shall consist of a Senate and House of Representatives.

Section 2. The House of Representatives shall be composed of Members chosen every second Year by the People of the several States, and the Electors in each State shall have the Qualifications requisite for Electors of the most numerous Branch of the State Legislature.

No Person shall be a Representative who shall not have attained to the Age of twenty-five Years, and been seven Years a Citizen of the United States, and who shall not, when elected, be an Inhabitant of that state in which he shall be chosen.

Representatives and direct Taxes shall be apportioned among the several States which may be included within this Union, according to their respective Numbers, which shall be determined by adding to the whole Number of free Persons, including those bound to Service for a Term of Years, and excluding Indians not taxed, three fifths of all other Persons. The actual Enumeration shall be made within three Years after the first Meeting of the Congress of the United States, and within every subsequent Term of ten Years, in such Manner as they shall by Law direct. The Number of Representatives shall not exceed one for every thirty Thousand, but each State shall have at Least one Representative; and until such enumeration shall be made, the State of New Hampshire shall be entitled to chuse three, Massachusetts eight, Rhode-Island and Providence Plantations one, Connecticut five, New York six, New Jersey four, Pennsylvania eight, Delaware one, Maryland six, Virginia ten, North Carolina five, South Carolina five, and Georgia three.

When vacancies happen in the Representation from any State, the Executive Authority thereof shall issue Writs of Election to fill such Vacancies.

The House of Representatives shall chuse their Speaker and other Officers; and shall have the sole Power of Impeachment.

Section 3. The Senate of the United States shall be composed of two Senators from each State, chosen by the Legislature thereof, for six Years; and each Senator shall have one Vote.

Immediately after they shall be assembled in Consequence of the first Election, they shall be divided as equally as may be into three Classes. The Seats of the Senators of the first Class shall be vacated at the Expiration of the second Year, of the second Class at the Expiration of the fourth Year, and of the third Class at the Expiration of the sixth Year, so that one-third may be chosen every second Year; and if Vacancies happen by Resignation, or otherwise, during the Recess of the Legislature of any State, the Executive thereof may make temporary Appointments until the next Meeting of the Legislature, which shall then fill such Vacancies.

No Person shall be a Senator who shall not have attained to the Age of thirty Years, and been nine Years a Citizen of the United States, and who shall not, when elected, be an Inhabitant of that State for which he shall be chosen.

The Vice President of the United States shall be President of the Senate, but shall have no vote, unless they be equally divided.

The Senate shall chuse their other Officers, and also a President pro tempore, in the absence of the Vice President, or when he shall exercise the Office of the President of the United States.

The Senate shall have the sole Power to try all Impeachments. When sitting for that purpose they shall be on Oath or Affirmation. When the President of the United States is tried, the Chief Justice shall preside: And no person shall be convicted without the Concurrence of two thirds of the Members present.

Judgment in Cases of Impeachment shall not extend further than to removal from Office, and disqualification to hold and enjoy any Office of honor, Trust, or Profit under the United States: but the Party convicted shall nevertheless be liable and subject to Indictment, Trial, Judgment, and Punishment, according to Law.

Section 4. The Times, Places and Manner of holding Elections for Senators and Representatives, shall be prescribed in each State by the Legislature thereof; but the Congress may at any time by Law make or alter such Regulations, except as to the Places of Chusing Senators.

The Congress shall assemble at least once in every Year, and such Meeting shall be on the first Monday in December, unless they shall by Law appoint a different Day.

Section 5. Each House shall be the Judge of the Elections, Returns and Qualifications of its own Members, and a Majority of each shall constitute a Quorum to do Business; but a smaller number may adjourn from day to day, and may be authorized to compel the Attendance of absent Members, in such Manner, and under such Penalties, as each House may provide.

Each House may determine the Rules of its Proceedings, punish its Members for disorderly Behaviour, and, with the Concurrence of two thirds, expel a Member.

Each House shall keep a Journal of its Proceedings, and from time to time publish the same, excepting such Parts as may in their Judgment require Secrecy; and the Yeas and Nays of the Members of either House on any question shall, at the Desire of one fifth of those Present, be entered on the Journal.

Neither House, during the Session of Congress, shall, without the Consent of the other, adjourn for more than three days, nor to any other Place than that in which the two Houses shall be sitting.

Section 6. The Senators and Representatives shall receive a Compensation for their Services, to be ascertained by Law, and paid out of the Treasury of the United States. They shall in all Cases, except Treason, Felony, and Breach of the Peace, be privileged from Arrest during their Attendance at the Session of their respective Houses, and in going to and returning from the same; and for any Speech or Debate in either House, they shall not be questioned in any other Place.

No Senator or Representative shall, during the Time for which he was elected, be appointed to any civil Office under the Authority of the United States, which shall have been created, or the Emoluments whereof shall have been increased, during such time; and no Person holding any Office under the United States shall be a Member of either House during his continuance in Office.

Section 7. All Bills for raising Revenue shall originate in the House of Representatives; but the Senate may propose or concur with Amendments as on other bills.

Every Bill which shall have passed the House of Representatives and the Senate, shall, before it become a Law, be presented to the President of the United States; If he approve he shall sign it, but if not he shall return it, with his Objections, to that House in which it shall have originated, who shall enter the objections at large on their Journal, and proceed to reconsider it. If after such Reconsideration two thirds of that House shall agree to pass the bill, it shall be sent, together with the Objections, to the other House, by which it shall likewise be reconsidered, and if approved by two thirds of that House, it shall become a Law. But in all such Cases the Votes of both Houses shall be determined by Yeas and Nays, and the Names of the Persons voting for and against the Bill shall be entered on the Journal of each House respectively. If any Bill shall not be returned by the President within ten Days (Sundays ex-cepted) after it shall have been presented to him, the Same shall be a Law, in like Manner as if he had signed it, unless the Congress by their Adjournment prevent its Return, in which Case it shall not be a Law.

Every Order, Resolution, or Vote to which the Concurrence of the Senate and House of Representatives may be necessary (except on a question of Adjournment) shall be presented to the President of the United States; and before the Same shall take Effect, shall be approved by him, or being disapproved by him, shall be repassed by two thirds of the Senate and House of Representatives, according to the Rules and Limitations prescribed in the Case of a Bill.

Section 8. The Congress shall have Power To lay and collect Taxes, Duties, Imposts and Excises, to pay the Debts and provide for the common Defence and general Welfare of the United States; but all Duties, and Excises shall be uniform throughout the United States;

To borrow money on the credit of the United States;

To regulate Commerce with foreign Nations, and among the several States, and with the Indian Tribes;

To establish an uniform rule of Naturalization, and uniform Laws on the subject of Bankruptcies throughout the United States;

To coin Money, regulate the Value thereof, and of foreign Coin, and fix the Standard of Weights and measures;

To provide for the Punishment of counterfeiting the Securities and current Coin of the United States;

To establish Post Offices and post Roads;

To promote the Progress of Science and useful Arts, by securing for limited Times to Authors and Inventors the exclusive Right to their respective Writings and Discoveries;

To constitute Tribunals inferior to the Supreme Court;

To define and punish Piracies and Felonies committed on the high Seas, and Offenses against the Law of Nations;

To declare War, grant Letters of Marque and Reprisal, and make Rules concerning Captures on Land and Water;

To raise and support Armies, but no Appropriation of Money to that Use shall be for a longer Term than two Years;

To provide and maintain a Navy;

To make Rules for the Government and Regulation of the land and naval forces;

To provide for calling forth the Militia to execute the Laws of the Union, suppress Insurrections and repel Invasions;

To provide for organizing, arming, and disciplining the Militia, and for governing such Part of them as may be employed in Service of the United States, reserving to the States respectively, the Appointment of the Officers, and the Authority of training the Militia according to the discipline prescribed by Congress;

To exercise exclusive Legislation in all Cases whatsoever, over such District (not exceeding ten Miles square) as may, by Cession of particular States, and the acceptance of Congress, become the Seat of the Government of the United States, and to exercise like Authority over all Places purchased by the Consent of the Legislature of the State in which the Same shall be, for the Erection of Forts, Magazines, Arsenals, Dock-yards, and other needful Building;—And

To make all Laws which shall be necessary and proper for carrying into Execution the foregoing Powers, and all other Powers vested by this Constitution in the Government of the United States, or in any Department or Officer thereof.

Section 9. The Migration or Importation of such Persons as any of the States now existing shall think proper to admit, shall not be prohibited by the Congress prior to the Year one thousand eight hundred and eight, but a tax or duty may be imposed on such Importation, not exceeding ten dollars for each Person.

The privilege of the Writ of Habeas Corpus shall not be suspended, unless when in Cases of Rebellion or Invasion the public Safety may require it.

No bill of Attainder or ex post facto Law shall be passed.

No capitation, or other direct, Tax shall be laid unless in Proportion to the Census or Enumeration herein before directed to be taken.

No Tax or Duty shall be laid on Articles exported from any State.

No Preference shall be given by any Regulation of Commerce or Revenue to the Ports of one State over those of another: nor shall Vessels bound to, or from, one State, be obliged to enter, clear, or pay Duties in another.

No Money shall be drawn from the Treasury, but in Consequence of Appropriations made by Law; and a regular Statement and Account of the Receipts and Expenditures of all public Money shall be published from time to time.

No Title of Nobility shall be granted by the United States: And no Person holding any Office of Profit or Trust under them, shall, without the Consent of the Congress, accept of any present, Emolument, Office, or Title, of any kind whatever, from any King, Prince, or foreign State.

Section 10. No State shall enter into any Treaty, Alliance, or Confederation; grant Letters of Marque and Reprisal; coin Money; emit Bills of Credit; make any Thing but gold and silver Coin a Tender in Payment of Debts; pass any Bill Attainder, ex post facto Law, or Law impairing the Obligation of Contracts, or grant any title of Nobility.

No State shall, without the Consent of the Congress, lay any Imposts or Duties on Imports or Exports, except what may be absolutely necessary for executing its inspection Laws; and the net Produce of all Duties and Imposts, laid by any State on Imports or Exports, shall be for the use of the Treasury of the United States; and all such Laws shall be subject to the Revision and Control of the Congress.

No state shall, without the Consent of Congress, lay any duty of Tonnage, keep Troops, or Ships of War in time of Peace, enter into any Agreement or Compact with another State, or with a foreign Power, or engage in War, unless actually invaded, or in such imminent Danger as will not admit of delay.

Article II

Section 1. The executive Power shall be vested in a President of the United States of America. He shall hold his Office during the Term of four years, and, together with the Vice president, chosen for the same Term, be elected, as follows:

Each State shall appoint, such Manner as the legislature thereof may direct, a Number of Electors, equal to the whole Number of Senators and Representatives to which the State may be entitled in the Congress: but no Senator or Representative, or Person holding an Office of Trust or Profit under the United States, shall be appointed an Elector.

[The Electors shall meet in their respective States, and vote by Ballot for two persons, of whom one at least shall not be an Inhabitant of the same State with themselves. And they shall make a List of all the

Persons voted for, and of the Number of Votes for each; which List they shall sign and certify, and transmit sealed to the Seat of the Government of the United States, directed to the President of the Senate. The President of the Senate shall, in the Presence of the Senate and House of Representatives, open all the Certificates, and the Votes shall then be counted. The Person having the greatest Number of Votes shall be the President, if such Number be a Majority of the whole Number of Electors appointed; and if there be more than one who have such Majority, and have an equal Number of Votes, then the House of Representatives shall immediately chuse by Ballot one of them for President; and if no Person have a majority, then from the five highest on the List the said House shall in like Manner chuse the President. But in chusing the President, the Votes shall be taken by States, the Representation from each State having one Vote; a quorum for this Purpose shall consist of a Member or Members from two-thirds of the States, and a Majority of all the states shall be necessary to a Choice. In every Case, after the Choice of the President, the Person having the greatest Number of Votes of the Electors shall be the Vice President. But if there should remain two or more who have equal votes, the Senate shall chuse from them by Ballot the Vice President.]

The Congress may determine the Time of chusing the Electors, and the Day on which they shall give their Votes; which Day shall be the same throughout the United States.

No person except a natural-born Citizen, or a Citizen of the United States, at the time of the Adoption of this Constitution, shall be eligible to the Office of President; neither shall any Person be eligible to that Office who shall not have attained to the Age of thirty-five Years, and been fourteen Years a Resident within the United States.

In Case of the Removal of the President from Office, or of his Death, Resignation, or Inability to discharge the Powers and Duties of the said Office, the same shall devolve on the Vice President, and the Congress may by Law provide for the Case of Removal, Death, Resignation, or Inability, both of the President and Vice President, declaring what Officer shall then act as President, and such Officer shall act accordingly, until the disability be removed or a President shall be elected.

The President shall, at stated Times, receive for his Services a Compensation, which shall neither be increased nor diminished during the

Period for which he shall have been elected, and he shall not receive within that Period any other Emolument from the United States, or any of them.

Before he enter on the execution of his Office, he shall take the following Oath or Affirmation:—"I do solemnly swear (or affirm) that I will faithfully execute the Office of President of the United States, and will, to the best of my Ability, preserve, protect, and defend the Constitution of the United States."

Section 2. The President shall be Commander in Chief of the Army and Navy of the United States, and of the Militia of the several States, when called into the actual Service of the United States; he may require the Opinion, in writing, of the principal Officer in each of the executive Departments, upon any subject relating to the Duties of their respective Offices, and he shall have power to Grant Reprieves and Pardons for Offenses against the United States, except in Cases of Impeachment.

He shall have Power, by and with Advice and Consent of the Senate, to make Treaties, provided two thirds of the Senators present concur; and he shall nominate, and by and with the Advice and Consent of the Senate, shall appoint Ambassadors, other public Ministers and Consuls, Judges of the supreme Court, and all other Officers of the United States, whose Appointments are not herein otherwise provided for, and which shall be established by Law: but the Congress may by Law vest the Appointment of such inferior Officers, as they think proper, in the President alone, in the Courts of Law, or in the Heads of Departments.

The President shall have Power to fill up all Vacancies that may happen during the Recess of the Senate, by granting Commissions which shall expire at the End of their next Session.

Section 3. He shall from time to time give to the Congress Information of the State of the Union, and recommend to their Consideration such Measures as he shall judge necessary and expedient; he may, on extraordinary occasions, convene both Houses, or either of them, and in Case of Disagreement between them, with respect to the Time of Adjournment, he may adjourn them to such Time as he shall think proper; he shall receive Ambassadors and other public Ministers; he shall take care that the Laws be faithfully executed, and shall Commission all the Officers of the United States.

Section 4. The President, Vice President and all civil Officers of the United States, shall be removed from Office on Impeachment for, and Conviction of, Treason, Bribery, or other high Crimes and Misdemeanors.

Article III

Section 1. The judicial Power of the United States, shall be vested in one supreme Court, and in such inferior Courts as the Congress may from time to time ordain and establish. The Judges, both of the supreme and inferior Courts, shall hold their Offices during good Behaviour, and shall, at stated Times, receive for their Services, a Compensation, which shall not be diminished during their Continuance in Office.

Section 2. The judicial Power shall extend to all Cases, in Law and Equity, arising under this Constitution, the Laws of the United States, and Treaties made, or which shall be made, under their Authority; — to all Cases affecting Ambassadors, other public Ministers and Consuls;—to all cases of admiralty and maritime Jurisdiction;—to Controversies to which the United States shall be a Party; — to Controversies between two or more States;—between a State and Citizens of another   State;— between Citizens of different States:—between Citizens of the same State claiming Land's under Grants of different States, and between a State, or the Citizens thereof, and foreign States, Citizens or Subjects.

In all Cases affecting Ambassadors, other public Ministers and Consuls, and those in which a State shall be Party, the supreme Court shall have original Jurisdiction. In all the other Cases before mentioned, the supreme Court shall have appellate Jurisdiction, both as to Law and Fact, with such Exceptions, and under such Regulations as the Congress shall make.

The trial of all Crimes, except in Cases of Impeachment, shall be by Jury; and such Trial shall be held in the State where the said Crimes shall have been committed; but when not committed within any State, the Trial shall be at such Place or Places as the Congress may by Law have directed.

Section 3. Treason against the United States, shall consist only in levying War against them, or in adhering to their Enemies, giving them Aid and Comfort. No Person shall be convicted of Treason unless on the Testimony of two Witnesses to the same overt Act, or on Confession in open Court.

The Congress shall have Power to declare the Punishment of Treason, but no Attainder of Treason shall work Corruption of Blood, or Forfeiture except during the Life of the Person attained.

Article IV

Section 1. Full Faith and Credit shall be given in each State to the public Acts, Records, and judicial Proceedings of every other State. And the Congress may by general Laws prescribe the Manner in which such Acts, Records and Proceedings shall be proved, and the Effect thereof.

Section 2. The Citizens of each State shall be entitled to all Privileges and Immunities of Citizens in the several States.

A Person charged in any State with Treason, Felony, or other Crime, who shall flee from Justice, and be found in another State, shall on demand of the executive Authority of the State from which he fled, be delivered up, to be removed to the State having Jurisdiction of the Crime.

No Person held to Service or Labour in one State, under the Laws thereof, escaping into another, shall, in Consequence of any Law or Regulation therein, be discharged from such Service or Labour, but shall be delivered up on Claim of the Party to whom such Service or Labour may be due.

Section 3. New States may be admitted by the Congress into this Union; but no new State shall be formed or erected within the Jurisdiction of any other State; nor any State be formed by the Junction of two or more States, or parts of States, without the Consent of the Legislatures of the States concerned as well as of the Congress.

The Congress shall have Power to dispose of and make all needful Rules and Regulations respecting the Territory or other Property belonging to the United States; and nothing in this Constitution shall be so construed as to Prejudice any Claims of the United States or of any particular State.

Section 4. The United States shall guarantee to every State in this union a Republican Form of Government, and shall protect each of them against Invasion; and on Application of the Legislature, or of the Executive (when the Legislature cannot be convened) against domestic Violence.

Article V

The Congress, whenever two-thirds of both Houses shall deem it necessary, shall propose Amendments to this Constitution, or, on the Application of the Legislatures of two-thirds of the several States, shall call a Convention for proposing Amendments, which, in either Case, shall be valid to all Intents and Purposes, as part of this Constitution, when ratified by the Legislatures of three-fourths of the several States, or by Conventions in three-fourths thereof, as the one or the other Mode of Ratification may be proposed by the Congress; Provided that no Amendment which may be made prior to the Year One thousand eight hundred and eight shall in any Manner affect the first and fourth Clauses in the Ninth Section of the first Article; and that no State, without its Consent, shall be deprived of its equal Suffrage in the Senate.

Article VI

All Debts contracted and Engagements entered into, before the Adoption of this Constitution, shall be as valid against the United States under this Constitution, as under the Confederation.

This Constitution, and the Laws of the United States which shall be made in Pursuance thereof; and all Treaties made, or which shall be made, under the Authority of the United States, shall be the supreme Law of the Land; and the Judges in every State shall be bound thereby, any Thing in the Constitution or Laws of any State to the Contrary notwithstanding.

The Senators and Representatives before mentioned, and the Members of the several State Legislatures, and all executive and judicial Officers, both of the United States and of the several States, shall be bound by Oath or Affirmation to support this Constitution; but no religious Test shall ever be required as a qualification to any Office or public Trust under the United States.

Article VII

The Ratification of the Conventions of nine States shall be sufficient for the Establishment of this Constitution between the States so ratifying the same.

Done in Convention by the Unanimous Consent of the States present the Seventeenth Day of September in the Year of our Lord one thousand seven hundred and Eighty seven, and of the Independence of the United States of America the Twelfth. In Witness whereof We have hereunto subscribed our Names.

Articles in Addition to, and Amendment of, the Constitution of the United States of America, Proposed by Congress, and Ratified by the Legislatures of the Several States, Pursuant to the Fifth Article of the Original Constitution.

[The first ten amendments went into effect in 1791]

Amendment I

Congress shall make no law respecting an establishment of religion, or prohibiting the free exercise thereof; or abridging the freedom of speech, or of the press; or the right of the people peaceably to assemble, and to petition the Government for a redress of grievances.

Amendment II

A well regulated Militia, being necessary to the security of a free State, the right of the people to keep and bear Arms shall not be infringed.

Amendment III

No Soldier shall, in time of peace, be quartered in any house, without the consent of the Owner, nor in time of War, but in a manner to be prescribed by law.

Amendment IV

The right of the people to be secure in their persons, houses, papers, and effects, against unreasonable searches and seizures, shall not be violated, and no Warrants shall issue, but upon probable cause, supported by Oath or affirmation, and particularly describing the place to be searched, and the persons or things to be seized.

Amendment V

No person shall be held to answer for a capital or otherwise infamous crime, unless on a presentment or indictment of a Grand Jury, except in cases arising in the land or naval forces, or in the Militia, when in actual service in time of War or public danger; nor shall any person be subject for the same offence to be twice put in jeopardy of life or limb; nor shall be compelled in any criminal case to be a witness against himself, nor be deprived of life, liberty, or property, without due process of law; nor shall private property be taken for public use, without just compensation.

Amendment VI

In all criminal prosecutions, the accused shall enjoy the right to a speedy and public trial, by an impartial jury of the State and district wherein the crime shall have been committed, which district shall have been previously ascertained by law, and to be informed of the nature and cause of the accusation; to be confronted with the witnesses against him; to have compulsory process for obtaining witnesses in his favour, and to have the Assistance of Counsel for defence.

Amendment VII

In suits at common law where the value in controversy shall exceed twenty dollars, the right of trial by jury, shall be preserved, and no fact tried by a jury shall be otherwise reexamined in any Court of the United States, than according to the rules of the common law.

Amendment VIII

Excessive bail shall not be required, nor excessive fines imposed, nor cruel and unusual punishments inflicted.

Amendment IX

The enumeration in the Constitution, of certain rights, shall not be construed to deny or disparage others retained by the people.

Amendment X

The powers not delegated to the United States by the Constitution, nor prohibited by it to the States, are reserved to the States respectively, or to the people.

Amendment XI (1798)

The Judicial power of the United States shall not be construed to extend to any suit in law or equity, commenced or prosecuted against one of the United States by Citizens of another State, or by Citizens or Subjects of any Foreign State.

Amendment XII (1804)

The Electors shall meet in their respective States and vote by ballot for President and Vice-President, one of whom, at least, shall not be an inhabitant of the same State with themselves; they shall name in their ballots the person voted for as President, and in distinct ballots the person voted for as Vice-President, and they shall make distinct lists of all persons voted for as President, and of all persons voted for as Vice-President, and of the number of votes for each, which lists they shall sign and certify, and transmit sealed to the seat of the government of the United States, directed to the President of the Senate;—The President of the Senate shall, in the presence of the Senate and House of Representatives, open all the certificates and the votes shall then be counted; — The person having the greatest number of votes for President, shall be the President, if such number be a majority of the whole number of Electors appointed; and if no person have such majority, then from the persons having the highest numbers not exceeding three on the list of those voted for as President, the House of Representatives shall choose immediately, by ballot, the President. But in choosing the President, the votes shall be taken by states, the representation from each state having one vote; a quorum for this purpose shall consist of a member or members from two-thirds of the states, and a majority of all the states shall be necessary to a choice. And if the House of Representatives shall not choose a President whenever the right of choice shall devolve upon them, before the fourth day of March next following, then the Vice-President shall act as President, as in the case of the death or other constitutional disability of the President.—The person having the greatest number of votes as Vice-President, shall be the Vice-President, if such number be a majority of the whole number of Electors appointed, and if no person have a majority, then from the two highest numbers on the list, the Senate shall choose the Vice-President; a quorum for the purpose shall consist of two-thirds of the whole number of Senators, and a majority of the whole number shall be necessary to a choice. But no person constitutionally ineligible to the office of President shall be eligible to that of Vice-President of the United States.

Amendment XIII (1865)

Section 1. Neither slavery nor involuntary servitude, except as a punishment for crime whereof the party shall have been duly convicted, shall exist within the United States, or any place subject to their jurisdiction.

Section 2. Congress shall have power to enforce this article by appropriate legislation.

Amendment XIV (1868)

Section 1. All persons born or naturalized in the United States, and subject to the jurisdiction thereof, are citizens of the United States and of the State wherein they reside. No State shall make or enforce any law which shall abridge the privileges or immunities of citizens of the United States; nor shall any State deprive any person of life, liberty, or property, without due process of law; nor deny to any person within its jurisdiction the equal protection of the laws.

Section 2. Representatives shall be apportioned among the several States according to their respective numbers, counting the whole number of persons in each State, excluding Indians not taxed. But when the right to vote at any election for the choice of electors for President and Vice-President of the United States, Representatives in Congress, the Executive and Judicial officers of a State, or the members of the Legislature thereof, is denied to any of the male inhabitants of such State, being twenty-one years of age, and citizens of the United States, or in any way abridged, except for participation in rebellion, or other crime, the basis of representation therein shall be reduced in the proportion which the number of such male citizens shall bear to the whole number of male citizens twenty-one years of age in such State.

Section 3. No person shall be a Senator or Representative in Congress, or elector of President and Vice-President, or hold any office, civil or military, under the United States, or under any State, who, having previously taken an oath, as a member of Congress, or as an officer of the United States, or as member of any State legislature, or as an executive or judicial officer of any State, to support the Constitution of the United States, shall have engaged in insurrection or rebellion against the same, or given aid or comfort to the enemies thereof. But Congress may by a vote of two-thirds of each House, remove such disability.

Section 4. The validity of the public debt of the United States, authorized by law, including debts incurred for payment of pensions and bounties for services in suppressing insurrection or rebellion, shall not be questioned. But neither the United States nor any State shall assume or pay any debt or obligation incurred in aid of insurrection or rebellion against the United States, or any claim for the loss or emancipation of any slave; but all such debts, obligations, and claims shall be held illegal and void.

Section 5. The Congress shall have the power to enforce, by appropriate legislation, the provisions of this article.

Amendment XV (1870)

Section 1. The right of citizens of the United States to vote shall not be denied or abridged by the United States or by any State on account of race, color, or previous condition of servitude—

Section 2. The Congress shall have power to enforce this article by appropriate legislation.

Amendment XVI (1913)

The Congress shall have power to lay and collect taxes on incomes, from whatever source derived, without apportionment among the several States, and without regard to any census or enumeration.

Amendment XVII (1913)

The Senate of the United States shall be composed of two Senators from each State, elected by the people thereof, for six years; and each Senator shall have one vote. The electors in each State shall have the qualifications requisite for electors of the most numerous branch of the State legislatures.

When vacancies happen in the representation of any State in the Senate, the executive authority of such State shall issue writs of election to fill such vacancies: *Provided,* That legislature of any State may empower the executive thereof to make temporary appointments until the people fill the vacancies by election as the legislature may direct.

This amendment shall not be so construed as to affect the election or term of any Senator chosen before it becomes valid as part of the Constitution.

Amendment XVIII (1919)

Section 1. After one year from the ratification of this article the manufacture, sale, or transportation of intoxicating liquors within, the importation thereof into, or the exportation thereof from the United States and all territory subject to the jurisdiction thereof for beverage purposes is hereby prohibited.

Section 2. The Congress and the several States shall have concurrent power to enforce this article by appropriate legislation.

Section 3. This article shall be inoperative unless it shall have been ratified as an amendment to the Constitution by the legislatures of the several States, as provided in the Constitution, within seven years from the date of the submission hereof to the States by the Congress.

Amendment XIX (1920)

The right of citizens of the United States to vote shall not be denied or abridged by the United States or by any State on account of sex.

Congress shall have power to enforce this article by appropriate legislation.

Amendment XX (1933)

Section 1. The terms of the President and Vice-President shall end at noon on the 20th day of January, and the terms of Senators and Representatives at noon on the 3d day of January, of the years in which such terms would have ended if this article had not been ratified; and the terms of their successors shall then begin.

Section 2. The Congress shall assemble at least once in every year, and such meeting shall begin at noon on the 3d day of January, unless they shall by law appoint a different day.

Section 3. If, at the time fixed for the beginning of the term of the President, the President elect shall have died, the Vice-President elect shall become President. If a President shall not have been chosen before the time fixed for the beginning of his term, or if the President elect shall have failed to qualify, then the Vice-President elect shall act as President until a President shall have qualified; and the Congress may by law provide for the case wherein neither a President elect nor a Vice-President elect shall have qualified, declaring who shall then act as President, or the manner in which one who is to act shall be selected, and such person shall act accordingly until a President or Vice-President shall have qualified.

Section 4. The Congress may by law provide for the case of the death of any of the persons from whom the House of Representatives may choose a President whenever the right of choice shall have devolved upon them, and for the case of the death of any of the persons from whom the Senate may choose a Vice-President whenever the right of choice shall have devolved upon them.

Section 5. Sections 1 and 2 shall take effect on the 15th day of October following the ratification of this article.

Section 6. This article shall be inoperative unless it shall have been ratified as an amendment to the Constitution by the legislatures of three-fourths of the several States within seven years from the date of its submission.

Amendment XXI (1933)

Section 1. The eighteenth article of amendment to the Constitution of the United States is hereby repealed.

Section 2. The transportation or importation into any State, Territory, or possession of the United States for delivery or use therein of intoxicating liquors, in violation of the laws thereof, is hereby prohibited.

Section 3. This article shall be inoperative unless it shall have been ratified as an amendment to the Constitution by conventions in the several States, as provided in the Constitution within seven years from the date of the submission hereof to the States by the Congress.

Amendment XXII (1951)

No person shall be elected to the office of the President more than twice, and no person who has held the office of President, or acted as President, for more than two years of a term to which some other person was elected President shall be elected to the office of the President more than once.

But this Article shall not apply to any person holding the office of President when this Article was proposed by the Congress, and shall not prevent any person who may be holding the office of President, or acting as President, during the term within which this article becomes operative from holding the office of President or acting as President during the remainder of such term.

This article shall be inoperative unless it shall have been ratified as an amendment to the Constitution by the legislatures of three-fourths of the several states within seven years from the date of its submission to the states by the Congress.

Amendment XXIII (1961)

Section 1. The District constituting the seat of Government of the United States shall appoint in such manner as the Congress may direct:

A number of electors of President and Vice-President equal to the whole number of Senators and Representatives in Congress to which the District would be entitled if it were a State, but in no event more than the least populous State; they shall be in addition to those appointed by the States, but they shall be considered, for the purposes of the election of President and Vice-President, to be electors appointed by a State; and they shall meet in the District and perform such duties as provided by the twelfth article of amendment.

Section 2. The Congress shall have power to enforce this article by appropriate legislation.

Amendment XXIV (1964)

Section 1. The right of citizens of the United States to vote in any primary or other election for President or Vice President, for electors for President or Vice President, or for Senator or Representative in Congress, shall not be denied or abridged by the United States or any other State by reason of failure to pay any poll tax or other tax.

Section 2. The Congress shall have the power to enforce this article by appropriate legislation.

Amendment XXV (1967)

Section 1. In case of the removal of the President from office or of his death or resignation, the Vice President shall become President.

Section 2. Whenever there is a vacancy in the office of the Vice-President, the President shall nominate a Vice President who shall take office upon confirmation by a majority vote of both Houses of Congress.

Section 3. Whenever the President transmits to the President pro tempore of the Senate and the Speaker of the House of Representatives his written declaration that he is unable to discharge the powers and duties of his office, and until he transmits to them a written declaration to the contrary, such powers and duties shall be discharged by the Vice President as Acting President.

Section 4. Whenever the Vice-President and a majority of either the principal officers of the executive departments or of such other body as Congress may by law provide, transmit to the President pro tempore of the Senate and the Speaker of the House of Representatives their written declaration that the President is unable to discharge the powers and duties of his office, the Vice President shall immediately assume the powers and duties of the office as Acting President.

Thereafter, when the President transmits to the President pro tempore of the Senate and the Speaker of the House of Representatives his written declaration that no inability exists, he shall resume the powers and duties of his office unless the Vice President and a majority of either the principal officers of the executive departments or of such other body as Congress may by law provide, transmit within four days to the President pro tempore of the Senate and the Speaker of the House of Representatives their written declaration that the President is unable to discharge the powers and duties of his office. Thereupon Congress shall decide the issue, assembling within forty-eight hours for that purpose if not in session, If the Congress, within twenty-one days after receipt of the latter written declaration, or, if Congress is not in session, within twenty-one days after Congress is required to assemble, determines by two-thirds vote of both Houses that the President is unable to discharge the powers and duties of his office, the Vice President shall continue to discharge the same as Acting President; otherwise, the President shall resume the powers and duties of his office.

Amendment XXVI (1971)

Section 1. The right of citizens of the United States, who are eighteen years of age or older, to vote shall not be denied or abridged by the United States or by any State on account of age.

Section 2. The Congress shall have the power to enforce this article by appropriate legislation.

APPENDIX 3

Presidential Elections

Year	Candidate	Parties	Electoral Vote
1789	**George Washington**	No party designations	69
	John Adams		34
	Others		35
1792	**George Washington**	No party designations	132
	John Adams		77
	George Clinton		50
	Others		5
1796	**John Adams**	Federalist	71
	Thomas Jefferson	Democratic-Republican	68
	Thomas Pinckney	Federalist	59
	Aaron Burr	Democratic-Republican	30
	Others		48
1800	**Thomas Jefferson**	Democratic-Republican	73
	Aaron Burr	Democratic-Republican	73
	John Adams	Federalist	65
	Charles C. Pinckney	Federalist	64
	John Jay	Federalist	1
1804	**Thomas Jefferson**	Democratic-Republican	162
	Charles C. Pinckney	Federalist	14

1808	**James Madison**	Democratic-Republican	122
	Charles C. Pinckney	Federalist	47
	George Clinton	Democratic-Republican	6
1812	**James Madison**	Democratic-Republican	128
	DeWitt Clinton	Federalist	89
1816	**James Monroe**	Democratic-Republican	183
	Rufus King	Federalist	34
1820	**James Monroe**	Democratic-Republican	231
	John Quincy Adams	Democratic-Republican	1
1824	**John Quincy Adams**	Democratic-Republican	84
	Andrew Jackson	Democratic-Republican	99
	William Crawford	Democratic-Republican	41
	Henry Clay	Democratic-Republican	37
1828	**Andrew Jackson**	Democratic	178
	John Quincy Adams	National Republican	83
1832	**Andrew Jackson**	Democratic	219
	Henry Clay	National Republican	49
	William Wirt	Anti-Masonic	7
	John Floyd	National Republican	11
1836	**Martin Van Buren**	Democratic	170
	William H. Harrison	Whig	73
	Hugh L. White	Whig	26
	Daniel Webster	Whig	14
	W.P. Mangum	Whig	11
1840	**William H. Harrison**	Whig	234
	Martin Van Buren	Democratic	60
1844	**James K. Polk**	Democratic	170
	Henry Clay	Whig	105
	James G. Birney	Liberty	0
1848	**Zachary Taylor**	Whig	163
	Lewis Cass	Democratic	127
	Martin Van Buren	Free-Soil	0
1852	**Franklin Pierce**	Democratic	254
	Winfield Scott	Whig	42
	John P. Hale	Free-Soil	0
1856	**James Buchanan**	Democratic	174
	John C. Fremont	Republican	114
	Millard Fillmore	American	8
1860	**Abraham Lincoln**	Republican	180
	Stephen A. Douglas	Democratic	12
	John C. Breckinridge	Democratic	72

	John Bell	Constitutional Union	39
1864	**Abraham Lincoln**	Republican	212
	George B. McClellan	Democratic	21
1868	**Ulysses S. Grant**	Republican	214
	Horatio Seymour	Democratic	80
1872	**Ulysses S. Grant**	Republican	286
	Horace Greeley	Democratic; Liberal Republican	66
1876	**Rutherford B. Hayes**	Republican	185
	Samuel J. Tilden	Democratic	184
1880	**James A. Garfield**	Republican	214
	Winfield S. Hancock	Democratic	155
	James B. Weaver	Greenback-Labor	0
1884	**Grover Cleveland**	Democratic	219
	James G. Blaine	Republican	182
	Benjamin F. Butler	Greenback-Labor	0
1888	**Benjamin Harrison**	Republican	233
	Grover Cleveland	Democratic	168
1892	**Grover Cleveland**	Democratic	277
	Benjamin Harrison	Republican	145
	James B. Weaver	Populist	22
1896	**William McKinley**	Republican	271
	William J. Bryan	Democratic; Populist	176
1900	**William McKinley**	Republican	292
	William J. Bryan	Democratic; Populist	155
1904	**Theodore Roosevelt**	Republican	336
	Alton B. Parker	Democratic	140
	Eugene V. Debs	Socialist	0
1908	**William H. Taft**	Republican	321
	William J. Bryan	Democratic	162
	Eugene V. Debs	Socialist	0
1912	**Woodrow Wilson**	Democratic	435
	Theodore Roosevelt	Progressive	88
	William H. Taft	Republican	8
	Eugene V. Debs	Socialist	0
1916	**Woodrow Wilson**	Democratic	277
	Charles E. Hughes	Republican	254
1920	**Warren G. Harding**	Republican	404
	James M. Cox	Democratic	127
	Eugene V. Debs	Socialist	0

1924	**Calvin Coolidge**	Republican	382
	John W. Davis	Democratic	136
	Robert M. LaFollette	Progressive	13
1928	**Herbert C. Hoover**	Republican	444
	Alfred E. Smith	Democratic	87
1932	**Franklin D. Roosevelt**	Democratic	472
	Herbert C. Hoover	Republican	59
	Norman Thomas	Socialist	0
1936	**Franklin D. Roosevelt**	Democratic	523
	Alfred M. Landon	Republican	8
	William Lemke	Union	0
1940	**Franklin D. Roosevelt**	Democratic	449
	Wendell L. Willkie	Republican	82
1944	**Franklin D. Roosevelt**	Democratic	432
	Thomas E. Dewey	Republican	99
1948	**Harry S Truman**	Democratic	303
	Thomas E. Dewey	Republican	189
	J. Strom Thurmond	States' Rights	39
	Henry A. Wallace	Progressive	0
1952	**Dwight D. Eisenhower**	Republican	442
	Adlai E. Stevenson	Democratic	89
1956	**Dwight D. Eisenhower**	Republican	457
	Adlai E. Stevenson	Democratic	73
1960	**John F. Kennedy**	Democratic	303
	Richard M. Nixon	Republican	219
1964	**Lyndon B. Johnson**	Democratic	486
	Barry M. Goldwater	Republican	52
1968	**Richard M. Nixon**	Republican	301
	Hubert H. Humphrey	Democratic	191
	George C. Wallace	American Independent	46
1972	**Richard M. Nixon**	Republican	520
	George S. McGovern	Democratic	17
	Others		1
1976	**Jimmy Carter**	Democratic	297
	Gerald R. Ford	Republican	240
	Others		1
1980	**Ronald Reagan**	Republican	489
	Jimmy Carter	Democratic	49
	John Anderson	Independent	0
1984	**Ronald Reagan**	Republican	525
	Walter Mondale	Democratic	13

APPENDIX 4

Admission of States

Order of Admission	State	Date of Admission
1	Delaware	December 7, 1787
2	Pennsylvania	December 12, 1787
3	New Jersey	December 18, 1787
4	Georgia	January 2, 1788
5	Connecticut	January 9, 1788
6	Massachusetts	February 6, 1788
7	Maryland	April 28, 1788
8	South Carolina	May 23, 1788
9	New Hampshire	June 21, 1788
10	Virginia	June 25, 1788
11	New York	July 26, 1788
12	North Carolina	November 21, 1789
13	Rhode Island	May 29, 1790
14	Vermont	March 4, 1791
15	Kentucky	June 1, 1792
16	Tennesse	June 1, 1796
17	Ohio	March 1, 1803

18	Louisiana	April 30, 1812
19	Indiana	December 11, 1816
20	Mississippi	December 10, 1817
21	Illinois	December 3, 1818
22	Alabama	December 14, 1819
23	Maine	March 15, 1820
24	Missouri	August 10, 1821
25	Arkansas	June 15, 1836
26	Michigan	January 26, 1837
27	Florida	March 3, 1845
28	Texas	December 29, 1845
29	Iowa	December 28, 1846
30	Wisconsin	May 29, 1848
31	California	September 9, 1850
32	Minnesota	May 11, 1858
33	Oregon	February 14, 1859
34	Kansas	January 29, 1861
35	West Virginia	June 30, 1863
36	Nevada	October 31, 1864
37	Nebraska	March 1, 1867
38	Colorado	August 1, 1876
39	North Dakota	November 2, 1889
40	South Dakota	November 2, 1889
41	Montana	November 8, 1889
42	Washington	November 11, 1889
43	Idaho	July 3, 1890
44	Wyoming	July 10, 1890
45	Utah	January 4, 1896
46	Oklahoma	November 16, 1907
47	New Mexico	January 6, 1912
48	Arizona	February 14, 1912
49	Alaska	January 3, 1959
50	Hawaii	August 21, 1959

Index

Foreign relations *(cont.)*
  with Latin America, 286-288
  League of Nations, 210-211, 285-286
  Monroe Doctrine, 286, 288
  Nazi Germany, 292-294
  Pan-American Conferences, 287-288
  Panay incident, 296
  with Philippines, 291
  Platt Amendment, 287
  reciprocal trade policy, 288-289
  relations with Japan during World War
    I, 201-202
  Roosevelt Corollary to Monroe
    Doctrine, 162-163, 286
  Russian revolution and, 194-195
  self-determination in Europe after
    World War I, 209-210
  Spanish Civil War, 294-295
  Trade Agreements Act (of 1934), 288
  Treaty of Versailles, 283-284
  U.S. expansionism and, 126-144
    (*See also* Expansionism, U.S.)
  under Kennedy and Johnson, 442
  under Reagan, 515-527
  under Roosevelt, Theodore, 161-162
  under Wilson, 176-180
  Venezuelan debt crisis, 162
  World Court, 285
  as World War II approaches, 296-305
Fortas, Abe, 476
Four Power Treaty, 290-291
Fourteenth Amendment to Constitution,
    9-10
France:
  debt payments to U.S., 285
  Mexican intervention, 23-24
Franco, Francisco, 294-295
Frazier-Lemke Farm Bankruptcy Act,
    261
Freedmen's Bureau, 5, 8-9
Frick, Henry C., 75
Furman v. Georgia, 476

G

GAR (Grand Army of the Republic),
    104-105

Garfield, James A., 104, 130
Garner, John Nance, 301
Gemayel, Amin, 529
Geneva Summit, 412
George, Henry, 69-70
Germany:
  1953 East German uprising, 403
  air war against in World War II, 323-
    324
  anti-German hysteria in U.S., 201
  Arabic pledge, 189
  Berlin Blockade, 362
  Berlin Crisis (of 1958), 413
  between World War I and World War
    II, 292-294
  invasion of Soviet Union, 302
  Mandate system, 208-209
  occupation of following World War II,
    356-358
  reparations from after World War I,
    283-285
  submarine warfare during World War
    I, 187-188, 192-193
  Treaty of Versailles, 206-208
  West German rearmament, 404
  World War I and, 183-215
  Zimmermann telegram, 193
Ghost Dance War, 46
Ginsburg, Douglas, 522
Gladen, Washington, 93
Glass-Steagall Banking Act, 259
Glenn, John, 521
Gold, manipulation of by Fisk and
    Gould, 19
Gold rush, 50-51
Gompers, Samuel, 73-74
Good Neighbor Policy, 288-288
Goodnight-Loving Trail, 52
Gorbachev, Mikhail, 524-525
Gore-McLemore Resolutions, 191
"Gospel of Wealth," 69
Gould, Jay, 19
Government:
  Arthur administration, 104-105
  Civil Service reform, 105-106
  Cleveland's first term, 107-108
  Cleveland's second term, 109-112